Foundation PHP for Flash

Steve Webster

friendsof

DESIGNER TO DESIGNER™

Foundation PHP for Flash

© 2001 friends of ED

Trademark Acknowledgements

friends of ED has endeavored to provide trademark information about all the companies and products mentioned in this book by the appropriate use of capitals. However, friends of ED cannot guarantee the accuracy of this information.

Published by friends of ED

30 Lincoln Road, Olton, Birmingham.
B27 6PA. UK.
Printed in USA

ISBN 1-903450-16-0

Foundation PHP for Flash

Credits

Author
Steve Webster

Appendices
Kev Sutherland
Stef Lewandowski
Antonio Gould

Lead Reviewer
Matthew Gadd

Technical Reviewers
Gareth Heyes
Stef Lewandowski
Steve Parker
Jake Smith
Kev Sutherland
Peter Walker

Proof Readers
Lou Barr
Simon Collins
Joanna Farmer
Jenni Harvey
Fionnuala Meacher
Richard O'Donnell
Gaynor Riopedre

Content Architect
Alan McCann

Editors
Alan McCann
Jim Hannah
Richard O'Donnell

Author Agent
Gaynor Riopedre

Project Administrator
Fionnuala Meacher

Graphic Editors
Katy Freer
Deb Murray

Index
Simon Collins

Cover Design
Katy Freer

About the Author

Steve Webster is a Freelance Web Developer and has several years experience with Macromedia Flash and scripting & back-end development. A keen programmer since the age of 8 [and the good old days of the Sinclair Spectrum 48k], he has studied for an HND in Software Engineering. He is also a moderator in, among others, the Scripting & Backend forum at the excellent FlashKit site [www.flashkit.com], where he spends the majority of his time providing support and helping others with their projects.

Acknowledgements:

First and foremost I have to thank my long-term girlfriend Nicki. As always, your overwhelming support and encouragement kept me going through all those long nights and I couldn't have done it without you. I can't find the words to thank you enough letting me be what I had to be in order to get this book finished, and for putting up with me not being "all there" over the past few months.

What can I say, except: you are my rock and without you this dream would never have been realised. Maybe now we can get back to some sense of normality and enjoy the rest of our lives together...until the next time.

Eternal gratitude goes out to Alan and Gaynor for helping me through every stage of the book with saint-like patience, and for keeping the hounds at bay. I have learned, and hope to continue learning, a great deal from you, both about the technical aspect of writing and the human capacity for compassion and accommodation. You are true friends and I can only hope that we can continue working together (...I've still got that t-shirt by the way!)

I would also like to thank the rest of the friends of Ed team who helped make this book a reality. In particular I'd like to thank Matt and the rest of the technical review team who did such an outstanding job finding all of my deliberate mistakes - you're an author's dream!

To my family: thanks for supporting my passion for technology as I was growing up. Despite the occasional grumble that I was "spending too long in front of that infernal machine" you were always quick to praise and encourage my efforts, suffering many a "come and look at what I've done now" session.

All I can say is that I told you all that sitting in front of my computer would pay off eventually ... and I've finally made it. Hmmm ... almost an "I told you so" ;o)

Special thanks to my sister Sharon and her family for renting the sofa to me while I was between homes! It's probably the most uncomfortable sofa I've ever spent the night on but it beats cold hard streets!

Finally, thanks must go to Boris the Monkey. I must explain that Boris is the name I have given to a stuffed bear that my other half gave to me, and he kept me company during the late and sleepless nights that occupied the final throes of writing this book. He took all of my fits and tantrums in his cheerfully deadpan manner and never criticised me when I made a mistake. Boris - you rule!

...what do you mean it's time for me to go back in my cage? I haven't finished! Heeeeeeeeelllllllppppppppppp...............

No stuffed bears were harmed during the production of this book...honest!

Foundation PHP for Flash

4 PHP and Information Handling 113

5 Looking for Patterns 141

6 Remembering Visitor Information 177

10 Case Study 1 – User Poll   313

11 Case Study 2 – Event Planner   351

12 Case Study 3 – Forum   387

A Installing PHP and MySQL   439

B PHP and Object-Oriented Programming   469

C Resources   495

Index   499

Introduction

PHP and Flash were made for one another.

Sure, Flash can impress us on its own, but to create a changing, fully interactive Flash web site, you need to add some power behind the scenes. Put simply, PHP is the free and easy way to do it. With a list of functions as long as your arm PHP can always add dynamic sparkle to your Flash sites, and this book is your introduction to the sea of possibilities server-side scripting offers.

Foundation PHP for Flash will part that sea, and guide you through at your own speed.

How This Book Works

This book is aimed at designers, and specifically Flash designers, although my main aim is to teach you PHP in a friendly and designer-focused way. For that reason I've assumed, for the purpose of the case studies, that you'll know the basics of Flash and will be learning PHP to improve your Flash sites. But whether you're a Flash master or a novice, I'll nevertheless fully explain the Flash that we use throughout the book.

I believe in simplicity, so here's what we'll cover in each chapter:

- The basics of a particular aspect of PHP scripting

- A powerful reusable and adaptable Flash-integrated case study

The emphasis here is not on teaching you a ton of theory and then leaving you to figure out how to get some use from it, but rather to show you how PHP can make your life as a Flash designer better and easier.

I'll show you from start to finish what PHP is all about and, more importantly, how to use it in increasingly sophisticated and exciting web applications. Throughout each chapter we'll be working through simple code examples, working towards building everything your site could possible need, from registration and login movies, to a full Flash forum – a grand total of 12 full sample applications.

Styles You'll Come Across in the Book

We use a few layout conventions to make things clearer throughout the book.

- If I introduce a new **important term** or reference a future **Chapter No.** then these will be in bold.

- I'll use different styles to emphasize things that appear on the screen, `pieces of code`, `important pieces of code`, as well as hyperlinks and file paths.

> If there's something you shouldn't miss, I'll highlight it like this! When you see the bubble, pay attention!

- Lastly, I'll be running you through case studies and examples using worked exercises:

    1. If you see the exercise numbers, switch on your computer and get ready for action

    2. Follow the steps through and check the screenshots and diagrams for more hints

    3. When you get to the end, test it out!

What You'll Need For This Book

Of the few things we've so far mentioned about PHP you'll probably have been most drawn to the fact it's open source (in other words **free**). The most popular web server for running PHP, Apache, is also free. And the database solution MySQL, which PHP fully supports, yes, you've guessed it, it's open source too!

You'll want to download and install PHP now. I've supplied a comprehensive multi-platform installation guide in **Appendix A**. You should definitely check it out if you haven't yet got PHP running on your machine.

Essentially, you can use the book in a number of ways, either developing, running and testing your scripts on a local web server (eek! chicken/egg – if you don't know about server-side scripts and are a complete newbie, we'll cover all that in a moment) ... or you can upload your scripts and FLAs to a remote server – for example, one provided by your web host.

For the first option you'll need a local web server. For Windows, you could have PWS (Personal Web Server) or IIS (Internet Information Service – the network option) which should be available either on the Windows CD or from the Windows web site. For

Windows, Unix or Mac, you can also run Apache, a popular open source server. Full installation instructions on Apache can be found in **Appendix A**.

If you're hosting remotely, you might still want to test locally, but you'll need to have a host which supports PHP and MySQL (an increasing number do). See **Appendix C – Resources** for some suitable providers.

You'll also need to install the database solution MySQL, and again **Appendix A** has instructions.

Another thing you'll need is something to write your scripts with. PHP, like HTML, can be written in any text editor, like Notepad or SimpleText or even with one of the many PHP editing programs available. Such programs include syntax highlighting and color coding for easy scripting and a few examples can be found in the **Resources Appendix**. PHP files are simply saved with the extension .php.

All these technologies also come with full documentation, and if you have problems setting up, try our support forum at www.phpforflash.com. Which brings us neatly onto the topic of...

Support – Everybody Needs It

This friends of ED book is fully supported both at www.friendsofed.com and at our very own site at www.phpforflash.com. Source files for the book can be downloaded from either, and you can also visit our support forums for help, inspiration or just to chat. In fact, the forum at www.phpforflash.com is one of the case studies later on in the book, so pop along and have a sneak peek, and leave a message to say you like it!

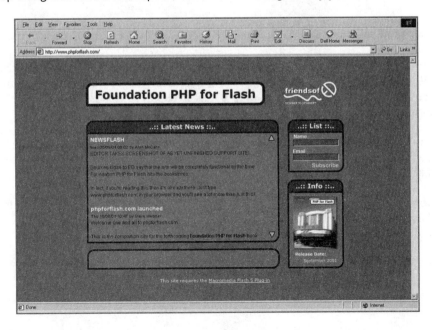

The PHP for Flash web site also contains additional files and tutorials, errata updates and plenty of neat demonstrations of the case studies in the book. Join our mailing list or submit FLAs for showcasing on the site – we'd love to see what you've achieved!

If it's the full designer's breakfast you want, the friends of ED site has interviews with top designers, information on other books and sample chapters, and much more. The book is just one part of the experience.

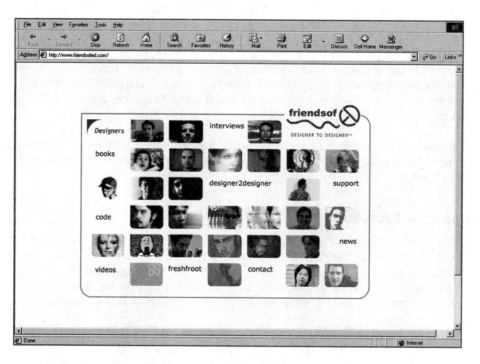

However, if you do run into trouble, and maybe have a problem with a certain file or tutorial or just get plain muddled, we're right here for you. Leave a message on the forum, use the online feedback form or drop a mail to support@friendsofed.com – we'll get you sorted in no time.

And even if you don't have problems, let us know what you think. Mail feedback@friendsofed.com or fill out the cute little reply card at the back of the book – that's what it's there for, and we'd love to hear from you!

Now that you're primed and ready, you're probably more and more curious about PHP and the kinds of things we'll cover, so let's move onto a quick history of the language and little more detail on what server-side scripting is.

PHP and Server-side Scripting

If you've been soaking up the information up to this point then you should already know that PHP is a server-side scripting language. That's all well and good, but I imagine that at least some of you are sat there wondering what on earth a server-side script is and what they're used for. Let's take a quick tour starting with how it all began - the story of how PHP came to being and why it has become one of the most popular and powerful server-side scripting languages available.

PHP was conceived in late 1994 and is the brainchild of Rasmus Lerdorf. It all started out when he created a collection of Perl scripts in order to keep track of the people who were looking at his online CV (or resume).

Inevitably others wanted to use these scripts on their own sites. In response to several requests, Rasmus released them as a package, called **P**ersonal **H**ome **P**age Tools, to a hungry audience in 1995. At this early stage PHP was little more than a collection of common online utilities – a guestbook, a counter and some other bits and bobs – with a simple macro parser bolted on to it.

In mid-1995 Rasmus completely rewrote the parser. He also added what was called the Form Interpreter, which basically gave PHP the ability to process HTML forms. These were collectively known as PHP/FI or PHP2. However, and for reasons probably best left unknown, the PHP bit now stood for: **PHP Hypertext Preprocessor** ...just to confuse everyone!

Although it is difficult to find any exact figures, it is estimated that by the end of 1996 PHP was being used on over 15,000 web sites, with that number growing to in excess of 50,000 by mid-1997. 1997 also saw the development of PHP switch from a one-man show to a whole group of developers committed to and responsible for the project and its organization. Again the parser was completely rewritten and this formed the foundations of PHP version 3. The language syntax was also refined, borrowing heavily from C and Perl to make it both more powerful and easier to learn. An API (Application Programming Interface) was also added to enable third party developers to extend the functionality of PHP by writing their own modules for it.

It was version 3 of PHP made web designers and developers sit up and listen. A server side scripting language that mere mortals could understand! No longer did you need to be a CGI genius to create page counters, guestbooks, registration forms and all those other server-side applications that form the meat of most modern web sites.

Version 3 changed the face of web development, making dynamic web content a reality with its simple syntax and ability to communicate with databases. The demands of the growing PHP community ensured that development of new functions and features continued with many developers contributing to PHP's functionality.

In parallel to several further releases bug fixes and enhancements of version 3, two developers, Zeev Suraski and Andi Gutman, both responsible for major contributions to the development of earlier versions of PHP, set about rewriting PHP from the ground up.

The outcome of the rewrite was the Zend engine, the heart of PHP4. The name Zend comes from the names of the two developers (Zeev and Andi). The Zend engine (PHP4) brought with it many new features including higher performance (up to a 1000% speed increase over PHP3), support for an even wider array of third-party libraries and extensions.

There is also increased object-oriented support, and **Appendix B** includes an advanced tutorial on this if you're feeling up to it in 500-or-so pages time!

The Client and the Server

Basically, a server-side script is a program that is executed on the server and can handle information requests, returning the appropriate document or generating a document on the fly, based on certain criteria – for example, it will generate a page that displays Welcome back Steve after you've logged in. It also allows us to access utilities on the server to provide us with extra functionality.

With the help of some diagrams, we can see the difference between a request for a normal file and a request for a server-side script.

The normal process for fetching a standard web page or file is as follows:

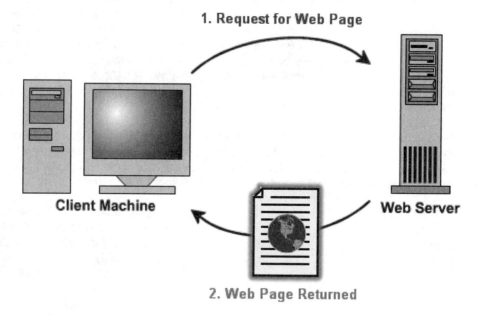

1. Request for Web Page

Client Machine

Web Server

2. Web Page Returned

Although this is a somewhat simplified view of the process, it covers the major stages involved with fetching a web page. First the **client** (you or your visitor's computer) makes a request to the **server** for a given web page. Then, assuming that the page exists, the server pulls the page from its storage location and returns it to the client.

This is the way that the majority of small web sites (and some larger ones) serve up their web pages and files. The pages involved are often referred to as "static pages" since their content can only be changed by editing the HTML file – and this can be a real pain if you've got a lot of content to change. Even the majority of Flash-based sites operate in this manner, although once the web page has been returned a separate request is issued for the SWF file.

However, when the page requested is a server-side script, such as PHP, the process is a little different.

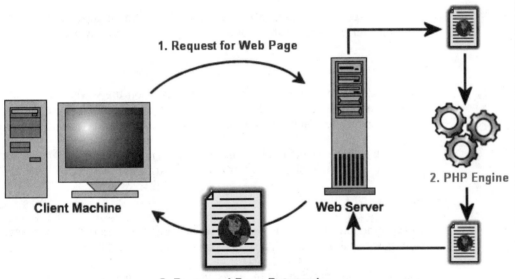

You can see that the request for the page is issued by the client as per usual since the client neither knows or cares whether it's asking for a server-side script or a normal file – like a hungry child in a sweet shop it just cries "I want one of those". When the server receives the request it pulls the file and passes it to the server-side (in this case PHP) engine.

The page passes though the PHP engine, with all code being executed before being returned to the client. It is at this stage of the process that the really exciting things get done: dynamic content can be generated, common files can be pulled in as part of the returned document, and utilities on the server can be executed. Information can also be pulled from a database or other source during this stage, though no external data source is shown here – we'll get to that from **Chapter 7** onwards.

Now that we know what PHP is, and we've discussed the advantages of adding server-side goodies to your 'static' sites, we can start to create our first PHP pages. We'll get into this properly when we see our first case study at the end of the next chapter, but for now, take a look at just how easy it all is.

The Basics of PHP

Normally, PHP code is embedded within an HTML file to produce dynamic web pages. Since we're only interested in how we can use PHP we will dispense with the HTML code in the scripts we create, although in our case studies between **Chapter 10** and **Chapter 12** we'll be using PHP along with HTML to create admin sections for our web applications!

1. If at this stage you've installed PHP and have access to an appropriate server, open up your preferred text editor and type in the following two characters:

    ```
    <?
    ```

    This is our opening tag – it tells the PHP processor on the server that we are now dealing with PHP script. All our scripts will need to contain these tags `<? ?>`, with our code going between them.

2. Now we'll introduce what is known as the `echo()` function, a simple way to ask PHP to send a certain piece of information or text to the client for display.

    ```
    echo();
    ```

    You've probably already guessed, but we put our text inside those brackets. Note how our line ends with a semi-colon – this is a must in PHP.

3. Add in a simple phrase in quote marks; you can write anything you like:

    ```
    echo("Hello and welcome to the site!");
    ```

4. Now close off your PHP script with the essential closing tag:

    ```
    ?>
    ```

    All that's left is to upload this or copy it to your PHP-enabled web server.

5. Save your file as `basic.php` in your root folder. You should have set this during installation. With Apache, it is usually by default in `htdocs` folder in the Apache

directory on your computer. If you're not testing locally at all, upload it to your site.

6. Lastly, type in the address to view your new file. Running locally for most of you this should be http://localhost/basic.php; check the **Appendix** if you have any problems. If you're using a remote web host, simply type in your address, e.g. www.phpforflash.com/basic.php.

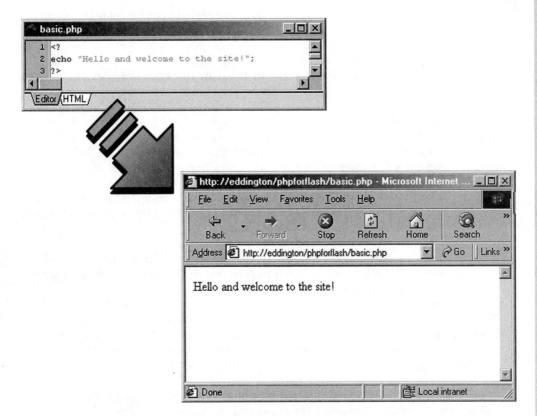

OK so this kind of basic thing can be done in a second in Flash or HTML, but those little PHP tags open a lot of doors for us, and enable us to do amazing things.

What if we wanted to greet visitors by name when they returned? It really is as simple as:

```
echo("Hello, $name, and welcome to the site!");
```

... where $name represents the value of a 'cookie', or little fragment of data we have stored containing our visitor's name. The cookie is set with just one line of PHP code and we'll be using them to the full in **Chapter 6**.

These $ values are worth big bucks to us. They are variables and can store all kinds of information, be it from a box where the user has typed something, the result of a server-side calculation (such as fetching the current time and date) or a whole array of data from a database.

Now what if we wanted to take that further — what else could we do with our visitor once we've greeted them by name?

- We could show him news articles, maybe — sorted by the latest article using the time function.

- Or how about news articles based on his interests — if we have asked him to provide us with preferences then we could use those to build a news page based on his favorite things.

- And what if we wanted to update the news? Would we have to rewrite the scripts? Nah ... why don't we just use a simple text file containing easily updatable info, and just load the news items in using PHP — the PHP file need never change. **Chapter 7** will show you how to tap into all kinds of external files.

- What if we allowed him to save certain pieces of news or content to view later? We just save his favorite items to the database along with his user details and he can retrieve them whenever he wants.

- And how about letting him search our news archive for a particular feature or keyword. We see how to search through text in **Chapter 5** and by **Chapter 9** it will be massive databases that we're searching.

Those <? ?> tags are our ticket to ever-changing, easy reusable and updatable information, and that information can be fed straight into our Flash projects. You can customize and personalize every aspect of your user's experience and bring people back to your site again and again.

In the first chapter, we'll be covering the bulk of the Flash side of things, although there will be plenty of Flash throughout the book. And to round off the next chapter, I'll take you through a great little user registration application, dissecting the Flash side bit by bit, and then showing you the true power of PHP scripts before we take the first steps towards fully understanding the crazy world of PHP.

PHP makes it easy to do practically anything your heart desires, and in 450 pages time you'll wonder how you ever lived without it.

Static is yesterday, PHP is today, and if you can read this book by tomorrow then it's yours for the taking!

1 Dynamic Data for Flash

What we'll cover in this chapter:

- *Bringing **external data** into Flash*

- *Loading **variables** using ActionScript*

- *Controlling the loading of data and movie clip **event handlers***

- ***Sending data** from Flash*

- *Our first glimpse of **Flash** and **PHP** combined – a registration application*

Foundation PHP for Flash

Before we dive head long into PHP, we're going to spend a chapter looking at the facilities available to us from within our Flash movies to interact with the server and load dynamic data. Although this chapter is mainly focused on the Flash side of things, you will find a sprinkling of PHP code here and there and an impressive practical case study at the end.

To follow our examples fully and to check your work against completed files, you'll need to pop along to www.phpforflash.com to download our comprehensive set of source code.

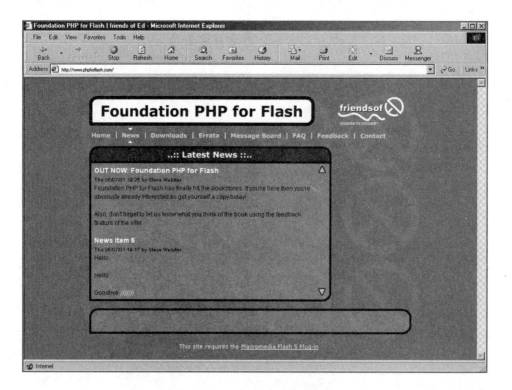

Before you download our files, you'll need to register your name and e-mail address with us. It'll only take two seconds and these details will also form the basis of your user profile on the PHP for Flash forum. If you'd like this kind of neat Flash PHP function on your site, I'll show you how in our extended tutorial at the end of the chapter. It'll give you an insight into just how well PHP and Flash work together and how simple it is to put real PHP power into your own Flash movies, sites and applications.

At the end of this chapter we'll strap on our water wings and dive straight into the deep end, but there's no reason to feel daunted. I'll be taking you through some Flash and PHP integration step by step and showing you what it does and in what chapter you can learn it – and you'll learn exactly what PHP can do for you and what this book will teach you.

If the deep end sounds a bit much ... well we all know what happens when you dive in the shallow end (you bang your head!). Don't worry, it'll all make sense soon enough.

So, you're already a Flash user (or you're learning) and your eyes light up at the word 'dynamic'. Let's have a look at how to inject some energy into those FLAs. Once we get that sorted then we can start down the road to creating some truly awesome dynamic Flash applications.

Loading External Data

The first thing we need to know is how to load dynamic data into our Flash movies. Once you know how to do this, anything is possible, and the kind of data you can load in is limited only by your imagination – it could be news, user feedback, forum posts, visitor information, anything you like!

The main way we will be loading external data into our Flash movies is using the `loadVariables()` command in ActionScript.

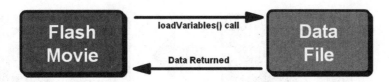

The syntax of this command is:

```
loadVariables(url, target [, variables])
```

where:

- **url** is an absolute or relative URL where the variables are located, for example www.phpforflash.com/variables.txt (or if the file resides in the same directory, just variables.txt)

- **target** is a level or movie clip to receive the variables, such as `_root.movieclip`.

- **variables** (sometimes referred to as the **method**) is an optional argument specifying a method for sending variables; there are two methods – POST and GET and we'll introduce these later.

When the `loadVariables()` command is called, the file identified by `url` is fetched by the Flash plug-in and the variables are loaded into our Flash movie. In order for this to succeed, the variables and their values must be specified within the file in the following format:

&var1name=value&var2name=value&var3name=value...

If we split this up we can see that it is a series of name and value pairings:

Variable 1	**Variable 2**	**Variable 3**
&var1name=value	&var2name=value	&var3name=value

For each of these name and value pairs, a variable is created on the timeline specified by `target`. These variables can then be used in the Flash movie as we would use a normal variable created using ActionScript.

A few examples of this in action might be to control the flow of the movie based on the values of these variables, or having them displayed in a textbox.

Before we go any further, let's knock up a quick demo movie that'll let us illustrate the use of the `loadVariables()` command using a simple text file.

The before and after screenshot shows you basically what we're aiming for:

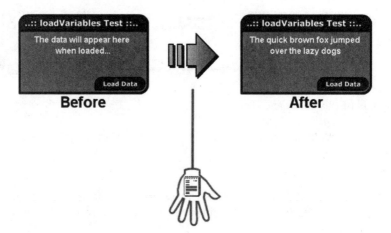

All we're going to do is load some text from a file into a Flash movie using `loadVariables` and have it displayed in a textbox.

Using loadVariables

First things first, let's sort out the Flash movie...

1. Create a new Flash movie and save it as `lvtest.fla`

2. Duplicate the layer structure shown below:

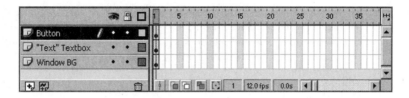

3. On the Window BG layer we'll want to create some funky styling. This isn't strictly a necessary step so you can pass on it if you're in a hurry, though I always feel that it's worth making things look cool! You can either follow the styling shown or get creative and design your own.

4. On the "Text" Textbox layer, create a multiline dynamic text box that's big enough to hold the text we want to load into it. Give this a variable name of `Text`. It's up to you whether you put in some informational text, such as The data will appear here when loaded.

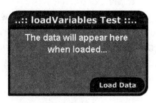
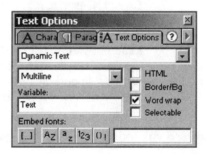

5. On the Button layer, create a simple button and attach the following ActionScript code:

```
on (release) {
    loadVariables("lvtest.txt", this);
}
```

> Here, we have not needed to use the optional **variables**, whilst **"lvtest.txt"** refers to what will be our variables file, and **this** means this movie, and tells Flash to load the variables into the current timeline.

That's the Flash movie sorted, so all that's left to do now is to create the text file with the data in it. For this it's best to use a simple text editor like **Notepad** or **SimpleText** but any program that will save as plain text will do the trick.

6. Looking back to step **4** on the previous page, we can see that the variable name we need to use is Text, so it's just a simple matter of assigning the text we want to appear in the textbox to that variable. Accordingly, your text file should look something like:

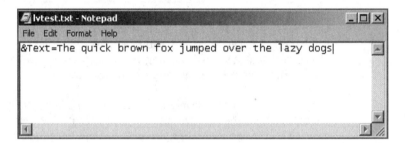

7. Save this as lvtest.txt in the same directory as your Flash movie and you're ready to rock and roll. Simply go back to the Flash editor, publish your movie and play with it in awe and wonder... well, maybe it doesn't seem *that* good but you've just taken the first step towards learning how to create truly dynamic Flash movies. Give yourself a pat on the back, and don't underestimate just how important this one tiny piece of script is. Now that you can load in these variables you can throw all kinds of data into your Flash movies.

Advice on using loadVariables

Although we've just been loading data *into* Flash using loadVariables, we can also pass information *from* our Flash movie out to a server-side script. The way that this information is handled by the server-side script varies depending on which language the script is written in. Although we'll cover this in more detail later, you might like to know that, for each ActionScript variable passed to a PHP script in this manner, an equivalent and identical PHP variable is automatically created.

Another important thing to note is, data loaded using a plain loadVariables command like the one shown above will often be **cached** by the browser. This means that, if you change the file, the browser won't bother to fetch the new version since, as far as it's concerned, it already has a perfectly good copy.

There are numerous methods that can be used to overcome this but the most simple is adding a random element to the name of the file you're loading:

```
loadVariables("lvtest.txt?" + int(Math.random * 100000),
➥ this);
```

`Math.random` creates for us a random number between 0 and 1 which we then multiply by 100,000 to get a random number somewhere between 0 and 99,999. Meanwhile `int` just makes sure it's a whole number!

Note, however, that if you test this movie using the Control>Test Movie option you will receive an error message. This is because the request for the file is going directly to the operating system instead of through the web browser. Since the former doesn't recognise the addition to the filename as data, it will throw up an error something along the lines of...

```
Error opening URL "file:///<PATH>lvtest.txt?13"
```

...where <PATH> is the directory in which your Flash movie resides.

It's also important to understand that data is not necessarily loaded *instantaneously* when `loadVariables` is called, and the movie doesn't automatically wait for the data to load before continuing with whatever it has to do next. Therefore, it's often best to have a method of detecting when all the data has been received by our Flash movie.

There are two methods that we can use in our Flash movies to detect when data has been loaded and we're going to look at them next.

The Movie Clip Event Handler

The first method of detecting when data has finished loading into our Flash movie involves getting to grips with the new `onClipEvent` handler. This was introduced in Flash 5 and can be attached to individual movie clip instances in order to, well, *handle* certain *events*.

The syntax for `onClipEvent` is simply this:

```
onClipEvent (event) {
    statements
}
```

Here, **event** can be any one of the many different events that an `onClipEvent` handler can look out for and you'll find all of them listed overleaf with details on when they are initiated.

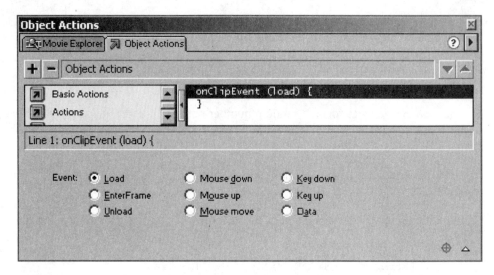

Event	Initiated
load	as soon as the movie clip instance appears in the Timeline.
enterFrame	as each frame of the movie clip instance is played. Actions execute *before* any actions attached to the frame.
unload	in the first frame *after* the movie clip instance is removed from the Timeline. Actions execute *before* any actions attached to the frame.
mouseDown	when the (left) mouse button is pressed.
mouseUp	when the (left) mouse button is released.
mouseMove	every time the mouse is moved.
keyDown	when a key is pressed
keyUp	when a previously pressed key is released.
Data	when data is received as a result of a loadVariablesor loadMovie call. In the case of loadVariables, this event is fired only once, when the last variable has been loaded. When used in conjunction with loadMovie this event is fired repeatedly as each section of the movie is loaded.

A given onClipEvent handler can only be set to look out for one of the above events, although a given instance of a movie clip can have as many onClipEvent handlers attached to it as you like. When the event specified by **event** occurs, the ActionScript **statements** inside the handler are executed.

It is worth noting that all statements executed in an onClipEvent handler are relative to the movie clip instance to which it is attached. This means that any variables used in the onClipEvent handler actually refer to variables on the timeline of the movie clip instance to which it is attached, and any movie clip functions that are called act on the same timeline. For example, if I were to call the gotoAndPlay(1) function from the event handler, the movie clip to which it is attached will `gotoAndPlay` frame 1. Obviously if you want to reference a different timeline for these actions then you need to specify that in the statement... `_root.gotoAndPlay(1)` and `_root.myVariable = 15` ... or use a `with` block.

As a quick example, an `onClipEvent` handler that looks like the following will increment the `count` variable every time a key is pressed:

```
onClipEvent (keyUp) {
    count++;
}
```

All of the events listed above are useful, and you'll probably end up using all of them at some time, but it is the last one, `data`, that we're particularly interested in. As you can see from the table, an `onClipEvent` handler that has been specified with the `data` event is executed when the last variable has been loaded as a result of a call to `loadVariables`.

To demonstrate the use of the `onClipEvent` handler we're going to modify our `lvtest.fla` movie to intelligently handle the loading of the data. This will let us display a loading... please wait frame while the data is loading, and once it has fully loaded we can switch to the frame where the data is displayed.

> Note that if you test this on your local machine you're only likely to get a tiny glimpse of the loading frame because the data will be loaded so quickly. To remedy this you'll probably have to upload the files to a web server and test them from there. Failing that, change the data being loaded in from "the quick brown fox..." to the entire text of War and Peace – that should do the trick!

Loading... Please Wait

The onClipEvent Way

1. The first step is to convert everything that we have on the main stage at the moment into a movie clip, since `onClipEvent` handlers can only be attached to movie clips. Do this by selecting everything you can see on the main stage and hitting F8 or selecting Convert to Symbol from the Insert menu. Make the behavior Movie Clip and give it an appropriate name as I have.

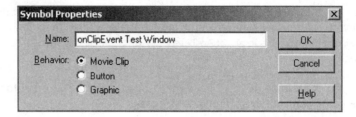

2. Now we need to edit our new movie clip and add a Loading frame to be displayed while the data is loading. Duplicate the layer and frame structure shown:

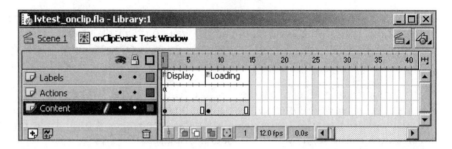

3. Go to the Loading keyframe and remove the button and the textbox since we won't want to show these while we're waiting for the data to load. In their place put some suitable text to let the user know that the data is being loaded (though yours doesn't have to be as delusional as mine!)

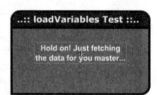

4. On the first frame of the Actions layer we need to put a stop action to stop the movie clip on the Display frame when the movie is first loaded.

5. While we're on the Display frame we may as well edit the code for the Load Data button so that, in addition to calling loadVariables, we tell the movie clip to goto the Loading frame and stop. Edit the code so that it reflects that shown below:

```
on (release) {
        loadVariables("lvtest.txt", this);
        gotoAndStop("Loading");
}
```

Now all that's left to do is to attach the onClipEvent handler to the instance of our movie clip on the main timeline and we're sorted.

6. Return to the main timeline and select the instance of our movie clip. If the Actions window is not already visible then make it so by right clicking on our movie clip and selecting Actions. Finally, enter the following code and test your movie (CTRL+ENTER).

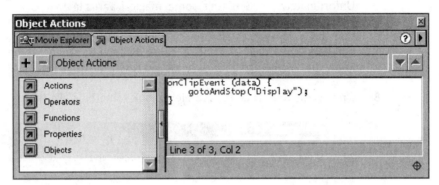

The Frame Loop Way

If we don't want to use onClipEvent, or if using it is impractical, then we can use a **frame loop** to wait for data. This would be implemented using simple ActionScript statements that hold up the movie until a certain variable has the correct value. Some may describe this as the "old way" of doing things, as this was the only method available in Flash 4 for performing such an action. However, it does have one key advantage over the previously described onClipEvent method; namely that it can be used to wait for data to be loaded into the _root of a movie, not just a movie clip.

We can easily convert the previous example to use a **frame loop** rather than the onClipEvent handler.

7. To do this, simply remove the onClipEvent code from the movie clip (basically undoing step **6**) and edit the movie clip so that it matches the diagram below:

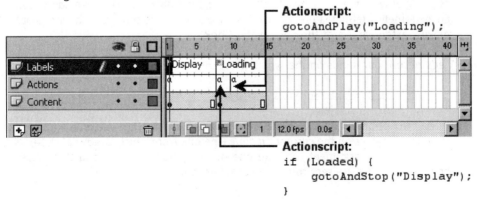

You can see that we're checking to see if the Loaded variable is set to true and, if so, we're breaking out of the frame loop and going to the Display frame.

Unfortunately, Loaded isn't some magical variable that is automatically set when the data is loaded, so we'll need to do this ourselves. The good news is that this is so easy it's almost unbelievable. We simply add &Loaded=1 to the end data we're loading in and, because it's the last variable to be loaded in, we know that all the variables have loaded when this variable is set.

8. Simply edit your lvtest.txt file to look something like this:

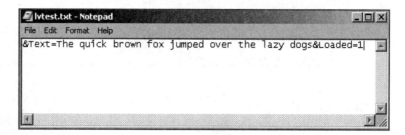

9. If you now test your movie again you'll find that it behaves exactly the same as the earlier example, with the only difference being that it's now using a frame loop to control the flow of the movie.

You will find uses for frame loops such as this one on your travels through Flashland but they will probably be few and far between. The rest of the code in this book uses the onClipEvent method, but now you know how to use frame loops you can write your code using either.

Sending Information from Flash

Back in the **Loading External Data** section we touched quickly upon the fact that, as well as being able to read in data , Flash can also send data out to server-side scripts. This is an extremely useful feature of the loadVariables command, and one that we'll be making extensive use of throughout this book.

Let's refresh our minds on the syntax of loadVariables:

```
loadVariables (url, target [, variables]);
```

Using the optional variables argument of the loadVariables command, we can send all of the variables on the current timeline (the one from which loadVariables is called). The variables argument can take one of two possible values, and that value dictates how the variables are sent to the server-side script.

This value, called the **method**, can be either **POST** or **GET**.

With the GET method, the data is passed as an appendage to the URL. You've probably seen at least one example of data passed this way on your journey through the tangled Web. A good example is the Google search engine at www.google.com. Once you've typed in your search criteria and hit the Search button you'll see a whole load of information added to the URL in your browser's address bar – that's data being passed using GET!

Address 🔁 http://www.google.com/search?q=Foundation+PHP+for+Flash+Friends+of+ED+Steve+Webster+Alan+McCann&btnG=Google+Search

The major flaw with using GET is that it can cause problems if you're trying to pass a large amount of data, as there are limits on the amount of information you can send this way.

The alternative method is known as POST and sends the data using buffers. This is the preferred method of passing data to server-side scripts, so let's take a look at a simple example of using `loadVariables` to send data to a server-side script.

Building a Download Registration Form

Now that we know how to pass information into and out of our Flash movies, it's time to start building a real world example, and you'll have already seen this in action at the start of the chapter when you went to our site and downloaded our source files.

The main purpose of this section is to show you how `loadVariables` and `onClipEvent` can be combined to build truly interactive and dynamic Flash applications. Having said that we'll be extensively using PHP code in this chapter to fetch and store data, but you're not expected to understand it at this stage – we'll leave that for the coming chapters. If you're curious though, I've fully commented the PHP code so you can have a good look to see what it's doing without having to know how it's doing it!

The application we're going to be building is our download registration form. This will basically allow you to keep track of who is accessing any part of your Flash site – in our case the **Downloads** section at www.phpforflash.com – although the example here has been adapted a little!

The first thing we should do is figure out what we're going to need. A few things that should spring to mind are:

- A data entry form

- Somewhere to store the data

- A method of moving the data between the form and the data store

- We might also want to be able to display the data already in the data store since information isn't much use unless you can look at it

To illustrate the skills we've just been learning we're going to use a Flash-based registration form to input our details, send them to a server-side script for storage in a database, and then get the server-side script to send all of the entries in the database back to our Flash movie for display. This way you can see everything in action.

The whole thing can be visualized using the following diagram:

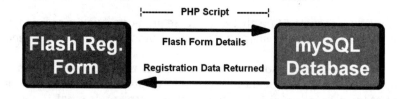

> Because this example uses a server-side script and a database to add the necessary functionality (being able to fetch and store data), you'll either have to be running a web server with all the relevant applications (PHP and MySQL) on your local machine, or have access to a remote server with the same relevant applications installed. For your convenience, comprehensive installation and configuration information is presented in **Appendix A** and you'll find a list of third party hosts that provide the facilities we need in **Appendix C - Resources**.

The main focus in the next exercise is going to be on building the Flash front-end to our download registration system. We're going to need at least 3 sections:

- A form to collect the data
- A please wait screen to display when submitting/reading the data
- Somewhere to display the returned registration data

Before we get really stuck in it might also be worth thinking about what kind of information we're going to want to collect from the user. Typical information for a download registration form to collect might be:

- Name
- E-mail Address
- Location

It is also likely we would want to store the date and time that a given form was submitted but this is best handled by the server-side script. Bear in mind that when you come to do your own projects, you can choose to ask your visitors for whatever information you need. You might need a date of birth, or a shoe-size – it's up to you, but for now we'll stick with name, e-mail address and location.

Let's take a look at the kind of thing we're aiming to create and then we can get Flashing!

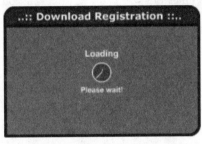

The diagram shows the three stages that the application will have to go through - Data Entry, Loading, and Display, so let's get started.

Designing Your Flash Form

1. Begin a new movie and save it as `register.fla`.

2. Select Insert > New Symbol from the main menu or press CTRL+F8 to create a new movie clip.

3. Enter the following details into the Symbol Properties window and hit OK.

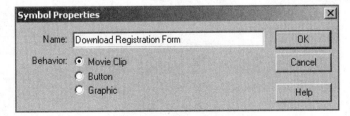

4. Within our new movie clip, duplicate the following layer and frame structure. Don't worry about the tween on the Section Items layer for now.

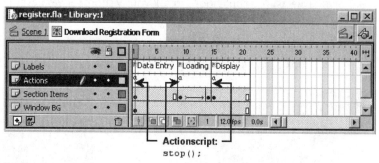

5. Add the stop actions to the appropriate frames as indicated above.

6. Again we're going to want to create some nice styling for the background of our download registration form. I've carried on using the same style from previous examples but you can use whatever you like.

7. On the Data Entry frame of the Section Items layer we're going to need some text boxes so that we've got somewhere to enter the data. It's also nice to have some text explaining what the form is for.

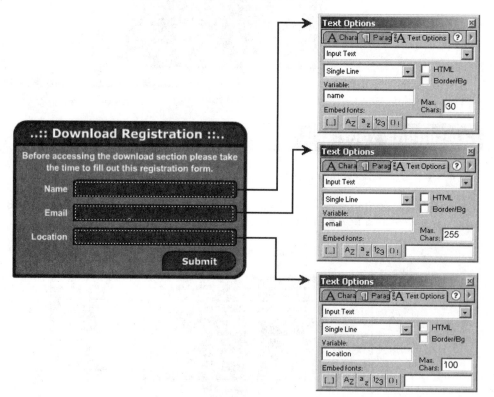

You can see from the previous diagram the necessary settings for each of the textboxes. You'll see I'm also adding in a maximum value for each text box – this prevents the user from exceeding the database field's 255 character limit.

8. We're also going to need some kind of a submit button that'll call `loadVariables` and send our movie clip to the Loading frame. All I've done is to copy the button from the previous example, changing the text and the code attached to it.

9. You can see from the screenshot below that I've added code to stop the form from being submitted if any of the textboxes have not been filled in, and that we're sending the variables from the Flash movie using the POST method. Do likewise and alter the copied button's ActionScript to reflect the screenshot:

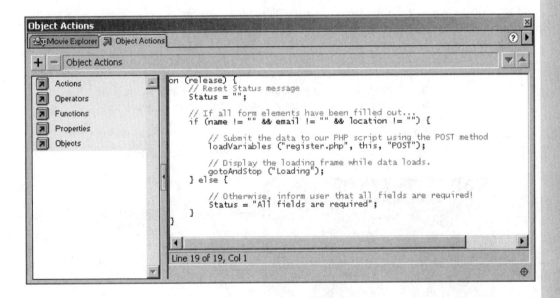

```
on (release) {
    // Reset Status message
    Status = "";

    // If all form elements have been filled out...
    if (name != "" && email != "" && location != "") {

        // Submit the data to our PHP script using the POST method
        loadVariables ("register.php", this, "POST");

        // Display the loading frame while data loads.
        gotoAndStop ("Loading");
    } else {

        // Otherwise, inform user that all fields are required!
        Status = "All fields are required";
    }
}
```

10. Now we come to the Loading frame. I have built a clock face animation as a separate movie clip and placed it on the Section Items layer to show that the movie is waiting for something. You can copy this from the Library of the finished FLA if you want to use it. Because it is a separate movie clip it will play when our Data Registration Form movie clip is stopped on the Loading frame.

11. Coming back to the **tween** between frames 9 and 14 on this layer, simply fade out the clock face animation. I think it's always better to have some kind of transition between different sections of a movie, and it is good to give the user visual feedback that something is happening and that their machine hasn't crashed!

Now it's time to construct the final section of our movie clip – the Display section.

12. Study the diagram below, adding the following to your frame:

- A multiline dynamic text box with the variable name `list`
- A button to scroll upwards and one to scroll downwards
- Some ActionScript to empower these buttons

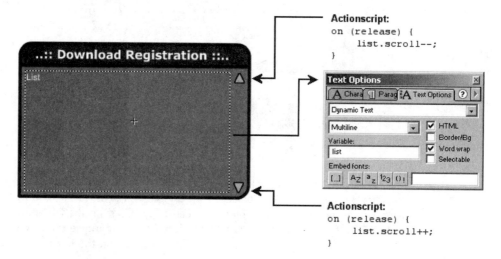

Actionscript:
```
on (release) {
    list.scroll--;
}
```

Actionscript:
```
on (release) {
    list.scroll++;
}
```

Finally, we need to add an `onClipEvent` handler to our movie clip instance on the main stage to get it to go to the Display frame when data is received.

13. Return to the main timeline and select the instance of our movie clip. If the Actions window is not already visible then make it so by right clicking on our movie clip and selecting Actions.

14. Enter the following code:

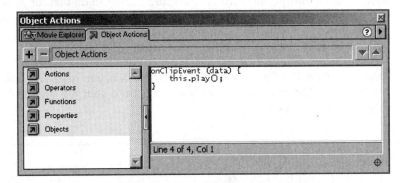

That's the Flash movie finished. Take a well-deserved breather and then we can plough on with the server-side scripts.

The Server-Side Scripts

All that's left for us to do now is write a couple of server-side scripts; one to create the database structure, and the other to handle the passing of information between the Flash form we've just created and the database.

Because of the nature of the relationship between PHP and MySQL you will need to find out the following information in order to get them to communicate:

- Database host address
- Your allocated username
- Your password

You may also need to find out the name of the database allocated to you if you do not have the ability to create databases yourself. This is generally only applicable to those hosting their sites on virtual servers.

If you're using a third party to host your website then you'll need to get hold of their technical support people if you cannot find this information on their website. If you're hosting the site locally then the default values provided in the scripts below should work for you. See the installation/configuration tips in **Appendix A** if you have any problems.

Don't forget that the source code to all the examples in this book is available in the source files if you don't feel like copying it from these pages, and also remember that it can be found at www.phpforflash.com.

Before we can store any information in the database we need to create the database and table to store the information in. I've created a script to do that for you easily and quickly. The file, called `register_setup.php` in the source files, should be copied to your web server (either remotely or to your web root folder if you're running a server like IIS or Apache on your machine) and then run through your web browser.

Once you have the file in the correct place and if you have PHP and MySQL properly installed (see **Appendix A**), simply type the path to your file straight into your browser's address bar and hit ENTER.

> *If you are using IIS or PWS then the files should be put in your C:/Inetpub/wwwroot folder. You might want to create a sub-folder called phpforflash to house your book files. Then use the following address http://localhost/phpforflash/register_setup.php. Essentially, localhost (or the name of your computer if it has one) replaces the Intepub/wwwroot in the path.*

You'll soon be able to understand exactly what this code does, and we'll be covering everything later in the book. For now, sit back and let the file run itself, and set up your phpforflash database and a simple downloadLog table.

As I said earlier you may need to edit the variables at the beginning of the script to match the details of your particular set-up...

```
/* MySQL details */
$dbhost = "localhost;
$dbuser = "your_username";
$dbpass = "your_password";
$dbname = "your_allocated_database";
```

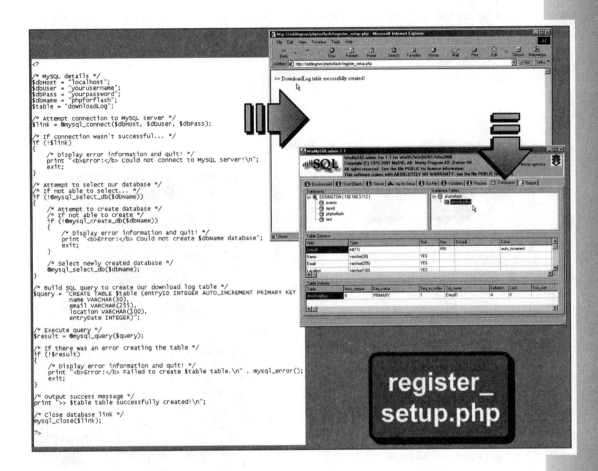

```
<?
/* MySQL details */
$dbHost = "localhost";
$dbUser = "yourusername";
$dbPass = "yourpassword";
$dbName = "phpforflash";
$table = "downloadLog";

/* Attempt connection to MySQL server */
$link = @mysql_connect($dbHost, $dbUser, $dbPass);

/* If connection wasn't successful... */
if (!$link)
{
    /* Display error information and quit! */
    print "<b>Error:</b> Could not connect to MySQL server!\n";
    exit;
}

/* Attempt to select our database */
/* If not able to select... */
if (!@mysql_select_db($dbName))
{
    /* Attempt to create database */
    /* If not able to create */
    if (!@mysql_create_db($dbName))
    {
        /* Display error information and quit! */
        print "<b>Error:</b> Could not create $dbName database";
        exit;
    }

    /* Select newly created database */
    @mysql_select_db($dbName);
}

/* Build SQL query to create our download log table */
$query = "CREATE TABLE $table (entryID INTEGER AUTO_INCREMENT PRIMARY KEY
            name VARCHAR(30),
            email VARCHAR(255),
            location VARCHAR(100),
            entryDate INTEGER)";

/* Execute query */
$result = @mysql_query($query);

/* If there was an error creating the table */
if (!$result)
{
    /* Display error information and quit! */
    print "<b>Error:</b> Failed to create $table table.\n" . mysql_error();
    exit;
}

/* Output success message */
print ">> $table table successfully created!\n";

/* Close database link */
mysql_close($link);

?>
```

register_setup.php

The Main Registration Script

Now we come to the main server-side script for this application. This one will handle the communication between the Flash form and the database where we're storing our data. Its job is to take the data from the Flash form and store it in the database, then fetch all the information in the database and return it back to the Flash form.

The script has many of the same elements as `register_setup.php`. It still has to connect to our database and talk to it, but this script will also interact with Flash!

As before the purpose of this exercise is to put what you've already learned to good use and to give you a glimpse of the kind of thing that will be second nature to you in 450 pages time! Just follow the diagrams on the next two pages and you'll see how straightforward it really is...

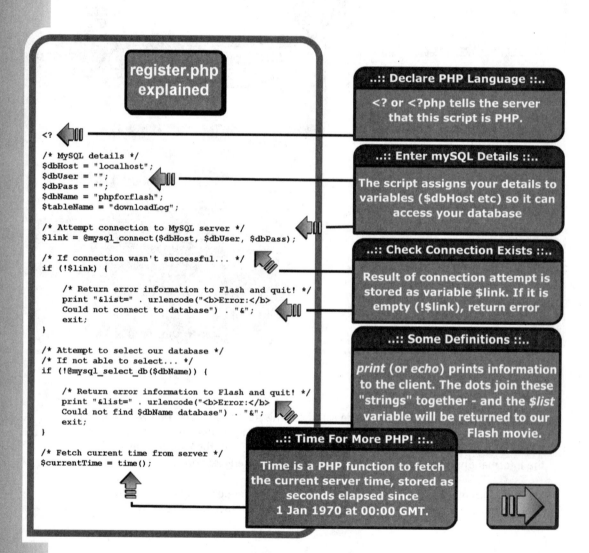

register.php explained

..:: Declare PHP Language ::..

<? or <?php tells the server that this script is PHP.

```
<?

/* MySQL details */
$dbHost = "localhost";
$dbUser = "";
$dbPass = "";
$dbName = "phpforflash";
$tableName = "downloadLog";

/* Attempt connection to MySQL server */
$link = @mysql_connect($dbHost, $dbUser, $dbPass);

/* If connection wasn't successful... */
if (!$link) {

    /* Return error information to Flash and quit! */
    print "&list=" . urlencode("<b>Error:</b>
    Could not connect to database") . "&";
    exit;
}

/* Attempt to select our database */
/* If not able to select... */
if (!@mysql_select_db($dbName)) {

    /* Return error information to Flash and quit! */
    print "&list=" . urlencode("<b>Error:</b>
    Could not find $dbName database") . "&";
    exit;
}

/* Fetch current time from server */
$currentTime = time();
```

..:: Enter mySQL Details ::..

The script assigns your details to variables ($dbHost etc) so it can access your database

..:: Check Connection Exists ::..

Result of connection attempt is stored as variable $link. If it is empty (!$link), return error

..:: Some Definitions ::..

print (or *echo*) prints information to the client. The dots join these "strings" together - and the *$list* variable will be returned to our Flash movie.

..:: Time For More PHP! ::..

Time is a PHP function to fetch the current server time, stored as seconds elapsed since 1 Jan 1970 at 00:00 GMT.

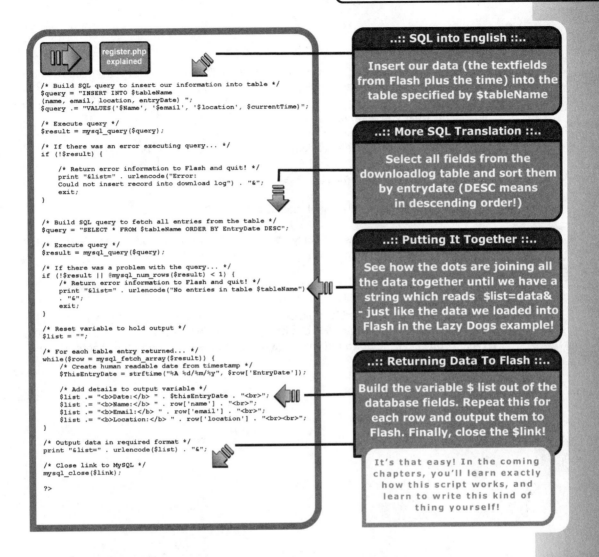

register.php explained

```
/* Build SQL query to insert our information into table */
$query = "INSERT INTO $tableName
(name, email, location, entryDate) ";
$query .= "VALUES('$Name', '$email', '$location', $currentTime)";

/* Execute query */
$result = mysql_query($query);

/* If there was an error executing query... */
if (!$result) {

    /* Return error information to Flash and quit! */
    print "&list=" . urlencode("Error:
    Could not insert record into download log") . "&";
    exit;
}

/* Build SQL query to fetch all entries from the table */
$query = "SELECT * FROM $tableName ORDER BY EntryDate DESC";

/* Execute query */
$result = mysql_query($query);

/* If there was a problem with the query... */
if (!$result || @mysql_num_rows($result) < 1) {
    /* Return error information to Flash and quit! */
    print "&list=" . urlencode("No entries in table $tableName")
    . "&";
    exit;
}

/* Reset variable to hold output */
$list = "";

/* For each table entry returned... */
while($row = mysql_fetch_array($result)) {
    /* Create human readable date from timestamp */
    $ThisEntryDate = strftime("%A %d/%m/%y", $row['EntryDate']);

    /* Add details to output variable */
    $list .= "<b>Date:</b> " . $thisEntryDate . "<br>";
    $list .= "<b>Name:</b> " . row['name'] . "<br>";
    $list .= "<b>Email:</b> " . row['email'] . "<br>";
    $list .= "<b>Location:</b> " . row['location'] . "<br><br>";
}

/* Output data in required format */
print "&list=" . urlencode($list) . "&";

/* Close link to MySQL */
mysql_close($link);

?>
```

..:: SQL into English ::..

Insert our data (the textfields from Flash plus the time) into the table specified by $tableName

..:: More SQL Translation ::..

Select all fields from the downloadlog table and sort them by entrydate (DESC means in descending order!)

..:: Putting It Together ::..

See how the dots are joining all the data together until we have a string which reads $list=data& - just like the data we loaded into Flash in the Lazy Dogs example!

..:: Returning Data To Flash ::..

Build the variable $ list out of the database fields. Repeat this for each row and output them to Flash. Finally, close the $link!

It's that easy! In the coming chapters, you'll learn exactly how this script works, and learn to write this kind of thing yourself!

All that's left to do now is to upload or copy all the files we've created to your web server and test. In practice you might not necessarily want to show visitors the details of all the other visitors but it's a good demonstration of the techniques presented in this chapter.

Summary

In the course of this chapter we have covered all the Flash techniques you'll need to know to create some stunning Flash applications. Don't worry if these techniques seem a little confusing at first – once you start using them on a regular basis you won't even have to think about what you're doing!

We're only one chapter in, and already we've looked at:

- Importing and exporting variables and data from Flash

- Controlling the display of loaded data

- Two methods of withholding your data until it is fully loaded – movie clip event handlers and frame loops

- Using Flash as the front-end to a practical and dynamic PHP application

Now that we've covered the Flash basics, it's time to take a look at what programming for the Internet involves and how PHP can bridge the gap between your Flash movie and the server. If you're feeling up to the challenge then turn the page (mind the chapter divider!)

2 Getting Started with PHP

What we'll cover in this chapter:

- *Beginning your PHP journey; **naming conventions** and **comments***

- *Using **variables** to store and call information*

- *Tying your code together with **operators***

- *Using **statements** to build complex arguments*

- *Storing and calling your data using **arrays***

- *Putting it all together in a simple login application*

Now that we've had our first experiences of PHP and know a little bit about how it works, it's time to start getting our hands dirty. In this chapter we're going to take a look at the basic elements of the PHP language and how we can use them to allow us to provide dynamic content for our Flash sites – because that's what we really want isn't it?

I'll use these pages to create a solid foundation upon which the rest of the chapters in this book can build – and trust me, we'll soon be reaching the dizzy heights of PHP heaven! After I've shown you the basics of good PHP scripts, I'll round it off with a nice User Login application.

A great deal of what you learn in this chapter will probably seem familiar to you if you're particularly experienced with ActionScript. This is because ActionScript has the same basic constructs as PHP, meaning that variables, arrays and so on may well be old news to you. Having said that though, it's worth pointing out that the way in which PHP handles these constructs can be quite different from ActionScript, so you'll want to pay attention even if you're an ActionScript whiz kid!

A Word About Naming Conventions

Before we get started it's worth spending a moment thinking about **coding style**. What I mean by coding style is not how you type or what you wear when you're writing your code – I mean how your code *looks*.

```php
<?

/* MySQL details */
$DBhost = "localhost";
$DBuser = "";
$DBpass = "";
$DBname = "phpforflash";
$Table = "DownloadLog";

/* Attempt connection to MySQL server */
$Link = @mysql_connect($DBhost, $DBuser, $DBpass);

/* If connection wasn't successful... */
if (!$Link)
{
    /* Display error information and quit! */
    print "<b>Error:</b> Could not connect to MySQL server! \n";
    exit;
}

/* Attempt to select our database */
/* If not able to select... */
if (!@mysql_select_db($DBname))
{
    /* Attempt to create database */
    /* If not able to create */
    if (!@mysql_create_db($DBname))
    {
```

> *That code looks pretty, but could you find your way around it? You've probably guessed, but coding style has nothing to do with fancy fonts or neat colour coding, but everything to do with proper commenting and smart naming conventions.*

Coding styles can apply to all aspects of the way your code reads but the one that has the most impact on making your life easier as a coder is the way that you name your variables.

Over the years I have been programming I've tried many different naming conventions, and have ended up creating my own style by hashing together my favorite bits of each. In the end it is not important *which* method you adopt, just that you use it consistently throughout your scripts.

One of the most popular naming conventions is called **camel notation**. Using this notation, variable names that are made up of just one word are written in lowercase letters, for example `name`. If more than one word is used for the variable name then the first letter of each extra word is capitalized – `dateOfBirth` for example. Camel notation is the default style used in ActionScript and for this reason I'm going to be using camel notation throughout the course of this book, both for the ActionScript and the PHP code.

```
notations.php

 1  <?
 2
 3  // Camel Notation
 4  // Lower case with subsequent words in initial capitals
 5
 6      $variableName = "value";
 7
 8  // Hungarian Notation
 9  // Prefixes variable name with variable type abbr.
10
11      $strVariableName = "value";
12
13  // Simple
14  // Uses all lowercase letters for variable names.
15  // Separates word with underscore
16
17      $variable_name = "value";
18
19  ?>

Editor \ HTML
```

If you've done a fair amount of ActionScripting using the Expert mode, you'll either have developed your own coding style or adopted one from somewhere else. If you feel more comfortable scripting this way then feel free to carry on doing so. After all, if it ain't broke, don't fix it! However, if you experience problems with any of the examples in this book then make sure you check you've changed every occurrence of a variable to your style.

It is also important to note that PHP is a **case-sensitive** language. This means that variables named $test, $Test and $TEST are actually all different variables. Because of this, you need to be extra careful when naming variables and above all that's why you should pick a style and keep to it.

Comments

Another thing we should cover before going any further is the use of comments. You'll notice in the few small scripts I've shown you already, have contained comments, whether used for guidance in the script from **Chapter 1** or to demonstrate notations above.

Comments are a web designer's best friend! If you've coded in ActionScript or had experience of any web language before, even HTML, you'll probably be familiar with what a comment is, but just for the sake of completeness... essentially, a comment is a little note that we add to your code to remind you what a given piece of code does. They are completely ignored by the PHP processor, and they are used to annotate your scripts to help you and other designers to understand what is going on without having to decode the whole script.

In PHP there are two methods:

```
// This is a simple comment
```

...and...

```
/* This is a particularly long comment, so we've taken the
trouble to encase it in these symbols, at the beginning and
end */
```

We'll be mostly using the first set, but we used the second in the example in **Chapter 1**.

Good variable names can reduce the need for comments. If you call a variable $name, then you don't need a comment explaining what's in it, but you might want one saying what we're going to do with that variable. It is important to strike a good balance between using descriptive variable names and using comments to ensure that your scripts are as readable as possible.

Now ... did someone mention variables?

Variables

The first and most fundamental thing we need from PHP is the ability to hold information – a dynamic scripting language without this ability is about as practical as a chocolate teapot!

Like ActionScript, the main way to hold information in PHP is with the use of **variables**. I won't dwell too much on what a variable is since you'll have used them in Flash before, but you can basically visualise a variable as a cardboard box in which you can store information of all shapes and sizes. The information that a variable holds is generally known as its **value**.

My analogy suffers a bit when you consider that boxes generally don't have names, unless you're *really* short of friends. In PHP we give each variable a unique and meaningful name so that we can refer to it, and its value, later in our scripts. There are some constraints that PHP imposes on how you name your variables but we'll come back to that a little later.

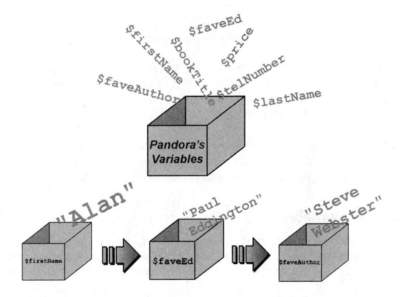

In the diagram above, you can see the variables $firstName, $faveEd and $faveAuthor and the values that these 'boxes' contain. Let's have a look at a real example of a variable being initialised and used in PHP:

```
<?
  // Store book title as variable and then display it
  $bookTitle = "Foundation PHP for Flash";
  echo($bookTitle);
?>
```

As you've probably already guessed, all this code does is print Foundation PHP for Flash, but let's take a closer look at what's happening here...

On the first and last lines of the script we have the opening and closing PHP tags. As we've already discussed, everything between these two tags is considered to be PHP code and is executed by the PHP processor on the server side.

The second line (after the comment) shows an example of variable initialisation in PHP.

```
$bookTitle = "Foundation PHP for Flash";
```

Something that may strike you as peculiar is the dollar symbol in front of the variable name. This is an old Perl convention that has been carried over to PHP, and will probably cause you a few problems as you get to grips with the language since ActionScript does not require you to use the dollar signs. However, PHP insists on it and doesn't suffer laxity on our part!

Basically, the line reads like this: *Store the string named Foundation PHP for Flash into a variable named $bookTitle.*

The next line uses the echo function we met earlier to output the contents of the variable $bookTitle. Notice that this is slightly different to the way we used echo before. In the last chapter we were simply printing a sentence on the screen (called a *string literal*). This time we are passing the variable $bookTitle which contains the string we want to print.

Of course, in this case the effect is the same, but once we assign these variables we can change their value easily and quickly, and once we're at the stage of $bookTitle = "whatever you type" then we're really empowering our Flash movies!

Naming your Variables

As we mentioned earlier, PHP imposes some constraints on how we name your variables. The simple rule to remember is that you can only use alphanumeric characters and the underscore character in your variable names, and that the first character *must not* be a number!

You can see an example of some good and bad variable names below...

```
?>
    // This file is in the downloads as badvarnames.php
    $1stNumber = 15;        // Bad! Cannot start with a number!
    $your name = "Steve";   // Bad! Spaces not allowed!
    $sun&moon = true;       // Bad! Alphanumeric and _ only!

    $firstNumber = 15;      // Good!
    $your_name = "Steve";   // Good!
    $sunAndMoon = true;     // Good!
    $_test = "Good";        // Good! Can start with _
?>
```

These are pretty much the same rules that govern how you name your variables in ActionScript so you might already be pretty familiar with them.

Aside from *how* we name our variables, it is also important *what* we name them. For example...

```
$name = "Steve Webster";
```

...makes far more sense than...

```
$a = "Steve Webster";
```

It's generally a good idea to name your variables somewhere along the lines of what you're going to be using them for. Firstly it will help you remember what they are called when you're halfway through your script and need to use it, and secondly you'll be able to make sense of it when you come back to the script in a few months to add some new functionality!

Loading Variables from PHP

Before we roll smoothly onto the next section let's take a look at how we can replace the text file from our `lvtest_onclip.fla` example with a PHP script to achieve the same effect. When we built our Registration FLA in Chapter 1, we used that technique, but this time, we're going to follow the process through step by step. This exercise will put that technique to use in our very first `loadVariables` test.

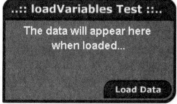

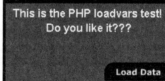

Before   **After**

Since we're using one of the examples from the first chapter as the basis for this example we can simply save that file under a different name so we don't have to recreate the movie.

1. Open the `lvtest_onclip.fla` movie from **Chapter 1** and save it as `phplvtest_onclip.fla`.

2. The only part of the movie that we need to change is the name of the file called by loadVariables. Edit the ActionScript on the Load Data button to call it lvtest.php instead of lvtest.txt...

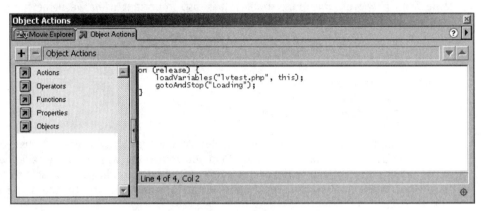

3. Now to create the PHP file. Using whichever is your favored text editor, or indeed your PHP editor if you have one, enter the following code and save it as lvtest.php.

```php
<?
  // lvtest.php

  // Store message into variable
  $text = "This is the PHP loadvars test! Do you like it?";

  // Output to Flash movie in name/value pair format
  echo "&text=" . urlencode($text);
?>
```

4. Here we've used the urlencode function to make sure that any special characters in $text are passed properly to the Flash movie. This is discussed in **Chapter 4** along with related functions.

5. That's it! Note that unlike loading a simple text file you'll have to upload or copy the HTML, SWF and PHP files to your web server in order for the example to work properly. This is because the PHP code needs to be executed by the server.

If you try and test the file locally you'll get some weird results where the PHP code is not executed. If you look at the PHP script you should be able to see what's happening!

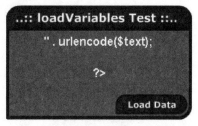

OK, now maybe you're thinking "what's the difference between loading the variables from the text file and the PHP file". Well, now I've shown you how to load those variables from a PHP file, we are no longer confined to loading the set sentence This is the PHP loadvars test…

We can set $text to equal whatever we want; it might be a username, a preference, a piece of news … now that the variable in passed in and out from a PHP script it has become dynamic and is ready to use in an amazing number of ways. That $text variable might even represent a value pulled from a database. In **Chapter 9** I'll show you just how to do that but you've already seen it in action – in the registration example from **Chapter 1**.

Data Types

Now we know what variables are and how we use them, we're going to look at the type of information that a basic variable can hold – known as its **data type**.

PHP has three basic data types that we can use:

- **Integers** are used to store whole numbers (in other words, numbers with no fractional part) within a range of approx. -2,000,000,000 to +2,000,000,000. An example of an integer might be 5.

- **Doubles** (also known as float or real numbers) are used to represent numbers that have a decimal value or an exponential part, for example 2.765 or even 2.0.

- **Strings** are used to represent non-numerical values and are encased in quote marks, such as "I am a non numerical value" or even "2"!

PHP is what is known as a **weakly typed language**. This means that, like ActionScript, the data type of a variable can be changed by re-assignment or can be interpreted as appropriate depending on the way in which it is used. It does differ from ActionScript slightly but the basic idea is the same.

We can see how easily PHP variables are interpreted according to use with the following piece of code.

```php
<?
    $first = "1";
    $second = "2";

    $result = $first + $second;
    echo "The result was: $result";
?>
```

Firstly we initiate two variables, $first and $second, with string values of "1" and "2" respectively. The variables are then added together, with the result being stored in the $result variable. Finally, we output the value of $result with a call to the echo function.

Generally, the process of adding two strings together results in the two strings being joined is known as **concatenation**. With this in mind, it would be perfectly reasonable to assume that the value assigned to $result would be "12" as a result of the concatenation or joining of the two strings. Indeed, this is exactly what would happen if we recreated this code in ActionScript.

However, in PHP the "+" symbol is a mathematical operator designed to work with numbers. So what actually happens is that the strings first get translated into the appropriate number types (integers in this case) and are then mathematically added together. This means that the value of $result is actually 3 (an integer) rather than "12" (a string). The values and data types of the $first and $second variables have not been modified; they were simply translated for the purposes of addition.

If we wanted to concatenate the strings then we would have to use PHP's concatenation operator; which is a full stop (or period). So, if we change the code to read...

```php
<?
    $first = "1";
    $second = "2";

    $result = $first . $second;
    echo "The result was: $result";
?>
```

...then $result would be assigned the string "12" as originally expected.

In the next section we're going to be looking at some of the bare necessities of a PHP script, including operators, statements and arrays. Don't worry if these seem scary at first; they're not, and once you understand how these basic concepts weave together your PHP variables, you're well on the way towards writing your own advanced scripts and designing amazing interactive sites!

Operators

Operators are used to build up mathematical and other expressions. We've already used operators in this section and you've undoubtedly used them in basic math and in your ActionScript code.

Let's take a look at what we mean by operator...

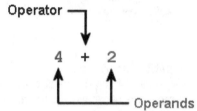

Addition is one of the simplest operators and the diagram above shows the different parts of the expression. This particular expression is built from two **operands** and a single addition **operator**. Obviously the more complex your expressions the more operands and operators you are likely to have, but you can always boil an expression down to a collection of operations such as the above.

PHP has a number of different operators so I'll take you through the main ones in the next few short sections. Since we've just seen one of them in action, let's see the arithmetic ones first.

Arithmetic Operators

Operator	Operation	Example	Result
+	Addition	6 + 2	6 + 2 = 8
-	Subtraction	6 - 2	6 - 2 = 4
/	Division	6 / 2	6 / 2 = 3
*	Multiplication	6 * 2	6 * 2 = 12
%	Modulus	7 % 2	7 % 2 = 1

You should recognize all of the above symbols from math, though they may have brought back a few bad memories! The last one might be new though. The modulus operator (%)

returns the remainder of the left operand divided by the right, so it's (7 % 2) = (3 remainder 1) and so the result is 1.

> *If you're wondering why we would need this one, then you'll find out in* **Chapter 12**, *where the modulus operator will be needed in our final in-depth case study – a PHP-based Flash forum!*

Negation Operator

The minus sign (–) can also be used with a single operand or number to negate the number (in other words, to make a positive number negative, and a negative number positive).

```
<?
    $num1 = 57;          // 57
    $num2 = - $num1;     // -57
    $num3 = - $num2;     // 57
?>
```

Assignment and Concatenation Operators

As we've already seen, the assignment operator, (=), is used to assign a particular value or the result of an expression to a variable. We've also already met the string concatenation operator earlier in this chapter. It is represented by a period (.) and is used to join two strings together.

```
<?
    $first = "Hello, ";
    $second = "Birmingham!";

    echo $first . $second;
// Prints "Hello, Birmingham!"
?>
```

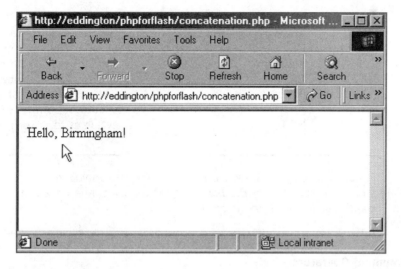

Comparison Operators

The comparison operators are used to compare two values or variable values.

Operator	Meaning	Example	Evaluates to true if...
==	is equal to	$a == $b	$a is equal to $b
!=	is not equal to	$a != $b	$a is not equal to $b
<	is less than	$a < $b	$a is less than $b
>	is greater than	$a > $b	$a is greater than $b
<=	is less than or equal to	$a <= $b	$a is less than or equal to $b
>=	is greater than or equal to	$a >= $b	$a is greater than or equal to $b

> *There are so many uses for these operators and you shouldn't underestimate them. The equal to operator == could, for example, check that a password matches the one in the database, whilst the greater than operator > could be used to grant extra admin permissions to someone whose $accessLevel was greater than 3.*

Logical Operators

Logical operators are used to evaluate a single expression, or series of expressions, extracting a Boolean true or false answer as the result. They are used in conjunction with the comparison operators, or with Boolean variables, to form complex expressions.

Operator	Meaning	Example	Evaluates to true if...
&&	AND	$a && $b	$a and $b evaluate to true
||	OR	$a || $b	$a or $b evaluate to true
and	AND	$a and $b	$a and $b evaluate to true
or	OR	$a or $b	$a or $b evaluate to true
xor	Exclusive	OR	$a xor $b $a or $b evaluate to true, but not both
!	NOT	! $a	$a evaluates to false

In our login example later, we'll be using OR (||) to validate our login form, to ensure that if the password OR the username have been left empty, our script returns an error.

Compound Operators

Compound operators are used to perform arithmetic and assignment operations simultaneously. They can save you time when you're coding but can make the expression harder to read.

Operator	Example	Equivalent to
++	$a++	$a = $a + 1
——	$a——	$a = $a - 1
+=	$a += $b	$a = $a + $b
-=	$a -= $b	$a = $a = $b
/=	$a /= $b	$a = $a / $b
*=	$a *= $b	$a = $a * $b
.=	$a .= $b	$a = $a . $b
%=	$a %= $b	$a = $a % $b

You might by now have realised (or recognise from ActionScript) that the ++ and — operators are perfect for incrementing or decrementing a value, which might be a user number or ID or anything you like!

OK, by now the only operators you may be interested in are the kind that begin with "Operator – can I have the number of the nearest math tutor", but don't worry; now we've introduced these operators it'll become second nature using them in our scripts and they have limitless potential.

Just copy the last few pages, stick them on your wall for reference and you'll never get stuck again. Then take a breather – you've earned it, and when you're ready, read on...

Using Statements

Thinking back to when I was knee-high to a grasshopper, I pretty much did what I was told. My parents would holler orders at me (usually along the lines of "put that down" and "get that out of your mouth") and I'd faithfully obey! This continued for who knows how many years until my vocabulary picked up that word that every parent dreads…"no"! Suddenly I was able to make decisions (not that my parents appreciated my obvious genius) and I'd generally repeat the word a few times for good measure. Oh how my parents pined for what was later dubbed "the days before no".

And this is exactly what has to happen to our PHP. It's about time our scripts grew up and learned some new skills; **selection** and **iteration**. Using these two constructs we're going to give our scripts the ability to make decisions based on certain criteria, and save ourselves a great deal of time and effort by using **loops** to repeat a single statement or even a series of statements.

Selection

In all but the most basic of PHP scripts we're going to want to make decisions, and to execute statements based on those decisions. PHP provides two basic types of selection statement and we're going to meet both of them here.

If... statements

The `if` statement allows the execution of one or more lines of code based on a given set of conditions. **If** those conditions evaluate to **true** then the statements are executed, otherwise execution passes to the next statement after the `if` block. PHP's `if` statement is written and behaves in exactly the same way as the `if` statement in ActionScript.

The syntax for an `if` statement in PHP is as follows:

```
if (condition) {
   statements
}
```

If we look at the flowchart we can see the operation of the `if` statement. If the expression shown as condition evaluates to `true` then the `statements` are executed.

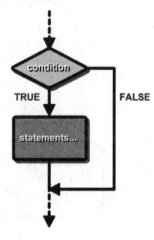

If the expression evaluates to `false` then execution passes out of the `if` statement.

To build the expression we use either one or a combination of the comparison operators and/or logical operators. An example of an `if` statement is shown below.

```
if ($name == "Steve Webster") {
    echo "You are the author of this book! Get on with
writing Chapter 2!";
}
```

```
ifonly.php                                                            _ □ X
1  <?
2  $name = "Steve Webster";
3  if ($name == "Steve Webster") {
4          echo "You are the author of this book! Get on with writing Chapter 2!";
5  }
6  ?>
Editor HTML
```

http://eddington/phpforflash/ifonly.php - Microsoft Internet E...

File   Edit   View   Favorites   Tools   Help

Back   Forward   Stop   Refresh   Home   Search

Address http://eddington/phpforflash/ifonly.php   Go   Links

You are the author of this book! Get on with writing Chapter 2!

Done   Local intranet

Note that as with a lot of the code snippets throughout the book, you'll have to add opening and closing tags, and occasionally set variables if you want to test them as above.

if..else.. statements

These are an extension of the standard if statement, and allow you not only to specify code to be executed if the given condition is met, but also to include code to be executed if the condition is not met. If we digress back to my childhood again, this is the age-old "**if** (you eat your sprouts) {you can have some ice cream}, **else** {it's no dessert for you}"!

The syntax for an if..else.. statement is shown below:

```
if (condition) {
     statements
}
else {
     statements
}
```

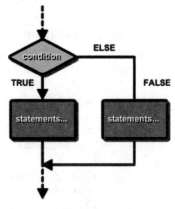

Looking at the syntax above and the flowchart diagram we can follow what happens in an if..else.. statement.

Firstly condition is evaluated. If the expression evaluates as true then the first block of statements is executed. Otherwise, the second block of statements is executed.

Continuing on with the previous example, we could expand it to use an if..else.. statement, like so...

```
if ($name == "Steve Webster") {
    echo "You are the author of this book! Get on with
writing Chapter 2!";
}
else {
    echo "You are NOT the author of this book! Could you
phone him and tell him to get on with writing Chapter 2!";
}
```

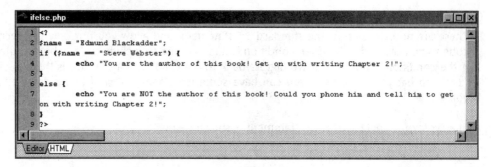

It is worth noting that the else section is completely optional. If the condition specified in the if statement is not met then execution simply passes to the next program statement. Needless to say though, you can't have an else without an if.

if..elseif..else.. statements

This variation on the standard if statement allows you to specify alternative conditions to be checked if the one in the if block is not met.

The syntax looks like:

```
if (condition) {
    statement
}
else if (condition) {
    statement
}
else {
    statement
}
```

It's worth noting that you have as many elseif blocks as you like and that the else block on the end is optional.

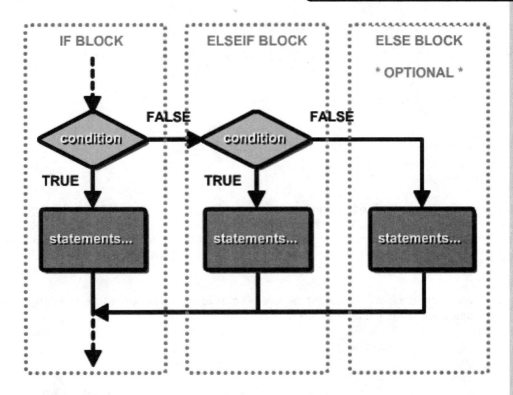

switch statements

The `switch` statement is useful for testing a single expression against a number of different values. While this can be done with `if` statements, it quite often leads to multiple nested `if` statements, which, at the best of times, are hard to follow.

Consider the nested `if` statements below:

```
if ($language == "PHP")
{
    echo("Good choice - PHP is cool! You don't by any chance
use Flash too?");
}
else
{
    if ($language == "Perl")
    {
        echo("Not bad. You might want to learn PHP
though!");
    }
    else
    {
```

continues overleaf

```
            if ($language == "ASP")
            {
                    echo("ASP eh? Have you checked out
www.asptoday.com!");
            }
            else
            {
                    echo("You're not using PHP, Perl or ASP!");
            }
        }
    }
```

In this fragment of code we are comparing the value in the $language variable to a series of three string values. With what you've learned about if statements so far you should be able to follow this code without too much of a problem. However, consider what would happen if we had to compare a variable or expression against 20 values ... hmmm, it starts getting complicated.

Enter the almighty **switch** statement. The following code would perform the same operation as the multiple if statements above.

```
switch($language)
{
    case "PHP":
            echo("Good choice - PHP is cool! You don't by any
chance use Flash too?");
            break;

    case "Perl":
            echo("Not bad. You might want to learn PHP
though!");
            break;

    case "ASP":
            echo("ASP eh? Have you checked out
www.asptoday.com!");
            break;

    default:
            echo("You're not using PHP, Perl or ASP!");
            break;
}
```

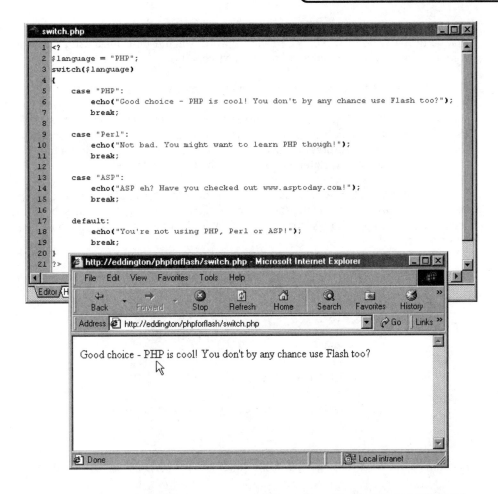

```
switch.php
1  <?
2  $language = "PHP";
3  switch($language)
4  {
5      case "PHP":
6          echo("Good choice - PHP is cool! You don't by any chance use Flash too?");
7          break;
8
9      case "Perl":
10         echo("Not bad. You might want to learn PHP though!");
11         break;
12
13     case "ASP":
14         echo("ASP eh? Have you checked out www.asptoday.com!");
15         break;
16
17     default:
18         echo("You're not using PHP, Perl or ASP!");
19         break;
20 }
21 ?>
```

Note: as in some of the previous examples, if you're testing this, you'll have to give the PHP script some tags, and also define your variables. In a real situation, this variable could come from a database or a cookie (see **Chapter 6***) or from an input box. Imagine a simple Flash movie where you ask the user what scripting language they use, and that variable is passed to the PHP script as* $variable.

The variable or expression to be tested is placed between parentheses after the switch keyword. Then for each value you want to compare the variable/expression against you have a case keyword followed by the value and a colon (:).

You then list the statements you wish to be executed if the variable/expression matches that particular value followed by a break keyword. You must include a break in a switch statement otherwise PHP will jump to the next condition.

The default section of the switch statement is much like the else section of an if statement. If no matching case has been found for the variable/expression given then the statements in the default section are executed. It is perfectly valid not to include a default section in a switch statement, in which case, if no matching case has been found for the variable/expression given, then no statements are executed and execution passes out of the switch statement and onto the next line of code.

It is worth noting that a switch statement can only test for equality. That is, it can only test to see if the given variable/expression is equal, "==", to the values in the case statements. If you tried to test for a range of values in a case statement it would generate an error:

```
switch($age)
{
    // WRONG! Will not work!
    case <15:
        echo("You're never too young to use PHP!");
        break;

    // CORRECT! Will work!
    case 21:
        echo("You're never too young to use PHP!');
        break;
}
```

Also, unlike many other languages, PHP will let you use variables in case conditions.

Iteration

Iteration (or **looping**) is a means by which we can execute a block of one or more statements, repeating them a specified number of times or until a condition is met.

Imagine that we had to output all the numbers from 1 to 10. The following code will do this for us.

```
echo "1\n";
echo "2\n";
echo "3\n";
echo "4\n";
echo "5\n";
echo "6\n";
echo "7\n";
```

```
echo "8\n";
echo "9\n";
echo "10\n";
```

However, this isn't very efficient and typing it out like this would get really tedious if we had to print all the numbers from 1 to 1000. In situations like this, looping is the designer's best friend. PHP offers three different looping statements, just as in ActionScript, and they are **while**, **do..while**, and **for**. We'll discuss each of these in turn but we won't dwell on them for too long since you might already be familiar with them from ActionScript.

> *The* \n *at the end of the string passed to the* echo *statement is used to insert a carriage return (or new line) at the end of the output line. We use the newline character because we want each key/value pair on its own line. However, an HTML page won't recognise these and so later we will be adding*
 (HTML line break tags) to the \n *if we are displaying it straight into a browser.*

while loops

Let's look at an example of a while loop.

```
$count = 1;

while ($count <= 10) {
    echo $count . "\n";
    $count++;
}
```

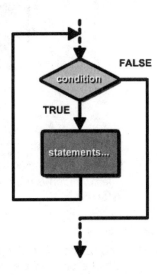

> *In plain English this is saying "while $count is less than or equal to ten, print it to the screen". Let's have a closer look at exactly what this code does.*

On line 1 we initialize the $count variable. Following that, we have the whole while loop. Firstly, we have the while keyword followed by a condition in parentheses.

We then have the block of code to be executed if the condition evaluates to true. As discussed earlier in the Operators section, the ++ operator that is applied to the $count variable above simply adds 1 to the variable. We need to do this in the loop, otherwise the value of $count will never change from that assigned in the first line of this script and we will be stuck in the while loop forever!

Also worthy of note is that in this situation the $count variable is often referred to as the loop control variable.

You may have guessed by now that this loop gives exactly the same output as the 10 statements above. I think you'll agree that it's much more efficient.

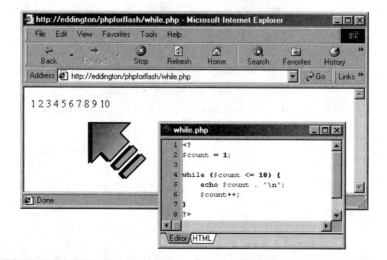

> A while *loop is known as a 'zero or more times' or* **pre-test loop** *because the condition is evaluated before the first iteration of the loop (or at the start).*

do..while loops

A do..while loop is really just a variation on the while loop, with the only difference being that the condition is evaluated at the end of the statement as opposed to the beginning. This makes it a 'one or more times' loop because the statements in the loop are guaranteed to execute at least once. This type of loop is also known as a **post-test loop** since the condition is evaluated at the end of the loop.

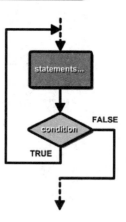

We could rewrite the example from the previous section using a do..while loop like so:

```php
$count = 1;

do {
    echo $count . "\n";
    $count++;
} while ($count <= 10);
```

There are a couple of things to note about a do..while loop. Firstly, you'll see that the while(**condition**) section has been moved to the bottom of the loop and, the do keyword has been inserted in its place. Note that a semi-colon has been added to the while section. This is essential and PHP will show an error if it is omitted.

for loops

The last of PHP's looping statements is the for loop. Generally, for loops are used when you know how many times a given loop needs to be executed.

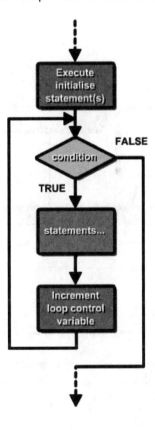

The syntax of a `for` loop is slightly more complex than that of the `while` and `do..while` loops:

```
for(initialize; condition; control)
{
    statements
}
```

The `for` loop takes three expressions inside its parentheses, separated by semi-colons. The first expression `initialize` is used to initialize the loop control variable. The second expression `condition` is used to specify the condition, which if `true` will continue the loop. The final section, labeled here as `control`, is used to manipulate the loop control variable. Often this is just a simple increment or decrement expression.

OK, so that sounds a bit scary, let's take a look at a real one:

```
for($count = 1; $count <= 10; $count++)
{
    echo $count . "\n";
}
```

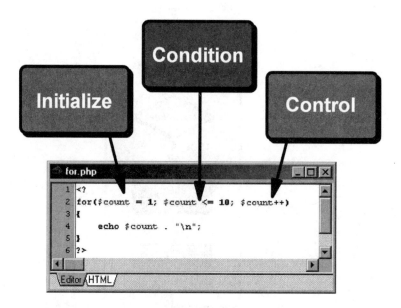

Yes, you've guessed it! This does exactly the same as the two preceding examples. If you look closely at the examples you'll see that all we've done is move all the statements referring to the loop control variable within the `for` loop.

Arrays

The easiest way to think of an array is as a list of variables all referenced by the same name. In order to access the individual variables (or elements) in an array we use what is known as array index notation.

In PHP, the simplest array consists of a series of elements with indices starting from zero and incrementing sequentially. Let's look at an example of such an array. Suppose that we wanted to create an array to hold 10 names. The structure might look something like:

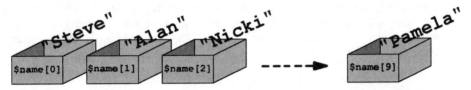

Here we have 10 array elements, with each element being represented by a box with the name of the array and the appropriate element index contained in square brackets. This is how individual elements of an array are referenced in PHP, as well as in Flash.

Creating Arrays

Now that we know what an array is, we need to know how to create one. PHP provides a number of different methods for creating an array and we'll discuss the most common ones here.

With arrays in PHP, as with variables, you do not need to declare them before you can use them. Instead, an array is created when a value is first assigned to it.

The simplest way of creating an array is to assign values to the array in the following manner:

```
$name[] = "Steve Webster";
$name[] = "Alan McCann";
$name[] = "Kev Sutherland";
```

This creates an array called $name that has 3 elements. Since we didn't explicitly state the element indices when assigning the values to the array, they are automatically placed at positions 0, 1 and 2 in the array. The same thing could have been achieved with the following code:

```
$name[0] = "Steve Webster";
$name[1] = "Alan McCann";
$name[2] = "Kev Sutherland";
```

The difference here is that we are explicitly stating the element indices when assigning the values to the array. Note that in PHP, you can have elements in the array holding different data types. This is because as we mentioned before, PHP is a **weakly typed** language. So the following is perfectly valid (although it doesn't make much sense):

```
$name[0] = "Steve Webster";   // A string
$name[1] = 15;                // An integer
$name[2] = -24.17;            // A double
```

It is good practice to assign array elements sequentially (at sequential indices) as this makes looping through an array much easier. However, there are times when we might want to put elements at non-sequential indices. These are known in other languages as sparse arrays and commonly used in the writing of spreadsheet programs.

```
$name[77] = "Kev Sutherland";
$name[0] = "Steve Webster";
$name[34] = "Alan McCann";
```

The above is perfectly valid but it is worth paying special attention to what happens to subsequent simple array assignments. In this case, the highest array index is 77. Now if we add another element using the simple array assignment method like so:

```
$name[] = "Jim Hannah";       // Assigned to $name[78]
```

The new element is entered into the array at an index one higher than the current highest array index, in this case 78.

Arrays can also be created (initialized) using the `array` construct. To use this construct we simply pass it the values that we want to assign to our new array and store the returned value into a variable. For example, the following code will create an array identical to the one we first encountered in this section.

```
$name = array("Steve Webster", "Alan McCann", "Kev
Sutherland");
```

So far we have only created arrays with integers as indices. However, we can also have an element whose index is a string value. For example, we could create the following array:

```
$book['Title'] = 'Foundation PHP for Flash';
$book['Publisher'] = 'friends of ED';
$book['Subject'] = 'Web Design';
$book['Rating'] = 10;
```

We could then output the title of the book as follows:

```
echo($book['Publisher']);    // Prints "friends of ED"
```

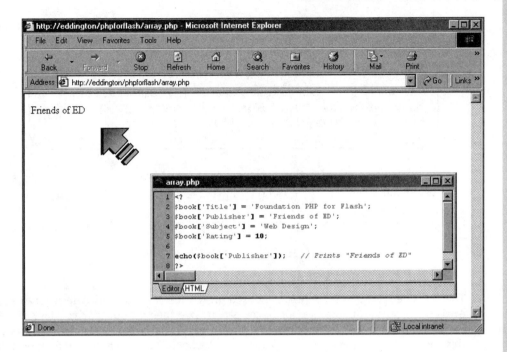

Looping Through a Sequential Array

So far you may be thinking that you could do without arrays and just use individual variables to store the values that you need. However, the real power of an array becomes apparent when we use it in conjunction with looping.

Imagine that your script had to store and print four names to the browser window. Using individual variables this could be accomplished with the following code:

```
$name1 = 'Steve Webster';
$name2 = 'Alan McCann';
$name3 = 'Kev Sutherland';
$name4 = 'Jim Hannah';

echo($name1);
echo($name2);
echo($name3);
echo($name4);
```

This may not be too bad for just four names, but imagine what would happen if we had to store and print 100 names ...you'd have to have one echo statement for every name that had to be printed. If we use an array in conjunction with a `for` loop then this task can be made much simpler:

> *Have a look at the example below and see if you can figure out what's happening. Everything there has been covered already, and you should be becoming a bit more comfortable with PHP code.*

```php
$name = array('Steve Webster', 'Alan McCann', 'Kev
Sutherland', 'Jim Hannah');

for ($index = 0; $index < count($name); $index++)
{
    echo($name[$index]) . "<br>\n";
}
```

The first line creates a sequentially indexed array with our four names in it ($name[0], $name[1] and so on, just like our boxes earlier). We then introduce a `for` loop using a variable called $index as the loop control variable. Probably the most interesting part of this loop is the $index < count($name) section. The count function returns the number of elements in the array (in this case 4) and that value is checked against the value of $index every time we go through the loop.

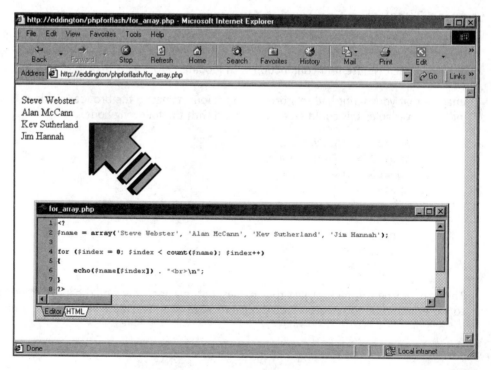

Note that `count` returns the number of elements in the array, not the highest index of the array. If we go back to this example:

```php
$name[77] = 'Kev Sutherland';
$name[0] = 'Steve Webster';
$name[34] = 'Alan McCann';
```

Then `count($name)` would return the number of elements in the array (3) and not the highest index of the array (77).

Looping Through a Non-Sequential Array

As we've discovered we need to treat non-sequentially indexed arrays in a special way. A non-sequential array can be one whose integer indices – [1] [2] [3] and so on – do not form a sequence, or an array whose elements are indexed though a string value (as seen previously). Luckily for us, PHP provides facilities for working with these types of array.

An array, whether sequential or non-sequential, has a built-in pointer. This pointer keeps track of the current array element. When an array is first created, the pointer will point to the first element in an array. We can read the value of this array element by using the `current` function, and the element's index with the `key` function.

We can illustrate the use of these functions if we return to our previous example:

```php
$name[77] = 'Kev Sutherland';
$name[0] = 'Steve Webster';
$name[34] = 'Alan McCann';

$currentvalue = current($name);
$currentindex = key($name);

echo("$currentindex: $currentvalue");
```

Because the array has just been created the pointer is pointing to the first element in the array. So, this code will print 77: Kev Sutherland. This may be a little unexpected but this was the first element in the array (regardless of its index) because it was the first to be assigned to the array.

Note though that neither `current` nor `key` will advance the internal pointer. For that job we need to enlist the help of the `each` and `list` functions. An example of a loop that will print out all of the values in our non-sequential `$name` array could be:

```php
reset($name);
while (list($key, $value) = each($name))
{
    echo("$key: $value<br>\n");
}
```

The reset function returns the internal array pointer to the first element of the array. We may not need to do this (the array may have just been created) but it's worth using anyway so that we definitely know where the pointer is!

The each function is passed an array. It then returns the key and value of the current element and moves on to the next array element. When the last element of an array is reached it returns false. Because this function returns two values, it has to return them as an array, which is where the list function comes into play.

The list function basically breaks apart the return value of the each function (an array) and stores them in two variables ($key and $value).

The output would look like this:

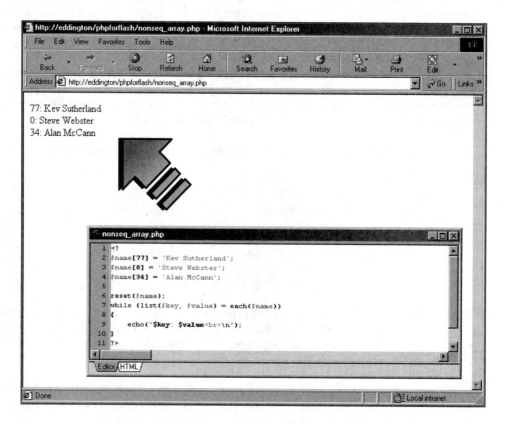

This same loop would work for our string indexed array:

```
$book['Title'] = 'Foundation PHP for Flash';
$book['Publisher'] = 'friends of ED';
$book['Subject'] = 'Web Design';
```

```
$book['Rating'] = 10;

reset($book);
while (list($key, $value) = each($book)) {
    echo("$key: $value<br>\n");
}
```

For which the output would look like:

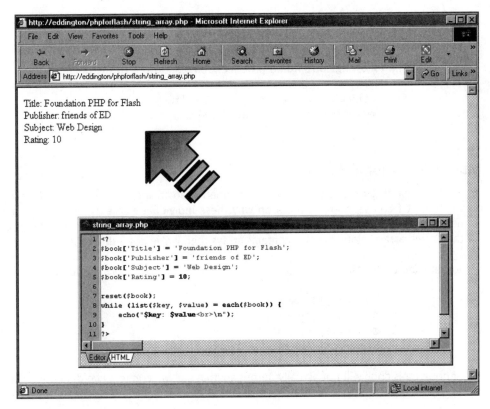

We can also use the `foreach` loop that was introduced with PHP version 4. This is the preferred method of looping through all of the values in an array

There are two syntaxes; the second is a minor, but useful, extension of the first:

1.

```
foreach($array as $value) {
statements
        }
```

continues overleaf

2.

```
foreach($array as $key => $value) {
    statements
}
```

The first form loops over the array given by $array. On each loop, the value of the current element is assigned to $value and the internal array pointer is advanced by one (so on the next loop, you'll be looking at the next element).

The second form does the same thing, except that the current element's key (or index) will be assigned to the variable $key on each loop.

The following code would produce identical output to the previous…

```
foreach($book as $key => $value) {
    echo("$key: $value<br>\n");
}
```

Multi-Dimensional Arrays

At the beginning of this section we mentioned that an array is simply a collection of variables. Of course, there's no reason why these individual elements of an array cannot be arrays themselves. This creates what is commonly known as a two-dimensional array. If the nested arrays' elements also contains arrays then we've got a three-dimensional array!

To help you understand this better take a look at the following piece of code:

```
$users[0]['name'] = "steve";
$users[0]['pass'] = "nottelling";
$users[1]['name'] = "joe";
$users[1]['pass'] = "itsasecret";
```

Although this code will not actually output anything, it will create a two dimensional array.

This could be visualized by the diagram below.

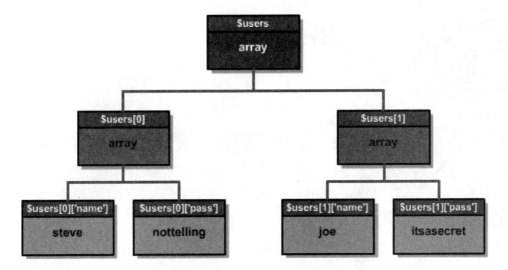

Here we can see the tree-like structure of the two dimensional array we've created. You can see from this that the two elements of the $users array are, in fact, arrays themselves, each representing a given user. Each of these arrays holds the name and password for each user.

When combined with **looping**, multi-dimensional arrays provide a powerful container for our information. The following code would output the above array, indicating the structure.

```
// Loop to traverse elements of $users array
foreach($users as $key => $value) {
    // Output
    echo "User $key\n";

    // Loop to traverse each sub-array
    foreach($value as $key2 => $value2) {
        echo "  $key2: $value2<br>\n";
    }
}
```

The last two pieces of code, if put together in a script, would produce the following output:

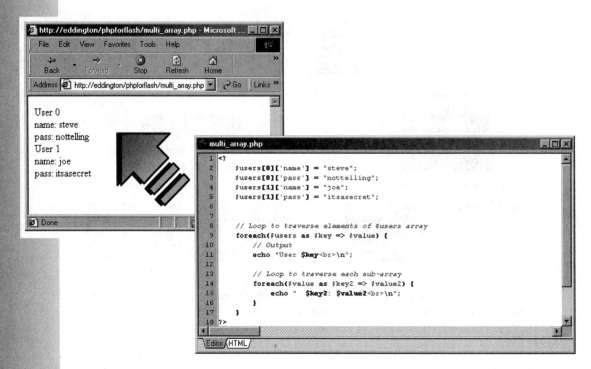

We could also use the same theory to loop through arrays with more dimensions, simply by adding more `foreach` loops.

Sorting Arrays

Now that we know how to create arrays and how to loop through them, it would be nice to be able to get them into some kind of order. We'll only cover the simplest of sorting routines for arrays here, as we're only likely to want to sort our arrays numerically or alphabetically. If you're interested in more advanced array sorting methods in PHP then take a look at the Arrays section of the PHP manual.

The simplest of the array sorting functions is **sort**. This function rearranges the elements of an array so that they are sorted into numeric and alphabetical order. It also reassigns the array's indices to reflect the new order.

For example, consider the following piece of code:

```php
$reviewers = array("Gareth", "Stef", "Pete", "Jake");

sort($reviewers);

foreach($reviewers as $id => $reviewer) {
    echo "Reviewer $id: $reviewer<br>\n";
}
```

This would output:

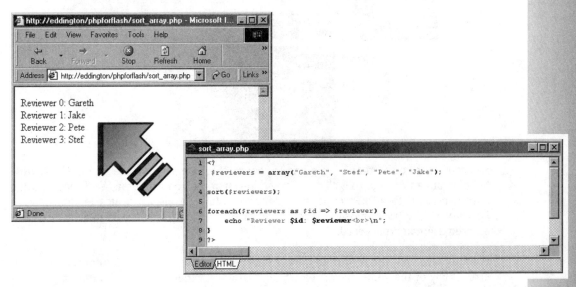

You can see that the array has been sorted alphabetically. However, as mentioned previously, the array indices are also reassigned, so this method of sorting may not be convenient for non-sequential or string indexed arrays. To combat this problem we can use the `asort` function. This changes the order of the array elements but does not alter their indices.

PHP also provides two related functions, **rsort** and **arsort**, that work in exactly the same was as `sort` and `asort` respectively except that they order the array in reverse.

Putting It Into Practice

We've covered a massive amount of ground in this chapter but it wouldn't be complete without a practical example to round it all off. In this section we're going to create a simple user authentication system for our Flash movies.

So that we're not fumbling around in the dark, let's take a look at the finished article.

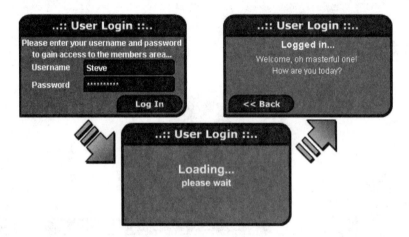

You can see from this that we're going to require three sections for the movie. Firstly we'll build a data entry page to collect the login information from the user. We'll then fire this information off to a PHP script for verification while we display a nice loading screen. Finally we'll display a message received from the PHP script, which is individual to the entered username/password.

We also have an error section to handle incorrect username/password information – one error if any of the fields are left empty, and another if there are no valid matches.

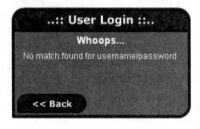

Right, that's enough chit-chat – let's get cracking!

Building our Flash Login Interface

The first thing we need to do is to create a movie clip. Since we're going to be using the `onClipEvent` handler to detect when we've received data from the PHP script we'll need to have everything encapsulated in a movie clip.

1. Create a new movie clip by selecting Insert > New Symbol from the main menu or by pressing CTRL+F8 – you know the drill by now! As always, give it a suitable name (I've used Login Window) and hit the OK button.

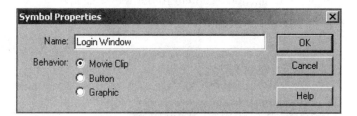

2. Next we need to create the layer and frame structure for the sections of the movie clip. Use the screenshot below as a guide.

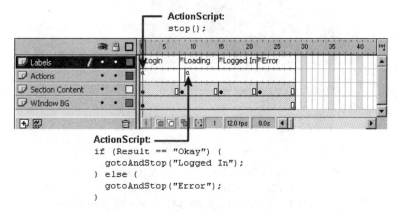

```
ActionScript:
stop();
```

```
ActionScript:
if (Result == "Okay") {
  gotoAndStop("Logged In");
} else {
  gotoAndStop("Error");
}
```

Don't forget to add the ActionScript as shown!

3. Before we move on to create the individual sections of the movie clip let's create a nice stylish background to run through the whole interface. After a chapter of PHP basics, statements, loops and arrays, I bet you'll relish the chance to get arty! I've kept up my theme from earlier examples but you can use whatever you fancy...

Create your styling on the Window BG layer.

Having created a suitably awesome background, we need to start adding the functional content to our movie clip. We'll start out with the Login frame:

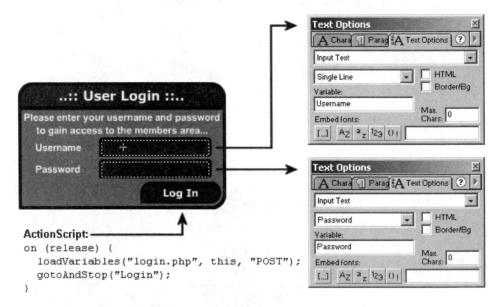

ActionScript:
```
on (release) {
  loadVariables("login.php", this, "POST");
  gotoAndStop("Login");
}
```

4. The main areas of this section that we need are the two text boxes and the button. It's also nice to add a bit of text telling the user what we want from them, or else they may just sit staring blankly at it all day! Add these as in the screenshot, not forgetting to ActionScript some functionality into the button!

5. Moving on to the Loading frame, this is probably about as simple as it gets. All I've got here is some text telling the user what is happening. If you've got some time to kill you might want to put a groovy animation in here to keep them interested, such as the clock animation we used in **Chapter 1**.

Now we need somewhere to display the data that the PHP script returns to our Flash movie. The script will return a custom message in the message variable so as a bare minimum we'll need a text box of the same name. I've also thrown in a Back button as well so that you can try out different username/password combinations without having to refresh the movie – think of it as an early Logout button!

6. On the Logged In frame duplicate the following structure, with a dynamic text field to hold our customized message and a Back button.

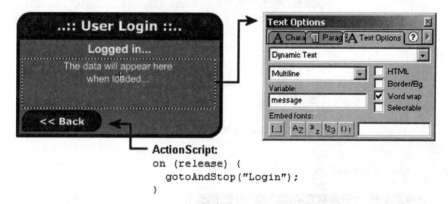

```
ActionScript:
on (release) {
   gotoAndStop("Login");
}
```

If the username/password information entered into the form does not match any of the ones we're going to code into the PHP script, we need a section of the movie clip to tell the user just that. The PHP script will return error information in a variable named errorMsg so, again, we'll at least want a text box with that name.

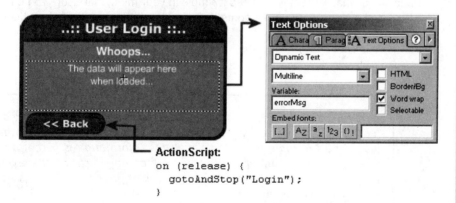

```
ActionScript:
on (release) {
   gotoAndStop("Login");
}
```

7. For this, simply replicate the Logged In frame, changing the small header at the top to reflect the fact that it's an error page, and changing the name of

the text box to `errorMsg` so that our error message will be displayed.

Now there's only one bit left to add: the `onClipEvent` handler to tell our movie clip when the data has been loaded.

8. From the main timeline, drag a copy of our newly created movie clip from the Library onto the stage and attach the following code to the new instance.

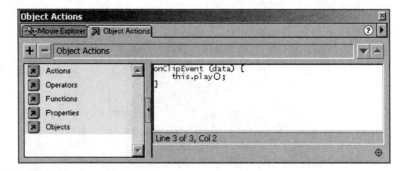

Now for the PHP bit...

Scripting the Login Engine

All that's left for us to do now is to bash out the PHP script to run the whole show. As you probably expected, we're going to be using a lot of the techniques covered in this chapter. Although I'll be walking you through the code, don't feel intimidated if you don't understand what we're doing – keep it simple in your mind, make sure you understand the basics, and eventually the more complicated code will unravel itself like a budding flower.

This is where it all comes together.

> *Throughout the book, if you ever get stuck at a certain concept or function and can't remember where it was covered, don't forget the index and the table of contents – all the information is here if and when you need it, and if you're still stuck on any particular item you can check the PHP manual at* www.php.net *or visit us at* www.phpforflash.com/support!

1. The first part of the script deals with storing the usernames and passwords, along with the custom messages, of each authorized user. We use three separate arrays to store this information, with each array holding separate data items.

```
<?

$usernames[] = "Steve";
$passwords[] = "nottelling";
$messages[] = "Welcome, oh masterful one!\nHow are you
today?";

$usernames[] = "Matt";
$passwords[] = "itsasecret";
$messages[] = "Hello Sir Matt, knight of the purple jelly
table! Did you bring my rubber wallpaper?";

$usernames[] = "Bill";
$passwords[] = "pimple";
$messages[] = "Is that little penguin scaring you again?";
```

```
login.php                                                        _ □ X
1  <?
2     /*********************************************************
3        File: login.php
4
5        From: Chapter 2
6              Foundation PHP for Flash by Steve Webster
7        URL:  http://www.phpforflash.com
8     *********************************************************/
9
10    // Create and fill username and password arrays.
11    // We also want to return a custom message for each user so
12    // we'll fill another array with those messaged
13    $usernames[] = "Steve";
14    $passwords[] = "nottelling";
15    $messages[] = "Welcome, oh masterful one!\nHow are you today?";
16
17    $usernames[] = "Matt";
18    $passwords[] = "itsasecret";
19    $messages[] = "Hello Sir Matt, knight of the purple jelly table! Did you bring my
   rubber wallpaper?";
20
21    $usernames[] = "Bill";
22    $passwords[] = "pimple";
23    $messages[] = "Is that little penguin scaring you again?";

  Editor HTML
```

> Note that the usernames and passwords we are setting here will be case-
> sensitive so be careful how you type them!

Next we need to have some code to check we have been passed both a username and a password. We do this first since there's no point in continuing if either one or the other, or both, isn't present. Note that this could have been performed in the Flash movie before we sent the information to our PHP script. Indeed, that is generally a better method of doing such things. However, for the sake of a tutorial, let's nail it all to PHP.

2. To do this we use the `if` statement that we met in the **selection** section, along with some **logical operators** and the functions we met in the **variables** section to determine that they have a value.

```php
// Check that a username and password have been passed...
if (!isset($username) || empty($username) ||
    !isset($password) || empty($password)) {

    // If not tell Flash movie that we've failed and exit
    print "&result=Fail&errorMsg=" . urlencode("You need to
supply a username and password");
    exit;
}
```

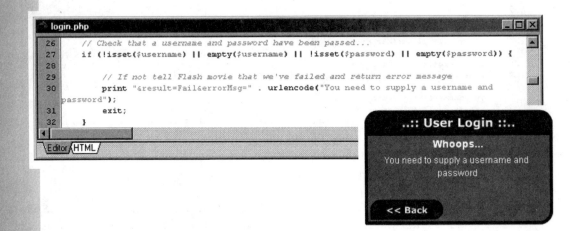

```php
26     // Check that a username and password have been passed...
27     if (!isset($username) || empty($username) || !isset($password) || empty($password)) {
28
29         // If not tell Flash movie that we've failed and return error message
30         print "&result=Fail&errorMsg=" . urlencode("You need to supply a username and
password");
31         exit;
32     }
```

..:: **User Login** ::..

Whoops...

You need to supply a username and password

<< Back

There are two bits of code here we haven't met before. Firstly the `isset` and `empty` functions are used to check that a given variable exists and has a value respectively. The other is the `exit` statement. This statement ends the PHP script prematurely at the point where it is specified. This is useful, as we have used it here, when an error has occurred and there's no point in going on.

3. Now we set up a variable that we're going to use to indicate whether a match was found for the username and password passed into our script from the Flash movie. This is initially set to `false`.

```
// Set a variable so we can indicate
// whether a match was found or not

    $matchFound = false;
```

Now comes the juicy bit – **looping** through the `usernames` and `passwords` arrays we created earlier to see if we can find a match for the ones from the Flash movie.

4. We do this using a `for` loop since we can tell how many iterations (loops) we're going to need by counting the number of elements in any of the three arrays.

```
    // Now we loop through each entry in our arrays
    // looking for a valid match
    for ($count = 0; $count < count($usernames) &&
$matchFound == false; $count++) {

        // If username and password matches entry...
        if ($username == $usernames[$count] && $password ==
$passwords[$count]) {

        // Get the user's message and indicate we've found a
match
            $message = $messages[$count];
            $matchFound = true;
        }
    }
```

You'll notice from the above code that we're checking for a combination of conditions within the `for` loop statement. Firstly we're checking to make sure that our loop control variable `$count` has not exceeded the total number of elements in the `$usernames` array, since we can't check the details against users we don't have.

However, we're also checking that the value of $matchFound is still false. This means that once we've found a match the loop terminates – there's no point in checking the details against the rest of the users if we already have a match.

If a match is found, we copy the value of the relevant element of the messages array so that we can output it to Flash later. We also set the $matchFound variable to true so we can break out of the loop.

5. Finally, we check the value of the $matchFound variable so that we can determine whether a valid username/password combination has been entered.

```
// If we found a match...
if ($matchFound) {

    // Tell movie login was okay and return custom msg
    print "&result=Okay&message=" . urlencode($message);
} else {

    // Otherwise, tell Flash movie we failed
    print "&result=Fail&errorMsg=" . urlencode("No match
found for username/password");
}

?>
```

```
login.php                                                              _ □ ×
33
34       // Set a variable so we can indicate whether a match was found or not
35       $matchFound = false;
36
37       // Now we loop through each entry in our arrays looking for a valid match
38       for ($count = 0; $count < count($usernames) && $matchFound == false; $count++) {
39
40           // If username and password matches entry...
41           if ($username == $usernames[$count] && $password == $passwords[$count]) {
42
43               // Get the user's message and indicate we've found a match
44               $message = $messages[$count];
45               $matchFound = true;
46           }
47       }
48
49       // If we found a match...
50       if ($matchFound) {
51
52           // Tell the Flash movie that login was successful and return custom message
53           print "&result=Okay&message=" . urlencode($message);
54       } else {
55
56           // Otherwise, tell Flash movie we failed
57           print "&result=Fail&errorMsg=" . urlencode("No match found for username/password");
58       }
59
60       ?>

 Editor  HTML
```

That's it! Upload or copy the whole lot to your web server, fire up a browser window and have fun! Remember, to add users or change passwords, just change them in the array – it's as easy as that.

> *In later chapters, you'll learn how to adapt this kind of thing to work with a database of users, and that's when things will really start to kick off!*

Summary

We'll kick off the summary with simple truth: *the ground we've covered in this chapter is absolutely massive*. If you've got to this stage, then you should realize that you've already got a fairly firm grounding in the basics of PHP.

We've discussed:

- Good naming conventions and comments – making your code readable

- Variables, and loading variables from a PHP script into Flash

- Operators and how to use them

- Using statements – selection and iteration

- Arrays, sequential and non-sequential – how to call data from them and sort them

- Bringing it all together in a practical PHP and Flash application

We've been able to skim through the basics of PHP relatively quickly because of the similarity between PHP and ActionScript and because you should already have been familiar with concepts such as variables, arrays, selection and iteration. All we had to do was work out how they were used in PHP and identify any quirks!

So, where to next? Well, I don't know about you but I'm off to shove my head in a bucket of ice and let it cool down for a while. The nature of the content covered in this chapter was fairly dry, and you may have found it hard going because of that, but like I said, it's only Chapter 2 and you're well on your way. I'd suggest you give yourself a hearty pat on the back and take the rest of the day off… you've certainly earned it!

3 Making PHP Work for You

What we'll cover in this chapter

- *Introducing **functions** – essential to writing good, reusable PHP code*

- ***Passing data** to and from, into and out of functions*

- *Making reference to functions in our code; **including** external files*

- *A fully reusable Tell-a-Friend application*

Up until this point we've been writing our scripts in a strictly monolithic fashion. Essentially this means that all our code has been thrown together in the same section of the same script. While this is fine for the relatively small scripts that we've written so far, once we begin to write larger scripts, or even start working on a whole site, it will lead to a lot of redundant, unmanageable and non-reusable code.

Avoiding these three pitfalls at all costs is the mark of a good PHP developer; so let's take a quick moment at the start of this chapter to explore why.

- **Redundant Code.** The word 'redundant' is used a lot when talking about bad programming practice and has been used in many different contexts to convey different messages. Of these, the one we're concerned with here is the unnecessary repetition of code throughout a script.

- **Unmanageable Code.** Another point against redundant code is the fact that it can make your code unmanageable. Taking the previous example of a script that needs to authenticate a username and password at several points throughout the script, imagine what would happen if we needed to change the way that the password was validated - we'd have to go through our script and edit every instance of our verifying code. Unmanageable code is *unmaintainable* code, and needs to be avoided!

- **Non-Reusable Code.** Continuing with our example, imagine that we have several scripts on our site that need to perform the same username and password authentication. Each script would have a repeat of the authentication code, making it both redundant *and* unmanageable.

You're obviously going to want to stay as far away as possible from these coding nightmares. Thankfully, PHP provides the ability to create user-defined functions so that we only have to write code for a particular purpose once, referencing it throughout our script. PHP also allows us to pull in code from external files, meaning that we can store code that is common to more than one script in a single file.

club *php*

No Redundant Code

No Unmanageable Code

No Non-reusable Code

No Denims

Functions Available!

Admission - $6

The webmaster reserves the right to refuse entry

Having met and understood this fearsome trio of coding no-nos, it's time to take an in-depth look at our best defence – the trusty **function**. Put simply, functions are little chunks of reusable code that, once defined, can be called upon whenever and wherever we need them.

> *Functions in PHP work in pretty much the same way as their ActionScript counterparts - right down to the syntax used to create and call them. This similarity exists because believe it or not, both PHP and ActionScript both have a common ancestor – the C programming language!*

Just in case you haven't met functions in ActionScript, or any other language for that matter, we'll spend a paragraph or two recapping on what a function is and what it allows us to do.

Introducing Functions

Functions help to divide monolithic scripts into parts that are easier to understand and modify, splitting a big problem into smaller parts. They help to clarify the structure of the script, avoid code duplication and make it easier to modify the script.

This is basic to any good design. Once you break the general idea into smaller ideas, locating areas of repetition is easier and you can then turn these areas into functions.

OK, so you know what a function is in theory, but if you're still a little mystified as to why these functions are so useful, I'll draw on personal experience and lead you on a tale of bikes, yellow stickers and forgetfulness...

I have a motorcycle. It's only a little Peugeot Speedfight 100 but it gets me from A to B (with an occasional detour to C), and it infuriates the heck out of car drivers when I zip past them in traffic jams – most satisfying! Anyway, I am forever losing the keys for my little scooter, resulting in an almost daily *hunt the keys* session.

Now, I could solve the problem by making 20 copies of the keys and dotting them all over the house - I'd be sure to stumble across a copy within a few minutes of searching. However, if I ever need to change my keys (perhaps when I get myself a nice new Ducatti 1100) I will have to change all 20 copies of my keys too.

A better solution would be to have a single set of keys and to constantly store them on the key-rack by my front door. Then I could dot some yellow sticky notes around the house telling me that my keys are on the key-rack by the front door. That way, when I find one of these notes I go straight to the key-rack and pick up my keys. If I ever need to change the keys I don't need to change the notes, since the notes just tell me where I can find my keys!

This is the basic idea behind functions, storing a piece of code to fulfil a purpose (the keys) in a single place and then referencing it throughout our code (the sticky notes).

So now you know what functions do (and what kind of bike I have) let's see how they work. Here's the procedure for creating a function in PHP:

```
function functionName([parameters]) {
    statements
}
```

As with a lot of the elements of the PHP language we've met so far, this is exactly the same as the syntax for creating functions in ActionScript, so it might be pretty familiar to you if you're already a Flash user.

A simple function in PHP might look something like:

```
function outputName() {
    echo "My name is Steve Webster.";
}
```

```
echo "I'll tell you my name.<br>\n";
outputName();
```

This obviously isn't too useful a function since all it does is print a name, but it does give you a simple look at a real PHP function. The last line of the above code is an example of how to call a function. This is done simply by using the name we gave the function earlier in the script, followed by a pair of parentheses, with a semi-colon to finish off the line.

When the function is called, or invoked, execution passes to the first statement in the function. The statements inside the function execute as normal until either the end of the function or until the `return` keyword is encountered. At this point the execution passes back to the next statement *after* the function call.

It's like that detour to C on the A to B journey through a script or page. When the PHP processor hits the function, it heads off at a tangent to fulfil the function step by step, and then comes back once the function has been completed and carries on with the rest of the page.

We can visualize this using the diagram below:

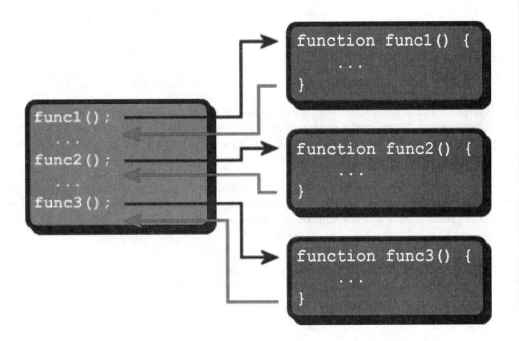

Variable Scope

With the introduction of functions into our scripts, we encounter the issue of **variable scope**. The scope of a variable determines which parts of the script have access to it.

Until now, all the variables we've used are what are known as **global variables**, meaning that they are accessible throughout the script. However, variables that are created inside a function have limited scope and are only accessible within the function itself, and these are known as **local variables**.

Moreover – and though you might not think it – variables that exist outside of the function (global variables) are not automatically accessible within our functions. This was introduced to combat the security implications of automatically creating global variables from data passed in via GET and POST.

The distinctly *non*-global nature of global variables can be illustrated with the following piece of code:

```php
function increment() {
    $number++;
}

$number = 1;

echo $number . "<br>";        // Will print 1
increment();
echo $number . "<br>";        // Will print 1
```

Because the `$number` variable is not visible inside the `increment` function, it is not incremented as we might expect it to be. Instead, a new `$number` variable is created *locally* to the `increment` function, and it is this variable which is incremented, leaving our global variable untouched!

All is not lost however, and we can access global variables from within our functions by specifying them within the function preceded by the `global` keyword. We could rewrite the previous piece of code to take advantage of this feature:

```php
function increment() {
    global $number;

    $number++;
}

$number = 1;

echo $number . "<br>";        // Will print 1
```

```
    increment();
    echo $number . "<br>";              // Will print 2
```

We could also have accessed the global $number variable by using the built-in $GLOBALS array. This array holds all of the script's global variables and allows us to manipulate them without having to use the global keyword.

```
    function increment() {
        $GLOBALS['number']++;
    }

    $number = 1;

    echo $number . "<br>";              // Will print 1
    increment();
    echo $number . "<br>";              // Will print 2
```

Obviously the sample functions presented here are not necessarily the most useful, but they're just to illustrate the techniques that you will need as a PHP designer.

Variable Lifetime

Like all things on our wonderful planet, variables have a lifetime, and when that lifetime is over, they cease to exist. Unlike the aforementioned planet dwellers though, the lifetime of a variable is governed not by the passage of time but by when the variable goes out of scope.

This whole concept can be made a little easier if we look at a piece of code.

```
    function updateCount() {
        $count++;
        print "Count: $count<br>\n";
    }

    updateCount();   // Will print "Count: 1"
    updateCount();   // Will print "Count: 1"
```

If you look at the code above, it doesn't matter how many times we call the updateCount function, the output will always be the same. This may seem a little strange until you realize that at the end of the updateCount function, the *local* $count variable goes out of scope and dies. When the function is called again, a fresh $count variable is created.

We can force PHP to remember the value of certain variables by specifying the variable name with the `static` keyword.

```php
function updateCount() {
    static $count = 0;

    $count++;
    print "Count: $count<br>\n";
}

updateCount();   // Will print "Count: 1"
updateCount();   // Will print "Count: 2"
```

You can see from the above code that this time $count retains its value between function calls (although it is still a local variable and not accessible outside the function). What happens is that the first time updateCount is called, $count is initialized to 0, and on subsequent calls this initialization is passed over. However, you have to remember that the now static $count variable will only retain its value during the execution of the whole script. If the script is reloaded then the $count variable will again be initialized to 0.

Passing Data to Functions

The example given above shows a simple function that doesn't take any arguments. While this is still useful, functions really start to come into their own when we can pass information to them.

> *Passing arguments is really passing information. When variables are listed in a function definition they are known as parameters and they tell PHP what information the function expects. When the function is called in the script, data is passed using arguments (which is just another name for the bits between the parentheses)*

To pass information we use the **parameters** part of the function definition syntax. Here, as in ActionScript, all we do is list the information we want to be passed in the form of variable names. We can then use these variable names inside our function to reference the information passed in.

```php
function outputDetails($name, $jobTitle, $age) {
    print "Your name is $name, you are a $jobTitle and you
are $age years old<br>\n";
}

outputDetails("Steve Webster", "PHP Guru", 22);
outputDetails("Alan McCann", "Content Architect", 23);
```

You can see the benefits of being able to pass data into functions by looking at the above code. By making the name and age parts of the output dependent on the arguments of the function, we can change the output by changing the arguments we feed to the function in the function call.

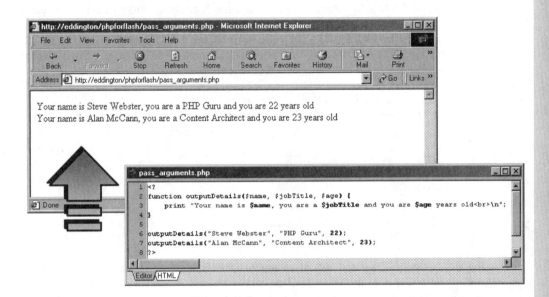

Returning Data from Functions

As well as being able to pass data into our functions, we can return information from them. This is accomplished by using the `return` keyword, followed by the value we want to return (or the variable name that contains that value).

For example, a function to square a number could look like:

```php
function square($number) {
    return $number * $number;
}

echo "4 squared = " . square(4) . "<br>\n";// 16
echo "10 squared = " . square(10) . "<br>\n";    // 100
```

The `square` function takes the data passed in via the `$number` parameter, squares the number by multiplying it by itself, and returns the result. This means that we can pass this function any number and it will return that number's square.

The return keyword can be used anywhere in the function and causes the exiting of the function at that point. In addition, we can have multiple return statements in a function, and this is often used with the **selection** statements to indicate the success or failure of an operation.

But, because of the fact that execution of a function is aborted when a return keyword is encountered, we are restricted to a single active return statement in a function, and thus restricted to a single return value. As a workaround, we could use an array as a return value in order to allow us to return more than a single value. For example, a function that will both double and square an argument could look like:

```
function doubleAndSquare($number) {
$returnArray['double'] = $number * 2;
$returnArray['square'] = $number * $number;

return $returnArray;
}

$values = doubleAndSquare(5);
print "Doubled: " . $values['double'] . "<br>\n"; // 10
print "Squared: " . $values['square'] . "<br>\n"; // 25
```

Using this technique, we can return as much information from a function as possible. However, returning data in the form of an array may not always be practical. In the next section we'll look at a way of having data from within the function available outside of it.

Passing Data by Reference

By default, all arguments are passed by value. This means that a copy is made of any variable used as an argument to a function. This ensures that playing around with the variable inside the function will not affect the value in the original.

If we do want the function to be able to play with the value in our global variables then we need to pass them by reference. We specify this by using an ampersand in front of the variable name in the parameter list:

```
function doubleAndSquare($number, &$double, &$square) {
          $double = $number * 2;
          $square = $number * $number;
}
          $valueDouble = 0;
          $valueSquare = 0;

doubleAndSquare(5, $valueDouble, $valueSquare);
print "Doubled: " . $valueDouble . "\n";          // 10
print "Squared: " . $valueSquare . "\n";          // 25
```

```
&$doubleNumber        &$squ
                       r  a
                       e  r
                          e
                       b muN
```

Notice that the ampersand is *only* placed before the variable names in the list of parameters for a function (in the function definition) and not in the list of arguments (where the function is invoked).

Passing by reference allows us to modify the value of global or other variables to which the function does not have direct access. This isn't possible with the standard way of passing information since this means that a copy of the variable is just made. Any modifications are applied to the copy and then thrown away when the function ends. References allow us to get around this.

> *There are a couple of ideals you should try and conform to when creating functions. Firstly, a function should only complete a single purpose, and its name should reflect that purpose without being too long-winded – remember our conventions from* **Chapter 2**. *It should have strong* **cohesion**, *meaning that all the internal operations should be closely related – geared towards completing a single operation. Plus they should not be strongly related to, or heavily dependent on, other functions, a technique known as* **loose coupling**. *By having strong cohesion and loose coupling we make our code as reusable and easy to maintain as possible.*

Including External Files

In addition to writing commonly used code into functions, it would be handy if we could put these functions in an external file and add them into our scripts when we want to use them. If you have ever designed a web page in HTML and have used Cascading Style Sheets, you might have used a similar technique to reference the style file in every page throughout your site.

PHP provides two functions for including external files in our PHP scripts, called include and require. Both functions take a filename to include as a single argument and, in PHP4, they now both operate in much the same way. The main difference between include and require is that include is evaluated every time it is encountered (at every iteration of a loop) at runtime, while require is evaluated only once at the pre-processor stage.

In both cases, the file specified is assumed to be a standard HTML file, so we'll still have to use our PHP tags when we're specifying common code.

The syntax for the functions is:

```
require(filename);
include(filename);
```

Let's take a look at the include function in action...

File **common.php** – this will be our included file:

```
<?
    function square($number) {
        return $number * $number;
    }
?>
```

File **includetest.php** – this will pull in the **common.php** script and use it to call the **square** function

```
<?
    include("common.php");
    echo "4 squared = " . square(4);
?>
```

Here we specify the square function in the common.php file, and include that in our includetest.php file using the include function. This allows us to use the square function in our code as though it was a normal function defined in the includetest.php file.

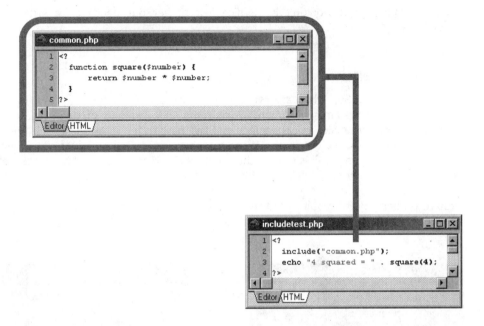

As stated previously, in PHP4 it pretty much doesn't matter which of these two we use to include our common code. However, the rest of this book favors the `include` function as it has the same name as a similar function in ActionScript.

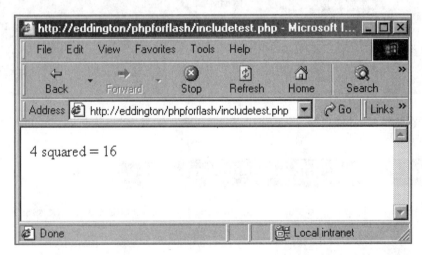

So there we have it – the code in its isolated form, and yet we can't really be said to have applied it to anything that allows us to do anything dramatically different from the previous chapter. We just know how to do things in a more efficient way. Now don't get me wrong – this is a supremely important thing to do. Efficiency is nine-tenths of the law in programming. But wouldn't it be nice just to get our hands on a little sample application?

Tell Your Friends

Oh, go on then. So, what are we going to build? My answer to this is a site recommendation system. Put simply, we're going to build one of those *Tell-a-Friend* utilities that seldom make an appearance on Flash based sites. A visitor fills out this form with their details and the details of a friend that they want to tell about the site. When the data is submitted, an email is sent to the friend telling them all about how great the site is and to go take a look.

You're probably getting quite used to this by now, but before we set out building this application let's look at where we're headed.

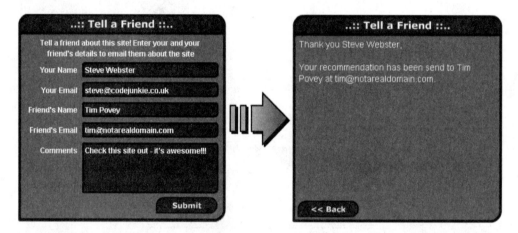

Obviously in addition to the screens shown above we're going to have an email being sent out to the friend.

Building the Tell-A-Friend Interface

As usual, we're going to start out by building the Flash front-end for the site.

1. Create a new movie clip by selecting Insert > New Symbol from the main menu or by pressing CTRL+F8. Give it a suitable name – like the one shown overleaf – and hit the OK button.

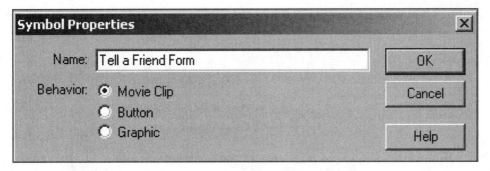

2. Next we need to create the layer and frame structure for the sections of the movie clip. As in the previous chapter, just follow my screenshots, remembering to add in the all-important ActionScript.

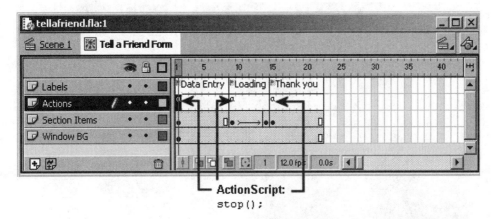

ActionScript:
```
stop();
```

3. For the sake of continuity I've carried on using the same style from previous examples, so as you've already seen, this is what my Window BG layer looks like:

4. On the Data Entry frame of the Section Items layer we're going to need some textboxes so that we've got somewhere to enter the data. It's also nice to have some text explaining what the form is for.

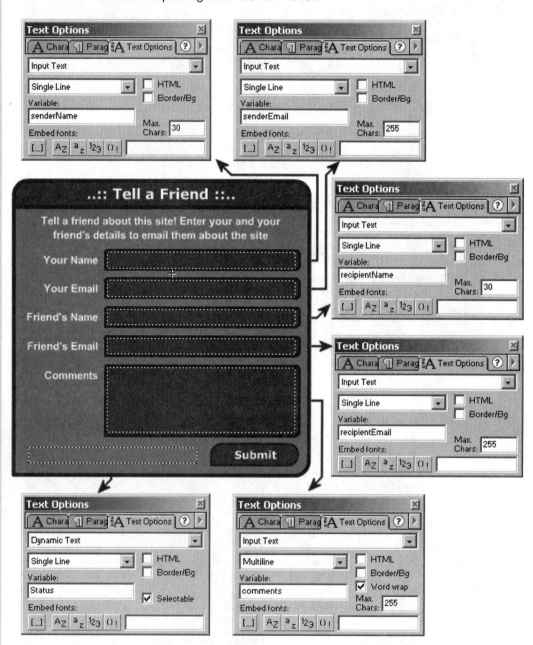

5.   We're also going to need some kind of a submit button that'll call `loadVariables` and send our movie clip to the Loading frame. All I've done is to copy the button from the previous example, changing the text and the code attached to it.

6.   You can see from the screenshot below that I've added code to stop the form being submitted if any of the text boxes have not been filled in, and that we're sending the variables from the Flash movie using the POST method.

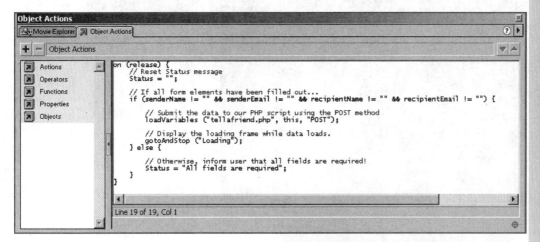

```
on (release) {
    // Reset Status message
    Status = "";

    // If all form elements have been filled out...
    if (senderName != "" && senderEmail != "" && recipientName != "" && recipientEmail != "") {

        // Submit the data to our PHP script using the POST method
        loadVariables ("tellafriend.php", this, "POST");

        // Display the loading frame while data loads.
        gotoAndStop ("Loading");
    } else {

        // Otherwise, inform user that all fields are required!
        Status = "All fields are required";
    }
}
```

7.   Now we come to the Loading frame. I have used the same clock face animation as in the Download Registration Form example in **Chapter 1**.

8.   Lastly, we need to construct the final section of our movie clip – the Thank you section. What we need here is a multiline text box to display the response from the PHP script, and a Back button so the user can go back and recommend more friends!

9. Study the diagram below and recreate the main points:

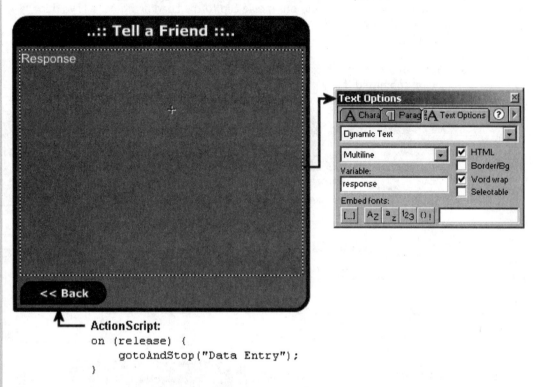

ActionScript:
```
on (release) {
    gotoAndStop("Data Entry");
}
```

The only thing left is the `onClipEvent` handler to our movie clip instance on the main stage to get it to go to the Display frame when data is received.

10. Return to the main timeline and select the instance of our movie clip. If the Actions window is not already visible then make it so by right clicking on our movie clip and selecting Actions. Enter the following code:

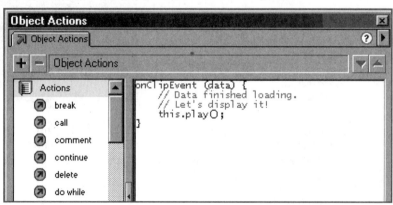

Adding the PHP Script

Now we've got the skeleton of the project, let's flesh out the Flash.

1. We'll kick off the script by initializing a few variables that we might want to change from time to time.

```
<?
 // tellafriend.php

 $siteName = "Foundation PHP for Flash";
 $siteURL = "http://www.phpforflash.com";
 $siteContact = "admin@phpforflash.com";
```

```
tellafriend.php                                          _ □ X
 1  <?
 2      /***********************************************************
 3          File: tellafriend.php
 4
 5          From: Chapter 3
 6              Foundation PHP for Flash by Steve Webster
 7          URL:  http://www.phpforflash.com
 8      ***********************************************************/
 9
 10     $siteName = "Foundation PHP for Flash";
 11     $siteURL = "http://www.phpforflash.com";
 12     $siteContact = "admin@phpforflash.com";
 ◄ │                                                           ► │
 \Editor \HTML/
```

2. Next, we'll construct the e-mail message using the variables we've been passed from the Flash movie. In this piece of code we take advantage of the fact that, when assigning a string value to a variable, we can span that string over multiple lines, and have all the line breaks included in the string.

```
$mailMessage = "Hello $recipientName,

$senderName ($senderEmail) came across the $siteName
website at
$siteURL and though that you might like to take a look for
yourself!

$senderName also left the following additional comments
for you:
```

continues overleaf

```
$comments;


If you believe you have received this email in error then
please
contact $siteContact and let us know!

Also, please note that we cannot be held responsible for
the comments
added by the sender.
_____";
```

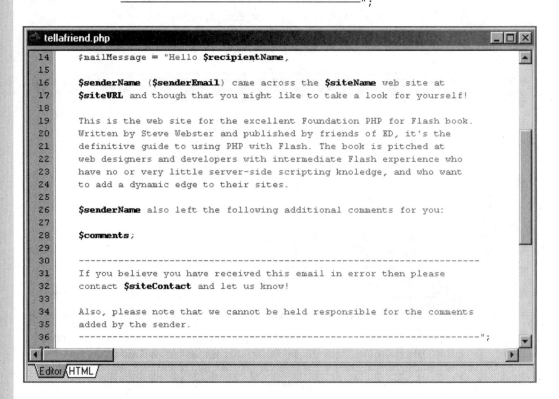

```
tellafriend.php                                                    _ □ ×
14    $mailMessage = "Hello $recipientName,
15
16    $senderName ($senderEmail) came across the $siteName web site at
17    $siteURL and though that you might like to take a look for yourself!
18
19    This is the web site for the excellent Foundation PHP for Flash book.
20    Written by Steve Webster and published by friends of ED, it's the
21    definitive guide to using PHP with Flash. The book is pitched at
22    web designers and developers with intermediate Flash experience who
23    have no or very little server-side scripting knoledge, and who want
24    to add a dynamic edge to their sites.
25
26    $senderName also left the following additional comments for you:
27
28    $comments;
29
30    ----------------------------------------------------------------------
31    If you believe you have received this email in error then please
32    contact $siteContact and let us know!
33
34    Also, please note that we cannot be held responsible for the comments
35    added by the sender.
36    ----------------------------------------------------------------------";
```
Editor / HTML

3. Now we're going to build up the variables for sending the e-mail. This is simply
    a case of things like a properly formed To and From field, as well as a Subject
    for the e-mail.

```
// Build up e-mail header fields
$mailFrom = "From: $siteName <$siteContact>";
$mailTo = "$recipientName <$recipientEmail>";
$mailSubject = "Recommendation from $senderName";
```

4. Next, we're going to send the e-mail using the `mail` function.

```
// Send e-mail
mail($mailTo, $mailSubject, $mailMessage, $mailFrom);
```

> `mail (to, subject, message [, additional_headers])`
>
> *This function basically attempts to send an e-mail to the e-mail address specified in* to *with a subject of* subject *and a body of* message. *The optional* additional_headers *part allows you to set things like the From address, as we'll see later in this example.*

5. Finally, we send our response back to the Flash movie.

```
$response = "Thank you $senderName,\n\nYour recommendation
has been send to $recipientName at $recipientEmail.";

// Respond to Flash movie!
print "&result=Okay&response=$response&";

?>
```

```
tellafriend.php                                                    _ □ ×
38      // Build up email header fields
39      $mailFrom = "From: $siteName <$siteContact>";
40      $mailTo = "$recipientName <$recipientEmail>";
41      $mailSubject = "Recommendation from $senderName";
42
43      // Send email
44      mail($mailTo, $mailSubject, $mailMessage, $mailFrom);
45
46      $response = "Thank you $senderName,\n\nYour recommendation has been send to
$recipientName at $recipientEmail.";
47
48      // Respond to Flash movie!
49      print "&result=Okay&response=$response&";
50
51  ?>

Editor HTML
```

Try it out and tell all your friends about us!

Summary

This chapter was all about learning how to program good, reusable and maintainable PHP scripts. It is important from the outset to get used to writing your scripts with the topics covered in this chapter in mind, as this will save you a lot of time when you come to update your scripts.

We've explored:

- Functions and reusable, maintainable code

- How functions affect variables and their scope and lifetime

- Passing data in and out of functions

- Including external files

As a bonus, you've now got a Tell-a-Friend movie clip that you can include in any site – now that's what I call reusable!

Now that you've finished this chapter, I'd suggest you go and take a breather. Go out for a walk, sit in the garden teasing the dog, or just collapse in front of the TV – anything but sit in front of your computer reading this book. When you come back you'll be fully refreshed and eager to tackle the next chapter!

4 PHP and Information Handling

What we'll cover in this chapter:

- *The basics of using **strings** in PHP*

- *Joining strings together and using **variables** in strings*

- *The most important and useful **string-related functions***

- *Building a simple but effective **text highlighting** application*

At some point or another in our scripts, we're going to want to be able to analyze and manipulate strings. We've already touched upon strings briefly at various points in the previous chapters, but in this chapter we're going to roll up our sleeves and get down and dirty with them! We'll be looking at how we can convert our strings into a given format, as well as some of the string manipulation functions available to us in PHP.

Rather surprisingly, there's a lot more to strings than initially meets the eye. We've already got the basics pinned down – namely that we can use strings in our scripts to store textual information – and we've already seen some examples of strings in action in earlier chapters. Adding to your familiarity with strings we'll see that strings are also available to use in ActionScript and, although their implementation and use is quite different from PHP, you'll at least have an understanding of the concept of strings and the kinds of operations that can be performed on them.

Once we've covered the basics of strings in PHP, we'll move on to looking at string manipulation functions. PHP provides a multitude of string manipulation functions – some totally obscure that I've never found a use for, and others so useful that life without them would be unbearable! Well, okay...maybe not quite *that* bad, but it would make our lives as web designers a heck of a lot harder without them.

OK, enough chit-chat from me – let's get those strings in tune!

The Basics

A string is basically a series of characters, textual data if you will... In PHP, there is no practical limit on the length of your strings, and you can shove as much information into them as you like, although your hosting company may not thank you for gobbling up all their RAM if you decide to test that theory.

In PHP, a string is anything between a pair of matching single or double quotes.

```
"This is a string"

'So is this!'
```

It's worth noting, however, that the quotes must be a matching pair or PHP will throw a wobbly! This is a common error to make when you're first starting out coding with PHP, and we've all done it at sometime or another.

Single quoted strings are slightly more efficient in terms of their operation because PHP doesn't have to process them for a multitude of special characters or perform variable expansion in them, so use them wherever you can. If you're required to output such fanciful things as variable values or want to make use of escape sequences (which we'll come to later) then you'll need to use a double quoted string!

Under normal circumstances, when PHP encounters a matching quote to that which was at the beginning of the string it will assume that the end of the string has been reached, and process anything afterwards as normal PHP code. This obviously presents a problem if we want to include these characters within our strings, but thankfully a workaround is provided.

Character Escaping

If you have a look at the two strings listed below, you can see examples of the kinds of problems we could come across when dealing with quotations in strings.

```php
$string1 = "Why won't "this" work?";

$string2 = 'Why won't this work?';
```

In the first string, the single quote being used as an apostrophe in the word won't doesn't cause any problems since the string is using double quotes as its delimiters. The error in this particular string is contained in the double quotes surrounding the word this. When PHP encounters the first double quote after the start of the string, as far as it's concerned that's the end of the string. As a result of this, the word this becomes a bunch of junk characters that PHP doesn't understand.

In the second string, unlike the first, we've got a problem with the single quote being used as an apostrophe in the word won't. Again, this turns the characters after it into incomprehensible junk that'll generate an error if used in a script.

In order to have quotation marks, and certain other special characters, as part of our strings we need to precede them with the backslash character – a technique known as **character escaping**. Take a look at the strings below to see escaping in operation.

```php
$string1 = "This one \"will\" work!";

$string2 = 'So will \'this\' one!';
```

By **escaping** each of the troublesome characters with a backslash we've created a pair of valid and trouble-free strings.

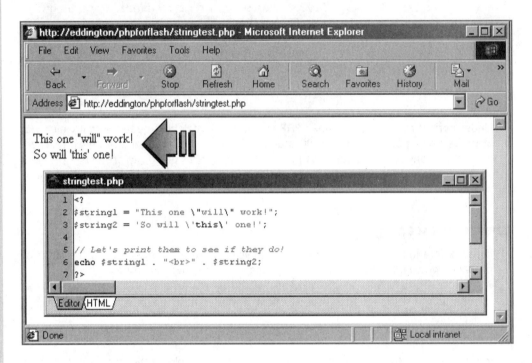

Joining Strings Together

We met the **string concatenation** operator back in **Chapter 2** but it's worth revisiting it here to view it in context. One or more strings can be concatenated (or joined) using the string concatenation operator – a simple full stop or period (.).

```
$firstName = "Steve";
$lastName = "Webster";

$fullName = $firstName . ' ' . $lastName;;
echo $fullName; // Prints "Steve Webster"
```

The above piece of code takes the values of the $firstName and $lastName variables, concatenates them with a space in between (denoted by ' ') and stores the resultant value in the $fullName variable. The value of $fullName at the end of this code will be "Steve Webster", and this is a relatively common operation to perform on user data.

Using Variables in Strings

PHP allows us to include the values of variables inside double quoted strings. This means that we don't have to use the concatenation operator in simple operations such as the one outlined above.

For example, the following two lines of code will produce the same value in the $fullName variable...

```php
$firstName = "Steve";
$lastName = "Webster";

$fullName = $firstName . ' ' . $lastName;
$fullName = "$firstName $lastName";

echo $fullName;  // Will print "Steve Webster"
```

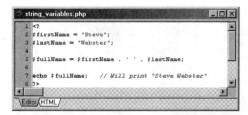 

Basically, what PHP does when it encounters the $ character in a double-quoted string is encase everything immediately after to form a valid variable name. In order to explicitly specify the **end** of a variable name in the string we'll need to enclose the entire variable name, including the $, in curly braces.

```php
$drink = "ED Cola";

echo "I think $drink's great" . "<br>\n";
echo "I need to get some chilled $drinks from the shop" .
➡ "<br>\n";
echo "I have many {$drink}s every day" . "<br>\n";
```

The first `echo` statement will produce the expected output since the single quote character cannot be part of a valid variable name.

The second one will not, however, because PHP treats the 's' on the end of `$drink` as part of the variable name. Since `$drinks` is not defined, the output will look like this:

I need to get some chilled from the shop

This problem is solved in the last `echo` statement by encasing the variable name in curly braces.

$drinks is not a recognized variable name and so is ignored

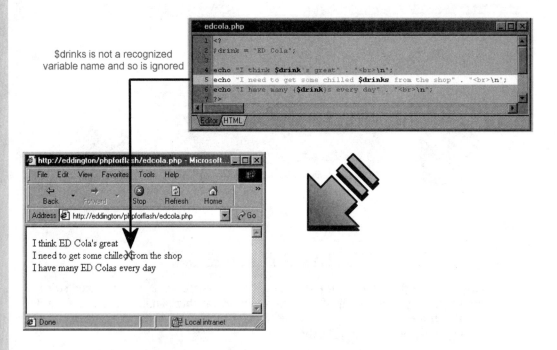

The PHP processor handles double and single quoted strings differently. The main difference is that PHP will interpret double quoted strings, while single quoted strings are treated almost exactly as written.

For example, what we failed to mention when we previously covered the escaping technique was that we can insert many special characters into our strings by escaping certain *other* characters. This allows us to represent characters that cannot be represented visually (non-printable characters) such as carriage-return and tab. Take a look at the table below to see some of the possibilities.

Sequence	Translated to...
\n	Linefeed (LF)
\r	Carriage Return (CR)
\t	Horizontal Tab
\\	Backslash character
\$	Dollar sign

> *Note that, because the backslash and dollar signs have special meanings within a string, they need to be escaped in order to obtain the desired result, even though they can be represented visually in the source file.*

However, these escape sequences are only translated when used in double quoted strings. This is because their single quoted counterparts aren't processed for this kind of information. The only exceptions to this rule are the escaped single quotes we met earlier and the escaped backslash.

Let's look at an example and all should become clear...

```
echo "Line1\nLine2\nLine3";
```

```
echo 'Line1\nLine2\nLine3';
```

The first `print` statement will give us the output we expect:

```
Line1
Line2
Line3
```

> *Note, as mentioned in **Chapter 2**, these linefeeds will not show up in your browser (but do work when passed into Flash) and so if you test the following through a browser you'll only see spaces between the text not line breaks!*

However, since \n has no special meaning inside of a *single quoted* string, the output will be given exactly as written:

```
Line1\nLine2\nLine3
```

The moral of the story is to use the right quotes for the right job!

String Related Functions

At the time of writing, PHP has 72 string related functions, and there's no way we're going to be able to cover them all here – it would be such a stupidly long and boring chapter that hospitals could use it as cheap anaesthetic. Instead, we're going to be concentrating on the most useful functions, as these are the ones you'll find yourself needing to use most often.

> For those who want to know how to do such wildly quirky things as calculating the Levenshtein distance between two strings, you can find a complete list of PHP's string functions either online at www.php.net or in the electronic manual supplied with PHP.

print() and echo()

The print and echo functions take exactly the same arguments and perform exactly the same operation as one another.

```
print(string)
echo(string)
```

They take the **string** and output it to the client (namely the web browser). In use, they might look something like this:

```
print('This is  output to the client');
echo("Welcome back $firstName");
```

Because the string being passed to the print function requires no processing with regards to special characters or variables, we have encased it in single quotes. Similarly, because we want to insert the value of the variable $firstName in the string passed to the echo function, we need to encase it in double quotes.

An interesting point to note is that neither print nor echo are strictly functions, they are language constructs. This means that they can happily be used without the parentheses.

```
print "Welcome back $firstname";
echo 'This is output to the client';
```

As with naming conventions, it is best to pick one style and stick with it throughout your scripts. You'll save yourself a lot of hassle and your scripts will be easier to read too.

printf() and sprintf()

The printf and sprintf functions allow us to produce a string that is formatted according to a set of instructions. Their operation differs slightly in that printf will output the resultant string to the client, returning true or false depending upon the success of the operation, while sprintf returns the resultant string without printing it to the client, so that it can be stored in a variable or used in an expression.

```
printf(format string [, args...]);

sprintf(format string [, args...]);
```

We use the **format string** to give the function our instructions for formatting the list of arguments (**args**) in the resultant string. It will generally contain a mixture of standard characters, which are included in the resultant string as they are written, and something known as **conversion specifications** that actually do the job of formatting the arguments.

A conversion specification begins with a "%" followed by up to five specifiers. They are, from left to right:

- An optional **padding** specifier that says what character will be used for padding the results to the right string size. This may be a space character or a 0 (zero character). The default is to pad with spaces. An alternate padding character can be specified by prefixing it with a single quote mark.

- An optional **alignment** specifier that says if the result should be left-justified or right-justified. The default is right-justified; a "−" character here will make it left-justified.

- An optional **width** specifier − a number that says how many characters (minimum) this conversion should result in.

● An optional **precision** specifier that says how many decimal digits should be displayed for floating-point numbers. This option has no effect for other types than double. (Another function useful for formatting numbers is `number_format`.)

● A **type** specifier says how argument data should be treated. A partial list of the most commonly used type specifiers is given below:

%   a literal percent character. No argument is required.

d   the argument is treated as an integer, and presented as a signed decimal number.

u   the argument is treated as an integer, and presented as an unsigned decimal number.

f   the argument is treated as a double, and presented as a floating-point number.

s   the argument is treated as, and presented as, a string.

A typical statement *without* using `printf` might look something like the following:

```
$month = 1;
$day = 7;
$year = 2042;

echo "$month/$day/$year";
```

The above piece of code would output the date represented by the variables in the m/d/yyyy format:

1/7/2042

```
printf.php                                    _ □ ✕
1  <?
2  $month = 1;
3  $day = 7;
4  $year = 2042;
5
6  echo  "$month/$day/$year";
7  ?>
  Editor HTML
```

However, we may want to show the date in mm/dd/yyyy format which is where the printf function comes into play. If we swapped the echo line above for the following printf function call we'd get the desired output.

```
printf("%02d/%02d/%d", $month, $day, $year);
```

This will output:

01/07/2042

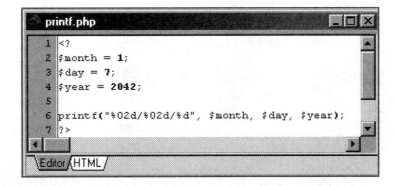

```
printf.php                                    _ □ ×
1  <?
2  $month = 1;
3  $day = 7;
4  $year = 2042;
5
6  printf("%02d/%02d/%d", $month, $day, $year);
7  ?>

Editor HTML
```

This shows how printf and sprintf can be used to accomplish things that would otherwise be near-impossible or just down right annoying. We're using the optional width specifier in the conversion specifications for the $day and $month variables to ensure that the resultant string has at least two characters for each, padding them with a zero if necessary.

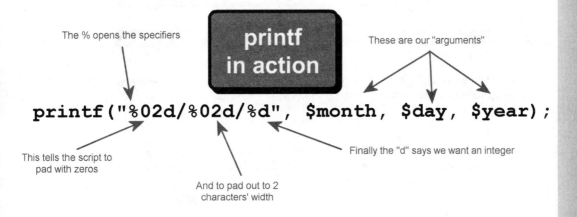

The % opens the specifiers

**printf
in action**

These are our "arguments"

```
printf("%02d/%02d/%d", $month, $day, $year);
```

This tells the script to
pad with zeros

And to pad out to 2
characters' width

Finally the "d" says we want an integer

If we wanted to store the nicely formatted output in a string then we'd use the `sprintf` function.

```
$month = 1;
$day = 7;
$year = 2042;

$date = sprintf("%02d/%02d/%d", $month, $day, $year);

// Will print 01/07/2042
echo $date;
```

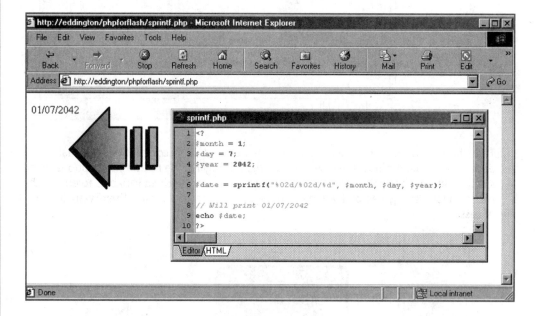

Although we're going to end our discussion of `printf` and `sprintf` here, you'll find them cropping up in a few of the examples later on in the book.

urlencode()

Along with the basic output functions we've met already, `urlencode` is going to be one of the most constant features of our scripts. We've seen this already in previous chapters and the format looks something like:

```
urlencode(string);
```

What this does is take all non-alphanumeric characters, with the exception of "-", "_" and '.' in the **string**, and replaces them with a % symbol followed by two hex digits. In addition, spaces are swapped for the "+" character.

This is a format known as application/x-www-form-urlencoded and is used for the information passed between a web browser and a server-side script such as PHP. It allows special characters to be passed as they were intended instead of being interpreted and processed by either the web browser or server software.

> *The function also returns the urlencoded version as a string, which can then be passed around (or into Flash as we saw in* **Chapter 1***).*

An example may clear things up a little:

```
$myString = "Hello isn't PHP just wicked?";
echo urlencode($myString);
```

The above piece of code will produce the following output:

Hello+isn%27t+PHP+just+wicked%3F

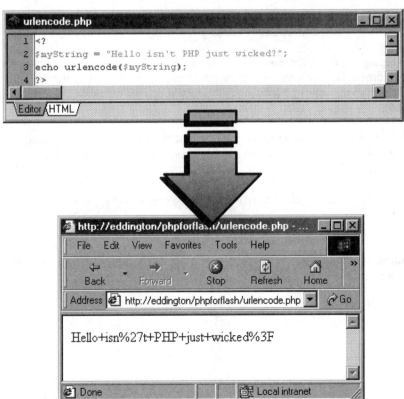

You can see that the spaces have been replaced with the "+" character and special characters such as the apostrophe and question mark have been translated into some kind of cryptic code. This may look like scribbledehobble to us, but the web browser and (more importantly from our point of view) Flash understand this just fine!

urlencode has a partner function, urldecode, which performs exactly the same operation, only in reverse. There are also two related functions called rawurlencode and rawurldecode, that are essentially the same except they translate spaces into a % symbol followed by two hex digits (%20).

> You might have seen %20 in action if you've ever been to a web page where the owner has used a space in the file name or address!

The earlier string encoded with rawurlencode would look like:

```
Hello%20isn%27t%20PHP%20just%20wicked%3F
```

explode()

This rather smashing function splits a string into an array, using another string to specify the boundaries at which to split it.

```
explode(separator, string [, limit]);
```

The **string** is split at the **separator**, with each substring becoming an element of the array returned. The optional **limit** argument allows you to specify the maximum number of elements in the returned array, with the final element containing the portion of string not split.

The following example is similar to the one that appears in the PHP manual, and has been used here both because it is an extremely fitting example and because I have a massive pizza fetish!

```
$pizza = "piece1 piece2 piece3 piece4";

$pieces = explode(' ', $pizza);
```

As you've probably guessed, $pieces ends up as an array with 4 elements once the $pizza string has been exploded using a single space as the separator.

It's worth noting that each space character is thrown away in this operation, and does not appear in any of the array elements. Also note that the original string ($pizza) is not modified in any way, shape or form by explode.

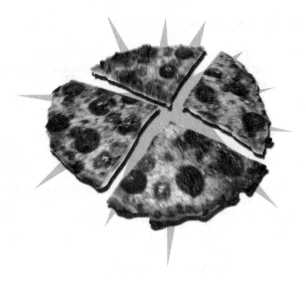

implode()

The explode function's partner in crime is called (unsurprisingly) implode.

```
implode(glue, pieces);
```

...where the **glue** is a string value and the **pieces** represent an array. This function joins all the elements of the array pieces together, inserting glue in between each to form the returned string.

As an example, we could put the formerly split string back together again using the following code.

```
$newPizza = implode(' ', $pieces);
```

Well that example was purely theoretical because those four pieces of pizza have already been eaten by me and my editors!

> *These two functions together are useful for storing an array of information as a single string and then getting is back out again. It's use is really shown in* **Chapter 7**, *where* implode *allows us to store all the information about a given user on a single line, and* explode *let's us get at the individual bits again*

substr()

The substr function will return part of a given string based on the information passed in its arguments. Let's take a look at the prototype:

```
substr(source, start [,length]);
```

Here, **source** is the string to be parsed, **start** is the position at which to begin the returned string, and the optional **length** specifies the end of the returned string – note that the latter two need to be integers.

> *It is also important to note that the first character in any given string is at position 0 rather than 1.*

In its simplest form, this function in use would look something like the following:

```
$fullName = "Steve Webster";
echo substr($fullName, 6); // Will print: Webster
```

Bringing into play the length argument, we could change this to:

```
$fullName = "Steve Webster";
echo substr($fullName, 6, 3); // Will print: Web
```

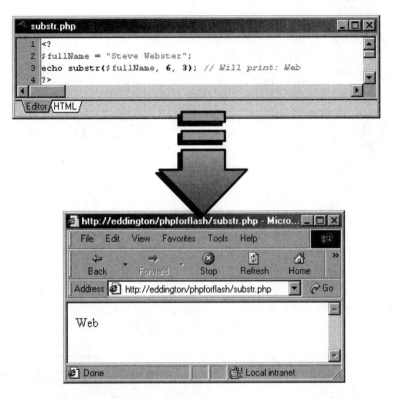

If length is negative, substr will count backwards from the end of the source string.

```
$fullName = "Steve Webster";
echo substr($fullName, 6, -5); // Will print: We
```

In practice, substr can be used to chop a sting down into something more manageable. For example, if we had an FLA where we have a text box that'll only display roughly 50 characters because of it's size then we can use substr to give us the first 50 characters of a given string to be put in there. This is useful for giving a quick snippet of a piece of information, and can be used in conjunction with a More... button to show the full string.

strlen()

This function simply returns the number of characters in a given string (answering that age old question of how long is a piece of string).

```
strlen(string);
```

> This is actually a very useful function and can be used to check the length of data being sent to PHP before we attempt to insert it, for example, into a database.

strstr()

This function will search for one string inside of another.

```
strstr(haystack, needle);
```

The function returns the substring of **haystack** from the first occurrence of **needle** to the end. If no match is found it returns `false`.

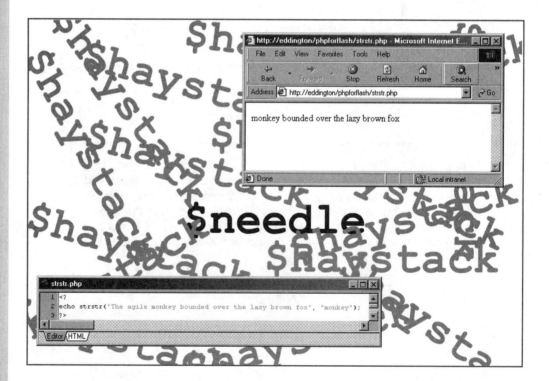

This function also has a case insensitive relative called stristr. We use these last two functions later on in the chapter.

> *Searching for one string within another is invaluable and can be used for search engines as well as for validating input!*

str_replace()

This function is used to perform search and replace operations on a string.

```
str_replace(needle, replacement, haystack);
```

str_replace will replace all occurrences of **needle** in string **haystack** with **replacement**. The resultant string is returned, but haystack is not modified in this operation.

Let's take a look at an example:

```
$text = "The cow jumped over the moon";
echo "Before: $text <br>\n";

$text = str_replace("cow", "troll", $text);
echo "After: $text <br>\n";
```

Try this out and your browser should look like the one in the screenshot:

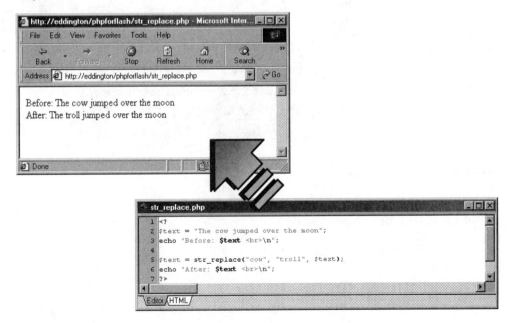

You can also use a variable to represent the replacement value instead of a string:

```
$replacement = "cookie monster";
$text = "The cow jumped over the moon";
echo "Before: $text <br>\n";

$text = str_replace("cow", $replacement, $text);
echo "After: $text <br>\n";
```

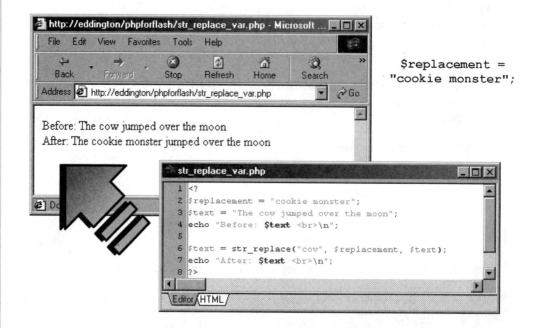

```
$replacement =
"cookie monster";
```

> This is an extremely useful function for weeding out particular words,
> phrases, or variables. You could even use it to replace swear words with
> asterisks!

strtolower() and strtoupper()

These two functions both take a single string argument and return a modified version of
that string. They look roughly like this:

```
strtolower(source);

strtoupper(source);
```

In the case of strtolower, all the alphabetical characters in the string **source** are converted to lowercase. I won't insult your intelligence by explaining what strtoupper does!

Both of these functions are available as methods of the string class in ActionScript, so you should be somewhat familiar with their operation already!

Let's take a look at what they'll do to a string...

```
$string = "Friends of ED";

$string = strtolower($string);

// Will print friends of ed
echo $string . "<br>\n";

$string = strtoupper($string);

// Will print FRIENDS OF ED
echo $string;
```

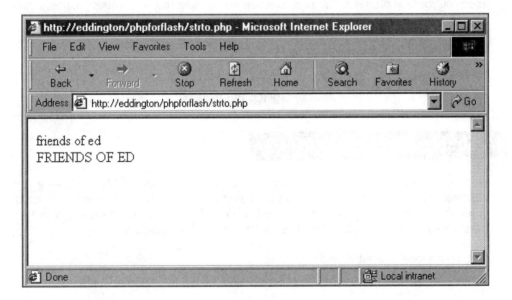

The main use I've found for these functions is when checking for e-mail addresses already present in a mailing list or user registration application. Since the regular string comparison using the == operator is case-sensitive, we need to find a way of making sure that everything is in the same case when checking for things such as this. This is because steve@codejunkie.co.uk and Steve@codejunkie.co.uk are actually different strings but they'll both send email to the same account because e-mail addresses are not case-sensitive. By using strtolower on the e-mail address we can solve this problem!

stripslashes()

The default installation of PHP has a configuration option set that will automatically escape any special characters that comes from either POST or GET methods, or via a cookie. Because of this we either need a way of removing these backslashes from our strings, or we have to program our way around the fact that these backslashes are going to be there.

Thankfully, PHP provides us with a function that will remove these slashes so we can go about our normal business. The final function we're going to cover in this chapter simply goes like this:

```
stripslashes(source);
```

This function simply takes our **source** string, strips out all the slashes, and returns the resultant string. The original source string is not modified in any way.

A Simple Text Highlighter

Well, it's sample application time again. For the purposes of demonstrating the information garnered in this chapter we're going to build a fairly simple text based search application. This will employ some of the features discussed in this chapter, and include others we'll meet later in the book – especially in the three case studies.

Let's take a look at what we'll be building...

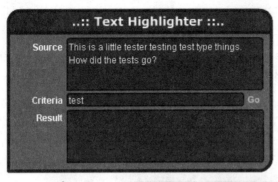

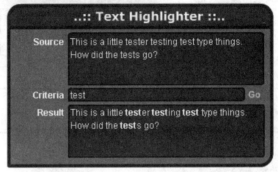

What we'll be doing is using PHP to highlight all occurrences of the string given by `criteria` in the `source` string. We'll then store the result in `result`.

We're going to make the structure of the FLA far simpler than previous ones, creating everything on the main timeline, and in a single frame, rather than encapsulating everything in a movie clip.

If you're hungry for more movie clip action then fear not – we'll be creating two of them in the next chapter! For now, let's see some more of those string functions...

1. With no movie clip to create, the first thing we should do is to set out the layer and frame structure.

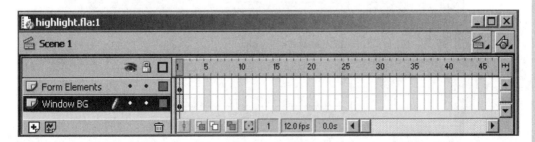

I've just used separate layers as usual for the movie background and the various form elements.

2. After creating whatever styling you feel like on the Window BG layer it's time to create the form elements. Use the diagram below as a guide:

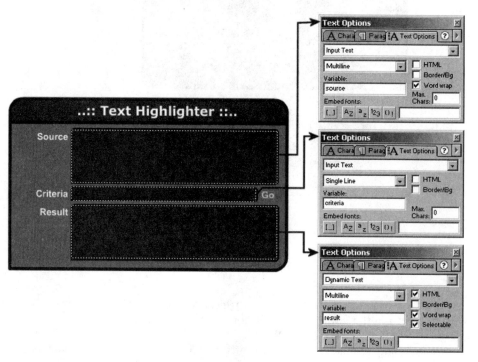

The important thing not to miss out here is to ensure that the HTML check box is checked for the `result` text box. This is because we're going to use HTML tags to highlight any matches found.

3. The final step on the Flash side is to add the code for the Go button.

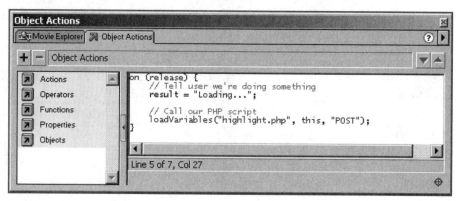

Here we're setting `result` to show the user that we're in the process of loading their data, and then calling the `loadVariables` function to send information to, and fetch information from, the PHP script.

4. That's it for the Flash movie, and the PHP script is so simple that it really demonstrates the power of the string functions available to us with this scripting language.

```php
<?
        // highlight.php
        // Chapter 4 - Foundation PHP for Flash

    // Perform search and replace
    $result = str_replace($criteria, "<b>$criteria</b>",
$source);

    // Output result to Flash
    print "&result=" . urlencode($result);
?>
```

```
highlight.php                                         _ □ X
 1  <?
 2  // highlight.php
 3  // Chapter 4 - Foundation PHP for Flash
 4
 5      // Perform search and replace
 6  $result = str_replace($criteria, "<b>$criteria</b>", $source);
 7
 8      // Output result to Flash
 9  print "&result=" . urlencode($result);
10  ?>

 Editor HTML
```

You can see that we're using the `str_replace` function to replace each occurrence of the value of the `$criteria` variable passed in from Flash in the variable $source. What we're replacing $criteria with is actually $criteria itself surrounded by HTML bold tags - **...** - meaning that the word is highlighted when returned and displayed in Flash!

Summary

So there we have it. That's enough specialist information about strings to keep a professional tennis player in rackets! We've looked at some really important and fundamental PHP principles here, and by this stage you should be comfortable with them.

We've looked at:

- Strings and how they are constructed

- The convenience of character escaping

- How to join strings together

- Using variables in strings

- The most important string-related functions

Finally, as usual, we flexed our PHP muscles a little with an exercise and believe me this kind of practice will stand you in good stead for your PHP future!

5 Looking for Patterns

What we'll cover in this chapter

- *What a **regular expression** is, in its simplest form*

- *How we can advance things a little for **better results***

- *PHP **functions** that make regular expressions more powerful*

- *How to make **simple** and **advanced** search applications*

Okay, now you should be feeling that we're really getting on, and we're now going to be steering the good ship PHP out into some deep blue water. In this next chapter we're going to take a look at **regular expressions**, and we'll check out exactly what kind of manipulation they perform on our strings.

Simply speaking, regular expressions provide a way to match patterns in our strings. We can start simply by selecting a particular letter (I don't know, say, "a") to match. Or we can get a bit more adventurous and match a whole range of letters or even non-letters. It depends on how brave we are feeling, or how complex our programming needs to be.

Let's dip our toes in the deep end for a moment – without diving in quite yet. Have a look at the expression below which, believe it or not, is a regular expression for checking the validity of an e-mail address (You don't need me to tell you how useful this could be).

```
^([a-zA-Z0-9._-]+)@([a-zA-Z0-9-])+(\.[a-zA-Z0-9-]+)+$
```

See what I mean? But we're not going to hide from them here. We're going to tackle them head on and by the time we've finished this section you should be able to understand exactly what's going on in there and why it works. Honestly!

Despite their top-of-the-range, *supercode* appearance, regular expressions by themselves are pretty useless without functions. It is the functions that take them and apply them to our strings, and towards the end of this section we'll have a look at the most useful of PHP's regular expression functions and how we can use them in our scripts.

Basic Pattern Matching

First, however, we need to know how to build regular expressions in the first place! Whole books have been dedicated to the theory and construction of regular expressions so don't expect to become a guru of them overnight, or indeed in the course of this section. Regular expressions take quite a while to learn, but once you've got the basics down you can pick the rest up as you go along!

Before we go anywhere, you need to be aware that we specify regular expressions in PHP as strings, passing them to functions to perform the required operations. This is quite different to languages such as Perl where regular expressions are part of the constructs of the language.

Let's kick things off with a discussion of the basics. *A regular expression is essentially a pattern that describes the nature of the string we're trying to find.* It's similar to how you might search for a word in a text document. The pattern can be as simple or as complex as you like. It might range from a literal string to a complex series of character classes. There are all sorts of other wondrous things you can search for – but more of that later.

As each new feature of the PHP regular expression is covered, we'll take a look at an example of it in action, showing some strings for which that regular expression would return a match. You'll find the portion of the string that matches the regular expression shown in **bold** so you can see clearly what's going on.

Beginning and ending with ...

Anyway, let's take a look at a straightforward example.

```
"^one"
```

> Please note that the double quotation marks are just to show that what we've got here is a string, and is not actually part of the pattern itself.

Although this is a pretty basic example, we've included a single special character in here. The ^ character, also known as a **carat**, indicates that the pattern should only match strings *beginning* with one. This means that when we apply this regular expression to a string, it will match "**one** green bottle" but not "I want one of those green bottles".

Such special characters are known as **anchors**, and the ^ anchor also has an opposite, the $ anchor.

```
"night$"
```

This indicates that the pattern should only return a match for strings that *end* with night. When applied to a string, this would match "in the middle of the **night**", but not "night and day" or even "had a nightmare".

If we want to be really restrictive we can use both of the previously mentioned anchors.

```
"^elephant$"
```

The regular expression above would *only* return a match for the string "**elephant**", with everything else being ignored. This means that none of the following strings would match: "elephants are cool", "I love elephants" or "international elephant appreciation society".

We can also be completely *unrestrictive* with regards to the position of the matched string.

```
"elephant"
```

The above would match "I have a little baby **elephant**", "**elephant**s have long memories" and even "meet Nigel, my **elephant**ine friend".

Having given you far too personal an insight into the special characters in my life, it's time to be moving swiftly on. There are other **special characters** we can use in our regular expressions that would make them more flexible and powerful.

Wildcards

We can specify how many times a given character may occur in a string that we want to be matched by using one of the regular expression **wildcard modifiers**. These can add a greater flexibility to our search.

The wildcard modifiers are *, + and ? and they apply to the preceding character or group of characters. Each of the modifiers has a different meaning:

* Match zero or more occurrences
+ Match one or more occurrences
? Match only zero or one occurrence

The wildcard modifiers are applied to the preceding character. Take a look at this example:

```
"co+"
```

A regular expression that looks like this will match any string that has a 'c' followed by one or more 'o' characters. It would gladly match "This is **co**ol" and "I'll fetch my **co**at" but would overlook "What a lovely card".

If we swapped the + for a * then all three strings would return a match because only the 'c' is mandatory. This is because the * makes the previous character match zero or more occurrences of itself, so would even match a string that doesn't contain an 'o' at all.

An example of the final wildcard modifier might look something like:

```
"snakes?"
```

This would match both "There's a **snake** in my boot" and "**snakes** are cool".

You might be thinking that we could do away with the wildcard modifiers in the previous examples, and you'd be right. To take the last one as an example, if we'd simply used

```
"snake"
```

...for our regular expression then it too would have matched "There's a **snake** in my boot" and "**snake**s are cool". However, you can see that the final 's' in the word "snakes" remains unmatched and this may not be desirable. For example, if we wanted to include the space after the word in the above regular expression then it would look something like

```
"snake "
```

Because we're specifying that we want a space after the word snake then "snakes are cool" would not return a match because it doesn't fit the pattern. However, by using our wildcard modifiers we could make this work.

```
"snakes? "
```

This translates to something like:

> *Match any string that contains the word "snake", possibly followed by an "s", but always with a space at the end..*

> *Of course it goes without saying that if we need to match for any of the special characters then we simply need to escape them with a backslash.*

Another point to be aware of is that using the * and + modifiers can end up with a match on a completely zany string. For example, if we were looking for something to match both "about" and "abbey", it would be reasonable to expect the following regular expression to handle the job for us.

```
"ab*"
```

However, while it would match both of the desired strings, it would also match pointless strings like:

```
"abbbbbbbbbbbbbbbout"
```

This clearly may be undesirable and we need to find a more restrictive way of handling this kind of situation.

Bounds

Luckily for us, we can use a feature of regular expressions known as **bounds**. This allows us to specify a minimum and maximum number of occurrences for a given character.

A simple bound in use might look something like:

```
"ab{2}"
```

Here we're saying that we want to match any string that has an "a" followed by exactly two "b"s The above example shows how to match an exact number of occurrences of a given character, but we can also use bounds to specify a range for the number of occurrences, using a **minimum range** value and a **maximum range** value.

Take a look at this example:

```
"ab{1,2}"
```

This regular expression will match a string with an "a" followed by a minimum of one "b" and a maximum of two "b"s. It would have the result we were looking for earlier, namely matching "**ab**out" and "**ab**bey" but not "abbbbout".

If we omit the maximum range value, but leave the comma, then we have a way of specifying that we want *at least* a certain number of occurrences of a given character. If we wanted to match at least three occurrences of a character then our regular expression would look something like:

```
"ab{3,}"
```

It would be a mistake to try and do exactly the same with the first number of a range, since it's impossible to have less than zero occurrences of a character. We would get the desired effect by using zero as the minimum range number:

```
"ab{,3}"           //  Not good
"ab{0,3}"          //  Much better
```

Matching Any Character

So far we've been using our regular expressions to match specific characters or character sequences. While this is useful, it's often desirable to have a true wildcard character, one that will match *any* character.

For this kind of operation we can use a full stop or period, (.), in our scripts. This is used to represent any non-newline character in our strings. So:

```
"co.l"
```

...would match both "**coal**ition" and "**cool**", the period representing an "a" in the first example, and an "o" in the latter.

When used in conjunction with either bounds or the wildcard modifiers, we can produce some extremely flexible regular expressions. For example, the following regular expression will match any word that begins with a "b" and ends in an "e" and has at least one character in between.

```
"b.+e"
```

So this would match "I've got a new **bike**", "**blondie** is great" and "I love **brie**" but not simply "be" (because the + denotes that we need at least one character in between "b" and "e").

Quantifying Character Sequences

All of the previous examples involve matching multiple occurrences of individual characters, but what if we wanted to extend the same functionality to character sequences?

The answer is that we need to enclose the characters in parentheses. So, if we wanted to match any string that had a "b" followed by one or more sequences of "an" then the regular expression might look something like:

```
"b(an)+"
```

This would match both "**ban**" and "**banan**a".

The same idea can be used with all of the elements of regular expressions we've met so far, and you can even use them inside the parentheses.

Using OR

Yet more flexibility is afforded in the shape of '|'. In our regular expressions we can use the '|' symbol to mean OR.

> You'll remember in **Chapter 2** we covered the OR operator and it was represented by || - note that inside regular expressions we use just the one because they appear inside strings.

So, let's take it back to our first example:

```
"^one"
```

This, as you will recall, matches anything *beginning* with "one", such as "one green bottle". Now let's shoehorn in an OR operator:

```
"^one|^two"
```

...which, as you may have guessed, will return anything beginning with "one" or "two".

We can also apply this to previously covered techniques, so the following regular expression will match any string that contains "cool" or "coalition".

```
"co(ol|oalition)"
```

Character Classes and Ranges

Another funky keyboard-saving feature of regular expressions is that of **character classes** and **ranges**.

Character ranges are specified using what is known as a **bracket** expression. This uses square brackets to enclose the range, and the characters to be matched can either be specified explicitly or using **range notation**. Let's take a look at a few examples:

`"[abd]"`	Will match a string that contains an "a", "b" or "d"
`"[a-z]"`	Will match a single lowercase letter "a" to "z"
`"[0-9]"`	Will match any single digit

We can also combine ranges to produce more complex expressions:

`"[a-zA-Z]"`	Will match a single upper or lowercase letter.
`"[a-zA-Z0-9]"`	Will match any alphanumeric character.

In the same manner we can specify character ranges that we *don't* want to match by using the carat symbol, '^', as the first symbol in a bracket expression. Now, let's just relax about the fact that this is totally different from our previous use of carat. If these quirks don't kill us (and they won't), they can only make us stronger.

`"[^a-zA-Z]"`	Will match any non-alphabetic character.
`"[^a-zA-Z0-9]"`	Will match any non alphanumeric character

We also need to be concerned with representing the '–' symbol in a character range since it has a special meaning – that of denoting a range (like `[a-z]` or `[0-9]`).

In order to have the dash as part of a character range we need to ensure that it is either the first character after the opening bracket (or after the carat if we're using it as above) or the last character before the closing bracket.

So if we wanted to match any string with an alphanumeric character followed by a dash then we'd use either of the following expressions:

```
"[a-zA-Z0-9-]"
```

```
"[-a-zA-Z0-9]"
```

Character classes are similar but arguably more useful than character ranges. They can save us time trying to construct the same thing using other regular expression techniques.

You'll find a listing of the most useful character classes below:

Character Class	Matches...	Same As
[[:alpha:]]	any letter	[a-zA-Z]
[[:digit:]]	any digit	[0-9]
[[:alnum:]]	any letter or digit	[a-zA-Z0-9]
[[:space:]]	any whitespace	[\t\r\n\c]
[[:upper:]]	any uppercase letter	[A-Z]
[[:lower:]]	any lowercase letter	[a-z]
[[:punct:]]	any punctuation mark	[.!,;:]

These can be used anywhere a normal character can be used. For example, if we wanted to match any letter followed by any punctuation mark we could use the following expression:

```
"[[:alpha:]][[:punct:]]"
```

> Now, if you take a look back at the first page of this chapter, and at that first bit of code we were introduced to, don't you find it starting to form itself into some kind of coherent sense?

Escape This Madness!

With all these symbols having special meanings you're probably wondering what we're going to do if we want to actually use them as search characters in our regular expressions.

Well, we're back to our good old friend...**escaping**. We need to escape these special characters using the backslash symbol. So, if we wanted to match *any sequence of characters that are enclosed in square brackets* we could use the following regular expression...

```
"\[.+\]"
```

This may be a little more understandable if we split it apart...

```
"\[
```

The opening bracket, escaped to show that we want it to be included in the search string as opposed to signifying the start of a character range.

.+

These are treated as special characters since the backslash used at the beginning of the string only escapes the immediately following character.

\] "

The escaped closing bracket.

So this would match "[hello]" and `how are [you]` but not "I'm fine thanks" or even "why do you [ask" (the last one isn't matched because there's no closing bracket).

> *As I stated in an earlier chapter, we only really need to escape the first (or opening) bracket here. The reason for this is that once we've escaped the opening bracket, the closing one has no special meaning. However, this is considered bad programming practice as it can lead to confusion when dealing with complex expressions.*

Breaking Down Our E-mail

Now that we know what regular expressions are and how to construct them we're going to return to the complex regular expression presented at the beginning of this chapter and see if we can make total sense of it.

Just to refresh our memories, here's what it looked like:

```
^([a-zA-Z0-9._-]+)@([a-zA-Z0-9-])+(\.[a-zA-Z0-9-]+)+$
```

This regular expression is one that can be used to validate an e-mail address. We're not concerned whether the e-mail address actually exists, just that it's in the correct format. Before we get started let's have a think about the different ways to represent an e-mail address. The list below shows some of the more common formats:

> steve@codejunkie.co.uk
> joe.bloggs@bloggs369.com
> billy-bloggs@terra-nova.com
> james_archer@another.co.it

1. From this we can determine some common points between different formats of e-mail address. There are three parts to an e-mail address. We have the **username**, followed by an @ symbol and the address ends with the **domain** part. This last section is split into a **domain name** (codejunkie) and a **top-level domain** (.co.uk).

Now we know what we're looking for we can start to break apart our regular expression.

```
^([a-zA-Z0-9._-]+)@([a-zA-Z0-9-])+(\.[a-zA-Z0-9-]+)+$
```

2. Before we delve into the workings of the expression, the first thing we should notice is that the whole expression is topped and tailed by the ^ and $ characters. This shows that we're only interested in a match if our expression makes up the entire string.

3. Once we've removed these, the next section that needs dealing with looks like this:

```
([a-zA-Z0-9._-]+)
```

This part of the regular expression matches the username part of the e-mail. You can see that we're using character ranges to specify the valid characters for this part of the address, which can consist of alphanumeric characters as well as a ".", "_" or "-". The "+" outside of the closing square bracket shows that we're after *one or more* occurrences of one of these characters.

> *Note that we didn't need to escape the period in the above expression because it has no special meaning inside of a character class – it just matched a period!*

4. Next we've got a plain @ symbol on its own. This represents the @ symbol in an e-mail address and nothing special needs to be done with this.

Obviously this leaves the rest of the regular expression to match the domain portion of the e-mail address.

```
([a-zA-Z0-9-])+(\.[a-zA-Z0-9-]+)+
```

If we split this up and deal with it a piece at a time it will be easier to understand.

5. Firstly we've got the following section:

```
([a-zA-Z0-9-])+
```

This is quite similar to the username section described above, except that we're only looking for characters that fall in the alphanumeric category and dashes. Again, we're using the "+" symbol to denote that we're looking for one or more occurrences of these characters.

6. The final part is a little more complicated:

   ```
   (\.[a-zA-Z0-9-]+)+
   ```

   We're using parentheses here to show that we're after a sequence of characters, and the "\." bit tells PHP that we want the first character of that sequence to be a period.

   Following this we've got a character range as for the first part of the domain section shown previously. We add a closing parenthesis to show that that is the end of the character sequence we're looking for.

   Lastly, we add a "+" to show that we're looking for one or more occurrences of this character sequence.

7. If we overlay a valid e-mail address onto this expression you can see how each section relates...

   ```
   Steve                @codejunkie          co.uk
   ^([a-zA-Z0-9._-]+)   @([a-zA-Z0-9-])      +(\.[a-zA-Z0-9-]+)+$
   ```

Regular expressions are extremely powerful and you'd be at a disadvantage to not understand them. That said, they are complex beasts so don't feel too concerned if it takes a while for the penny to drop!

PHP Regular Expression Functions

Okay, so now we've figured out how to create regular expressions, let's look at what we can do with them. PHP provides a whole array of functions that we can use to evaluate regular expressions in our scripts.

ereg() and eregi()

The ereg function is probably the most used of PHP's regular expression functions.

```
ereg (pattern, string [, regs])
```

In its simplest form this function simply returns true if the regular expression **pattern** was found in **string**, or false if no match was found.

If matches are found for parenthesized sub-strings of a pattern, and the function is called with the optional third argument **regs**, the matches will be stored in the elements of the array regs.

$regs[1] will contain the sub-string which starts at the first left parenthesis; $regs[2] will contain the sub-string starting at the second, and so on. $regs[0] will contain a copy of string.

With ereg, searching is case sensitive. If we want to perform a case insensitive search then we would need to use ereg's partner-in-crime – **eregi.**

eregi (**pattern, string** [, **regs**])

eregi performs in exactly the same way as ereg, except for the fact that the search is performed without regard for letter case.

So we could use this function, along with the complicated regular expression we've just been building, to check that a given e-mail address is valid.

```
<?
$email1 = "steve@codejunkie.co.uk";
$email2 = "not a@valid email";

$regexp = "^([a-zA-Z0-9._-]+)@([a-zA-Z0-9-])+(\.[a-zA-Z0-9-
]+)+$";

if (eregi($regexp, $email1)) {
    print "E-mail address '$email1' is valid <br>\n";
} else {
    print "E-mail address '$email1' is invalid <br>\n";
}

if (eregi($regexp, $email2)) {
    print "E-mail address '$email2' is valid <br>\n";
} else {
    print "E-mail address '$email2' is invalid <br>\n";
}
?>
```

This should output the following:

E-mail address 'steve@codejunkie.co.uk' is valid
E-mail address 'not a@valid email' is invalid

```
email_validate.php                                        _ □ ×
1  <?
2  $email1 = "steve@codejunkie.co.uk";
3  $email2 = "not a@valid email";
4
5  $regexp = "^([a-zA-Z0-9._-]+)@([a-zA-Z0-9-]+)+(\.[a-zA-Z0-9-]+)+$";
6
7  if (eregi($regexp, $email1)) {
8      print "E-mail address '$email1' is valid <br>\n";
9  } else {
10     print "E-mail address '$email1' is invalid <br>\n";
11 }
12
13 if (eregi($regexp, $email2)) {
14     print "E-mail address '$email2' is valid <br>\n";
15 } else {
16     print "E-mail address '$email2' is invalid <br>\n";
17 }
18 ?>
```
Editor HTML

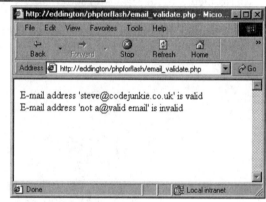

http://eddington/phpforflash/email_validate.php - Micro... _ □ ×

File   Edit   View   Favorites   Tools   Help

Back   Forward   Stop   Refresh   Home

Address http://eddington/phpforflash/email_validate.php   Go

E-mail address 'steve@codejunkie.co.uk' is valid
E-mail address 'not a@valid email' is invalid

Done   Local intranet

ereg_replace() and eregi_replace()

These functions are used to perform a search and replace operation using regular expressions. This can be extremely useful for doing a batch replacement of certain words or symbols in a given string.

As with ereg and eregi, these two functions are identical except for the fact that **eregi_replace** will perform its operation regardless of letter case. For this reason we're only going to cover **ereg_replace** here.

The format for this function is:

```
ereg_replace(pattern, replacement, string)
```

This function scans the **string** for matches to **pattern**, then replaces the matched text with **replacement**. The modified string is returned. If no matches are found in string then it will be returned unchanged.

So if, for example, we were running a message board for children and didn't want them to be able to display their e-mail address, we could use these functions to filter out e-mail addresses and replace them with a message saying that e-mail addresses are not allowed.

```
<?
$msg = "Hi Nicki, my new email: steve@codejunkie.co.uk";
$regexp = " ([a-zA-Z0-9._-]+)@([a-zA-Z0-9-])+(\.[a-zA-Z0-9-
]+)+";

$msg = ereg_replace ($regexp, "[Email addresses not
allowed]", $msg);

print $msg;
?>
```

The above code will give the following output:

Hi Nicki, my new email: [Email addresses not allowed]

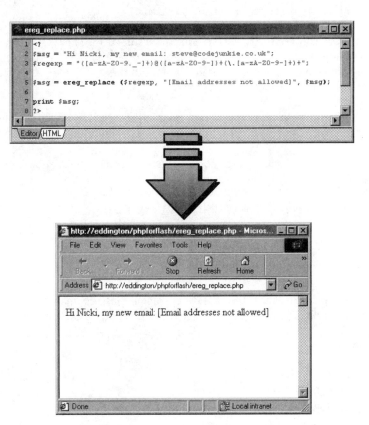

Of course this could be simply worked around by adding spaces between one or more letters in the email address, since space is not part of a valid email address and therefore not part of our regular expression. We could rewrite the expression to take spaces and other characters into account but we could end up censoring perfectly innocent content. It's a case of striking a balance between being diligent and keeping the system user friendly – not an easy task.

split() and spliti()

These functions are used to split a string into an array. In this respect they are much like the explode function we met in the previous chapter. However, they differ in that they take a regular expression as the boundary at which to split the string.

Again, spliti is just a case insensitive version of split so there's no need to cover that here.

The format for the function is:

```
split (pattern, string [, limit])
```

This returns an array of strings, each of which is a sub-string of string formed by splitting it on boundaries formed by the regular expression pattern. If limit is set, the returned array will contain a maximum of limit elements with the last element containing the whole rest of string. If an error occurs, split returns false.

So if we wanted to split a string into an array of sentences we'd need to split it at any end of sentence punctuation, such as a full stop, question mark or exclamation mark.

```
$string = "This is cool. PHP is real cool! How about some
lunch? I'm having some";

$sentences = split("[.!?]", $string);

foreach($sentences as $count => $sentence) {
    print "$count: $sentence <br>\n";
}
```

Here you'll see we're using the [.!?] character class to match all end of sentence punctuation marks. Then we use a foreach loop to output each sentence in turn.

This will output

```
0: This is cool
1: PHP is real cool
2: How about some lunch
3: I'm having some
```

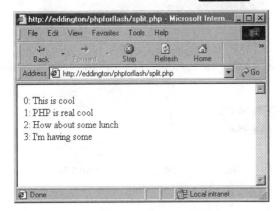

It is worth noting that splitting a string by a regular expression is less efficient than doing so by a simple string, so if you maybe do not require the power of regular expressions in this instance then use `explode` instead.

Again, we've covered some pretty heavy ground in this chapter but now it's time to exercise that gray matter. We're going to be building a fully searchable news archive where the user can choose between doing a simple string-based search, and performing a regular expression search.

The phpforflash.com News Archive

Here, we're going to see how to scour through the archives at www.phpforflash.com, where, incidentally, the final application is available for download.

Below you'll find a diagram of the one I made earlier.

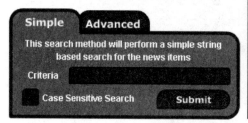

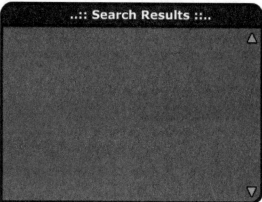

This movie consists of two movie clips; one for the **search box** on the left, and another for the **search results** on the right. We're going to build each of these in turn before moving onto the PHP scripts.

Building The Flash Front End

The first thing we have to do is to build the Flash interface - made up from two movie clips which we're going to build here.

1. Before we go anywhere with the two main movie clips we'll need to build a custom check box for the case sensitive option of the search box. If you don't feel like building your own you can use the CheckBox smart clip that comes as part of Flash, which can be found by selecting Window > Common Libraries > Smart Clips.

2. To make your own, start as usual by creating a new movie clip and giving it a suitable name, in this case Check Box.

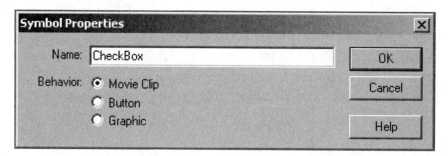

3. Next we need to create the layer and frame structure for the sections of the movie clip. Use the following screenshot as a guide.

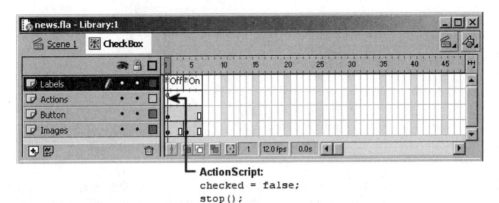

ActionScript:
```
checked = false;
stop();
```

4. On the Images layer, create images of a checked and unchecked box in the relevant frames as shown below.

5. On the Button layer we're going to create an invisible button. An invisible button is a button where only the Hit state has anything on it. They are useful on many occasions and we'll be using them again later in this application.

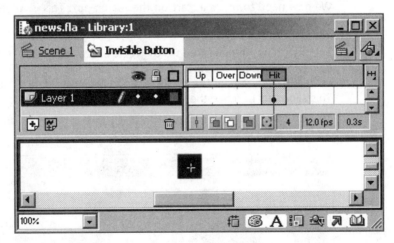

6. Once you've created the invisible button you need to add an instance to the Button layer and resize and place it so that it is in the same position and is the same size as the check box images we've just created.

7. All that's left to do now for this part is to add the following ActionScript code to the button.

```
on (release) {
    if(checked == true) {
        checked = false;
        gotoAndStop("Off");
    }
    else {
        checked = true;
        gotoAndStop("On");
    }
}
```

This code is what actually does the legwork of our little check box. When the mouse is pressed over the invisible button, this code checks to see what state the check box is currently in. If the checked variable is set to true, then, at the moment, the check box appears On. In this case we set the checked variable to false and go to the Off frame.

Otherwise, the checked variable must either be set to false or, if this is the first time the user has clicked on our check box, checked has no value. In this case we set the checked variable to true and go to the On frame.

That's it – we now have a custom check box to use in our Flash movies. Return to the main stage and drag a copy of your check box from the library.

We now need to make a start on the search box. This is where the lion's share of the work is going to be done.

8. The first thing we need to do is to create a new movie clip. Although we're not going to be using the onClipEvent handler for this application it is nice to keep different parts of the movie separate by encapsulating them in movie clips. This allows us to make the whole movie easier to manage.

Create another new movie clip and call it SearchBox.

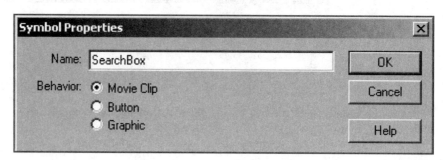

9.   The layer and frame structure of the movie clip should be as follows:

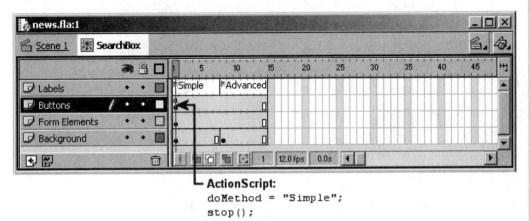

ActionScript:
```
doMethod = "Simple";
stop();
```

Don't forget to add the ActionScript as shown as it sets up the initial search method and stops the movie clip.

10.   In order to get the tabbed dialog look I've simply drawn two different images on the Background layer; one with the Simple tab shown as active and at the front, and the other with the Advanced shown active.

Take a look at the images below to see what I mean:

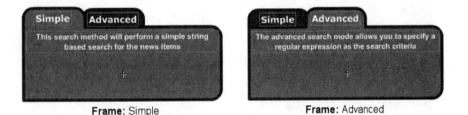

Frame: Simple   **Frame:** Advanced

You'll see that I've also added a textual explanation of the different search modes to help the user understand what each does. It's generally a good idea to build this kind of thing into your user interfaces where users might be a little lost as to what to do. Go ahead and create something similar, though I'm sure you can improve on mine.

11. Now we need to create the functional elements of the interface. Take a look at the following screenshot of the Form Elements layer:

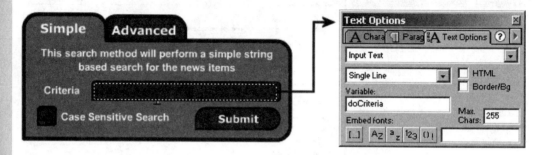

The first thing you'll want to do is to add the text box so that the user can type in their search criteria. Give this a variable name of doCriteria. It's also sensible to limit the amount of data that can be entered here as shown in the screenshot above.

12. We're going to need an instance of our Check Box movie clip so that the user can select whether or not they want their search to be case sensitive. Drag an instance from the Library onto the Form Elements layer and give it an instance name of cbCaseSensitive – this will let us reference it from ActionScript so that we can check it's status.

13. The final element is the Submit button. This is a simple button with the following ActionScript attached:

```
on (release) {
    if (doCriteria != "") {
        if (cbCaseSensitive.checked) {
            doCase = true;
        } else {
            doCase = false;
        }

    _root.NewsDisplay.searchResults = "Searching";

    loadVariables ("fetchnews.php", _root.NewsDisplay,
"POST");
    }
}
```

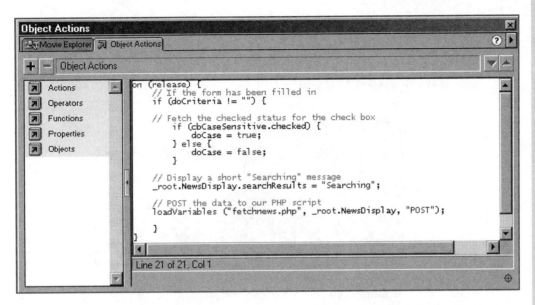

```
on (release) {
    // If the form has been filled in
    if (doCriteria != "") {

        // Fetch the checked status for the check box
        if (cbCaseSensitive.checked) {
            doCase = true;
        } else {
            doCase = false;
        }

        // Display a short "Searching" message
        _root.NewsDisplay.searchResults = "Searching";

        // POST the data to our PHP script
        loadVariables ("fetchnews.php", _root.NewsDisplay, "POST");

    }
}
```

The one part of this code that may need explaining is the following line...

```
if (cbCaseSensitive.checked) {
```

This checks the value of the `checked` variable in our instance of the Check Box movie clip we created earlier. If its value is `true` then the user wants to perform a case sensitive search, otherwise they want a case insensitive search, so we set `$doCase` accordingly.

All this chunk of code does is check that the user has entered at least something in the search criteria box. If they have, the `checked` status of our Check Box is examined and the `doCase` variable is set accordingly, which we'll use in our PHP script. Finally, we call the PHP script that'll handle the search, sending the data using the `POST` method, and tell `loadVariables` that we want any data that is returned put into the `_root.newsDisplay` movie clip (which we'll get to in a moment).

14. The very last thing that we need to take care of in our SearchBox movie clip is to add a couple of invisible buttons to allow the user to switch between Simple and Advanced search modes.

    Don't forget to make sure that these are added to the SearchBox movie clip itself and not just the instance on the main timeline!

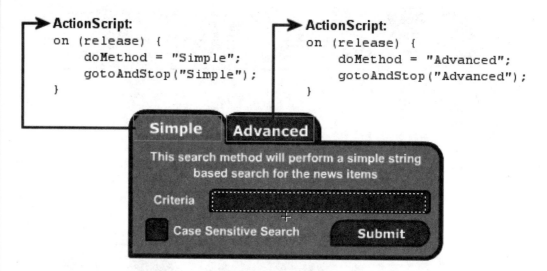

ActionScript:
```
on (release) {
    doMethod = "Simple";
    gotoAndStop("Simple");
}
```

ActionScript:
```
on (release) {
    doMethod = "Advanced";
    gotoAndStop("Advanced");
}
```

15. This is a simple case of taking two instances of our invisible button on the Buttons layer and stretching them to cover the tabs. Then all you have to do is add the relevant ActionScript which simultaneously sets the appropriate search mode and sends the movie clip to the correct frame.

Now that we've got our search box we need to create the movie clip to display the search results.

16. Return to the main timeline by selecting Edit > Movie from the main menu.

17. Create a new movie clip and call this one NewsDisplay.

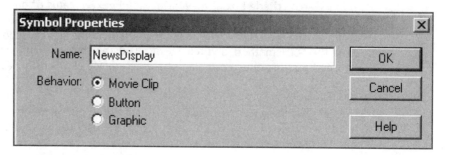

Because this is a relatively simple movie clip, everything is in a single frame on a single layer.

18. Create a background layer – in fact you can borrow and amend a Window BG layer from previous exercises – add a dynamic text box, with the variable name searchResults and two nice scroll buttons. Eventually, your layout will resemble the screenshot below.

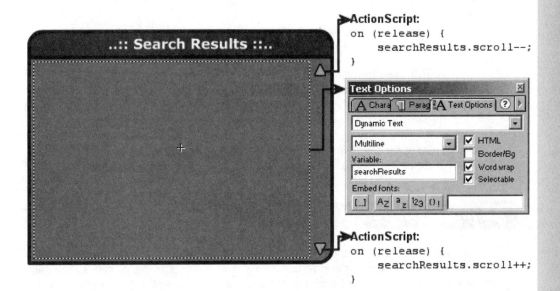

ActionScript:
```
on (release) {
    searchResults.scroll--;
}
```

ActionScript:
```
on (release) {
    searchResults.scroll++;
}
```

> *Note how we've set the text box up to render and display HTML so that we can add text formatting to the search results.*

19. The final thing we need to do on the Flash side of things is to drag an instance of each of our SearchBox and NewsDisplay movie clips onto the main stage.

Although we don't need to give an instance name to the instance of our SearchBox movie clip, we do need to name the instance of NewsDisplay. If you think back to when we were creating SearchBox, we added the following loadVariables call to the Submit button

```
loadVariables ("fetchnews.php", _root.NewsDisplay, "POST");
```

20. You can see from this that we're telling Flash to load any data returned from fetchnews.php to the _root.NewsDiplay movie clip. If we want the search results to be displayed we'll need to set the name of our instance of the NewsDisplay movie clip to NewsDisplay.

That's it for the Flash front end unless you want to add something yourself. I've just plonked a bit of text on mine to tell the user what it is about.

Adding a Portion of PHP

It's now time to move on to the PHP scripts that actually do all the work of searching and returning news data. We're going to use a couple of techniques we picked up in earlier chapters to break the tasks of defining and searching/returning the news items into two. This will make the whole system more manageable and is a great excuse to put everything we've learned so far into practice.

news.php

The first script we're going to look at is news.php. This is where we'll enter all the news items that we want to be searchable. We'll use a multi-dimensional array to store the information and then use the include function in our other script to import the data.

1. Rather than boringly list the whole contents of my news.php script I'll show you how to build up a couple of news items and then let you loose to create your own wacky news. This is achieved by the code outlined below.

```
<?
    $newsItems[0]['Title'] = 'Put your news title in here';
    $newsItems[0]['Body'] = 'This would be the news text';

    $newsItems[1]['Title'] = 'News Item 2 Title';
    $newsItems[1]['Body'] = 'Another load of news text';

?>
```

From this, and, the PHP material we covered in **Chapter 2**, you should be able to add as many news items as you like.

2. You'll want to create at least five items to enable you to test the search properly but if you don't feel particularly creative you can download all of the files for this chapter, including a complete news.php script, from www.phpforflash.com.

> *Remember that in single quotes strings the only thing you need to worry about escaping with a backslash are any extra single quotes you use (\') and the backslash character itself (\\).*

fetchnews.php

This is the PHP script that is called from our Flash movie, and it's here we're going to be searching the news items and returning the results.

3. The first thing we need to do is to load in the news items from news.php. We'll do this using the include function we met in **Chapter 3**. You're beginning to see how it all comes together.

```
<?
    // Load news items in from external file
    include("news.php");
```

4. With that done, we need to un-escape the special characters in our $doCriteria string, that is being passed in from our Flash movie, or we'll have problems when it comes to searching for a match. We also need to initialise a variable to hold any matching news items that we find.

```
    // Unescape special characters in $doCriteria string
    $doCriteria = stripslashes($doCriteria);

    // Initialize our variable to hold search results
    $searchResults = "";
```

5. Next, we need to determine which search method was selected and perform the relevant search operation. We do this in the form of some function calls that we'll get around to writing next.

```
    // If we're performing a simple search...
    if ($doMethod == "Simple") {
        // Call simple search function & store return value
        $searchResults = SimpleSearch();
    } else {
        // Call advanced search function & store return value
```

continues overleaf

```
                        $searchResults = AdvancedSearch();
            }
```

You can see from this that we're going to be returning the search results from the function called, and that we're storing this information in our $searchResults variable so that we can set it up for sending back to Flash.

6. Finally we output the results to Flash. We include a summary of the search options used before encoding and outputting the search results.

```
// Output search header
print "&searchResults=";
print urlencode("Method: $doMethod\nCriteria:
$doCriteria\nCase: $doCase\n\n");

// Output search results
print urlencode($searchResults) . "&";
```

```
fetchnews.php                                                          _ □ X
 1  <?
 2  // fetchnews.php
 3  // Chapter 5 - Foundation PHP for Flash
 4
 5  // Load news items in from external file
 6  include("news.php");
 7
 8  // Un-escape any special characters in our search criteria string
 9  $doCriteria = stripslashes($doCriteria);
10
11  // Initialise our variable to hold search results
12  $searchResults = "";
13
14  // If we're performing a simple search...
15  if ($doMethod == "Simple") {
16      // Call the simple search function and store return value
17      $searchResults = SimpleSearch();
18  } else {
19      // Call the advances search function and store return value
20      $searchResults = AdvancedSearch();
21  }
22
23  // Output search header
24  print "&searchResults=";
25  print urlencode("Method: $doMethod\nCriteria: $doCriteria\nCase: $doCase\n\n");
26
27  // Output search results
28  print urlencode($searchResults) . "&";
Editor  HTML
```

With the main part of our script written, it's time to sort out the search functions.

You can see from the previous section of code that we have two functions; SimpleSearch and AdvancedSearch. As the names might suggest, SimpleSearch will perform a basic, string-based search for the given criteria, while AdvancedSearch will treat the search criteria as a regular expression and perform, you guessed it, a more advanced search.

7. Kicking off with the SimpleSearch function, the first thing we need to do is to define the following code as a function and to set up any global variables that we need.

```
// Function to perform a simple string search
function SimpleSearch() {

    // Global variables
    global $newsItems;
    global $doCriteria;
    global $doCase;
```

8. Once this is done we need to set up a loop so that we can search through all of the news items in the $newsItems array. We'll use a for loop for this, using the count function to get the number of news items in the array.

```
// For each news item in array...
for($count = 0; $count < count($newsItems); $count++) {
```

9. We'll want the function to be able to search through both the Title and Body elements of the current news item, so we use the foreach function to fetch and process each value in turn. Using this method also allows you to add more elements to the $newsItems array we constructed in the news.php script and have them searchable too.

```
// Loop through each element of news item...
foreach($newsItems[$count] as $value) {
```

10. Next we need to determine if we're performing a case sensitive or case insensitive search. We need to do this because it impacts on which function we need to call.

```
// If we're performing a case sensitive match...
if ($doCase == "true") {
```

```
fetchnews.php                                              _ □ X
31  // Function to perform a simple string search
32  function SimpleSearch() {
33      // Global variables
34      global $newsItems;
35      global $doCriteria;
36      global $doCase;
37
38      // For each news item in array...
39      for($count = 0; $count < count($newsItems); $count++) {
40
41          // Loop through each element of news item...
42          foreach($newsItems[$count] as $value) {
43
44              // If we're performing a case sensitive match...
45              if ($doCase == "true") {
```
Editor / HTML /

11. So, if we're performing a case sensitive simple string-based search then we'll want to use the strstr function, which finds the first occurrence of a string, that we met in the previous chapter. We pass to this function the current element of the current news item ($value) and the search criteria ($doCriteria) and check the return value to see if a match was found.

```
// Use case sensitive function to check for match
// If match found...
if (strstr($value, $doCriteria)) {
```

12. If we find a match then we'll want to add the current news item to the search results. At the same time we use HTML tags to format the output so that the news item's title is shown as a bold blue, while the body is shown in whatever color we specified for the searchResults text box in our Flash movie.

```
// Store news item details for output
$searchResults .= '<font color="#003366"><b>';
$searchResults .= $newsItems[$count]['Title'];
$searchResults .= '</b></font><br>';
$searchResults .= $newsItems[$count]['Body'];
$searchResults .= '<br><br>';

// Move on to next news item
break;
```

We also use the break keyword to break out of the foreach loop and move on to the next news item. We need to do this because there's little point in searching the remaining elements in a news item for which we've already found a match. We'd also end up with each news item being added to the search results multiple times if a match was found in more than one element – not good enough!

If no match is found then no action is taken and we simply move on to the next element of the current news item, or to the next news item if the current element is the last.

13. The code below also shows the operation of a case insensitive match. No explanation is offered for this, save to say that the only thing that is different between this section of code and the previous one is that, instead of calling strstr, we call stristr for a case insensitive search.

```
        }
    } else {

        // Use case insensitive function to search
        // If match found...
        if (stristr($value, $doCriteria)) {

            // Store news item details for output
            $searchResults .= '<font color="#003366"><b>';
            $searchResults .= $newsItems[$count]['Title'];
            $searchResults .= '</b></font><br>';
            $searchResults .= $newsItems[$count]['Body'];
            $searchResults .= '<br><br>';

            // Move on to next news item
            break;
        }
    }
}
}
```

```
fetchnews.php                                                    _ □ X
47        // Use case sensitive function to check for match
48        // If match found...
49        if (strstr($value, $doCriteria)) {
50
51            // Store news item details for output
52            $searchResults .= '<font color="#003366"><b>';
53            $searchResults .= $newsItems[$count]['Title'];
54            $searchResults .= '</b></font><br>';
55            $searchResults .= $newsItems[$count]['Body'];
56            $searchResults .= '<br><br>';
57
58            // Move on to next news item
59            break;
60        }
61    } else {
62
63        // Use case insensitive function to check for match
64        // If match found...
65        if (stristr($value, $doCriteria)) {
66
67            // Store news item details for output
68            $searchResults .= '<font color="#003366"><b>';
69            $searchResults .= $newsItems[$count]['Title'];
70            $searchResults .= '</b></font><br>';
71            $searchResults .= $newsItems[$count]['Body'];
72            $searchResults .= '<br><br>';
73            // Move on to next news item
74            break;
75        }
76    }
77    }
78    }
Editor HTML
```

14. Now we need to determine if any match was found at all. If no match was found then we place a message, telling the user this, into our $searchResults variable. We do this by using the strlen function to check the length of the $searchResults variable. If the length is zero then we didn't find any matches.

```
// If we didn't find a single match...
if (strlen($searchResults) == 0) {
  // Set "no match" message
  $searchResults = "No match found";
}
```

15. Finally we return the $searchResults string and exit the function.

```
// Return search results...
return $searchResults;
}
```

```
  fetchnews.php                                          _ □ X
  80      // If we didn't find a single match...            ▲
  81      if (strlen($searchResults) == 0) {
  82          // Set "no match" message
  83          $searchResults = "No match found";
  84      }
  85
  86      // Return search results...
  87      return $searchResults;
  88  }
                                                           ▼
  ◄                                                        ►
  Editor HTML
```

16. The AdvancedSearch function works in exactly the same way, except that we use the regular expression functions to perform a search on the strings instead. You can read the comments in the code for further explanation but it is essentially the same as SimpleSearch. You should also notice a good many things popping up that we have covered in previous chapters – merely a sign of your overall PHP proficiency increasing!

```php
// Function to perform a regular expression search
function AdvancedSearch() {
  // Global variables
  global $newsItems;
  global $doCriteria;
  global $doCase;

  // For each news item in array...
  for($count = 0; $count < count($newsItems); $count++) {

    // Loop through each element of news item...
    foreach($newsItems[$count] as $value) {

      // If we're performing a case sensitive match...
      if ($doCase == "true") {

        // Use case sensitive function to check for match
        // If match found...
        if (ereg($doCriteria, $value)) {

          // Store news item details for output
          $searchResults .= '<font color="#003366"><b>';
          $searchResults .= $newsItems[$count]['Title'];
          $searchResults .= '</b></font><br>';
          $searchResults .= $newsItems[$count]['Body'];
          $searchResults .= '<br><br>';
```

continues overleaf

```
                          // Move on to next news item
                          break;
                        }
                  } else {
                     // Use case insensitive function to search
                     // If match found...
                     if (eregi($doCriteria, $value)) {

                         // Store news item details for output
                         $searchResults .= '<font color="#003366"><b>';
                         $searchResults .= $newsItems[$count]['Title'];
                         $searchResults .= '</b></font><br>';
                         $searchResults .= $newsItems[$count]['Body'];
                         $searchResults .= '<br><br>';

                         // Move on to next news item
                         break;
                     }
                  }
               }
            }

            // If we didn't find a single match...
            if (strlen($searchResults) == 0) {
               // Set "no match" message
               $searchResults = "No match found";
            }

            // Return search results...
            return $searchResults;;
         }
```

That's everything. All that's left to do now is to upload and/or copy the whole lot to your web server and play happily in the knowledge that you've created something this advanced!

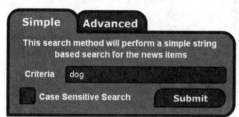

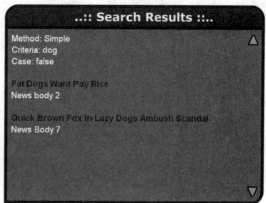

There are a couple of things that strike me as missing from this application, and these were left out on purpose to give you something to do between chapters.

Firstly, there are some elements missing from the news items. In addition to a title and a body, news items will often list an author for that item, as well as when it was posted. Secondly, it would be nice to give the user the option of displaying all of the news items. Although this can be done by using a single period in the Advanced Search mode (because a single period in a regular expression will match any character) but it isn't exactly elegant to make the user do it themselves.

Summary

Now, I guess I don't have to tell you that it's not been easy, and it's certainly nobody's idea of a picnic – but you should now have a thorough understanding of some of the more complex aspects of the PHP language.

We have looked at:

- Regular expressions and what a puzzle they appear to be

- Basic pattern matching

- Getting more flexible with wildcard modifiers

- Shaping things up with bounds

- Taking a few shortcuts with character classes and ranges

- PHP Regular Expression Functions

...and all that with a couple of really handy exercises. What more could you ask? Well, just look at the next chapter!

6

Remembering Visitor Information

What we'll cover in this chapter

- Introducing **Cookies**

- **Creating** and **manipulating** cookies using PHP's **setcookie** function

- Setting **restrictions** on cookies such as an expiry date

- Putting it all together with a **cookie cutter** Flash application

One of the most helpful features any web site can have is being able to remember visitor information. The common things we might like to remember about our visitors are:

- Visitor name or other personal details
- Username and/or password
- Site Preferences
- Shopping cart items

Remembering this kind of information can help us make the visitors time at our site a lot easier and a lot more productive. I'm sure you've been to sites that had a little check box which offered to remember your username and password next time you logged in from the same computer.

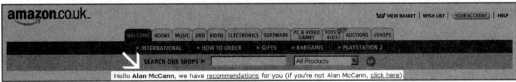

Screenshot taken from www.amazon.co.uk

From recalling your name to storing your address and shopping preferences, one of the easiest methods of remembering visitor information in PHP is with the use of...

Cookies

Cookies, originally known as 'the magic cookies', were first developed by Netscape for incorporation in its web browser software, and can be used to remember little titbits of information about a given user.

The great thing about cookies is that they are stored on the user's own system, meaning that we don't have to deal with how and where to store them ourselves. Although it occasionally varies, most web browsers store their cookies as small text files on the user's hard drive.

In its simplest form, we can use the cookie to remember the visitor's name and to provide them with a personalized greeting the next time they visit the site. At the more extreme end we can use cookies to develop shopping cart type applications, using them to remember items and quantities that a user has selected so far. The fact that this information will be stored when the visitor leaves the site, and will be available when they return, marks the advantage of using cookies over global variables on your Flash sites.

> *You've seen all those Flash sites with a* Skip Intro *button, but how about a cookie that remembers whether or not you've already seen the intro and skips it automatically on subsequent visits – with PHP this is easy and you'll see just how easy later on!*

According to the cookies specification drawn up by Netscape, there are some restrictions imposed on the use of cookies to ensure that the system isn't abused. Firstly, a web browser should only store a total of 300 cookies, and only allow a given server to store a maximum of 20. In addition, a single cookie should not exceed 4kb in size. If we need to retain more information, it should be done so on the server-side (in a database for example) with some kind of identifier being stored as a cookie instead.

Another security feature, but this time for the sake of data privacy rather then integrity, is that cookies are only sent to servers which are permitted to receive them and, typically, only the web page that created the cookie is able to view it. When we start playing around with cookies you'll see that it's possible to limit which servers, and under what conditions, the cookies are sent out to.

Cookies are used on a huge number of web sites. If your web browser supports it, turn on cookie prompting and take a spin around your favorite sites – you'll be surprised how many are using cookies to store information about your visits.

To do this, follow the screenshot, and set a Custom Level in the Security tab from Tools > Internet Options. You can choose to be prompted before a cookie is set, and you can now go cookie hunting!

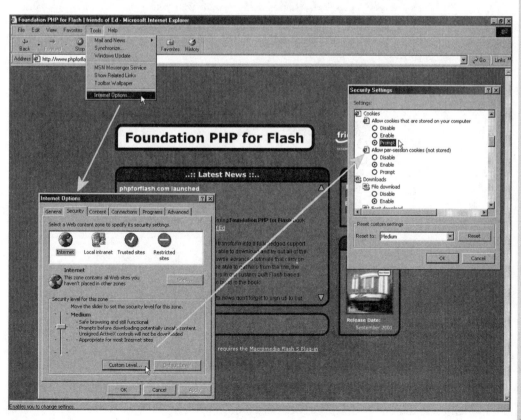

Remember when you're doing this though that cookies are not inherently evil surveillance devices – they can only store personal information about you which you provide to the site yourself.

Restrictions on Cookies

There are four pieces of information we can supply with a cookie so that it's just what we need.

Expiry Date

Every cookie has a date at which it will expire – an expiration date if you like! When a cookie has expired it will no longer be sent to the server and in most cases will be removed from the user's system. If no expiry date is specified when the cookie is set, then the cookie will be removed at the end of the current browser session (when the user closes the browser). This method is useful for creating temporary cookies to remember whether a user is logged in or not.

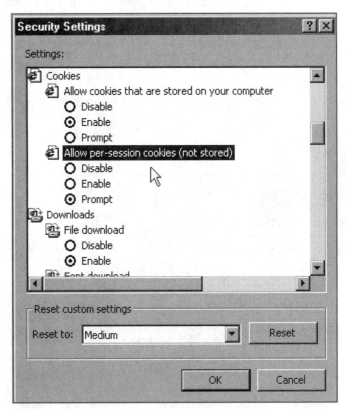

If you look back to our cookie options, you'll see that there is a setting to also prompt when these temporary per-session cookies are being used.

Domain

When a web browser searches for valid cookies to send to the server, the **domain** attribute is checked against the domain name of the server to which the cookie will be sent. A match is determined by performing a tail check, which compares the cookies domain attribute against the end of the server's domain name.

For example, a domain attribute of .codejunkie.co.uk would match www.codejunkie.co.uk and another.partof.codejunkie.co.uk. If a match is found, the **path** attribute is then analyzed.

A cookie can only be set for a given domain if the request comes from a host within that domain. The default value of the domain attribute for a cookie is the host name of the server that generated the request.

Path

The **path** attribute of a cookie is used to specify the subset of URLs in a domain for which the cookie is valid. If a match is found here then the cookie is considered valid for the current site and is sent along with the standard HTTP header.

As an example, if a cookie had a path of /news then it would be available to /newsletter.php, as well as all files in both /newsamples/ and /news. In fact, the cookie will be available for anything that begins with /news, be it a directory or a file. To make the cookie available for the whole domain set the path to "/".

If no path is given for a cookie then it will take the path from the file requesting the setting of the cookie.

Secure

The final restriction is the **secure** attribute of the cookie. If a cookie is marked as secure then it will only be sent if the communication channel with the host is a secure one.

This means that secure cookies will only be sent to servers when the connection uses the **Secure Socket Layer** (**SSL**) protocol, in other words URLs that begin with https:// rather than http://.

PHP Likes Cookies...

As you might have guessed, if only by their very inclusion in this book, cookie support is fully integrated into PHP, allowing us to use cookies in our scripts with very little effort. For example, reading cookies from within PHP is as easy as accessing variables. This is because any cookies that are valid for the current document are automatically made available as global variables, in exactly the same way that POST and GET data is. This happens before any of the code in the PHP script is executed.

This ease of use extends to setting cookies from PHP too. This can be achieved by a single function call, which in its simplest form accepts two arguments; a name and a value for our cookie. Cunningly enough, the function concerned is called setcookie – even I can remember that one!

Setting cookies

Let's take a little look at setcookie...

```php
<?
    // Increment number of visits count
    // If count isn't set then it will be set to 1
    $count++;

    // Store the cookie on the user's system
    setcookie('count', $count);

    // Output message
    print "You have visited this site $count time(s).\n";
?>
```

```
setcookie.php                                              _ □ X
 1  <?
 2      // Increment number of visits count
 3      // If count isn't set then it will be set to 1
 4      $count++;
 5
 6      // Store the cookie on the user's system
 7      setcookie('count', $count);
 8
 9      // Output message
10      print "You have visited this site $count time(s).\n";
11  ?>

 Editor HTML
```

When the above script is first run the $count variable is initialized and assigned the value of '1' – this happens to all non-existent variables that are incremented in the manner used here. A cookie is then set on the client under the name of count. Finally a simple print statement is used to give feedback on the current value of $count.

Things start to get interesting when the script is loaded for a second time. Because a cookie exists by the name of count, a global variable by the same name is generated automatically with its value set to the value of the cookie. This is all done before any code in the PHP script is executed, so when we increment the $count variable, it will now hold a value one greater than the value stored in the cookie. Finally we're using setcookie() to update the cookie's value to the new $count and printing our visitor message again.

If you play with this you'll notice that each time you refresh your browser the number of times you've visited the site, or at least that page anyway, is updated and reflected in the message you see on-screen.

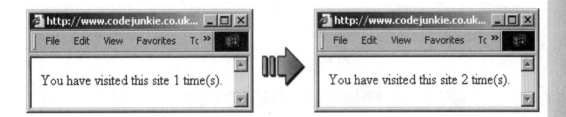

If this example doesn't work for you then double-check that you have cookies enabled in your browser

Common Pitfalls

When dealing with cookies, there are several common pitfalls that the designer can fall into which will either prevent cookies from working or produce error messages (maybe even both!)

Of all the pitfalls, by far the most common is outputting information before a call to setcookie. It is important to remember that cookies form part of the HTTP header, and accordingly calls to setcookie must appear before any standard output, such as that given by the print and echo statements. This also includes any white-space characters before the opening PHP tag.

If you see an error message like the following then it's time to backtrack and check your scripts for pre-`setcookie` output.

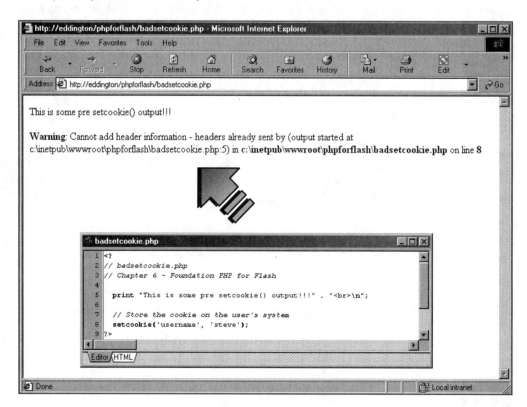

Another common pitfall is the assumption that, as soon as you call `setcookie`, the cookie will be immediately available to your script.

```
<?
  setcookie('username', 'steve');

  print "Username: $username";
?>
```

It may be considered reasonable to assume that the above script would produce the output you see on the right (opposite page).

However, the output will not be as expected on the first run due to the way that cookies work with server-side scripts. When a given script is requested, all valid cookies are sent to the server. Although calling `setcookie` tells the browser to create and store a cookie named `username`, the cookie won't get sent back to the server until the next time the script is requested. Thus, on subsequent runs of the script the output is fine.

 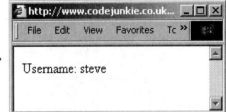

First Run   **Subsequent Runs**

Who Ate all the Cookies?

Having cookies available as global variables is all very well, but what if we wanted to process all the cookies that are available to us? How would we know which global variables were generated as a result of cookies and which came from other sources such as GET and POST data?

Besides this, using automatic global variable creation in PHP should be avoided wherever possible due to the security risk it poses. So unfortunately, despite its use as a teaching exercise, the method of setting cookies we have just examined will be replaced in our more advanced scripts. But what can we use to replace it?

The answer lies in the $HTTP_COOKIE_VARS array. Each cookie that is passed to the server is stored in this array, in addition to being created as a global variable. This allows us to process all, or a subset, of the cookies available using the array looping procedures we set out in **Chapter 2**.

Get your best typing gloves on and create the following PHP script or, alternatively, leave the gloves off and just open it from the source files.

```
<?
// setcookie.php
// Chapter 6 - Foundation PHP for Flash

   // Set up some cookies...
   setcookie('username', 'steve');
   setcookie('password', 'nottelling');
   setcookie('skipintro', 'true');

   // Determine the number of cookies currently set
   $cookieCount = count($HTTP_COOKIE_VARS);

   // If we've got more than one cookie...
   if ($cookieCount > 0) {
```

```
        // Output header
        print "Cookies found: $cookieCount <BR><BR>\n\n";

        // Loop through all cookies...
        foreach($HTTP_COOKIE_VARS as $cookieName =>
    $cookieValue) {

            // Output name/value
            print "$cookieName=$cookieValue <br>\n";
        }
    } else {
        // Otherwise output "no cookies" msg
        print 'No cookies available, hit refresh';
    }
    ?>
```

Here we're using the foreach loop (specific to version 4 of PHP) to work our way through the array of cookies, outputting each one in turn. When run, this script should give output similar to that shown below.

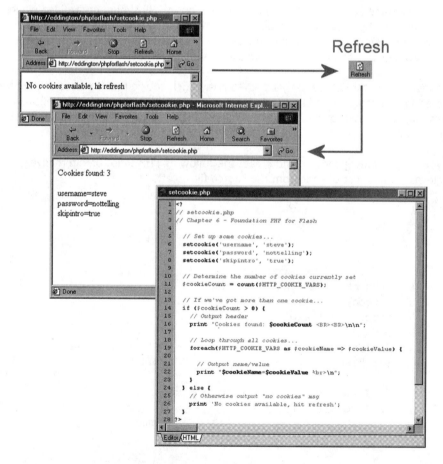

As you'll see, the first time you run it, you'll have to hit Refresh *as there are no cookies yet to display. This script shows us the power available to us in creating and calling cookies from PHP!*

The Life and Times of a Cookie

The previous example was all very well, but you'll find that if you close the browser window and then reopen it and reload the page, the visit counter has been reset to 1. Because we didn't provide an expiry date for our cookie the browser removed it at the end of the session, or when the browser window was closed. While this can be useful for storing information such as the login status of a user, we're also likely to want to store information in the cookie on a more permanent basis.

In order to increase the life of a cookie beyond the current session we need to provide a date on which we want the cookie to expire. We can do this easily enough by adding an extra parameter in the call to setcookie, but unfortunately we can't just supply the date as a string.

A Brief History of time()

Rather than a human readable date such as 27/02/2002 21:15:00, we need to supply the desired expiry date of our cookie in the form of a **Unix timestamp**. This may sound daunting at first until you realise that a Unix timestamp is simply a number specifying the number of seconds that have elapsed since midnight on 01 January 1970 – also known, rather grandly, as the **epoch**.

For those of you who fear that we're going to have to calculate this ourselves, fear not! Nor is there a poor Unix user who has been counting these seconds since 1970 without toilet breaks. PHP provides us with a nice little function that will fetch the current time as a Unix timestamp. As with most of PHP's standard functions this one is intuitively named, and it's simply called **time()**.

The syntax for time is about as simple as we've met so far:

```
time();
```

Taking no arguments whatsoever, we can simply call time and store the returned integer in a variable for future use.

For example, we can use the following piece of code to fetch the current time as the number of seconds since the epoch and store it in the $now variable:

```
<?
   // Fetch current time as no. of seconds since epoch
   $now = time();
    print $now
?>
```

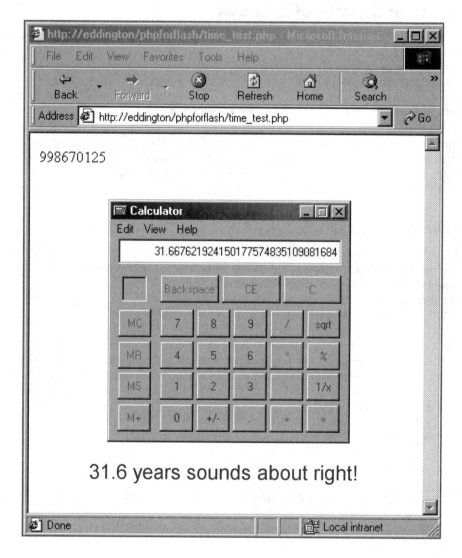

Cookies Do Time Travel

Now you may be wondering how this function can be used to set the expiry date of our cookie. There's little point in taking the return value of `time` and using it directly as our expiry date since the cookie would expire as soon as we've set it. What we need is a way of manipulating the timestamp so that we can fast-forward it to some date in the future.

As the return value of `time` is an integer, we can use the standard mathematical operators to play around with it, allowing us to set a timestamp for some date in the future.

```
<?
    // Fetch current time as no. of seconds since epoch
    $now = time();

    // Advance timestamp by 10 seconds.
    $future = $now + 10;

    // Display our time values
    print "Now: $now <br>\n";
    print "Future: $future";
?>
```

If you test the above code on your server you should have an output similar to the following.

Now: 997797605
Future: 997797615

> *Obviously when you run the above script you'll get different numbers because this number represents the time when I was writing this book (and the number in the previous example was greater because it represents the time when Alan was editing the book and added the screenshot!) Regardless of what your numbers are, the bottom one should be 10 greater than the top one, and that represents an extra 10 seconds.*

Anti-Ageing Cream for Cookies

Given the capabilities of the time function, and since we know (or can at least calculate) the number of seconds in a given period such as an hour or a day, we can now start extending the life of our cookies.

Let's breathe some life into the count example we met earlier in the chapter. The original file is included as count.php in the source files, and we're now going to make some amendments.

```
<?
    // Expiry date is current date plus 1 minute (60 secs)
    $expiryDate = time() + 60;

    // Increment number of visits count
    // If count doesn't already exist then to 1
    $count++;

    // Store the cookie on the user's system
    setcookie('count', $count, $expiryDate);

    // Output message
    print "You have visited this site $count time(s).\n";
?>
```

So long as you reload the site more frequently than once every minute the count will keep ticking – even if the browser has been closed and opened in between. Every time the script is run the expiry date of the cookie is updated to 1 minute in the future, ensuring that our cookie is valid for that period regardless of whether the browser has been closed or not.

You'll find that if you do not reload the page within 1 minute the count will reset to 1. This is because our cookie has expired and is no longer valid. You may find, however, that it takes considerably longer than 1 minute for the cookie to expire because the time function fetches the time according to the server. If the time on your system is 4 minutes behind the server time then you'll have to wait 5 minutes for the cookie to expire. In the same fashion you may find that the cookie expires as soon as it's set because your system time is in front of the server time.

For this reason it is best to steer clear of cookies that expire within a few minutes of the current time. Quite often this won't be a problem anyway because we'll either want to store the cookie indefinitely or store it for at least for a few days, but you should at least be aware of using time to store a cookie over relatively small periods.

Incorporating the Calendar

Using the `time` function is all well and good, but what would happen if we wanted our cookie to expire on a certain date. What we need is a method of generating a timestamp that represents a given date.

Thankfully, PHP provides us with the *mktime* function:

```
mktime(hours, minutes, seconds, month, day, year);
```

So, for example, if we wanted to generate a timestamp for a cookie that would expire at midnight on the *25th December 2002* the function call would look like:

```
$expiryDate = mktime(0, 0, 0, 12, 25, 2002);
```

Another function we can use to generate a Unix timestamp for a given date is *strtotime*. This function is far more user friendly in that it takes its date as a humanly readable string.

Creating the same timestamp as the code above using *strtotime* is a simple case of entering something like this:

```
$expiryDate = strtotime("12/25/2002 00:00:00");
```

It will also endeavor to convert dates represented in other formats but this is often a matter of trial and error to see how a given format works.

> *One thing to bear in mind is that the function leans towards U.S date formats, so "01/02/2002" will be taken as 2nd January 2002 rather than 1st February 2002 which is how you might read it if you're used to the European format.*

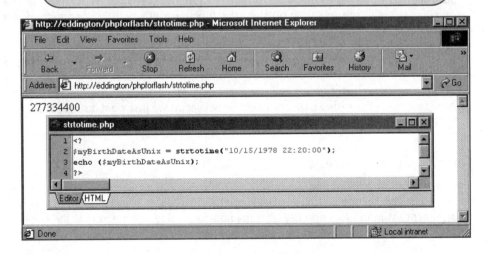

Deleting a Cookie

There may come a time when you've finished with a cookie on a given user's system and want to remove it. Although PHP doesn't provide any function specifically for removing cookies, we can produce much the same effect by updating the cookie's timestamp. By setting the expiry date of the cookie to one sometime in the past, we are forcing the cookie to expire and effectively removing the cookie from the user's system.

For example, the following line of code sets the expiry date of a cookie named `existingcookie` to one day (or 86400 seconds) ago.

```
setcookie('existingcookie', '', time() - 86400);
```

It is worth noting that any changes made to a cookie during the execution of a script are not reflected in either the `$HTTP_COOKIE_VARS` array or in the automatically created individual variables until subsequent runs of the script. This means that after the above line of code has been executed we can still use these values throughout the script.

Also worthy of note is the fact that deleting and setting (in that order) a given cookie in the same script in PHP4 is achieved as we would expect — first removing the old cookie and setting the new one. This is not the case however if you are using PHP3, where `setcookie` calls are actually performed in reverse order.

Cookie Paths and Domains

We can also use `setcookie` to restrict the cookie to a specific part of our site using the **domain** and **path** attributes. These are specified as additional arguments to the call to `setcookie`.

```
setcookie(name, value, expires, path, domain);
```

So if we wanted to set a cookie up to only be visible to the /samples path of our site (my codejunkie.co.uk site in this case) then the function call would look something like the following:

```
setcookie("test", "ing", 0, "/samples", ".codejunkie.co.uk");
```

Because we're explicitly adding the `path` and `domain` portions of the function call we also have to include the expiry date argument. However, as we just want a single session cookie in this case we can use zero as an expiry date to have it skipped.

The Cookie is Secure, Sir!

The last bit of information we can cram into our call to `setcookie` is an integer to represent the **secure** attribute of the cookie. This is just slapped onto the end of the argument list in the function call and any non-zero value will mean that the cookie is setup as a secure one. That said, it's generally best to use `true` if you want a cookie to be secure, or `false` if you want to explicitly set it to non-secure (as opposed to not including the argument at all which would have the same effect).

```
setcookie("test", "ing", 0, "/samples", ".codejunkie.co.uk",
true);
```

This would set a secure cookie for the same domain and path settings as previous, and it would only be sent to the server if the connection used the SSL protocol as discussed at the start of the chapter.

The Flash Cookie Cutter

Now that we've crammed all this wonderful cookie knowledge into our gray matter it's time to put it to good use in Flash.

In this section we're going to build what is commonly known as a **cookie cutter**. This application will let us view the cookies for our site, set new ones and update or remove existing ones. An application like this is a brilliant introduction to using cookies with Flash and can be used over and again.

Let's have a look at the final FLA, which you can find in the source files for this chapter:

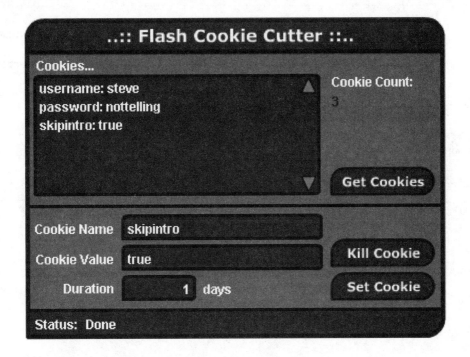

The user interface will be divided into two sections. The top section is where we'll be able to view all of the cookies currently set and the bottom section will be used to manipulate our cookies. Now let's open Flash and get cutting...

Cutting Cookies in Flash

1. As with most of the other applications that we've built thus far, we're going to be using the onClipEvent handler to detect when a given server-side operation has been completed. To this end we're going to want to put everything in a movie clip so the first thing we have to do is create one. Insert > New Symbol from the main menu or press CTRL+F8 to create the movie clip and give it a suitable name.

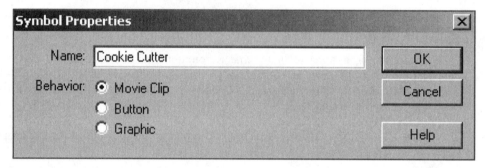

The timeline for this movie clip is going to be somewhat simpler than the previous ones with everything contained on a single frame. However, it's still a good idea to separate different elements of the movie clip onto different layers.

2. Recreate the layer structure shown below, where I've simply separated all the background elements from the form elements.

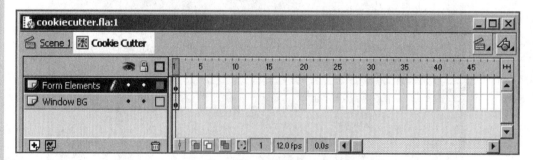

3. Again we're going to want to create a suitably stylish background for our movie clip. As always, I've remained faithful to the style introduced from the outset in this book, but you can make yours as extravagant or as simple as you like.

> Remember, all these applications are perfectly adaptable for you to use on your own sites, with your own design and whatever extra functionality you want. You could even try combining some of the sample applications you've met so far, and cookies are a great way of making visitor data available to all your site's Flash applications!

4. Now we need to add the form elements onto the Form Elements layer. Use the diagram as a guide…

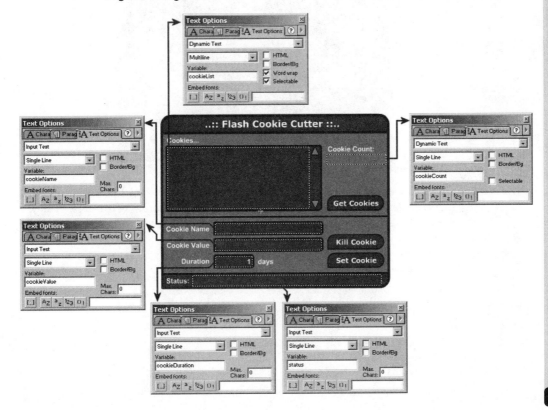

5. Next we to add the ActionScript for the various buttons on the form. We'll kick off with the small scroll buttons next to the `cookieList` text box. These simply manipulate the `scroll` property of the text box to scroll the text up or down when the relevant button is clicked. This will allow the user to easily view all the cookies if there are more than can be displayed at any one time in the text box.

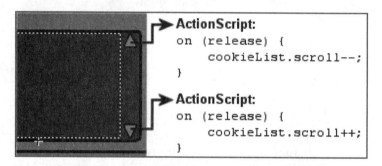

```
ActionScript:
on (release) {
    cookieList.scroll--;
}
```

```
ActionScript:
on (release) {
    cookieList.scroll++;
}
```

Now we can deal with the buttons that will interact with the PHP script we're going to be developing in a moment.

6. The Get Cookies button first sets the action that we want the PHP script to perform. It then clears the `cookieList` and `cookieCount` text boxes. Finally, it sets the `status` variable to reflect the operation being performed and calls the script.

```
on (release) {

    // Set the action we want
    action = "getcookies";

    // Now clear the text boxes
    cookieList = "";
```

```
cookieCount = "";

// Let user know what we're doing
status = "Fetching cookies for site...";

// And lastly, call the script
loadVariables("cookiecutter.php", this, "POST");

}
```

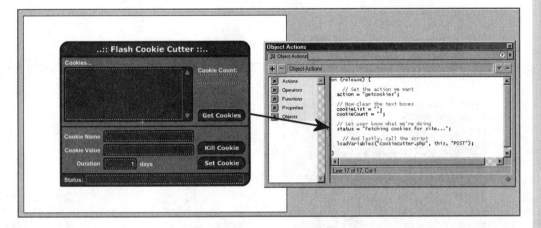

7. The operation of the Kill Cookie button is to remove the cookie specified in cookieName. Again we set the action variable to tell the script what we want it to do for us, call the script and set the status variable.

```
on (release) {

// Set the action we want
action = "killcookie";

// Let user know what we're doing
status = "Removing cookie...";

// And lastly, call the script
loadVariables("cookiecutter.php", this, "POST");

}
```

8. The final button we need to consider is the Set Cookie button. The code for this button only differs from the previous one in the values we are using for the variables.

```
on (release) {

    // Set the action we want
    action = "setcookie";

    // Let user know what we're doing
    status = "Setting cookie...";

    // And lastly, call the script
    loadVariables("cookiecutter.php", this, "POST");

}
```

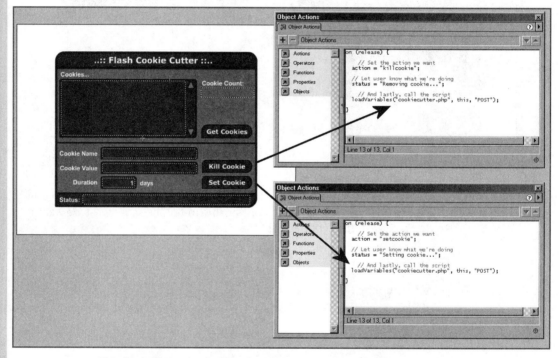

The final thing we need to do on the Flash side of things is to drag an instance of our Cookie Cutter movie clip onto the main stage and attach some code to it.

9. Once we have an instance on the main stage, we need to add the code to inform the user that the previous operation has been completed. We'll do this by simply using an onClipEvent(data) handler to set the status variable, indicating the success of the operation.

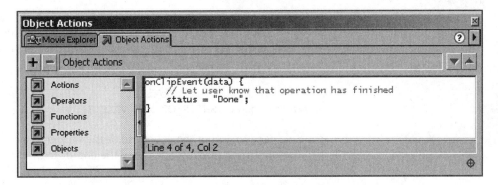

With the Flash front-end sorted, all that's left to do is to code the PHP script that will actually perform all the cookie manipulations for the application. The script will use a lot of the cookie related features of PHP we've met in this chapter, and is actually deceptively short.

Sharpening our Cookie Cutter with PHP

1. The first thing we need to do at this end is to decide what action is required of us by the Flash movie. This is specified in the $action variable and we're going to use the switch statements we saw in **Chapter 2** to test its value.

    ```
    <?
      // Determine what action to take
      switch ($action) {
    ```

    The first possibility is that the Flash movie has requested that a list of all the cookies be returned.

    ```
        // If we're fetching the cookies...
        case 'getcookies': {
    ```

2. If this is the case then we initialize a string variable to hold the list of cookies. We then loop through the $HTTP_COOKIE_VARS array using foreach and add each cookie's name and value to our string, putting each cookie on its own line.

    ```
          // Initialize variable to hold cookie list
          $cookieList = "";

          // Loop through cookies. Add them to cookielist var
          foreach($HTTP_COOKIE_VARS as $cookieName =>
    $cookieValue) {
              $cookieList .= "$cookieName: $cookieValue\n";
          }
    ```

3. We then fetch the total number of cookies for display in our cookieCount text box in Flash. Although it's not required, it is helpful to use the same name for the variable in PHP as the one we're using in Flash as it helps to eliminate mistakes!

```
// Fetch total number of cookies
$cookieCount = count($HTTP_COOKIE_VARS);
```

4. Finally for this action we need to output the list of cookies along with the cookie count to Flash, and use the break keyword to signify the end of this particular case block.

```
// Output cookie information back to Flash
echo "&cookieCount=$cookieCount";
echo "&cookieList=" . urlencode($cookieList);

// Done
break;
}
```

```
cookiecutter.php                                                    _ □ X
1  <?
2  // cookiecutter.php
3  // Chapter 6 - Foundation PHP for Flash
4
5  // Determine what action to take
6  switch ($action) {
7
8      // If we're fetching the cookies...
9      case 'getcookies': {
10
11         // Initialise variable to hold cookie list
12         $cookieList = "";
13
14         // Loop through all the cookies, adding them to the cookie list variable
15         foreach($HTTP_COOKIE_VARS as $cookieName => $cookieValue) {
16             $cookieList .= "$cookieName: $cookieValue\n";
17         }
18
19         // Fetch total number of cookies
20         $cookieCount = count($HTTP_COOKIE_VARS);
21
22         // Output cookie information back to Flash
23         echo "&cookieCount=$cookieCount";
24         echo "&cookieList=" . urlencode($cookieList);
25
26         // Done
27         break;
28     }
 Editor  HTML
```

5. If we're supposed to be setting a cookie, rather then fetching a list of them, then we need to add another `case` block to our `switch` statement.

```
// If we're setting a cookie...
case 'setcookie': {
```

6. Here we must determine whether the user wants to set a single session cookie (one that will be removed as soon as the browser window is closed) or whether we want to keep it for a number of days.

7. We can test for this by checking the variable `$cookieDuration` that has been passed from Flash. If it is set to 0 we can assume that the user wants this to be a single session variable and call `setcookie`, with just the cookie name and value specified.

```
// If specified duration is zero...
if ($cookieDuration == 0) {

// Set cookie for this browser session only
setcookie($cookieName, $cookieValue);
```

8. If, however, we have a meaningful value for `$cookieDuration` then we need to calculate the Unix timestamp for the specified number of days in the future. We do this by first multiplying the value of `$cookieDuration` by 86400 (the number of seconds in one day) to get the number of seconds until we want the cookie to expire. We then add this to the value returned by `time` to form a valid future timestamp.

We then simply call `setcookie` with the extra argument specifying the desired expiry date for the cookie.

```
} else {

// Otherwise convert days into a future date.
    $expiryDate = time() + ($cookieDuration *
➥86400);

// Set the cookie with the calculated expiry date
setcookie($cookieName, $cookieValue, $expiryDate);
}
```

9. We finish up by telling the Flash movie that we're done doing its bidding and, again, use the `break` keyword to signify the end of the current `case` block.

```
// Done
echo '&result=Okay';
```

continues overleaf

```
        break;
    }
```

```
 cookiecutter.php                                                    _ □ ✕
30     // If we're setting a cookie..
31     case 'setcookie': {
32
33         // If specified duration is zero...
34         if ($cookieDuration == 0) {
35
36             // Set cookie for this browser session only
37             setcookie($cookieName, $cookieValue);
38         } else {
39
40             // Otherwise convert the duration days into a future date.
41             $expiryDate = time() + ($cookieDuration * 86400);
42
43             // Set the cookie with the calculated expiry date
44             setcookie($cookieName, $cookieValue, $expiryDate);
45         }
46
47         // Done
48         echo '&result=Okay';
49         break;
50     }
```
`Editor HTML`

10. The final operation that we could conceivably be asked to perform is that of removing a cookie. If you remember back to the main chapter text all that needs to be done here is to update the cookie with an expiry date sometime way back in the past. For this, the simplest timestamp to use is 1 since that represents 1 second from the epoch, or midnight on 1st January 1970 – that'll be long enough ago I think!

```
    // If we're removing a cookie...
    case 'killcookie': {

        // Force cookie to expire
        setcookie($cookieName, '', 1);

        // Done
        echo '&result=Okay';
        break;
    }
}
?>
```

```
cookiecutter.php                                    _ □ ×

52      // If we're removing a cookie...
53      case 'killcookie': {
54
55          // Force cookie to expire
56          setcookie($cookieName, '', 0);
57
58          // Done
59          echo '&result=Okay';
60          break;
61      }
62  }
63  ?>

Editor  HTML
```

You should now have a fully working cookie cutter! And you've built it yourself – how good does that feel? All you need to do now is to upload or copy these files to your web server and load the Flash movie through your browser.

Further Development

If you want to develop this application further then you could try adding fields in the Flash movie to allow the user to set domain and path information for the cookies. Of course, this will also require a small edit to the Flash movie.

The same techniques presented here can be used to remember many different bits of information about your visitors and their time at your site. One of the possibilities is a clever Skip Intro button that when clicked will store a cookie on the users system, specifying that they don't want to see the intro if they return to your site. You can then check for this as soon as your movie loads and skip the intro automatically if appropriate.

You'll need to change the way the cookie information is returned from the script. Rather than returning the cookies as a list stored in a string, you'll want to return one variable for each cookie, with the name and value of the variable identical to the cookie's name and value respectively.

Alternatively, you could try setting a cookie at the very end of the intro so that the site knows that this user has already seen it and won't play it again. There are limitless possibilities.

Summary

In this chapter we've discovered a simple way of storing information on the user's computer and of using that information to influence the content of our Flash movies. This is our first look at maintaining a visitor's information between visits to the site so you can feel extremely proud of what you've accomplished here!

Beginning with a discussion on the nature of cookies in general we've also seen:

- What they are and how they work

- The restrictions that can be placed upon them

- How the `time` function can be used to set expiry dates

- How we can read and manipulate cookies with PHP and the `setcookie` function

- A working example of a cookie cutter application!

Because PHP makes handling cookies easy there wasn't a great deal to the script, and this can only be a good thing for busy designers who want to spend their time designing!

This is just the first step in storing information with PHP. In the next few chapters we'll look at some more advanced methods of handling and storing user data with PHP, and build some more excellent Flash applications.

7

Tapping Into External Files

What we'll cover in this chapter

- **Reading** from external files

- **Writing** new information to files and holding information for future use

- Putting all that to use in creating and maintaining a Flash-based **mailing list**

In the last chapter we took a look at cookies and how we can use them in PHP to remember visitor information between visits. This is all very well for relatively small amounts of non-critical information but they have a number of disadvantages in certain situations...

■ **Data Size**
Cookies are great for holding small pieces of information, and accordingly have a maximum size of 4kb. This means that storing large amounts of data using cookies is wholly impractical.

■ **Availability**
Cookies, by design, are only available to the site when a given user is actually visiting it. This would make it virtually impossible to use cookies to store information such as personalized news items for display on the site when users visit. Each visitor would have to have a copy of each news item, and we're then back to being limited by the maximum data size of a cookie.

■ **Information Retention**
Another problem with cookies is that we can never guarantee that they are going to be available to the site when the visitor returns. If the user has visited many sites in between and exceeded the maximum of 300 cookies, old cookies will start to be thrown away to make room for new ones. Similarly, if the user removes the cookies manually or needs to reinstall the software on their machine, the old cookies will not be available.

This means that we should not store any crucical information in a cookie because we cannot be sure that it will still be there when the visitor returns.

■ **User Preference**
And of course users can always disable cookies in their browser.

All these things mean that although cookies can be a great help, we cannot fully rely on them for holding and returning important information.

Having realised that the humble cookie has some serious limitations, we need to find another way of storing and retrieving data from our scripts. Over the coming chapters we'll be covering many of these methods but for this one we're going to focus on that old stalwart of data storage – the text file.

PHP provides us with a whole truckload of file handling functions. It currently has over 65 file and directory related functions, which should be enough to keep us contented.

We don't have room to cover all the functions here, and it would be a questionable exercise anyway since only a handful of them are going to be of any long-term use. Instead we're going to concentrate on the ones that will help us to perform the most common file operations:

- **Open**
  Opening a file with a view to reading and/or writing information to/from it.

- **Close**
  Closing the file when we're done with it.

- **Read**
  The actual operation of reading data from the file.

- **Write**
  Writing data to the file.

...and a few others thrown in for good measure including a quick look at related functions that handle directories. How can you resist?

Finally we're going to round the chapter off with yet another solid example. This time we're going to build a Flash-based mailing list application that you can add to any site. We'll include in this an admin section that will let you manage the mailing list and send out e-mails.

You can see the mailing list in action at www.phpforflash.com where you can also grab the example files for the chapter.

To whet your appetite in the meantime take a look at the screenshots of the application below – but no peeking ahead to see how it's done!

Opening Files

The most basic thing we're likely to want to do to an external file is open it. This is achieved through a single function in PHP: fopen().

The syntax for the fopen function is as below:

```
fopen (filename, mode [, use_include_path]);
```

Before we get into the nitty-gritty of this function's parameters we need to consider the return value of the function.

If the targeted file is successfully opened, this function returns what is known as a **file handle**. This is basically an integer that uniquely identifies the open file so we can use it in subsequent file-related function calls. If the file is not opened successfully then the function will return `false`.

Let's look at the component parts in more detail.

filename

If you glance up at the above syntax for `fopen`, you will note that **filename** is a string that specifies the name of the file that we want to open. We can use the `fopen` function to open any file that exists on the server's file system, or via HTTP or FTP on the Internet. The method used depends on the beginning of the `filename` string.

http://

If `filename` begins with "http://", a connection is opened to the specified server and a handle to the specified file is returned.

PHP does not handle HTTP redirects, so you must fully qualify the filename you want to open. As an example, suppose we wanted to open a file name index.html from http://www.phpforflash.com.

We would have to set `filename` to...

http://www.phpforflash.com/index.html

...in order to open the file, even though simply entering http://www.phpforflash.com in our web browsers takes us automatically to the index.html file.

If you're a bit concerned about people opening and modifying files from your site then fear not. For obvious reasons, files opened via HTTP are read-only.

ftp://

If `filename` begins with `ftp://`, an FTP connection to the specified server is opened and a handle to the requested file is returned. If the server does not support **passive mode** ftp, this will fail.

You can open files for either reading or writing via FTP but not both simultaneously. This restriction is particular to FTP.

If `filename` begins with anything else, the file is opened from the file system, and a pointer to the opened file is returned.

It is worth noting that neither the http:// *nor* ftp:// *at the beginning of the file have to appear in any particular letter case.*

The remainder of the filename may or may not be case sensitive depending on the operating system on which the file being targeted resides. For example, windows servers will treat file.ext, File.ext *and* FILE.EXT *in exactly the same way, while to Unix or Linux based servers these are three totally different files.*

Returning to the syntax of the `fopen` function, you will see that `filename` is followed by the **mode** parameter.

mode

Essentially, its the modes job is to tell PHP exactly what kinds of operation we want to perform on the file. There are several possible values this string can take and they are listed below, along with the operation(s) they represent:

Value	Meaning
r	Open file for reading only. Place file pointer at the beginning of the file.
r+	Open file for reading and writing. Place file pointer at the end of the file.
W	Open for writing only. If the file already exists then delete its contents. If the file does not exist, attempt to create it.
w+	Open file for reading and writing. If the file already exists then delete its contents. If the file does not exist, attempt to create it.
A	Open file for appending – write only. Place the file pointer at the end of the file. If the file does not exist then attempt to create it.
a+	Open file for appending – read and write. Place the file pointer at the end of the file. If the file does not exist then attempt to create it.

The mode *may also contain the letter "b" – signifying that the file should be opened in binary mode. This is useful only on systems that differentiate between binary and text files (that is to say it's of no use in Unix). If not needed, this will be ignored. When dealing with binary files it is better to use the "b" flag because although Unix treats ASCII and binary files the same, it is better to make your code cross compatible.*

include_path

Finally, taking one last glance back at the syntax for `fopen`, you will see an optional third parameter. You can set it to "1", if you want to search for the file in the `include_path`, too. The `include_path` is an entry in the PHP configuration file and you can find out more at www.php.net.

Some Function Action

Let's take a look at a couple of instances of the `fopen()` function in action.

```
// Open news.dat from file system for reading only
$file = fopen("news.dat", "r");

// Create a new file for writing on the file system
$file = fopen("output.txt", "w");

// Open file for appending: read and write in data dir
$file = fopen("data/banned.inf", "a+");

// Open index.html from http://www.phpforflash.com
// MUST be read only
$file = fopen("http://www.phpforflash.com/index.html", "r");
```

If your server is running a Windows-based operating system then you need to take special care when specifying the path to the file that you escape the backslash characters. This is necessary because the filename is specified as a string and because the backslash character has a special meaning within strings (as we have already seen). Alternatively you can use the forward slash character, which has no special meaning and does not require escaping:

```
// Not good
$file = fopen ("c:\data\info.txt", "r");



// Good
$file = fopen ("c:\\data\\info.txt", "r");

// Good
$file = fopen ("c:/data/info.txt", "r");
```

Warnings

Before we go any further it's worth discussing the automatically generated error messages when an operation like a file open is performed. Depending on your configuration of PHP, if something goes wrong with the operation you may get error messages automatically shown within the output of the script.

An example can be seen below:

Warning: file("test.txt") - No such file or directory in /path/to/www.codejunkie.co.uk/public_html/file.php on line 3

Obviously this kind of output can cause havoc with either nicely designed HTML user interfaces or, in our case, the information sent back to Flash.

To suppress these error messages we can use PHP's error suppression operator – @ – before the function call. For example, to suppress an error message from the `fopen` function, the function call may look like:

```
$file = @fopen("test.txt", "r");
```

We can then test the value of `$file` and output a more pleasing error message if we choose to do so.

Closing Files

Now that we know how to open files we need to cover closing them! Any files that remain open at the end of your script will be automatically closed by PHP, but it's good programming practice to close a file when you're done with it. You will also need to close a file if you want to change the mode with which the file was opened.

PHP provides us with the `fclose()` function for this task.

```
fclose (file_handle);
```

`fclose` takes a single argument, which is the handle of the file to close. For this we use the previously returned value of `fopen`. The function returns `true` on success, or `false` on failure.

Now that we can open and close a file we can look at a real running example:

```php
<?
    // Attempt to open file for reading
    $file = @fopen("test.txt", "r");

    // If the file was opened successfully...
    if ($file) {

        // Output success message
        print "File opened successfully!\n";

        // Close file
        fclose($file);
    } else {

        // Otherwise output failure message
        print "File not opened!\n";
    }
?>
```

This code simply attempts to open the test.txt file from the same directory that the PHP script is in. If it succeeds then we print a message saying so and close the file. Otherwise, we simply print a failure message. It may seem like common sense but it's worth noting that we don't need to close a file if it wasn't opened successfully!

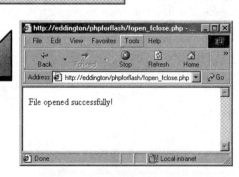

Displaying a File

Opening and closing files is all well and good, but it's not exactly exciting is it? What we need is a way of displaying the file to get it to work for its supper!

What we are going to look at is the PHP fpassthru() function. It sends the contents of the file to the client.

```
fpassthru(file_handle);
```

Again this function takes the handle of the file to be displayed and presents it as a single argument. On success the function will return true, on failure false.

This function outputs the contents of the file from the current file position (more on that later) to the end of the file. As an added bonus, fpassthru will close the file for us when it's done. We could modify the previous example to actually output the contents of the file if it is opened successfully, like so:

```php
<?
    // Attempt to open file for reading
    $file = @fopen("test.txt", "r");

    // If the file was opened successfully...
    if ($file) {

        // Output success message
        print "File opened successfully! <br>\n";

        // Output file contents
        fpassthru($file);
    } else {

        // Otherwise output failure message
        print "File not opened!\n";
    }
?>
```

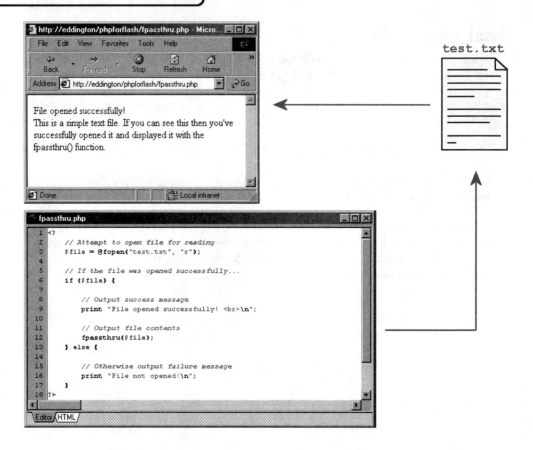

Note that we've removed the call to the `fclose` function since `fpassthru` handles closing the file for us.

When used in this context, text files will make the best target for the `fpassthru` function. However, we could also use it to output images:

```php
<?
    // Attempt to open file for reading
    $file = @fopen("picture.gif", "r");

    // If the file was opened successfully...
    if ($file) {

        // Output image
        fpassthru($file);
    } else {
```

```
                        // Otherwise output failure message
                        print "File not opened!\n";
                    }
            ?>
```

If you enter the URL for this script into your browser and the image exists, the result of this would be the same as typing the name of the image file in directly. However, if the file doesn't exist you get a nice message telling you so.

The same technique could also be used with another `fpassthru` function call to output an image not found message which would make it suitable for an HTML `<IMG>` tag, replacing those horrid boxes with red crosses in them!

PHP code:

```
        <?
                // Attempt to open file for reading
                $file = @fopen($filename, "r");

                // If the file was opened successfully...
                if ($file) {

                    // Output image
                    fpassthru($file);
                } else {

                    // Otherwise output failure message
                    $errorimg = fopen("whoops.gif", "r");
                    passthru($errorimg);
                }
        ?>
```

HTML code:

```
        <IMG src="getimage.php?filename=test.gif">
```

Here we're using a query string to pass the name of the desired image file via the `$filename` variable.

Reading From Files

`fpassthru` is a nice enough function, but it's not very useful if we don't want to actually output the contents of a file. What if we just want to read data in and use that in our PHP script? Can PHP handle that too? Of course it can!

PHP provides a number of functions for reading data from an external file and we're going to look at some of them in this section.

fread()

To read a string from an opened file we can use the fread function.

```
fread(file_handle, length);
```

$$\$text\ =\ fread(\ \boxed{\equiv}\ );$$

This function takes it upon itself to read the string, expecting it to be as long as **length** specifies, and expecting it to be buried in the file quoted by **file_handle**.

To take up one of our earlier examples, rather than outputting the whole file we could just output the first 26 characters of it (the first sentence only) with the following code:

```php
<?

    // Attempt to open file for reading
    $file = @fopen("test.txt", "r");

    // If the file was opened successfully...
    if ($file) {

        // Output success message
        print "File opened successfully! <br>\n";

        // Read first 26 bytes from file
        $output = fread($file, 26);

        // Output string
        print $output;
    } else {

        // Otherwise output failure message
        print "File not opened!\n";
    }

?>
```

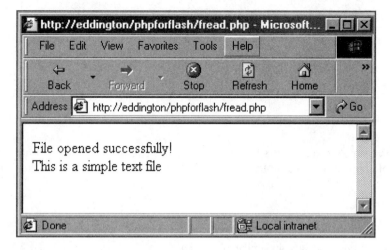

Note that if the end of the file is reached before `fread` has read `length` characters, the text up to that point will be returned.

fgetc()

Although `fread` can be used to read single characters at a time it's a bit like using a sledgehammer to crack a nut – a touch heavy!

A better solution would be to use the `fgetc()` function.

```
fgetc(file_handle);
```

This would be more efficient from an overheads point of view because it doesn't need to read ahead to determine the total length of the string. So to read the first character of the file from our example earlier we could use the following code:

```
<?
    // Attempt to open file for reading
    $file = @fopen("test.txt", "r");

    // If the file was opened successfully...
    if ($file) {

        // Output success message
        print "File opened successfully! <br>\n";

        // Read first character from file
        $output = fgetc($file);
```

continues overleaf

```
                    // Output string
                    print $output;
            } else {

                    // Otherwise output failure message
                    print "File not opened!\n";
            }
        ?>
```

Here we've simply replaced the call to fread with a call to fgetc. We could replicate the output of the previous example if we were to loop the reading and outputting code 26 times.

fgets()

The fgets function is largely similar to fread.

```
fgets(file_handle, length);
```

It has the same parameters and performs almost the same operation as fread. The difference is that if a newline character is encountered during the read operation then fgets will stop reading at that point. This makes the function ideal for reading through lines of a text file one at a time.

There is also a subtle difference in the interpretation of the **length** argument. While fread will read up to length characters from the file, fgets will only read up to length − 1 characters.

The following code will loop through our test file, outputting every five characters of the file on a separate line...

```
<?
    // Attempt to open file for reading
    $file = @fopen("test.txt", "r");

    // If the file was opened successfully...
    if ($file) {

        // Output success message
        print "File opened successfully! <br>\n";

        do
        {
            $output = fgets($file, 6);
```

```
        if ($output) {
            print "$output <BR>\n";
        }
    }

} else {

    // Otherwise output failure message
    print "File not opened!\n";
}

?>
```

Browser window:
```
http://eddington/phpforflash/fgets.php - Microsoft ...
File  Edit  View  Favorites  Tools  Help
Back   Forward   Stop   Refresh   Home
Address  http://eddington/phpforflash/fgets.php   Go

File opened successfully!
This
is a
simpl
e tex
t fil
e. If
you
can s
ee th
is th
en yo
u've
succe
ssful
ly op
ened
it an
d dis
playe
d it
with
the f
passt
hru()
func
tion.
Done                          Local intranet
```

Editor window (fgets.php):
```
1  <?
2      // Attempt to open file for reading
3      $file = fopen("test.txt", "r");
4
5      // If the file was opened successfully...
6      if ($file) {
7
8          // Output success message
9          print "File opened successfully!<br>\n";
10
11         do
12         {
13             $output = fgets($file, 6);
14
15             if ($output) {
16                 print "$output <br>\n";
17             }
18         }
19         while($output);
20
21     } else {
22
23         // Otherwise output failure message
24         print "File not opened!\n";
25     }
26  ?>

Editor / HTML
```

file()

The last of the file reading functions we're going to take a look at is the `file()` function, which creates a nice array out of our external file.

```
file(filename);
```

You can see from the above syntax that, rather than an open file handle, the `file` function takes as its single argument the **filename** (and path) of the file to be opened.

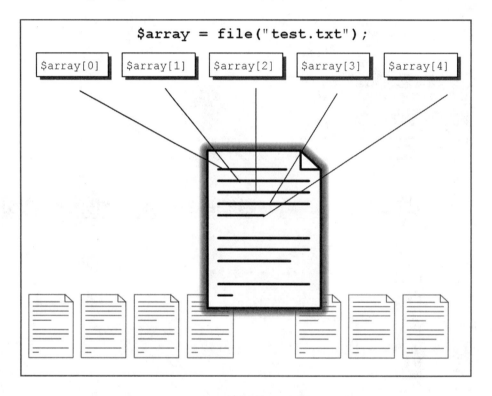

This is a handy all-in-one function that will open the file, load the file into an array, with each line represented by one element of the array, and then close it when it is done, returning the array. If the file could not be opened then the function returns `false`.

Note that each array element, having been constructed from a single line in the file, will still contain the newline characters that were present in the original file.

Using this function we could loop though all the lines in a given file, outputting them with line numbers.

```
<?
    // Attempt to open file for reading
    $lines = @file("file_to_array.txt");

    // If the file was opened successfully...
    if ($lines) {

        // Loop through all lines of file
        foreach($lines as $count => $line) {
            // Output count and line
            print "$count: $line <br>";
        }
    } else {

        // Otherwise output failure message
        print "File not opened!\n";
    }
?>
```

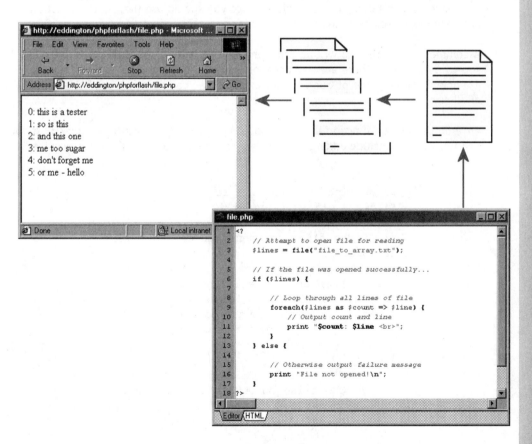

Writing to Files

The ability to read data from files is all well and good, but we need to find a way of getting the information there in the first place. We could just re-upload the file every time we wanted to change it, but that's akin to having a spa bath installed and never turning on the water jets.

PHP provides us with a couple of functions to enable us to write to files.

```
fputs(file_handle, string [, length]);
fwrite(file_handle, string [, length]);
```

The parameters for both functions are the **handle** for the file to be written to, the **string** to be written and, optionally, the number of characters from the string to be written.

The functions return true if the write operation is successful and, well, false if it is not.

The two are nearly identical and the only occasion when one is preferential over the other is when writing to **binary files**. In this instance you should use the fwrite function as it has been designated as a binary safe function.

A common use of the file writing functions is to write to a site-wide error log, allowing you to determine if there are any occasional or persistent problems with your site. For example, if we take one of our previous examples we can modify it so that a log is kept of all errors.

We'll do this using a function that you should be able to use in most of your PHP scripts. The function will include adding a timestamp so we can tell when the error occurred!

```
<?
    // Attempt to open file for reading
    $lines = @file("test.txt");

    // If the file was opened successfully...
    if ($lines) {

        // Loop through all lines of file
        foreach($lines as $count => $line) {
            // Output count and line
            print "$count: $line <br>";
        }
    } else {

        // Otherwise output failure message
        print "File not opened!\n";
        writeLog("Couldn't open test.txt");
```

```
    }

function writeLog($logEntry) {
    // Filename of log file
    $logFile = 'error.log';

    // Create human readable date/time string for
    // current time
    $dateStamp = strftime("%D %T", time());

    // Open log file for appending
    $file = @fopen($logFile, 'a');

    // If we've opened the file successfully
    if ($file) {
        / /Write the log entry and close file
        fwrite($file, "$dateStamp: $logEntry\n");
        fclose($file);

        //.Return success
        return true;
    } else {
        // Otherwise, return failure
        return false;
    }
}
?>
```

Here we're using a function to attempt to write errors to an error log file. We use the fopen function to attempt to open the file specified in $logFile for appending and test that the file was opened correctly. If it was, then we write our log file entry on a new line in the file and then close the file. We return true to indicate that the operation was a success.

If we fail to open the file then we simply return false since we can't write *that* error to a log file.

There's one function buried in here that we haven't met so far – strftime. This function converts the timestamp returned from the time function into a string with a format of our choosing.

It works very much like the printf and sprintf functions we met in **Chapter 4**, in that the various tokens given in the string (which make up the first argument) are converted into text representing certain parts of the timestamp. All of the tokens begin with a % sign and the ones we've used represent...

- **%D**   The date in mm/dd/yy format

- **%T**   The time in hh:mm:ss format

So, if the test.txt file cannot be found then an entry will be made in the error.log file that looks something like this:

```
08/11/01 15:57:23: Couldn't open test.txt
06/11/01 08:08:21: Couldn't open test.txt
06/11/01 07:11:50: Couldn't open test.txt
.....................................
```

> *Note that you'll need to make sure that you have the permissions to write to the error file or the folder it is in. Right-click and view the* Properties, *specifically the* Security *tab, to check. Also, if you actually have the* test.txt *file still in your root folder, you should temporarily move it or rename it to check that the errors are being generated.*

```
logfile.php                                              _□X
1  <?
2      // Attempt to open file for reading
3      $lines = @file("test.txt");
4
5      // If the file was opened successfully...
6      if ($lines) {
7
8          // Loop through all lines of file
9          foreach($lines as $count => $line) {
10             // Output count and line
11             print "$count: $line <br>\n";
12         }
13     } else {
14
15         // Otherwise output failure message
16         print "File not opened!\n";
17         writeLog("Couldn't open test.txt");
18     }
19
20     function writeLog($logEntry ) {
21         // Filename of log file
22         $logFile = "error.log";
23
24         // Create human readable date/time string for
25         // current time
26         $dateStamp = strftime("%D %T", time());
27
28         // Open log file for appending
29         $file = @fopen($logFile, "a");
30
31         // If we've opened the file successfully
32         if ($file) {
33             // Write the log entry and close file
34             fwrite($file, "$dateStamp: $logEntry\n");
35             fclose($file);
36
37             // Return success
38             return true;
39         } else {
40             // Otherwise, return failure
41             return false;
42         }
43     }
44 ?>
   Editor HTML
```

logfile.php

This is a good function to use across our site, and it would be worth taking a little time
out to develop our function to tell us the file that generated the error. This would only
require a small addition (an extra parameter passed into the function and a modification
of the call to fwrite) but would make the log file a lot more useful since we'll know the
source of all our problems.

Navigating Within Files

So far we've been reading and writing from and to the beginning of any files we've been playing with. While this is useful we will often want to navigate our way through the files we encounter to find the bits we're interested in.

Since each subsequent read operation advances our position within the file, we could use a loop reading one character at a time to move our way through all the data. However, this will only let us move forwards and we'd have to close the file and re-open it in order to reset the file pointer.

Thankfully, PHP provides a handful of functions that we can use to navigate our way through files more freely.

rewind()

The simplest of these functions is the rewind() function. As its name suggests, this function resets the file position to the beginning of the file.

```
rewind(file_handle);
```

You can see from the syntax above that file rewind function takes as its only argument the **file_handle** of the file to rewind. If the operation is successful the function returns true, and on failure it returns false.

fseek()

The fseek function allows us to navigate to any point in our file with a single function call.

```
fseek(file_handle, offset [, whence])
```

The fseek function sets the file position indicator for the file referenced by **file_handle**. The new position, measured in bytes from the beginning of the file, is calculated by adding the value of **offset** to the position specified by **whence**.

The possible values for whence are as follows.

SEEK_SET Sets file position relative to the start of the file. SEEK_CUR Sets file position relative to the current file position SEEK_END Sets file position relative to the end of the file.

Unusually for PHP functions, the fseek function will return "0" on success and "−1" on failure.

It's worth noting that it is perfectly valid to have a negative offset when setting the file position relative to either SEEK_CUR or SEEK_END but doesn't make much sense for SEEK_START since you can't seek before the start of a file.

It's also worth noting that you cannot perform fseek operations on file handles returned by fopen if they use the "http://" or "ftp://" formats.

So, for example, if we wanted to open a file and read just the last 10 characters (the very last word in our test.txt file) we would use the following code:

```php
<?
    $file = fopen('test.txt', 'r');

    if ($file) {
        fseek($file, -10, SEEK_END);
        $output = fread($file, 10);

        print "Output: $output\n";
        fclose($file);
    } else {
        print "Cannot open file";
    }
?>
```

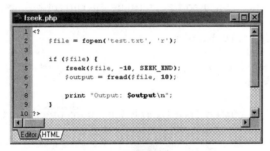

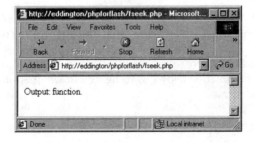

Here you can see we're using our newly acquainted `fseek` function to move 10 characters back from the end of the file (`SEEK_END`). We're then using a simple `fread` to read the final 10 bytes of the file in and a print statement to output the lot!

A few more examples of the `fseek` function in action are shown below. The comments alongside should give you a good indication of their use.

```php
// Move 5 characters from start of file
fseek($file, 5, SEEK_SET);

// Move 5 characters back from current file position
fseek($file, -5, SEEK_CUR);

// Move 11 characters past end of file
// Useful for files opened with write access to extend
// the file
fseek($file, 11, SEEK_END);

// Move to start of file. Same as rewind($file)
fseek($file, 0, SEEK_SET);
```

ftell() and feof()

The `ftell()` function is used to determine the current position within the file.

```php
ftell(file_handle);
```

Again, `ftell` takes a sole argument – the handle of the file from which to fetch the current file position.

Another useful function is `feof()`. This function is used to indicate whether or not the current file position is actually the end of the file.

```php
foef(file_handle);
```

This function returns `true` if the file specified is at EOF and `false` otherwise.

More Useful Functions

We round off our journey through file-related functions in PHP with a look at some useful functions that don't really fit into any other category we've covered.

A greater sensitivity of error message is afforded by the `file_exists` function. As its name dictates, this function allows us to figure out whether or not a file is actually on our server at all. The format is:

```php
file_exists(filename);
```

The function simply takes the **filename** of the file for which we want to check as a single argument. It will return true if the file exists, or false otherwise.

We can use this function to determine if a file exists before attempting to open it.

```php
$filename = "lums.txt";

if (file_exists($filename)) {
    $file = @fopen($filename, 'r');

    if ($file) {
        fpassthru($file);
    } else {
        print "File found but couldn't open";
    }
} else {
    print "Cannot find file $filename";
}
```

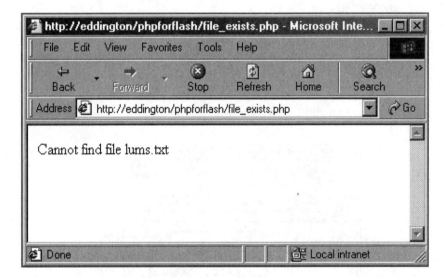

If you follow through the nested if..else *statements, you'll see that we first check it exists, and then we check if we can open it, outputting different messages if it doesn't exist or if it does but we just can't open it.*

Now, you may be forgiven for thinking that the `fopen` function would serve all our conceivable needs in terms of file existence. After all, you try to open a file, it doesn't open, it doesn't exist, right? Wrong! There are a number of reasons why a file might fail to open. You can see from the above example that using both functions in tandem allows us to give a more specific error message to the user.

There's also a couple of other functions we can use prior to calling `fopen` to help us decide whether the operation will succeed or not.

```
is_readable(filename);
is_writable(filename);
```

These functions are very self-explanatory, returning `true` if the file is readable and writable respectively, and `false` otherwise. Let's pretend we've found our `lums.txt` file, but someone's gone and made it read-only!

```
$filename = "lums.txt";

if (is_readable($filename)) {
    print "File is readable <br>\n";
} else {
    print "File is not readable <br>\n";
}

if (is_writable($filename)) {
    print "File is writable <br>\n";
} else {
    print "File is not writable <br>\n";
}
```

Having looked extensively at the file-related functions in PHP and how we can use them to store and retrieve information, it's time to put all that knowledge into practice with a sample application.

Building a Flash Mailing List Application

In this section we're going to be building a mailing list application. There are actually two parts to it – the **user side** and the **administration side**. The user side will handle all user interaction, which is basically just the subscription to our mailing list. The admin side will handle the sending out of e-mails to all the users subscribed on the mailing list.

As with most of the other applications we're going to use a movie clip to hold the entire application.

1. Create the movie clip, give it a suitable name like Mailing List and hit the OK button.

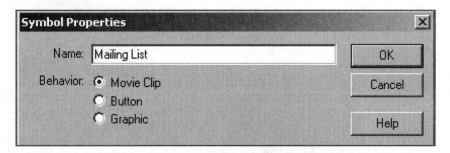

2. Next we'll build the timeline and frame structure for the movie clip. Use the screenshot below as a guide.

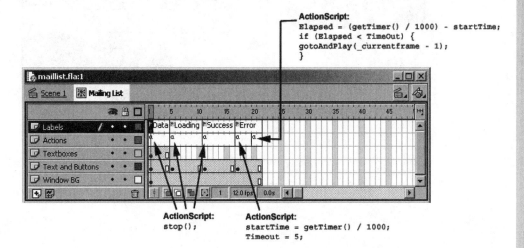

3. Again we're going to want to create a suitably stylish background for our movie clip. As always, I've used the phpforflash.com style introduced from the outset in this book but you've probably developed your own funky design calling card by now.

4. Now we need to add the form elements onto the Textboxes layer. Use the diagram below as a guide…

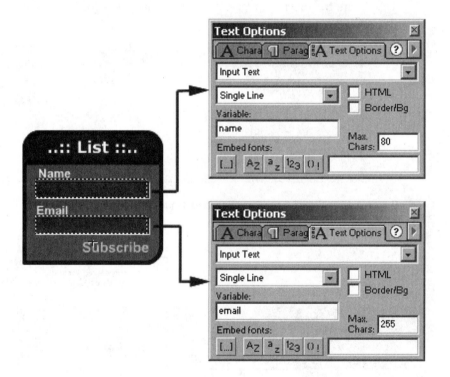

5. You'll also want to add some ActionScript to the Subscribe button shown above. This is to process the details entered and send us to the Loading frame

6. Now we move on to that Loading frame. Here I've re-used the waiting clock animation from previous examples.

7. We also need to create the elements for the Success frame. This is simply a message telling the user that they've been subscribed successfully to our mailing list.

8. The last frame we need to worry about is the Error frame. This is where any errors that occur will be displayed so we'll need a text box to display them. We'll name the variable errorMsg and use that to return error information from our PHP script.

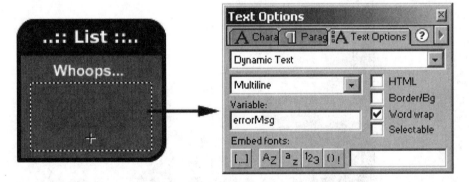

9. The final thing we need to do on the Flash side of things is to drag an instance of our Mailing List movie clip onto the main stage and attach some code to it.

10. Once you have an instance on the main stage we need to add the code to send the movie clip to the appropriate frame on success/failure of the operation. We can do this by checking the result variable that we'll set from our PHP script and using gotoAndStop to jump to the appropriate frame.

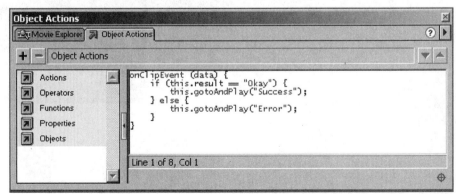

With that done we now need to build up the PHP script to handle the requests from the Flash movie. We'll use a lot of functions in this code to keep everything easily understandable.

Adding The PHP Script

Before we kick into the PHP script, we need to think about how we're going to store the user data in our text files. Since the `file` function will load each line of the given file into an array element it seems sensible to have one line per subscriber in the file. However, we need to store more than a single piece of data about each subscriber. The information we'll want to store is:

- Name
- E-mail Address
- Date Subscribed

So we need a way of fitting this all on to one line whilst still being able to get at the individual bits when we need to. The answer is to use some kind of separator and then use the `explode` function to split the string apart when we want to get at the individual bits.

We need to make sure that the separator we choose isn't likely to crop up in any of the data fields we want to store, or else it'll cause problems when we come to explode the string. A commonly used separator is the "|" character and this is the one we'll be using in this application.

Just so you're sure about what's going on here, take a look at a few entries from my text subscriber file:

```
Steve Webster|steve@codejunkie.co.uk|998254219
james|james@codejunkie.co.uk|998297924
billy|billy@codejunkie.co.uk|998299352
```

Here you can see how the different data fields are separated with their Unix timestamps at the end.

1. Right, with all that sorted we can get on and tackle the PHP script. This is our opening chunk of code:

```
<?
    // Check for required data
    if (!isset($email) || !isset($name) ||
            empty($email) || empty($name)) {
        fail("Both name and email are required");
    }
```

continues overleaf

```
// Make string lowercase
$email = strtolower($email);
```

The first thing we do is to check that the required data has been sent to us. Although we're doing this already in the Flash movie it's worth double checking the data as it helps to weed out any errors that could occur as a result of misnamed variables.

We then use the strtolower function we covered in **Chapter 4** to make sure that the e-mail address uses all lower case letters. We do this so that, when checking to make sure that a given user is already subscribed to the mailing list, we don't get any confusion between, say Steve@codejunkie.co.uk and steve@codejunkie.co.uk.

2. Next, we use a switch statement to check the value of the $action variable which will be sent from the Flash movie. We check it against two known actions and call the appropriate function if a match is found, and we use the default: block to return an error message if the value of $action is not a valid action.

```
// Determine operation to perform
switch($action) {
    case "subscribe":
        subscribe($name, $email);
        break;

    case "unsubscribe":
        unsubscribe($email);
        break;

    default:
        fail("Unknown action: $action");
}
```

That's the end of the main code for the maillist.php file and we now move onto the functions that actually do the legwork.

3. The first two functions we meet, although small, will be used throughout the rest of the script to report back to Flash on the status of the operation. The fail() function, as its name might suggest, will tell our Flash movie that the operation has failed and, by making $errorMsg a parameter of the function, we can use it to report all of our errors with a custom error message.

```
function fail($errorMsg) {
    $errorMsg = urlencode($errorMsg);
    print "&result=Fail&errorMsg=$errorMsg";
    exit;
}
```

4. The `success()` function works in much the same way, except we've no need to supply any more information than the fact that the operation succeeded. Thus, the function has no parameters and uses a simple print statement to feedback to Flash.

```
function success() {
    print "&result=Okay";
    exit;
}
```

Both functions use the `exit` keyword once they've sent their data to Flash to prevent any further execution.

5. Next we have a function that will determine if a given email address is subscribed to the list. This will be used in both the `subscribe()` and `unsubscribe()` functions to determine the current subscription state of a user. This allows us to return error information if a user is already subscribed in the case of `subscribe`, and if a user isn't subscribed in the case of `unsubscribe`.

```
function isSubscribed($email) {
    $matchFound = false;
    $subscribers = file('subscriber.dat');
```

Here we're setting up our `$matchFound` variable to `false`, and we'll use this variable to indicate whether or not a user is subscribed.

We then use the `file` function we've just met to load the contents of the `subscriber.dat` file into an array called `$subscribers`, with each subscriber being stored in an element of the array.

6. Now we check that the file has been opened successfully and that it actually has some data in it. If so, we use a `foreach` loop to go through each element of `$subscribers` in turn, storing the index and value of the current element in the `$count` and `$subscriber` variables respectively.

```
if ($subscribers) {
    foreach($subscribers as $count => $subscriber) {
```

7. We then use the `explode` function to separate the three data fields of the `$subscriber` string into an array.

```
$info = explode('|', $subscriber);
```

8. After exploding `$subscriber`, we check the value of `$info[1]`, which is the e-mail address for the current subscriber, against the e-mail address being

passed into the function. If there is a match then we set our $matchFound variable to true.

```
        if($info[1] == $email) {
            $matchFound = true;
        }
    }
}

return $matchFound;
}
```

Once we've finished looping through all subscribers in the file we close the `foreach` loop and the `if` statement, and return the value of our $matchFound variable.

9. We now move on to the `subscribe()` function.

```
function subscribe($name, $email) {

    if (isSubscribed($email)) {
        fail("$email already subscribed");
    }
```

You can see that we're receiving the $name and $email variables as arguments when the function is called. We're then using our `isSubscribed` function to check whether the e-mail address supplied is already subscribed to the mailing list. If the function returns `true`, then we call our `fail` function to tell Flash why we've failed.

10. It's now time to fetch the current time and date to use as our joined date for the subscriber, and attempt to open our `subscriber.dat` file in append mode.

```
    $joinDate = time();

    $file = @fopen('subscriber.dat', 'a');

    if (!$file) {
        fail("Error: Couldn't open subscriber file");
    }

    fputs($file, "$name|$email|$joinDate\n");
    fclose($file);

    success();
}
```

If the file was not opened successfully then we report that back to Flash. Otherwise we use the fputs function to output our subscriber information on a new line in the file, remembering to separate each of the data items with the "|" character. Another crucial point is the newline character added at the end "\n". This ensures that the next subscriber is added on the next line, maintaining the structure of our file.

All that's left to do then is to close the file and report the success of the operation back to our Flash movie.

11. The final function we need to handle is the unsubscribe() function. This is a little more complicated than the subscribe() function because of the fact that you cannot simply remove a line in the middle of a file. Instead we have to read the entire file by using file, delete the element that corresponds to the subscriber we want to remove, and then write the whole lot back to the file, overwriting the current contents.

```
function unsubscribe($email) {
    if (!isSubscribed($email)) {
        fail("$email not subscribed to mailing list");
    }
```

The first thing we need to do in our function is to check to see if the e-mail address being passed into the function actually exists in the subscriber file. If it doesn't exist there's no pointing trying to remove it so we return error information to Flash.

12. We then attempt to read the entire subscriber file into the $subscribers array. We check to make sure that there wasn't an error opening the file and, if there was, report an error to Flash.

```
$subscribers = file('subscriber.dat');

if (!$subscribers) {
    fail("Error: Couldn't open subscriber file");
}
```

13. We then use a foreach loop to check each of our subscribers in the file for a match to the email address given. If there is a match then we remove that element from the main $subscriber array using the unset() function.

```
foreach($subscribers as $count => $subscriber) {
    $info = explode('|', $subscriber);

    if($info[1] == $email) {
        unset($subscribers[$count]);
```

continues overleaf

```
            }
        }
```

14. Next, we attempt to open the subscriber.dat file for writing, using the "w" mode to ensure that any existing file is overwritten with our new one. We make sure that there wasn't an error opening the file and, if there was, report that back to Flash as an error.

```
$file = fopen('subscriber.dat', 'w');

if (!$file) {
    fail("Couldn't remove subscriber from file");
}
```

15. We then loop through the remaining elements in the $subscribers array, writing them to file.

```
foreach($subscribers as $subscriber) {
    fwrite($file, $subscriber);
}
```

16. Finally we close the file and report our great success back to Flash.

```
fclose($file);

            success();
}

?>
```

Well, we're on a roll, so let's carry on. There's one thing that we need to do, and our mailing list application is pretty much useless without it. We need to build some kind of facility by which we can at least send an e-mail to these subscribers - the whole point of our mailing list in the first place.

Designing the Admin Interface

Since this admin section is not going to be publicly visible there's no point in going through the hassles of building it in Flash - we should be man or woman enough to stomach plain HTML. This will also give you an insight into how comfortable PHP is working with both.

1. So, we'll first start off by building the HTML file that'll act as our user interface.

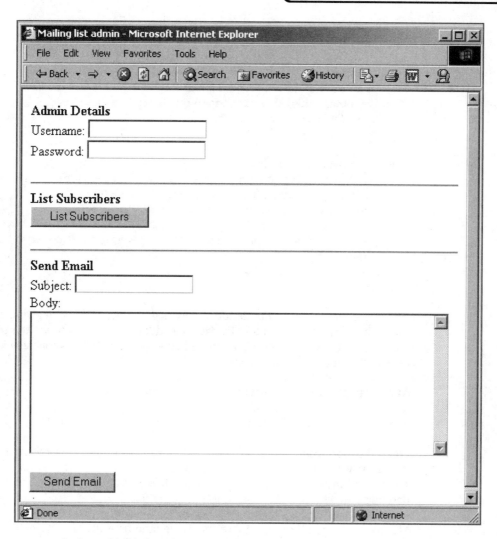

As I've said this is a simple HTML form and there shouldn't be anything new to you here – here's the code anyway, or you can find the file in the source code for this chapter:

```
<html>
  <head>
    <title>Mailing list admin</title>
  </head>
  <body>
    <form action="maillist-admin.php" method="POST">
      <b>Admin Details</b><br>
      Username: <input type="text" name="inUsername"><br>
```

continues overleaf

```
                    Password: <input type="password"
                ➡ name="inPassword"><br><br>

                    <hr>
                    <b>List Subscribers</b><br>
                    <input type="submit" name="action" value="List
                ➡ Subscribers"><br><br>

                    <hr>
                    <b>Send Email</b><br>
                    Subject: <input type="text" name="mailSubject"><br>
                    Body: <textarea name="mailBody" cols="60"
                ➡ rows="10"></textarea><br><br>

                    <input type="submit" name="action" value="Send Email">
                </form>
            </body>
        </html>
```

One of the interesting points to notice here is that, unusually, we're giving our submit buttons a name and a value. Not only does this allow us to set the text that appears on the submit button, these also get sent to PHP as variables - just as any other form element would.

As an example, take the following line of the above code:

```
<input type="submit" name="action" value="Send Email">
```

When the form is submitted, this will create a variable in the PHP (script names $action) with the value of "Send Email". Since we have more than one submit button in the HTML form we'll use this variable in the PHP script to determine which action the user wants us to perform.

2. Moving on to the PHP script, there should be little here that you haven't seen before.

```
<?
    // Define subscriber file
    $subsFile = 'subscriber.dat';

    // Define admin username and password
    $adminUsername = "steve";
    $adminPassword = "nottelling";
```

First up we store the name of the subscriber file in the $subsFile variable so we can refer to it through the rest of our script. Working in this way allows us to change the subscriber file we're using with the minimum amount of hassle.

We then set up the administration username and password that will be required to perform any of the operations in the script. We do this because we don't want Joe Public being able to come in and view all of our subscribers or send them e-mails.

3. Consequently, the next stage in the script is to check the supplied username and password against the admin details we've just defined. If the username and/or password does not match then an error message is displayed and execution of the script is halted.

```
// If supplied username/password do not match above
if ($inUsername != $adminUsername || $inPassword !=
➡ $adminPassword) {
    // Output error information and quit
    print "Invalid username or password";
    exit;
}
```

4. If the username and password are correct then we need to decide what action the user wants the script to perform. This is where our $action variable that we discussed earlier comes into play.

```
// Decide on what action we need to take
switch($action) {
    // Fetch list of subscribers
    case "List Subscribers":
        fetchList();
        break;

    // Send email to subscribers
    case "Send Email":
        sendEmail($mailSubject, $mailBody);
        break;

    default:
        print "Unknown action: $action";
        exit;
}
```

You can see that, depending on the action given, the appropriate function is called. In the case of sendEmail() we also pass in the elements of the HTML form that pertain to the e-mail - namely the supplied subject and body for the e-mail.

If no known match for $action is found then we output an error message and quit.

5. That's the end of the main section for the PHP script, and we now need to write the functions that are called by the above code.

```
function fetchList() {
    // Register global variables
    global $subsFile;
```

The first function to stand up and be counted is the fetchList() function, and all we're doing here is making sure that we've got access to the global variable $subsFile that contains the name of the subscriber list.

6. We then attempt to load the subscriber file as an array using the file function. If this function fails then we simply output an error message and halt the script.

```
// Attempt to open subscriber file
$subscribers = file($subsFile);

if (!$subscribers) {
    // Output error information and quit
    print "Couldn't open subscriber file or no
    ➥ subscribers listed";
    exit;
}
```

7. If all goes well we then use a foreach loop to traverse the array of subscribers. The first thing we need to do for each subscriber is to split the subscriber information using the explode function so that we can get at the individual pieces of information.

```
// For each subscriber line...
foreach($subscribers as $count => $subscriber) {

    // split subscriber info into array
    $info = explode('|', $subscriber);
```

8. We then take this information and assign it to meaningfully named variables to make the rest of the script more understandable.

```
// Assign array to meaningful variable name
$name = $info[0];
```

```
$email = $info[1];
$joined = $info[2];
```

9. Since the date on which the subscriber joined is stored as a Unix timestamp we need to convert this to a humanly readable time, and we do this using our trusty `strftime` function.

```
// Create a readable joined date out of timestamp
$joined = strftime("%D", $joined);
```

10. All that's left to do then is to output the current subscriber's information.

```
// Output information for each subscriber
print "<b>Subscriber $count</b><br>";
print "Name: $name<br>\n";
print "Email: $email<br>\n";
print "Joined: $joined<br>\n";
print "<br>\n";
    }
}
```

11. With regards to the `sendEmail` function, we start this in much the same way as we did with the previous one by making sure we've got access to the name of the subscriber file.

```
function sendEmail ($mailSubject, $mailBody) {
    // Register global variables
    global $subsFile;

    // Set up reply address for mailing list
    $mailFrom = "Mailing List <you@youremail.com";
```

12. We then define the name and e-mail address that we want the e-mail being sent to our subscribers to appear to be from. This is done in the

```
Name <Email>
```

...format that is the standard for e-mail programs to understand.

13. We then need to make sure that any automatically escaped quotation characters in the e-mail information passed into the script are removed before it's sent. We do this using the `stripslashes` function we met in **Chapter 4**, and we need to do this for both the subject and the body of the e-mail.

```
// Ensure that subject and body of email have
// automatically inserted escape slashes removed
```

continues overleaf

```
$mailSubject = stripslashes($mailSubject);
$mailBody = stripslashes($mailBody);
```

14. We then attempt to load the subscriber file, outputting error information if anything goes wrong. This is exactly the same as with the fetchList function earlier so we shouldn't need to go through this again.

```
// Attempt to read subscriber file
$subscribers = file($subsFile);

// If file open failed...
if (!$subscribers) {
    // Output error information and quit
    print "Couldn't open subscriber file or no
    ➥ subscribers listed";
    exit;
}
```

15. Again, as with the last function we use a foreach loop to process each subscriber in turn, first splitting the information and then assigning that information to meaningfully named variables.

```
// For each subscriber line...
foreach($subscribers as $subscriber) {
    // split subscriber info into array
    $info = explode('|', $subscriber);

    // Assign array to meaningful variable name
    $name = $info[0];
    $email = $info[1];
    $joined = $info[2];
```

16. Next up we build the e-mail address that the e-mail will be sent to. Again, we do this using the *Name <Email>* that's become the standard.

```
// Build to address including subscriber name
$mailTo = "$name <$email>";
```

The final thing we need to do for each subscriber is actually send the e-mail. We met the mail() function way back in **Chapter 3**, and we can use this function to send e-mails from our script.

```
// Send email to
mail($mailTo, $mailSubject, $mailBody, "From: " .
$mailFrom);
}
```

17. Finally for the function, indeed the script, we just output a confirmation message that the e-mail has been sent.

```
        print "Email sent to all subscribers";
    }

    ?>
```

That's all for this application. All that's left to do, as usual, is to upload or copy the whole lot to your web server. Don't forget to set the appropriate permissions for the subscriber.dat file so you have the appropriate write permissions.

One thing you might want to add is the ability for users to unsubscribe themselves from the e-mail. Armed with the information in this chapter have a go at adding this functionality. Hint: The function is already in the PHP script, we just need to build an interface for it!

Summary

Having reached the end of this chapter you should be fully proficient with the file-related functions in PHP. There is a lot to take in, especially if you're not familiar with basic file operations, but by working through each function in turn we've given ourselves a really good base from which to build.

We kicked off the chapter by looking at the basic operations. These were introduced as a foundation to the following sections, which would use them extensively, and we covered them in just about as much detail as was possible.

In full, we covered:

- How to open and close external files and even how to check if they actually exist

- How to display files and images, and create custom error messages

- Reading whole files or reading just one byte at a time

- Navigating files and other useful functions

Finally, we built a fully functional Flash based mailing list system. Here we used a lot of the techniques covered both in this chapter and so far throughout the whole book. It's a perfect addition to any website and can be practically dropped inas it stands!

Now that we've seen cookies in action and the benefits of using external text and log files, repetition it's time (and we're definitely ready) to hook up to a database and start using SQL to take our Flash movies into the stratosphere!

8

Introducing the Database

What we'll cover in this chapter

- **Fetching** information from databases – an introduction

- **SQL** and Relational Databases

- Basic SQL **functions**

- How we'll use MySQL as a **database option** for our PHP scripts and Flash movies

Before we can examine databases in depth, we need to take a sneak peek at how we can communicate with them to perform the tasks we want.

All we'll need to learn to talk to databases is a language known as **SQL** (pronounced *sequel*), which we will be implementing through the popular and powerful open source database product **MySQL** (confusingly enough pronounced *My-Ess-Cue-Ell*).

Now, what this constitutes is a minor diversion from our full-blooded rush on the subject of PHP. However, my advice is that if you engage with this chapter, employ MySQL and work through step by step, you will be head and shoulders above the rest of the class in the next chapter when PHP comes hurtling back.

The aim of this chapter is not to bore you with another language or to take your concentration away from PHP, but rather to enable you to fully understand, and then effectively use, this powerful language as a feature of your PHP scripts. As I've hinted at in previous chapters, once you can use databases to pull data into Flash, the sky's the limit.

So, kick off your shoes and start enjoying SQL!

An Introduction to SQL

SQL stands for **Structured Query Language** and it is the main language for interacting and manipulating databases. This may sound a little on the intimidating side but, unlike many programming languages, it's been strategically modelled around the English language, making SQL statements both easy to construct and easy to read.

Structured Query Language was first developed by IBM to bundle along with its own prototype RDBMS (Relational Database Management System) called **System R**. Details of the SQL language were subsequently published in various technical journals and in 1979 Oracle introduced the first commercially available implementation of SQL. Since then SQL has become widely implemented and is now accepted as the industry standard database access language.

What does all this mean to you and me? It means that if we devote a tiny chunk of gray matter to learning SQL then we should be able to use that knowledge with most database systems we come across. You can also bore your friends stupid by talking to them in SQL... though the novelty may wear off after the first handful of blank stares or violent attacks.

In this chapter we're going to focus on how to build SQL statements that will persuade any database server to perform to our heart's desire. Because SQL is something of a standard, we're going to do this without regard of implementation. What does that mean? Well, we're going to be concentrating on how to build good SQL statements that should work regardless of which database implementation we happen to be using.

However, before we get to play with, or even touch upon SQL, we need to cover a bit of theory behind databases. More specifically, we need to take a look at **relational databases**, why they exist, and what they can be used for.

Relational Databases

In the early 1970s, a learned fellow by the name of Dr E F Codd developed the relational database model. Dr Codd was an IBM scientist who devoted years of research to finding new ways to handle large amounts of data.

The problem with conventional methods, using so-called *hierarchical databases*, was that they were either too complex or required the developer to have an understanding of how the data was physically stored. This lead to great difficulties when altering the structure of the database or changing the storage medium, often resulting in applications having to be rewritten in order to access the data.

In the relational database model, data is stored in tables, with each table consisting of a number of records. As can be gathered from the name, the data in these tables is inter-related, a much more logical method of storing information.

A Brief History of MySQL

MySQL was developed in 1996 by a Swedish consultancy named TCX. They required a relational database system that was affordable, flexible, fast and could handle large amounts of data. Here are just some of the features that have helped make MySQL as successful as it is today:

Open Source

A key feature of MySQL is that it is provided open source, like good old PHP itself. This means that not only do you get a tip-top relational database management system, but you also get the source code for it. If there's a feature you'd like to see added to MySQL then there's no reason why you couldn't add it yourself by modifying the source code, assuming you have the technical wherewithal.

Support

Over the past few years the rise of Linux (an open source operating system) has instilled a confidence among businesses for open source products in the workplace. Indeed, the majority of the Internet is housed and served from computers running some flavor of Linux. This has led to a drastically increased user base for MySQL, ensuring its continued support and development.

MySQL is often confused as being a form of Structured Query Language. Rather, the MySQL tool uses, and in some cases expands upon, SQL to perform operations and manipulate its databases.

Database Theory

I know, I know, a quick glance down the page at the last few headings leaves you with a very short attention span. But stick with it. Before we get stuck into using MySQL, it would be a good idea to cover a little ground on database theory.

Let's look at a simple relational model of MySQL before we discuss each part in detail:

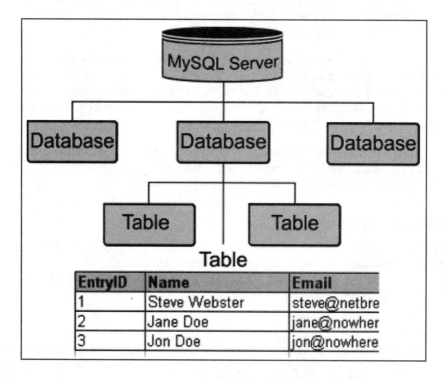

What can we gather from this? Well we can see that a single installation of MySQL can have many databases, and that each of the databases can have a number of tables. Each table contains specific data, which may or may not be related to the other tables in the database. The tables are made up of a number of columns and rows, much like a spreadsheet, and the point at which a column and row meet is called a field.

Each record in the table is stored in its own row, and each column has a name and a certain type of data that can be stored in it. A given field contains data designated by the column for that row or record in the table.

As mentioned previously, the tables in our databases can contain data that is related or completely separate from the other tables in the database. There is a concept known as **relationships** that can be used with related data in MySQL, but that is beyond the scope of this short introduction.

SQL for Kicks...

In this section we will discuss the use of Structured Query Language to create and manipulate our databases. We will take a look at the most common SQL commands and discuss how they will work with our chosen database management system. This is divided into sub-sections to deal with the different types of SQL statements.

In the following chapter we'll be focusing on MySQL as our database system of choice and we'll be taking a look at how we can access and manipulate data within it from PHP. Although MySQL uses the SQL language to manipulate and perform operations on its databases, it also expands upon SQL by introducing new commands not present in the language itself. For this reason we'll be taking special note of commands that are not part of standard SQL, in case we try to use them on a Microsoft database and receive nothing more than a giant raspberry.

Having got the introduction and the historical tracts out of the way we can get down to the serious business of taking in this supremely useful language.

> *For those who are cool enough to dive right in and use MySQL, you are going to have to install it on your system so you can play as we go along. Full instructions on installing and using MySQL can be found in* **Appendix A**. *If you'd rather just read on, and get into MySQL in the next chapter when we introduce it to Flash, turn your computer off and stick the night-light on...*

Creating a Database

Now, let's not attempt to breakdance before we can walk. Before storing any information in our database we need to actually create it. Now, you're probably thinking this involves starting from scratch and constructing this big relational monster – wrong. We simply do it with the CREATE command – I told you this stuff was easy!

The CREATE command is the main building tool of the SQL language and is used to create both databases and tables – the latter of which we'll come to in a moment.

The syntax for creating databases is one of the simplest you'll come across:

```
CREATE DATABASE databasename;
```

...where databasename is the name of the database to create.

> *Note that I have used upper case for the SQL commands in this case, and will continue to do so throughout the chapter. This is not essential – SQL accepts lower-case too – I am simply doing it to draw your attention to the syntax of the language.*

We need to pay special attention to the semi-colon at the end of the statement on the previous page. This signifies to whatever database system we're using that this is the end of the current statement, which allows long SQL statements to be split over multiple lines to make them more readable. The usefulness of this feature will become apparent later.

OK, let's enter this command. If you've been dabbling in the first appendix finding your MySQL feet then you'll have encountered the MySQL monitor – which is our way of controlling MySQL. Essentially, you need to follow the first part of the screenshot below in the command line. After we've typed `cd \mysql` then `bin\mysql`, we have started the MySQL monitor and it's waiting on our orders!

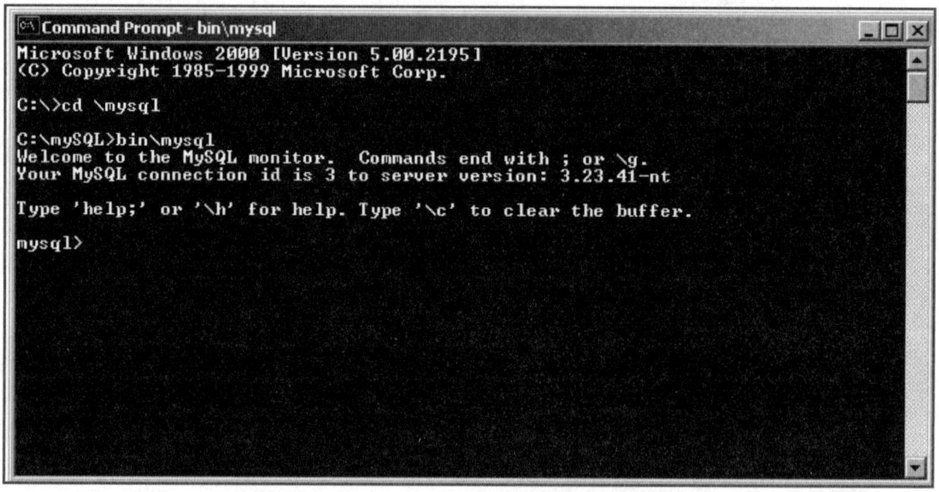

Now let's use the monitor to create a database named phpforflash:

```
CREATE DATABASE phpforflash;
```

We'll be using this database to store the information for the rest of this chapter. When you type this command into MySQL (shown opposite in the third-to-last line), you should see the following output:

```
Command Prompt - bin\mysql                                    _ □ X
Microsoft Windows 2000 [Version 5.00.2195]
(C) Copyright 1985-1999 Microsoft Corp.

C:\>cd \mysql

C:\mySQL>bin\mysql
Welcome to the MySQL monitor.  Commands end with ; or \g.
Your MySQL connection id is 3 to server version: 3.23.41-nt

Type 'help;' or '\h' for help. Type '\c' to clear the buffer.

mysql> CREATE DATABASE phpforflash;
Query OK, 1 row affected (0.07 sec)

mysql>
```

To take a look at the database we have just created, we would simply type:

    SHOW DATABASES;

Before we can do anything else to our database we need to make sure that our database system knows that we want to use it for subsequent operations, as many databases can be run concurrently. For this we will require the USE command and you can see the syntax below.

    USE databasename;

So, to select our database we would need to enter the following command into the MySQL monitor:

    USE phpforflash;

This is a common step to miss out when you're learning and playing around with SQL and can be the root cause of some very frustrating problems when trying to manipulate your newly created database. Everyone makes this mistake at least once so you'll be in good company when you do.

> *Remember, each MySQL command ends with a semi-colon.*

```
Command Prompt - bin\mysql                                    _ □ X
Microsoft Windows 2000 [Version 5.00.2195]
(C) Copyright 1985-1999 Microsoft Corp.

C:\>cd \mysql

C:\mySQL>bin\mysql
Welcome to the MySQL monitor.  Commands end with ; or \g.
Your MySQL connection id is 3 to server version: 3.23.41-nt

Type 'help;' or '\h' for help. Type '\c' to clear the buffer.

mysql> CREATE DATABASE phpforflash;
Query OK, 1 row affected (0.07 sec)

mysql> USE phpforflash;
Database changed
mysql>
```

Creating a Table

Now that we have had a look at creating our database, we're going to want to add some tables to actually hold the data. We can do this using the CREATE command we've just met, but we'll need to use it in a slightly different way.

The basic syntax for creating a table is slightly more complex than for creating a database, because we need to define a **name** and **data type** for all columns in our table.

> *In MySQL, a data-type is the type of information that a given column can hold — whether it's a string ("Hello"), a number (174) or something else such as a date or time. You cannot store a string in a column that has been designated to hold a number and vice versa. This is in contrast to the variables in both Flash and PHP, for which you do not have to specify a data-type, and the data-type can be changed throughout your script to suit your particular needs. We'll discuss some of the data-types available in MySQL a little further on in this section.*

The basic syntax for the CREATE TABLE command is:

```
CREATE TABLE tablename ( column_definitions );
```

Here, tablename is the name of the table to create and column_definitions describes all the columns for our table. The column_definitions element of the above command contains one or more of the following structures, each separated by a comma.

```
column_name type [NOT NULL | NULL] [DEFAULT def_val]
                 [AUTO_INCREMENT] [PRIMARY KEY]
```

Most of the elements of the above syntax should be self-explanatory by their names. For example, column_name is the name of the column we want to create, and type is the desired data type for the column.

> *Note however that this is not the complete syntax. What I've done is strip it down to show the options that are most likely to be used. If you're interested in all the juicy details then feel free to dip into the MySQL online manual.*

data types

"So," I hear you cry, "what kind of data types can we play around with?"

Well, this pretty much depends on how you're going to implement it. While some data types are common across all SQL-supporting database systems, others are **proprietary** and are only available on a specific system.

However, the data types presented below are the most commonly used of those available regardless of the database system you choose to use. For a complete list of data types supported by your chosen system then have a look in any documentation supplied with it – they'll be in there somewhere!

Anyway, enough of the rant! Bring on the data types...

INTEGER
Numerical value to hold an integer (that is to say, non fractional) value.

Range: -2,147,483,648 > 2,147,483,647

VARCHAR(n)
A variable length character field [string] of, at most, n characters.

The maximum length of a VARCHAR field is 255 characters.

CHAR(n)
A character type [string] of exactly n characters.

The maximum length of a CHAR field is 255 characters.

TEXT
A type to hold textual data with a maximum length of 65535 characters.

MEDIUMTEXT
A type to hold textual data with a maximum length of 16,777,215 characters.

DATETIME
A type used to store date/time information in the format 'YYYY-MM-DD HH:MM:SS'

TIMESTAMP
A type used to store date/time in the format 'YYYYDDMMHHMMSS'

If not explicitly assigned a value in an INSERT or UPDATE command, or if it is set to NULL, TIMESTAMP fields will be set to the current time.

This is a handy feature and means that we can use it as a simple last updated counter without having to worry about explicitly assigning it a value.

You'll probably recognize many of these types from our PHP scripts!

The elements after datatype are an important part of SQL. They allow us to set up some behavior rules for a given column. Note that these elements are shown in square brackets in my examples *only* to indicate that they are optional: The square brackets do *not* form part of the SQL command.

The particulars of each element are discussed below.

NOT NULL | NULL	Using either NOT NULL or NULL indicates if a value must be provided for this column in each row, or whether it can be left empty, respectively.
	If this is not explicitly defined in the statement then NULL is assumed.
DEFAULT def_value	This allows us to specify a default value for this column. If a row is added where no value is given for the column then def_value is used instead.
AUTO_INCREMENT	Using AUTO_INCREMENT we can specify that, unless a specific value is given for this column, then the value should be set to 1 greater than the highest value for this column.
	Obviously, this only makes sense when the column has a numerical data type and is most frequently used with table keys.
PRIMARY KEY	We use PRIMARY_KEY to designate that a particular column is to be used as the primary key for that table.
	Adding a primary key to a table improves the efficiency of any searching or sorting operations carried out on the table, but it can only be used on a column for which each row is assured of containing a unique value.
	It is good practice to ensure that each table has a PRIMARY_KEY column, even if we have to make up a column for it specifically. This is because it can be used to give a record a specific number or value.

We'll be meeting these in use as we go through the remaining chapters in this book, so it's worth familiarizing yourself with them at this early stage.

With the basics covered, let's see if we can create our very first table. Again, you can type each stage as it comes into the MySQL monitor or you can leave off the practical session untill we hit PHP again. We'll use this chapter to manually create the foundation for the content management system we're going to be creating in the next chapter, by which point we'll be able to store news items in a database and load them into Flash dynamically!

This example will cover a news section database table. If we think about what kind of information we might want to store in this, we should end up with at least a few of the following on our list:

- News Title
- Author Name
- Date of News Item
- News Body

Let's take a look at the whole SQL statement we'd use to create an appropriately structured database, and then we'll pick it apart piece by piece so that we understand what's going on.

```
CREATE TABLE news (
newsID INTEGER AUTO_INCREMENT PRIMARY KEY,
title VARCHAR(100),
author VARCHAR(30),
posted INTEGER,
body MEDIUMTEXT
);
```

Here we can see that we're creating a table called news, and that this table has five columns. Each column has been specified on a new line, making it easy to visualize the structure of the table.

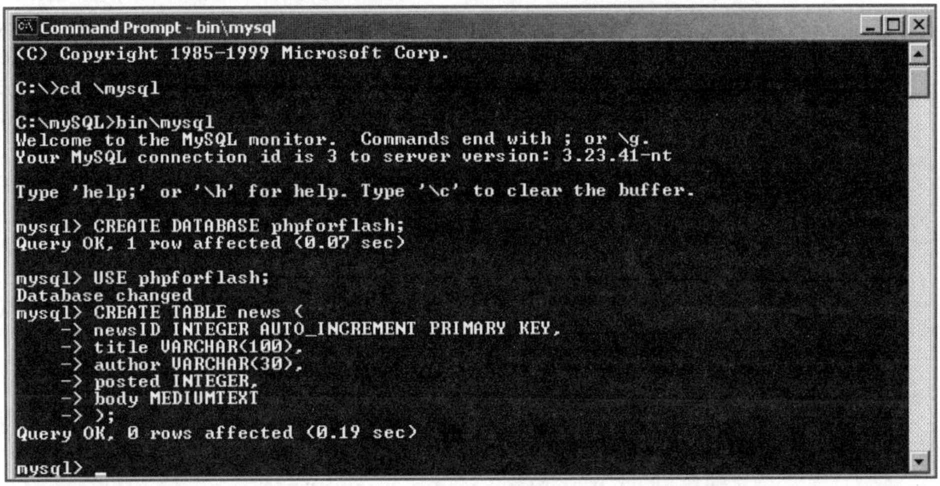

Go ahead and type that SQL query into your MySQL monitor (careful with the commas and semi-colons!) and we'll take a look at the elements that go towards creating this statement.

Dissecting the CREATE TABLE SQL Statement

1. OK, so let's take a look at that code in slow motion:

```
CREATE TABLE news (
newsID INTEGER AUTO_INCREMENT PRIMARY KEY,
title VARCHAR(100),
author VARCHAR(30),
posted INTEGER,
body MEDIUMTEXT
);
```

The first column specified is newsID. We're specifying that newsID is of type INTEGER, and that we want this column to be used as the **primary key** for the table. This ensures that each record added to the table will be assigned a unique number, allowing us to identify each separate news story.

```
CREATE TABLE news (
newsID INTEGER AUTO_INCREMENT PRIMARY KEY,
title VARCHAR(100),
author VARCHAR(30),
posted INTEGER,
body MEDIUMTEXT
);
```

2. Next we've got the title column, and as the name suggests we'll use this to store the title of our news item. I'm pretty sure that none of *my* news item titles will be more than 100 characters long so I have opted to go with this as a safe maximum length to use with VARCHAR. If you feel that yours will be longer or shorter then feel free to adjust it as you see fit. The benefits of limiting the length are simply a question of making our program run more quickly.

```
CREATE TABLE news (
newsID INTEGER AUTO_INCREMENT PRIMARY KEY,
title VARCHAR(100),
author VARCHAR(30),
posted INTEGER,
body MEDIUMTEXT
);
```

3. Following this, we have the author field that we'll use to store the name of the author who posted the news story. I've limited this to a maximum of 30 characters. Again, modify this length as you see fit.

```
CREATE TABLE news (
newsID INTEGER AUTO_INCREMENT PRIMARY KEY,
title VARCHAR(100),
author VARCHAR(50),
posted INTEGER,
```

```
body MEDIUMTEXT
);
```

4. This next field may seem a little strange at first. If we've got data types available to us that will store date and time information, why have I chosen to go with an INTEGER? The reason is that I want to be able to manipulate the date from PHP using the strftime function we met in the last chapter.

   Since strftime works on the return value of time, and since time returns an integer, I can use an INTEGER field to store the return value of time for later use. Cool, huh?

```
CREATE TABLE news (
newsID INTEGER AUTO_INCREMENT PRIMARY KEY,
title VARCHAR(100),
author VARCHAR(50),
posted INTEGER,
body MEDIUMTEXT
);
```

5. Finally we've got the body column in which we'll store the main bulk of the news for each item. I've used MEDIUMTEXT for this so that I can store shed loads of body text for each news item, should I need to – up to 16,777,215 characters! That's about 30 copies of this book!

6. If you're following along then we can take a peep to make sure that we've created our table by using the SHOW TABLES command. To ensure that we've created the table type the following into the MySQL monitor:

```
SHOW TABLES;
```

   This will produce a list of all the tables in the current database. The output should look like the one shown below:

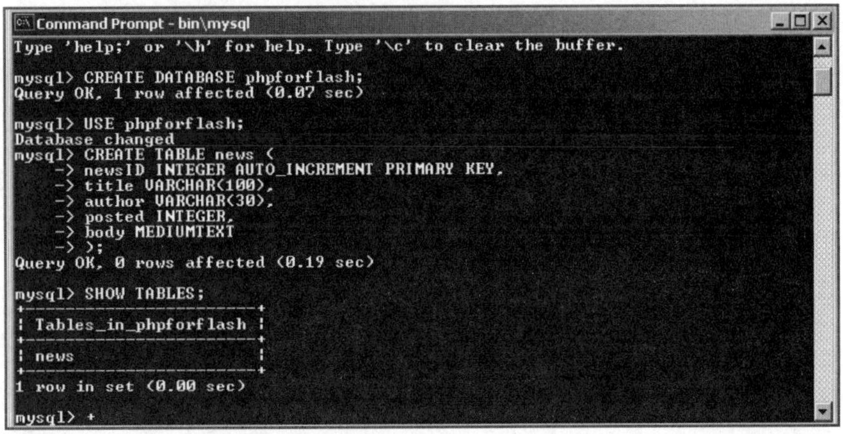

7. If you want to see what columns exist in your table then type the following into the MySQL Monitor:

```
DESCRIBE news;
```

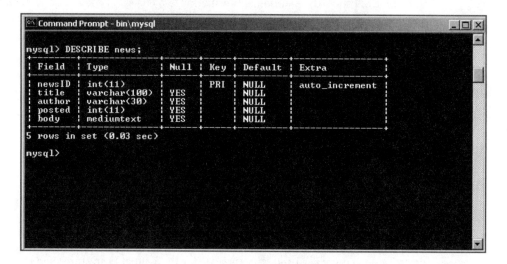

And there we have it – our first MySQL table. Would you say it was really so hard?

Removing Databases and Tables

While we're on the subject of *creating* databases and tables in SQL, it is worth mentioning the commands used to destroy or delete them too.

The **DROP** command can be thought of as the bulldozer of the SQL world. Its job is to destroy databases and tables we no longer want. Generally, we'll only want to do this when a database or table is not required anymore, for example if we've radically updated our site and it is no longer used.

> *Be very, very careful when you're using the* DROP *command; you'll see that there's no warning or confirmation request given, the data and structure of the database/table is just sent straight to join the great data bin in the sky.*

The syntax for that DROP command is pretty much the same for removing both databases and tables from MySQL.

```
DROP DATABASE databasename;

DROP TABLE tablename;
```

It may seem fairly obvious, but it's worth noting that dropping a database will also drop all the tables inside that database. Also, it's worth repeating that once the DROP command is issued there's no going back – your data is toast!

So, if we wanted to drop the table we just created in the last section, we'd issue the following MySQL command:

```
DROP TABLE news;
```

If you're playing along then you can try it out if you like – just make sure that you go back and re-create the table before moving on to the next section, because we'll use it with some of the other SQL commands. You have been warned!

```
Command Prompt - bin\mysql                                    _ □ ×

mysql> DESCRIBE news;
+---------+--------------+------+-----+---------+----------------+
| Field   | Type         | Null | Key | Default | Extra          |
+---------+--------------+------+-----+---------+----------------+
| newsID  | int(11)      |      | PRI | NULL    | auto_increment |
| title   | varchar(100) | YES  |     | NULL    |                |
| author  | varchar(30)  | YES  |     | NULL    |                |
| posted  | int(11)      | YES  |     | NULL    |                |
| body    | mediumtext   | YES  |     | NULL    |                |
+---------+--------------+------+-----+---------+----------------+
5 rows in set (0.00 sec)
mysql> DROP TABLE news;
Query OK, 0 rows affected (0.06 sec)

mysql>
```

Manipulating Our Databases and Tables

In this section we'll cover all the commands that we'll need to know to manipulate our databases. By manipulate, I mean we'll discuss how to add, remove and update data to/from/in our tables.

Again feel free to follow what I'm doing in the MySQL monitor if you have it open.

INSERT

The **INSERT** command is used to populate the rows in our tables with data. Each successful INSERT command will create a new row in the table.

The syntax of the INSERT command is:

```
INSERT [LOW_PRIORITY | DELAYED] [IGNORE]
INTO tablename [(columns)] VALUES (values);
```

Here, tablename is the name of the table into which we want to insert our data, and values is a comma-delimited list of values for the new row.

columns is an optional comma-delimited list of column names. The purely optional columns element can be used to specify both the columns to which data is being assigned in the values element, and in which order this data should appear. If columns is not specified then the values in values *must* be specified in the same order as the columns were, when the table was first created.

The LOW_PRIORITY option can be used to wait until no other client is reading the table before inserting the new row. This will cause the client to wait for completion of the statement before carrying on. If we don't want to wait we can use the DELAYED option, which will perform a similar operation as LOW_PRIORITY but will return control immediately back to the client.

The IGNORE option (which I'm sure sounds particularly appealing to some of you at this precise point in the book!) is used to ignore errors when trying to insert a new row into a table, where our new row may have the same value as another on a unique column. In this case the INSERT statement is ignored instead of generating a database error and no new row is added to the table.

Inserting a Row Into Our Sample Table

This should all make a lot more sense if we take a look at a simple statement to insert a new row of data into our news table.

1. Try entering the following:

```
INSERT INTO news VALUES (NULL, 'New Book Released',
'Steve Webster', 0, 'This is the news body');
```

Note that we set the first column (newsID) for this row to NULL, so that it will assign its own value. This will happen because of the AUTO_INCREMENT we added to the column definition when we created the table.

Also notice that we're setting the posted column for the new row to zero, because we'll need a return value from time to set this value properly. When we come to the next chapter and start looking at using PHP to interact with

MySQL we can perform this task, but until then this column will have no real meaning.

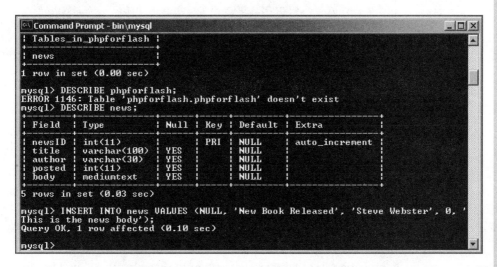

> *You can type this all in as one line as in the screenshot if you want, or you can take line returns after the commas to break it up; MySQL won't execute the command until it encounters the semi-colon.*

2. The `values` section of this statement contains all the data that we want to make up a new row of our `news` table. Note that the values are specified in the *same order* as the columns were declared earlier in this chapter. As mentioned earlier, if we do not include the `columns` section of the `INSERT` command then we must specify the data in this order to ensure that the data is put in the correct column for the row.

   The optional `columns` section is used when we either want to fill out just some of the fields for the new row of a table, or when we want to provide the data in a particular order in the `values` section. It is often worth doing this anyway just to make sure that we're adding the data to the appropriate columns.

3. So, if we rewrite the previous statement but this time with the `columns` section included, we would have:

```
INSERT INTO news   (title, author, body)
VALUES ('New Book Released', 'Steve Webster',
'This is the news body');
```

> Note that because we have specified which columns we want to fill out for this row in the columns section, we can exclude the newsID column from the values section. This is due to the fact that this is already designated as an AUTO_INCREMENT column and the value for it in our new row will be set automatically to 1 higher than the current highest value for that column.

We've also excluded the value for posted since, as discussed previously, it has no meaning in the current context. This will automatically be set to NULL for the new row.

4. Go ahead and use this technique to add seven more rows to the news table with different values. This will give us some data to work with in the later sections of this chapter. Don't forget to change the details (such as the name) for each row or they'll all be the same!

If inspiration fails you then try some of the sample values listed below:

Title	Author	Body
New Book Released	Steve Webster	This is the news body
Ace Author Agent Gets Married	Alan McCann	All the best for the future from everyone in the PHP team and Steve
Here Comes the Bride	Gaynor Riopedre	Funny coincidence is his name's ED
Layout of Book Heralded	Katy Freer	The Future's Pink!
PHP Changes Lives	Kev Sutherland	My Appendix was put in
Fifth Printing For Book	Richard O'Donnell	I left Chapter 5 on the train to Dorridge
PHP Sweeps World	Felicity Kendal	St Mirren for the cup
Knighthood For PHP Writer	Elizabeth Windsor	It's the best thing I've read since Bravo Two Zero

REPLACE

The **REPLACE** command is specific to MySQL (it is not part of the SQL language). Its syntax is almost identical to that of the INSERT command, and it performs a similar task.

However, as you might expect, if another row exists with the same value in a column that has been designated as a unique index (as the PRIMARY_KEY) then the new record replaces the old. If no such row exists then the new row will be added to the table as if an INSERT command were executed.

Thus, the general syntax is:

```
REPLACE [LOW_PRIORITY | DELAYED] [IGNORE]
INTO tablename [(columns)] VALUES (values);
```

The options work the same way as those for the INSERT command.

UPDATE

The **UPDATE** command is used to change the values of one or more columns in an existing row or rows.

The general syntax is:

```
UPDATE [LOW_PRIORITY] tablename
    SET colname=value [, colname=value...]
    [WHERE condition] [LIMIT n];
```

This command will update the rows in tablename that match the condition(s) specified in condition, up to a maximum of n rows. If no condition is specified then all rows in the table are updated, up to a maximum of n rows.

For each of these rows, the value in each column specified by colname is set to the corresponding value.

Note that you can use multiple colname=value expressions to update more than one column at a time. Simply separate each expression with a comma as shown in the syntax.

The part of the statement where condition is specified is known as the WHERE clause, and we'll meet this one further on down the road. condition can be a simple comparison or a complex series of expressions. For the purposes of this book we're only going to be performing simple comparisons here.

A simple example of update we can use to change the author of all stories written by Steve Webster to Alan McCann in our news table would look like this:

```
UPDATE news SET author='Alan McCann'
    WHERE author='Steve Webster';
```

DELETE

The **DELETE** command is used to remove one or more rows from a given table. Like the UPDATE command, this can be limited to rows that match a particular criteria using a WHERE clause within the statement, or can be set loose to delete all the rows in a given table. You can limit the number of affected rows by the use of the LIMIT block, also described previously.

The general syntax for the DELETE command is:

```
DELETE [LOW_PRIORITY] FROM tablename
    [WHERE condition] [LIMIT n];
```

If we omit both the WHERE and LIMIT clauses all rows in the given table will be removed - no warning will be given and our data will be long gone!

If we wanted to remove all entries in our news table where the author was Alan McCann, we would use the following statement:

```
DELETE FROM news WHERE author='Alan McCann';
```

Searching Our Databases and Tables

Once we've got our data into the database we'll want to be able to get it out again or search it for certain criteria. To perform these queries, let's meet another new command.

SELECT

The **SELECT** command is used to retrieve rows or columns of data in your web applications from your MySQL database. This is an extremely powerful command, and therefore has a fairly complex syntax. For this reason only the most commonly used aspects of the syntax are shown below:

```
SELECT columns FROM tablename
    [WHERE condition]
    [ORDER BY colname [ASC | DESC]]
    [LIMIT n];
```

> **Note:** the options must appear in the order shown above.

This will fetch all rows from tablename that match the optional condition, up to a maximum of n rows.

Most of the individual elements of the SELECT statement should be familiar to you by now from earlier commands, so we're only going to be looking at the bits that are different here.

The columns element can be either a list of columns whose information we want returned or an asterisk, in which case all columns are returned for matching rows.

The optional ORDER BY clause allows us to specify a column by which the results returned will be ordered. The optional element of this clause enables us to specify whether the results should be returned in ascending (ASC) or descending (DESC) order.

As with most things, this may make a heck of a lot more sense if we take a look at an example of SELECT strutting its stuff.

```
SELECT * FROM news;
```

Here the asterisk is used to fetch information for all columns in the table – we'll take a look at how we can narrow our statement down a little later on.

The above command will return all the columns for all of the rows in our news table. Because no WHERE clause has been specified the rows will be returned in the order in which they were added to the database.

```
MYSQL                                                                _ □ ×

mysql> USE phpforflash
Database changed
mysql> INSERT INTO news VALUES (NULL, 'Here Comes the Bride',
    -> 'Gaynor Riopedre', 0, 'Funny coincidence is his name is ED');
Query OK, 1 row affected (0.00 sec)

mysql> SELECT * FROM news;
+---------+------------------------------+-----------------+--------+-----------+
: newsID : title                        : author          : posted : body
:         :                              :                 :        :
+---------+------------------------------+-----------------+--------+-----------+
:       1 : New Book Released            : Steve Webster   :      0 : This is th
e news body
:       3 : Ace Author Agent Gets Married : Alan McCann     :      0 : All the be
st for the future from the PHP team and Steve :
:       4 : Here Comes the Bride         : Gaynor Riopedre :      0 : Funny coin
cidence is his name is ED
+---------+------------------------------+-----------------+--------+-----------+

3 rows in set (0.00 sec)

mysql> _
```

Beefing Up the Search

Making the statement a little more complex, we can just return the first 2 entries in the news table by adding a LIMIT clause.

```
SELECT * FROM news LIMIT 2;
```

We can also beef up our statement by limiting the information returned to just the values of the title and author columns.

```
SELECT title, author FROM news LIMIT 2;
```

Getting ever so slightly more useful, we can order the information returned by the value in the posted column. Since we're going to use this column to store the date and time that the news item was posted we can fetch the 2 latest news items by using the following statement.

```
SELECT title, author FROM news ORDER BY posted DESC
   LIMIT 2;
```

```
mysql> SELECT title, author FROM news ORDER BY posted DESC LIMIT 2;
+------------------------------+------------------+
| title                        | author           |
+------------------------------+------------------+
| New Book Released            | Steve Webster    |
| Ace Author Agent Gets Married | Alan McCann     |
+------------------------------+------------------+
2 rows in set (0.28 sec)
```

We can further modify this statement to return the five latest news items posted by Joe Bloggs in reverse date order.

```
SELECT title, author FROM news
   WHERE author='Joe Bloggs' ORDER BY posted DESC
   LIMIT 2;
```

We can, of course, specify more than one condition in the WHERE clause with the use of the logical AND, OR and NOT operators.

For example, to return the last 5 news items posted by either Joe Bloggs or Jane Bloggs then we'd use the following statement

```
SELECT title, author FROM news
   WHERE author='Joe Bloggs' OR author='Jane Bloggs'
   ORDER BY posted DESC LIMIT 2;
```

Summary

Well, this chapter has been a merry jaunt down SQL Avenue. It's not always been easy but I hope the remaining chapters in this book will have made it a worthwhile journey.

Storing relatively large amounts of data efficiently is the key to slick, dynamic websites. Without the techniques covered in this and the following chapter, we'd be stuck with conventional storage methods such as the humble text file or the flat file database we met in previous chapters.

We covered:

- Basic elements of the SQL language

- Creating and deleting databases and tables

- Inserting and updating information in our tables

- Searching our tables and returning specific information

If you're aching to put your newfound SQL knowledge to use then mosey on over the page to the next chapter, where our content management system (and more PHP with Flash) awaits.

We kicked off with a look at where relational databases came from and why we need them. This is the foundation upon which SQL was built so it was an essential topic to cover. In the next chapter we'll get our hands dirty with one of these relational database systems.

9

Integrating PHP with MySQL

What we'll cover in this chapter

- *Integrating a **MySQL database** with PHP scripts*

- *Connecting to MySQL from PHP; **selecting** and **creating** databases*

- *Executing **SQL queries** through PHP; **data definition** and **manipulation***

- *Creating a powerful **Content Management Application** with Flash, PHP and MySQL*

Having given ourselves a good foundation in Structured Query Language it's time to look at **MySQL** as an example of a specific database implementation using SQL. In particular, we'll be looking at how PHP can interface with MySQL to store and fetch data for our applications.

Luckily for us, interfacing with MySQL from PHP is very much the same as interfacing with any relational database system. PHP provides many built-in functions for accessing a myriad of databases such as Microsoft's popular **SQL Server** and **Oracle** and this means that porting an application from one database system to another can be as simple as changing the name of a few function calls.

We'll start off by looking at how we can access and manipulate data stored in MySQL databases using PHP. PHP supplies us with a hatful of functions for these tasks and we'll be exploring the most useful and popular of these.

To round off the chapter we shall be building a complete dynamic news system that you can use on any Flash site. This application will be the culmination of all our hard work in the last few database-driven chapters, but we'll be using techniques from almost every chapter to build it.

> *Don't forget that you can find the installation instructions for PHP and MySQL for Windows, Mac and Linux in* **Appendix A***.*

When PHP Met MySQL

OK, so it's time to see how we can use PHP to fetch and manipulate the data in our MySQL databases. We need to do this because Flash cannot access the MySQL databases itself so we have to use PHP as a kind of office gopher – fetching the information for us at our command.

At the time of writing, there are over 30 MySQL related functions built into PHP, many of which will perform similar or more obscure tasks to the SQL commands mentioned earlier. Covering all of these functions here would take a great many pages so we'll just discuss the most commonly used ones.

Connecting to the MySQL Server

The first thing we need to do in any PHP script we want to interact with MySQL is to connect to the MySQL server. We need to do this because your PHP scripts will not have access to MySQL unless they specifically ask for it. The syntax for this function is:

```
mysql_connect([hostname [, username [, password]]]);
```

The **hostname** is the name of the host running your MySQL server. If the MySQL server and the web server are running on the same machine then this can be set to localhost, and this is the default value if the hostname is not specified.

The **username** is the name of the user allowed to connect to the MySQL server. The **password** is the password assigned to that particular user.

The function will return a positive integer referencing the connection, called the link identifier, if the connection was successful, or false otherwise. We'll use the link identifier in future calls to MySQL related PHP functions.

Note that all three arguments are optional in a call to mysql_connect (symbolized by the square brackets I used). If no arguments are given then PHP will attempt to connect to a MySQL server running on localhost, and no username or password information will be sent. The stacked square brackets show that if you provide a username then you must provide the hostname argument, and if you provide a password then you must provide both the hostname and the username arguments.

> *Throughout this chapter we will use "user" and "pass" to represent your individual username and password for the database server respectively. You'll need to replace these with your own username and password. If you followed the installation tutorial in **Appendix A** then you'll need to use the username and password you entered there.*
>
> *If you're using a third party to host your system then you may need to contact their technical support department to get this information. You may also need to use a different host than "localhost", and again this information can be obtained from your hosting company.*

So, let's take a look at mysql_connect in action.

```
// Attempt to connect to the MySQL server
$link = @mysql_connect("localhost", "user", "pass");

// If the connection was successful...
if ($link) {
    // Output link identifier
    print "Link ID is $link";
} else {
    // Otherwise, output error information
    print "Error connecting to database server";
}
```

Because we're providing our own error message, we're using the error suppression operator, @, just before the call to mysql_connect to prevent PHP from throwing up any of its own error messages should the connection fail.

This little piece of code will attempt to connect to your MySQL database. If the connection is successful then the value of $link, which will contain the link identifier for the connection, is output.

If the connection fails and you get an error message then you'll need to make sure you're using the correct arguments in the call to mysql_connect. Double check the source of the details, and that they are entered correctly, and then try again.

On success, you should receive output similar to the following:

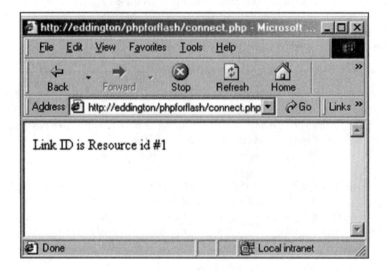

So, what does it mean? The 1 (or any other positive integer) in the output indicates that the connection to the MySQL server was successful. The following output would indicate a failure:

Error connecting to database server

Okay, so this isn't exactly rocket science but it's the first step in using data from a MySQL database in our Flash/PHP applications.

It is worth mentioning that you can open more than one connection using the mysql_connect function. This is something that seems obvious once you're told but is often missed when learning to get PHP interacting with MySQL. That said, this feature is seldom used, so you need only bear it in mind.

Disconnecting from the MySQL Server

Although our connection to the MySQL server is automatically closed when the script ends, it is good programming practice to close the connection manually when we've finished with it. Think of it as good manners. You wouldn't just up and leave if you'd been to someone's house for tea, would you?

The function we need to do this business is, rather unsurprisingly, called `mysql_close`. The format for this function is shown below.

```
mysql_close( [link_id] );
```

`mysql_close` takes a single optional argument of the link identifier of the connection to be closed. If no link identifier is specified then the most recently opened database connection is closed. If the operation was successful the function returns `true`, otherwise it returns `false`.

Let's go back and add a call to `mysql_close` to the previous example:

```
// Attempt to connect to the MySQL server
$link = @mysql_connect("localhost", "user", "pass");

// If the connection was successful...
if ($link) {
    // Output link identifier
    print "Link ID is $link";

            // Close the connection
            mysql_close($link);
            print "You are the weakest \$link ... good-
        bye!";
} else {
    // Otherwise, output error information
    print "Error connecting to database server";
}
```

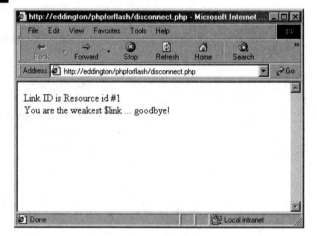

```
disconnect.php                                              _ □ X
 1  <?
 2  // disconnect.php
 3  // Chapter 9 - Foundation PHP for Flash
 4
 5  // Attempt to connect to the MySQL server
 6  $link = @mysql_connect("localhost", "", "");
 7
 8  // If the connection was successful...
 9  if ($link) {
10      // Output link identifier
11      print "Link ID is $link<br>\n";
12
13      // Close the connection
14
15      mysql_close($link);
16      print "You are the weakest \$link ... goodbye!";
17  } else {
18      // Otherwise, output error information
19      print "Error connecting to database server";
20  }
21  ?>
Editor HTML
```

http://eddington/phpforflash/disconnect.php - Microsoft Internet ... _ □ X

File   Edit   View   Favorites   Tools   Help

Back   Forward   Stop   Refresh   Home   Search

Address http://eddington/phpforflash/disconnect.php   Go

Link ID is Resource id #1
You are the weakest $link ... goodbye!

Done   Local intranet

Here we've added the call to mysql_close, but we've put it inside the if statement since there would be no point in trying to close a database connection that was not opened successfully.

Whilst creating and terminating connections to the MySQL server is no doubt useful – even essential – it's not quite the riveting stuff I promised you at the start of the chapter. So let's move on and look at how we can get MySQL to jump through some hoops at our command!

Selecting a Database

Once we're connected to the database server we're ready to start playing around with our databases. However, before we can get to the really juicy stuff we need to tell MySQL which database we want to be playing with.

If you've installed MySQL on your system and have followed along with the previous chapter then we'll already have a database we can play with named phpforflash. If you're hosting your site through a hosting company then you'll need to find out from them the name of the database you've been allocated.

The function we'll need to tell MySQL which database we're after is the mysql_select_db function.

```
mysql_select_db(db_name [, link_id]);
```

Here the string **db_name** is the name of the database we want to select, and the optional **link_id** specifies the link identifier of the connection we want to use for this action. If this argument is left off then the most recently opened connection is used.

If the database was selected successfully then the function returns true, and returns false otherwise.

Let's take a look at this in action...

```
// Attempt to connect to the MySQL server
$link = @mysql_connect("localhost", "user", "pass");

// If the connection was unsuccessful...
if (!$link) {
    // Output error information and exit
    print "Error connecting to database server";
    exit;
}

// Attempt to select database. If successful...
if (@mysql_select_db("phpforflash")) {
    // Inform user of success
    print "Database selected";
} else {
    // Otherwise inform user of failure
    print "Couldn't select database";
}

// Close the connection
mysql_close($link);
```

You'll see here that I've shuffled the code around a little. The reason for this is that, as we go through each of the PHP functions in this chapter we're going to be building up a complete script to read the entries from the news table we built up in the previous chapter. Don't worry if you didn't follow that through because we're going to be covering that from a PHP angle a little later in the chapter.

The most important part of this code from our perspective is the call to `mysql_select_db`. Here we're attempting to select our phpforflash database, testing the return value of the function using an `if` statement to find out whether or not the operation was a success. We then output an appropriate message and round off the script by closing the database connection.

If all goes well then you should see the following output.

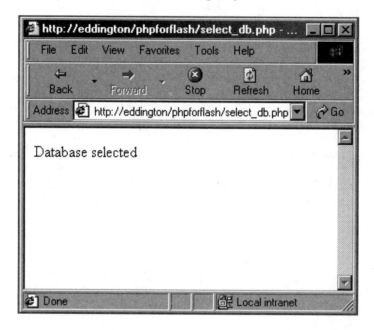

If you didn't play along with the previous chapter then you'll have got an error message instead of the above output. Fear not as this is simply because you haven't created the database yet and as such it can't be selected.

All of which is a perfect link to...

Creating a Database Through PHP

As we're wandering through these PHP functions it probably won't surprise you that there's a function for creating databases through MySQL too. You should also be familiar enough with the way that PHP functions are named to have a decent stab at guessing the name of this function.

The function is called `mysql_create_db` and it looks something like this:

```
mysql_create_db(db_name [, link_id]);
```

Here, **db_name** is the name of the database you want to create and, again, **link_id** is the link identifier for the connection to the MySQL server you wish to use (and is optional).

The function returns `true` if the database was created successfully, and `false` otherwise.

Anyone feeling particularly alert will realise that this is the same as the following SQL statement.

```
CREATE DATABASE db_name;
```

Since we're only going to need to create that database once we won't want to make this part of the script that we're building up. We'll just create a separate mini-script to create the database for us if it doesn't exist. We're going to return to this script a little later on in this chapter and add the code to create the table too so we can use it as a setup script for the application – cool huh?

Anyway, on with that mini-script:

```
// Attempt to connect to the MySQL server
$link = @mysql_connect("localhost", "user", "pass");

// If the connection was unsuccessful...
if (!$link) {

    // Output error information and exit
    print "Error connecting to database server";
    exit;
}

        // Attempt to create database. If successful...
        if (@mysql_create_db("phpforflash")) {

            // Inform user of success
            print "Database created";
        } else {

            // Otherwise, tell user there was an error
            print "Couldn't create database";
        }
```

continues overleaf

```
// Close the connection
mysql_close($link);
```

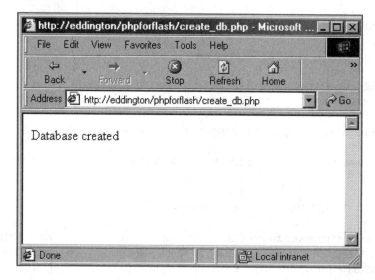

You'll see that this script uses a lot of the same code as the other one we're building up. That's mainly because we still need to be able to connect to and disconnect from the database server, and to provide feedback for the user on the success of the whole operation.

> *If you're hosting through a third party then you may not be able to create databases yourself in this manner, in which case you'll see an error message when running the above script. If this is the case, and you don't have a database automatically set up for you, then you'll need to contact your hosting company's technical support department and have them set one up for you.*

If the operation was a success and you've got access to the MySQL monitor, either from your own machine or on your hosted server via telnet then you should be able to see your newly created database using the SHOW DATABASES command we met in the previous chapter. This will produce a list of the databases on the MySQL server, among which should be the shiny new one we've just created.

```
Command Prompt - bin\mysql
Microsoft Windows 2000 [Version 5.00.2195]
(C) Copyright 1985-1999 Microsoft Corp.

C:\>cd \mysql

C:\mysql>bin\mysql
Welcome to the MySQL monitor.  Commands end with ; or \g.
Your MySQL connection id is 6 to server version: 3.23.39-nt

Type 'help;' or '\h' for help. Type '\c' to clear the buffer.

mysql> SHOW DATABASES;
+------------+
| Database   |
+------------+
| events     |
| mysql      |
| phpforflash|
| test       |
+------------+
4 rows in set (0.00 sec)

mysql>
```

Dropping a Database

Would it surprise you to find out you can also drop a database using a special function in PHP? I thought not! It probably won't surprise you that the function is called mysql_drop_db either.

                mysql_drop_db(**db_name** [, **link_id**]);

If you're not sure what the various arguments mean then look back at the two functions we've just met – they're exactly the same. As with the previous two, this function returns true on success and false otherwise.

We'll not play with this one, otherwise we're going to delete our nice newly created database. However, *if* we wanted to drop our phpforflash database we could use the following function call:

                mysql_drop_db("phpforflash");

Note that although it hasn't been shown, we'd need to be connected to the MySQL server using the code we've created previously before executing this statement.

> *If you happen to be playing along and have just deleted your database then you'll need to go back a step and recreate it as we're going to be using it for the remainder of this chapter!*

Executing SQL Queries with PHP

Having straightened out this database manipulation tangle, it's about time we turned our attention to tables. This is where our knowledge of SQL gleaned in the previous chapter will come in handy since there aren't any specific functions for performing table related tasks, such as inserting, updating, deleting and fetching data.

Instead, table manipulation is the job of a single function, mysql_query. We'll use this function in conjunction with the smattering of SQL knowledge we picked up in the previous chapter to both create our tables and work with the data within them.

The syntax of the function looks like this:

```
mysql_query(query_string [, link_id]);
```

The one argument of this function that needs closer examination is **query_string**. We use this argument to specify as a string the SQL statement that we want to perform on the currently selected database – also known as **querying** the database.

The return value of the mysql_query function will vary depending on the type of query we specify in query_string. There are basically two categories into which our SQL statements can fall – those that can be used to modify the tables themselves (known as **Data Definition Language** statements) and those that act on the data in a table (known as **Data Manipulation Language** statements) and we'll look at these now.

Data Definition: CREATE, DROP

The first thing we're likely to want to do once we've created a database is to populate it with tables. We can use the mysql_query function for this, passing an SQL query using the CREATE TABLE command to create our tables.

In the case of Data Definition Language (DDL) statements, the mysql_query function returns either true or false depending upon the success of the operation.

For example, if you remember back to the previous chapter we constructed the following query to create our news table.

```
CREATE TABLE news (
newsID INTEGER AUTO_INCREMENT PRIMARY KEY,
title VARCHAR(100),
author VARCHAR(30),
posted INTEGER,
body MEDIUMTEXT
);
```

We could use the same query from PHP to create the table using the `mysql_query` function. A quick snippet of the query being built and executed is shown below, and we'll look at a more detailed example in a moment.

```php
// Build table creation query
$query = "CREATE TABLE news (
          newsID INTEGER AUTO_INCREMENT PRIMARY KEY,
          title VARCHAR(100),
          author VARCHAR(30),
          posted INTEGER,
          body MEDIUMTEXT)";

// Attempt to create table. If successful...
if (@mysql_query($query)) {

    // Inform user of success
    print "Table created successfully";
} else {

    // Otherwise, tell user there was an error
    print "Error creating table";
}
```

This shows how to build up the query over a number of lines. It is worth noting that this isn't strictly necessary – you could specify the query as one long string if you like – but by building it up piece by piece we make our code a lot more readable. This is generally good programming practice as trying to find errors in a moderately complex query string when it's all specified on one line is not easy!

Note also the fact that we've omitted the semi-colon from the end of the query. The reason for this is that the entry in the PHP manual states that this is not required and should not be included. Don't confuse this with the semi-colon that delimits the end of the current PHP statement, as that's still required.

We're going to use the example code we created back when we met the `mysql_create_db` function, adding the code to create the table once we've attempted to create the database. This will then form the setup script for the sample application at the end of this chapter and can be uploaded to any web server to create the database and table structure for the application.

Before we dive headlong into this we'd better think about exactly what we want the script to do so we know where to place our new code. Before we do that let's just refresh ourselves as to what the code looked like.

```php
// Attempt to connect to the MySQL server
$link = @mysql_connect("localhost", "user", "pass");
```

continues overleaf

```
// If the connection was unsuccessful...
if (!$link) {

    // Output error information and exit
    print "Error connecting to database server";
    exit;
}

// Attempt to create database. If successful...
if (@mysql_create_db("phpforflash")) {

    // Inform user of success
    print "Database created";
} else {

    // Otherwise, tell user there was an error
    print "Couldn't create database";
}

// Close the connection
mysql_close($link);
```

An intuitive place to put our new table creation code would be inside the `if` statement once we've successfully created the database. This is a good starting place but it's far from the ideal position for our code. The reason for this is that it's perfectly reasonable for the database phpforflash to already exist but for it to be empty. In this case, the `mysql_create_db` function will return `false` and, if our table creation code is inside the `if` statement, it will never get executed.

Placing this kind of limitation on setup scripts is not generally a good idea. So what we want to do is to attempt table creation regardless of whether database creation succeeds or fails. This will leave us with a script looking something like the following:

```
// Attempt to connect to the MySQL server
$link = @mysql_connect("localhost", "user", "pass");

// If the connection was unsuccessful...
if (!$link) {

    // Output error information and exit
    print "Error connecting to database server";
    exit;
}

// Attempt to create database. If successful...
if (@mysql_create_db("phpforflash")) {
```

```
    // Inform user of success
    print "Database created<br>\n";
} else {

    // Otherwise, tell user there was an error
    print "Couldn't create database<br>\n";
}


        // Build table creation query
        $query = "CREATE TABLE news (
                newsID INTEGER AUTO_INCREMENT PRIMARY
        KEY,
                title VARCHAR(100),
                author VARCHAR(30),
                posted INTEGER,
                body MEDIUMTEXT)";

        // Attempt to create table. If successful...
        if (@mysql_query($query)) {

            // Inform user of success
            print "Table created successfully";
        } else {

            // Otherwise, tell user there was an error
            print "Error creating table";
        }

    // Close the connection
    mysql_close($link);
```

This code now attempts to create the table once the database creation code is done with. In this case, the only message that matters is the one that indicates the success or failure of the table creation.

> Note that if you followed along with the instructions in the previous chapter you'll get failure messages for both database and table creation with the above piece of code. This is because both the database and table already exist so don't worry too much – in this case the error messages are a good thing!

Data Manipulation: INSERT, REPLACE, UPDATE, DELETE

With Data Manipulation Language (DML) statements, the return value of the `mysql_query` function is `true` on success or `false` if the query could not be executed.

Since all these statements are used to manipulate data we can find out the number of rows affected by calling the `mysql_affected_rows` function. We won't be using this feature in our scripts but it's a useful function to have in your arsenal should you ever need it.

So, we can use the `mysql_query` function to insert and manipulate the news items in our news table. We'll start by inserting a row into our database, and because we're working from PHP we can finally fill in the posted column for our new row with the current time, as returned by `time`.

```php
// Attempt to connect to the MySQL server
$link = @mysql_connect("localhost", "user", "pass");

// If the connection was unsuccessful...
if (!$link) {
    // Output error information and exit
    print "Error connecting to database server";
    exit;
}

// Attempt to select database. If unsuccessful...
if (!@mysql_select_db("phpforflash")) {
    // Inform user of failure and exit
    print "Couldn't select database";
    exit;
}

// Define news item information
$title = "News from PHP";
$author = "Joe Bloggs";
$body = "This is a news item added from PHP";

// Fetch current time
$posted = time();

// Build query
$query = "INSERT INTO news (title, author, body, posted)
          VALUES('$title', '$author', '$body', $posted)";

// Attempt to insert row. If successful...
if (@mysql_query($query)) {
```

```
        // Inform user of success
        print "Row added to table";
    } else {

        // Otherwise, tell user there was an error
        print "Error adding row";
    }

    // Close the connection
    mysql_close($link);
```

You can see that once we've connected to the MySQL server and successfully selected our database we start to turn our attention to adding the new row of data to our news table. The first thing we do is to use the time function to fetch the current time as a Unix timestamp, storing the result in the $posted variable. We then build up our INSERT query to add some bogus data to our table, using $posted to insert the time that the article was posted in with the new row.

One thing of special interest with this code is how the query string is built up:

```
    // Build query
    $query = "INSERT INTO news (title, author, body, posted)
             VALUES('$title', '$author', '$body', $posted)";
```

Now, it may strike you as rather odd that we're using single quotes before and after the $title, $author and $body variables used in the query string. The reason we need to do this is because the data is stored in the table as strings. Once the variables have been expanded in the string we need those single quotes to tell MySQL that these are strings.

This may make a little more sense if we look at what happens once the variables have been expanded.

```
        "... VALUES('$title' ..."
```

...becomes...

```
        "... VALUES('News from PHP' ..."
```

However, if we left off the single quotes then things are a little different.

```
        "... VALUES($title ..."
```

...becomes...

```
        "... VALUES(News from PHP ..."
```

...which isn't a valid SQL statement because we need to enclose our string in single quotes.

A special exception to this rule is $posted. This doesn't need the single quotes since it is a number, and the data type for the posted column in our news table is INTEGER.

We'll be reusing a great amount of this code later in the chapter when we come to build our news application. For now, just run the script a few more times with different details for title, author and body, as this will give us some content to work with when we move on to the SELECT queries from PHP. You can go and check the data you've entered using the MySQL monitor.

Data Manipulation: SELECT

Although it is part of the Data Manipulation Language (DML) family of SQL commands, running the SELECT query from PHP deserves special attention. This is because the results of the query are not displayed directly on screen (as they were in the MySQL monitor) but are instead stashed away in a result set. The mysql_query function returns the result identifier for this result set when executing a SELECT query.

In order to fetch the results from this result set we need to use the mysql_fetch_array function. What this function does is to fetch the next row of the result set and return it as an array – moving to the next row afterwards. If no more rows are available this function returns false.

The general syntax for the mysql_fetch_array function is:

```
mysql_fetch_array(result_id [, result_type]);
```

Here, **result_id** is the result identifier returned by mysql_query. The **result_type** is an optional argument that allows you to specify the type of array returned and can have the following values:

MYSQL_NUM   The array returned will have numeric indices only. This is useful if you either don't know or don't want to rely on the column names for the table.

MYSQL_ASSOC   The array returned will have string indices only. Individual values can be accessed using the column name as the array index.

MYSQL_BOTH   The array will have both numeric and associative indices. This allows you either to access the individual values using either the column name or a number. This is the default value if the result_type argument is omitted.

We can also use the `mysql_num_rows` function to see how many rows were returned in the given resultset.

```
mysql_num_rows(result_id);
```

Once we have finished with the results we could use `mysql_free_result` to free up the memory associated with the result set. This is the syntax:

```
mysql_free_result(result_id);
```

This tends only to be used if you think your script is using too much memory when running. If this is not used, all result sets are freed once the script ends.

We should now have enough knowledge stashed away in our heads to write a small script to display the contents of our news table, using the `mysql_query` and `mysql_fetch_array` functions in tandem.

```php
// Attempt to connect to the MySQL server
$link = @mysql_connect("localhost", "user", "pass");

// If the connection was unsuccessful...
if (!$link) {
    // Output error information and exit
    print "Error connecting to database server";
    exit;
}

// Attempt to select database. If unsuccessful...
if (!@mysql_select_db("phpforflash")) {
    // Inform user of failure and exit
    print "Couldn't select database";
    exit;
}

// Build query
$query = "SELECT * FROM news";

// Execute query
$result = @mysql_query($query);

// Attempt to insert row. If successful...
if (!$result) {
    // Otherwise, tell user there was an error
    print "Error adding row";
}
```

continues overleaf

```
        // For each row in resultset...
        while ($row = mysql_fetch_array($result)) {

            // Convert 'posted' into dd/mm/yy hh:mm format
            $posted = strftime("%d/%m/%y %H:%M", $row['posted']);

            // Output news item data
            print "newsID: " . $row['newsID'] . "<br>\n";
            print "title: " . $row['title'] . "<br>\n";
            print "author: " . $row['author'] . "<br>\n";
            print "posted: " . $posted . "<br>\n";
            print "body: " . $row['body'] . "<br>\n";

            // Add a few line breaks to separate news items
            print "<br><br>";
        }

        // Close the connection
        mysql_close($link);
```

This code will loop through and display all news items in your table. We'll need to make a slight modification to this script in order to be able to send our information to Flash but we'll deal with that when we come to it.

Building a Content Management System

Having covered all the MySQL related PHP functions that we'll need throughout the rest of the book it's time to see them in action in a real application.

As hinted throughout this and the previous chapter, we're going to be building a dynamic news system for our site.

Since we don't want just anyone being able to update our news items, we're going to use two separate movies. One will be purely for displaying the data while we'll use the other to add news items. The PHP script for this second movie will be password-protected to stop malicious users (stop looking so guilty!) adding cheeky news stories to our sites.

Let's take a look at what we'll be building:

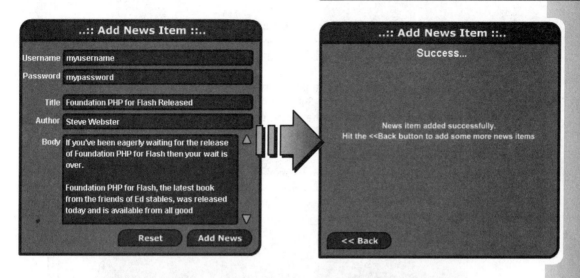

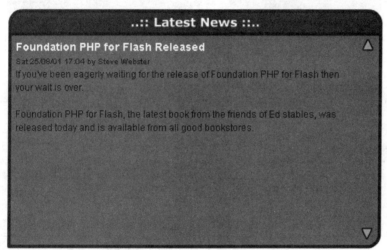

The Flash Movies Part 1 – news.fla

As usual we'll kick off by creating the Flash movies for the application before moving on to the PHP scripting that does all of the legwork.

OK, I imagine you'll be glad of the chance to get back to a bit of creative work as we splash down into Flash. First off, we're going to tackle the Flash movie that we'll use to display the news on our site.

1. As with most of the other applications that we've built so far in this book, we're going to be using the `onClipEvent` handler to detect when our Flash movie has received all of the data from the PHP script.

    So, we're going to want to put everything in a movie clip and the first thing we have to do is create one. Select Insert > New Symbol from the main menu or press CTRL+F8 to create the movie clip. Give it a suitable name and hit the OK button.

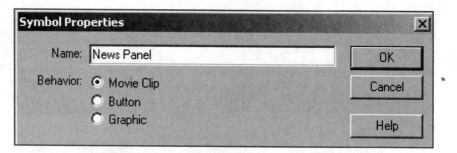

2. Our next step is to create the layer and frame structure for the movie clip. Use the screenshot below to guide you through.

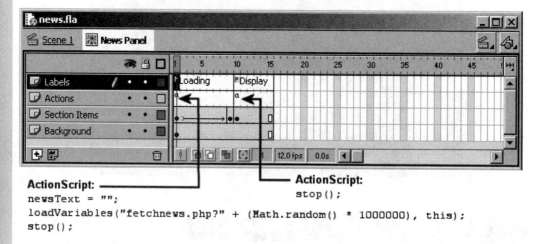

ActionScript:
```
newsText = "";
loadVariables("fetchnews.php?" + (Math.random() * 1000000), this);
stop();
```

ActionScript:
```
stop();
```

Don't forget to add the ActionScript shown above. The part that deserves special attention is the ActionScript on the Loading frame. This actually performs the task of calling the PHP script that will fetch our news items for us. Notice that we're using the technique discussed way back in **Chapter 1**, of adding a random number to the URL of the PHP file to prevent the web browser from serving us a cached version of the script output.

3. The Background layer contains the main background for the movie. Again I've stuck with the design I've been using throughout but you can make this as individual as you like.

4. The Loading frame is simply the animated clock hands that I've been using throughout this book. The tween between frames 1 and 9 on the Section Items layer is used to give a simple fade-out of the clock face.

5. The final frame we need to construct is the Display frame. This contains all of the elements necessary to display the news for our site.

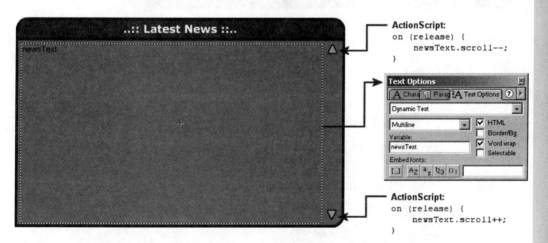

ActionScript:
```
on (release) {
    newsText.scroll--;
}
```

ActionScript:
```
on (release) {
    newsText.scroll++;
}
```

Here you can see we have a multiline text box with HTML enabled for displaying the actual news text and a couple of simple scroll buttons so that we're not restricted to the size of the text box for our news items.

6. The final thing we need to do for this movie is to return to the main timeline and drag a copy of our News Panel movie clip from the Library onto our main stage.

7. We then need to add the following ActionScript code to it so that we can move on to the Display frame once all the news items have been loaded in.

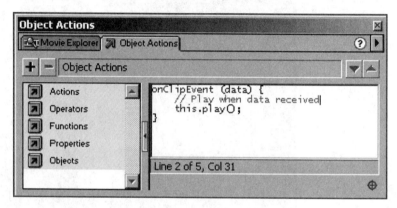

That's it for this movie – it's ready to rock and roll as soon as we get the database and the PHP script up and running. First though we need to sort out the movie clip that we'll use to add news items to our site.

The Flash Movies Part 2 – addnews.fla

This movie is a little more complicated than the previous one because of the amount of data we need to handle. Regardless, we still need to go through the same basic steps.

1. Again we're going to use an `onClipEvent` handler to control the flow of our movie clip once all data has loaded from a given call to `loadVariables`. This should be old hat to you by now – we're going to need to create a movie clip in which to encapsulate everything.

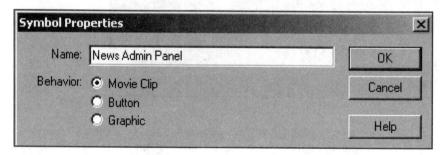

2. Next we need to create the layer and frame structure for this new movie clip.

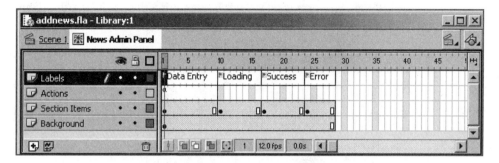

The ActionScript on the Actions layer of the Data Entry frame is a simple `stop()` action to prevent the movie clip from playing automatically. If we didn't have this then we wouldn't be able to enter our data, so it's an essential step.

3. Again the Background layer is made up of some simple styling to fit in with your site. As always, feel free to experiment here.

4. Next up is the Section Items layer of the Data Entry frame. This is where all of our information for adding a news item will be entered, so there's a lot to take in here. As well as the various details for the news item we'll provide text boxes for entering a username and password, and we'll use this in the PHP script to verify that the user has authority to add news items.

Use the screenshot below as a guide to creating the text boxes and buttons necessary for this section.

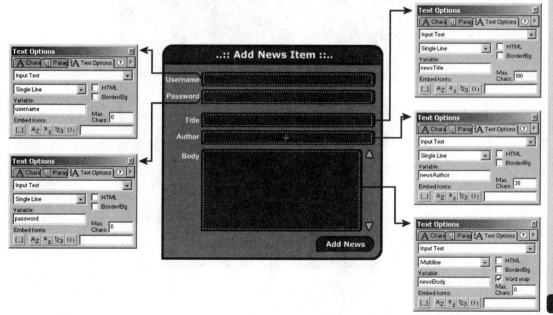

The detail noticeably missing from the previous diagram is the ActionScript for the three buttons in the frame. The two smaller arrows are used to scroll the newsBody text box and, since we've been using this technique throughout the book, I shall leave you to your own devices to add this code.

5. The one element that deserves special attention is the Add News button, as we'll use this to call our PHP script and send it the data to be added to the news table.

    The ActionScript for this button looks like the following:

```
on (release) {
    // If any required field not completed
    if (newsTitle == "" || newsAuthor == "" || newsBody ==
"") {
        // Set error message and show error
        errorMsg = "All fields required";
        gotoAndStop("Error");
    } else {
        // Otherwise call script and wait
        loadVariables("addnews.php", this, "POST");
        gotoAndStop("Loading");
    }
}
```

6. The Loading frame is yet again simply the animated clock face that we used in the previous movie.

7. The Success frame simply contains a message to let the user know that the operation has succeeded, as well as a button to take them back to the Data Entry frame where they can add more news items.

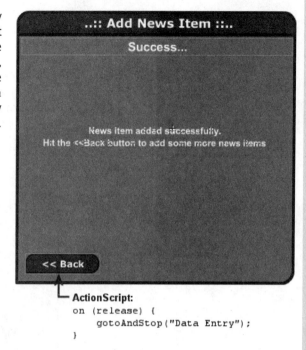

ActionScript:
```
on (release) {
    gotoAndStop("Data Entry");
}
```

8. The Error frame is much the same, except that we have a text box to display the error message returned from the PHP script.

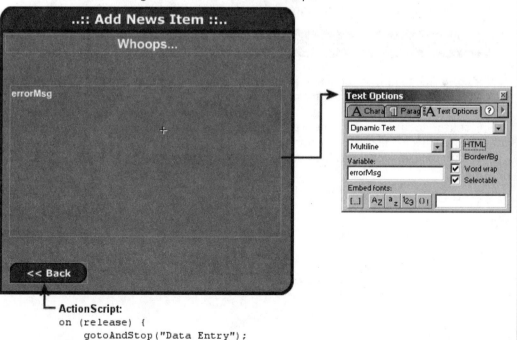

ActionScript:
```
on (release) {
    gotoAndStop("Data Entry");
}
```

9. The final thing we need to do for this movie is to return to the main timeline and drag a copy of our News Admin Panel movie clip from the Library onto our main stage.

   We then need to add the following ActionScript code to it so the movie goes to the correct frame on success or failure of the operation. Note that the `result` variable will be returned from the `addnews.php` script.

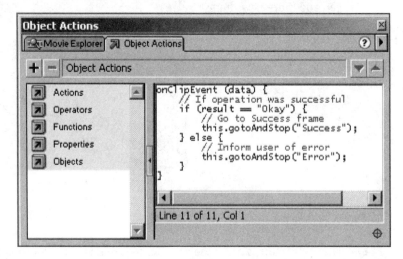

Now we've got the Flash under control, let's dive straight into the two PHP scripts.

The PHP Scripts Part 1 – newssetup.php

It's now time to turn our attention to the PHP scripts that will actually perform the fetching and storing operations to and from the database.

First up is just a refresher of the setup script we developed earlier in this chapter to create the database and the table structure for our news site. Since we've already built this script up over a number of stages there's little point in mulling over it again, so here's the script in full:

```php
<?

// Attempt to connect to the MySQL server
$link = @mysql_connect("localhost", "user", "pass");

// If the connection was unsuccessful...
if (!$link) {
```

```
        // Output error information and exit
        print "Error connecting to database server";
        exit;
    }

    // Attempt to create database. If successful...
    if (@mysql_create_db("phpforflash")) {

        // Inform user of success
        print "Database created<br>\n";
    } else {

        // Otherwise, tell user there was an error
        print "Couldn't create database<br>\n";
    }

    // Attempt to select database. If successful...
    if (@mysql_select_db("phpforflash")) {

        // Inform user of success
        print "Database selected<br>\n";
    } else {

        // Otherwise, tell user there was an error
        print "Couldn't select database<br>\n";
    }

    // Build table creation query
    $query = "CREATE TABLE news (
            newsID INTEGER AUTO_INCREMENT PRIMARY KEY,
            title VARCHAR(100),
            author VARCHAR(30),
            posted INTEGER,
            body MEDIUMTEXT)";

    // Attempt to create table. If successful...
    if (@mysql_query($query)) {

        // Inform user of success
        print "Table created successfully";
    } else {

        // Otherwise, tell user there was an error
        print "Error creating table";
    }
```

continues overleaf

```
// Close the connection
mysql_close($link);

?>
```

If you've not been playing along with all the bits of code as we've been moving through the last two chapters then you'll need to upload or copy this to your web server and load it through your web browser.

> *If this is beginning to feel familiar then you might remember this kind of setup script was used way back in Chapter 1 to set up our Registration movie!*

The PHP Scripts Part 2 – fetchnews.php

We now move on to the script that will fetch the news items for our `news.fla` Flash movie. We've already developed the bulk of this script too, but we'll go over each of the main parts so that we can familiarize ourselves with its operation.

1. First up we define our connection details for the database. By defining all this at the top of the script we make it easy to use the same script on other sites, since we won't have to go hunting through the script for each of these details.

```
<?
// Define database connection details
$dbHost = "localhost";
$dbUser = "user";
$dbPass = "pass";
$dbName = "phpforflash";
$table = "news";
```

2. Next, we attempt to connect to the database server using the `mysql_connect` function. Here we use the variables we created previously as the arguments for the function call, and test the return value to check that we've got a successful connection to the database. If we've failed then we output error information to Flash and exit the script.

```
// Attempt to connect to MySQL server
$link = @mysql_connect($dbHost, $dbUser, $dbPass);

// If the connection was unsuccessful...
if (!$link)
```

```
{
    // Report error to Flash and exit
    print "&newsText=" . urlencode("Couldn't connect to
server");
    exit;
}
```

3. We then attempt to select our database, outputting error information and exiting the script if unsuccessful.

```
// Attempt to select database. If unsuccessful...
if (!@mysql_select_db($dbName))
{
    // Report error to Flash and exit
    print "&newsText=" . urlencode("Could not select $dbName
database");
    exit;
}
```

4. Now we move on to the meat of the script.

```
// Build query to fetch news items from database
// Using ORDER BY to fetch newest items first
$query = "SELECT * FROM news ORDER BY posted DESC";

// Execute query
$result = @mysql_query($query);
```

As the comments show, we're first building up the query to fetch all the news items from the database and then using the mysql_query function to execute this query.

Notice that we're using the ORDER BY clause of the SELECT command to make sure that we receive the news items in reverse date order. We do this because it wouldn't be very user friendly to have to scroll all the way to the bottom of the news window to see the latest news.

5. Following this, we make sure that at least one news item has been returned and then initialize a variable to hold our news items that we're going to pass back to Flash.

```
// If query was okay AND we have at least 1 news item...
if ($result && @mysql_num_rows($result) > 0) {

    // Initialise variable to hold news items
    $newsText = "";
```

continues overleaf

```
// For each news item returned from query...
while($row = mysql_fetch_array($result))
{
```

6. We then create a `while` loop, using the `mysql_fetch_array` function to fetch a new row from the result of the SELECT query on each iteration of the loop.

7. The first thing we need to do to the current row is to extract the posted information and convert it from a Unix timestamp to a readable date. We do this using the `strftime` function that we met in **Chapter 7**.

```
// Format date in 'day dd/mm/yy hh:mm' format
$posted = strftime("%a %d/%m/%y %H:%M",
➥$row['posted']);
```

8. Next we add the title of the current news item to our `$newsText` variable that we'll be sending back to Flash. We're emphasizing the title of each news item so that it stands out from normal chapter text by using HTML tags to change its size and color.

```
// Add title to output in large white font
$newsText .= '<font color="#ffffff" size="14"><b>';
$newsText .= stripslashes($row['title']);
$newsText .= '</b></font><br>';
```

Worth nothing here is that we're using the `stripslashes` to remove any slashes that were automatically added to the chapter title when it was applied to the database.

9. We then need to add the by-line of the news item, which will consist of our humanly readable posted date that we constructed earlier along with the name of the author who posted the news item.

Note that again we're using HTML tags to alter this information's appearance, though this time we are making the text smaller than the default 12-point text that the main news body will be shown in.

```
// Add date posted and author name in small font
$newsText .= '<font size="10">';
$newsText .= $posted . " by " . $row['author'];
$newsText .= '</font><br>';
```

10. The final thing we do in the `while` loop is add the main news body, followed by a handful of HTML line breaks to separate each news item. Note that we're using `stripslashes` again here to remove any unwanted escaping from our strings.

```
        // Add news item body with a double linebreak
        $newsText .= stripslashes($row['body']);
        $newsText .= '<br><br>';
    }
```

11. Once all the news items have been added to the $newsText string we simply output that information back to Flash.

```
        // Output news items back to Flash
        print "&newsText=" . urlencode($newsText);
    }
```

12. The final thing we need to handle in our script is a nice error message for if we were unable to fetch any news items from the database. Then we just round the script off by closing the connection to the MySQL server.

```
    else
    {
        // Tell Flash no news items were found
        print "&newsText=" . urlencode("No news items yet");
    }

// Close link to MySQL server
mysql_close($link);
?>
```

That's it for this script and we now need to write the script to actually get the information into the table in the first place.

The PHP Scripts Part 3 – addnews.php

This script will perform a lot of the same basic actions as the previous one, so if you see a large menacing looking chunk of code you don't quite understand then check back with the previous script – it'll be in there.

1. As with the previous script, we're defining the various details of our database and connection at the top of the script to make it easy to change.

```
<?
// Define database connection details
$dbHost = "localhost";
$dbUser = "user";
$dbPass = "pass";
$dbName = "phpforflash";
$table = "news";
```

2. We then check that the username and password being passed in from the Flash movie are correct. If they're not then we output some error information back to Flash and exit the script. We do this before connecting to the database since there's no point in doing so if the user doesn't have the authorization to add news information.

```
// Check username and password
if ($username != "myusername" || $password != "mypassword")
{
    print "&result=Fail";
    print "&errorMsg=" . urlencode("Incorrect username
and/or password");
    exit;
}
?>
```

Obviously you may want to change myusername and mypassword to something a little harder to guess!

3. We then move on to the database connection code:

```
// Attempt to connect to MySQL server
$link = @mysql_connect($dbHost, $dbUser, $dbPass);

// If the connection was unsuccessful...
if (!$link)
{
    // Report error to Flash and exit
    print "&result=Fail";
    print "&errorMsg=" . urlencode("Could not connect to
database");
    exit;
}

// Attempt to select database. If unsuccessfull...
if (!@mysql_select_db($dbName))
{
    // Report error to Flash and exit
    print "&result=Fail";
    print "&errorMsg=" . urlencode("Could not select $dbName
database");
    exit;
}
```

You should recognize the main elements of the code above by now as we've been using them since the beginning of this chapter. This code basically attempts to connect to the database server and to select our desired database, outputting error information if anything goes wrong.

4. Time once again to fetch the current time as a Unix timestamp using the `time` function. We'll store this in the database so that, when the news item is read out again, we can reconstruct the date on which it was posted.

```
// Fetch the current time
$posted = time();
```

5. Following that, we build our SQL query to insert the news item into the database. We constructed a similar query earlier in the chapter so if you're not sure of the exact details then you need only flip back a few pages.

```
// Build Query
$query = "INSERT INTO news (title, author, body, posted)
          VALUES('$newsTitle', '$newsAuthor',
          '$newsBody', $posted)";
```

6. We then execute the query using the `mysql_query` function, storing the result in the `$result` variable.

```
// Execute Query
$result = @mysql_query($query);
```

7. Finally, we test the value of `$result` and output success or failure information back to Flash as appropriate, before rounding off the script by closing the connection to the MySQL server.

```
// If query was successful
if ($result)
{
    // Report success back to Flash movie
    print "&result=Okay";
}
else
{
    // Otherwise, tell Flash we stuffed up
    print "&result=Fail";
    print "&errorMsg=" . urlencode("Couldn't add news
item");
}

// Close the connection
mysql_close($link);
?>
```

There are several things you might want to add to this news system and, being the rotten little stinker that I am, I left them out so that you could put all the knowledge in this chapter to use and add them yourself.

The main things that stick out are:

- Ability to edit existing news items

- Ability to remove news items

- The fact that all news items are loaded at once

With the knowledge you've picked up in this chapter you should be adequately prepared to attempt adding all of the above functionalities to our news system. If you're still feeling a little daunted however you'll find a completed and documented version on the www.phpforflash.com web site.

Summary

It's only when you look back and see just how easy the Registration script from **Chapter 1** now seems that you can truly realize how much ground we've covered in these last few chapters, and just how much you've learned during the course of the book so far.

We've now taken our theory of the SQL language and put it into use with PHP and Flash to create a genuinely useful application.

We discovered how to:

- Communicate with MySQL using PHP scripts

- Create and maintain databases and tables

- Run SQL queries through PHP scripts to fetch data from our tables

Finally, we spent a massive amount of time developing our news system, using a culmination of the techniques we've learned so far throughout the book.

In the final few chapters, we're going to put all that together in some awe-inspiring practical applications. No more theory, just hard-edged useful, reusable scripts and FLAs for you to build, adapt and plug-in to your site.

I don't know about you but I'm off for an ED Cola break first...

10 Case Study 1 – User Poll

What we'll build in this chapter

- A **neat interface** in Flash for our user poll, easily slotted into any site or page

- A **reusable** file to contain our database connection and common functions

- Two great new scripts to fetch **polling information**, **register** and **store votes** and **display results**

- A **user-friendly** HTML admin page to enter new polls

Ladies and gentlemen, here we are, moving into the twilight hours of our PHP learning. We are all dressed up in our tuxedos and evening gowns, and the only thing we need is somewhere nice to go.

So how about Club PHP? I know some great case studies we can check out. These case studies will be more detailed than the sample applications we've been building so far, giving you a chance to stretch your knowledge and find out why Flash, PHP and MySQL make such a winning combination.

Each case study will be more complex than the last, but they are all well within our reach as PHP masters. We have risen through the ranks, and now is the time to make it pay off. If you find a part of the project that you don't quite understand then simply flip back to the relevant chapter and top up your knowledge-banks.

A learned fellow once gave us to understand that you can't get where you're going unless you know where you are. To remedy this, each of the case studies will be presented as complete projects. This means that before we dive in and start coding and messing about with Flash, we're going to take a step back and look at what we're trying to achieve.

We'll identify the project concept and make sure that it's a sound one. We'll then look at what we will need in order to achieve the goal, and how all of our various sections will fit together. Finally, we'll set about building the project, and maybe even apply a dash of testing too!

So, it's heads up, shoulders back, belly in, and let's go meet and greet the serious PHP crowd!

How To Start With Our User Poll

We're going to kick off our series of case studies with the good old **user poll**. You've probably come across these on your jaunts through the tangled Web, and they're a great way of gauging user opinion on some hot topic or other.

The questions posed in the poll can range from the serious "Who should be the next President?" to the sublimely pointless "ED Cola – Full Fat, Diet, or Caffeine Free?"

Since it's always a good idea to get inspired before embarking upon any project, take a few minutes to go cruising around a handful of web sites and see how many polls you can spot.

If we look at these polls then we can see some of the basic things we're going to need for our project:

- First and foremost we have the almighty **question**. Without the question the user isn't going to know what they're giving their opinion on, or even what their opinion is!

- Next up we've got the list of possible **answers** that the user can choose in response to the question.

- Finally, once we've voted we can often see the **results** of the poll as it currently stands.

Well, that doesn't sound too high brow, does it? We should be able to deal with this one – and with ammunition to spare!

Laying Down The Law...

Okay, to make our lives a little bit simpler we're going to lay down some ground rules for our project. Ground rules, as you know, are an all-important part of PHP etiquette. They stop our minds from drifting onto half-formed ideas.

First of all, we're going to be working on the assumption that each question will have only three possible answers. This is a good compromise, since it allows us to pose such questions as:

Do you like marbles?	What's your favourite food?	How old are you?
>> Yes	>> Ham	>> under 10
>> No	>> Jam	>> 10 to 29
>> What's a marble?	>> Spam	>> 30+

Also, for the purposes of this project we're not going to let the users have access to any other poll than the current one – even to view.

One last thing to note is that we're going to let a given poll run until we add a newer one. This can be a problem if we've got a poll that has a logical end (for example, "Who will win next season's Formula One Grand Prix?" becomes null and void once Michael Schumacher romps home for yet another championship win) but at least it keeps us on our toes updating our polls every now and again.

While these are all limitations, they're something you can add yourself if you really want to. If you feel up to the challenge but aren't sure where to start then you'll find some hints for doing this on the web site at www.phpforflash.com.

Executive Decisions...

Since we're fresh from the MySQL boot camp that was the last chapter, I think we should flex our newly acquired database muscles and store our poll information in a database.

With that and all the limitations for our project in mind, we can now start to sketch out the basics of what we need our little application to do.

First up, we need our Flash movie to fetch the details of the latest poll. Obviously Flash can't access the database itself so we'll have to employ the help of PHP to do the hands-on work for us.

- Once the information has been loaded, we can display the question and options to the user.

- Once the user makes a choice from the range of options, we then need to register that user's vote in the database. Again we'll use trusty old PHP here.

- When the vote has been registered we'll want to display the results of the poll as it currently stands. This information is returned to the Flash movie where we perform some jiggery-pokery on it, presenting the user with a suitably aesthetic set of results.

In addition to all this, it would be desirable to prevent any of the users from voting more than once in any poll. This can skew your results and you'd be surprised just how long users will sit around voting for the same thing over and over again just for kicks. Remember that scandalous vote on *Big Brother?* That was me!

There are a couple of methods we could use for this but we're going to stick with the faithful old cookie, despite the fact that a cookie is relatively easy to remove if a user *really* wants to vote more than once. No system we could develop would be 100% bullet proof so it's not really worth the effort.

Exercising Our Admin Rights

For the admin side of things we're going to want a simple method of adding new polls to the system and for listing all the polls to date along with their results. Since this is administration stuff that the user won't get to see, we don't need to use anything as flash as ... well ... Flash for the interface, we're big enough and ugly enough to handle plain old HTML.

> *Although the* www.phpforflash.com *site is completely designed in Flash, the admin section (for myself and Alan only) is plain HTML; it's the quickest and most basic method of creating such a thing and it works a treat. It'll also show you just how easily you can apply your new PHP skills to technologies other than Flash.*

This actually brings up quite an important point. Never make anything more complicated than it has to be – you'll only give yourself a headache!

Interfacing With Your Users

We should now have an idea of the kind of thing we're looking to build, and we've just filled in enough blanks to get us started on the project. We're now faced with the task of designing the user interface for our application. This is a crucial step and is best done with good old fashioned pen and paper.

We need to take into account all the steps that the application should go through that we discussed previously, and make sure that there is adequate provision for them.

Looking at the list of steps we came up with in the previous section, we can see that we're going to require two main sections for our user interface.

First up, we've got the section where we'll present the user with the poll question, and provide some buttons for the three possible choices. We also want to display the date that the poll was posted on.

With this in mind, I've sketched the following design...

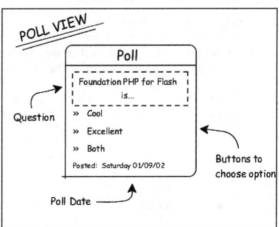

The sketch on the previous page includes all of the elements we require from our Poll View - with each of the options implemented as some kind of button to enable the user to choose between them.

Once the user has made their choice for the poll and that choice has been processed we want to show them the results so far in the poll.

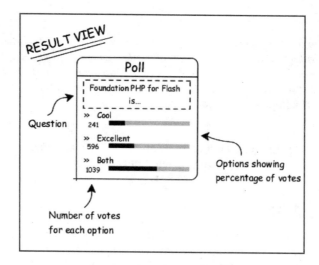

Here, we've repeated the question and the choices for the poll, but we're also using a couple of nifty methods for showing the results so far. The first of these is a series of simple text boxes containing the number of votes for each option, and this gives a good indication of how popular your poll is. In addition to this, we display the percentage of votes that each option has, using some percentage bars.

Fluffiness Aside – The Back End Scripts

Having sorted the design for the visual side of our application it's time to turn our attention to the back-end. Basically, all we want to do here is to determine our database requirements for the application so we have a good idea of where we're going when we come to build the table later on in the chapter.

Since we're only going to be storing very basic information, we can make do with a single table. Thinking about the information that we need to store in the database, I've come up with the following list:

- the question
- the date the poll was posted
- 1st option
- 2nd option

- 3rd option
- no. of votes for option 1
- no. of votes for option 2
- no. of votes for option 3

We'll also want to be able to uniquely identify each poll.

With the above list in mind, I've drawn up a table outline that shows not only how our table is going to be structured but also takes into account the type of information that we need to store for each column.

I use this kind of form in most of my database related projects, and they come in especially handy when you've got more than one table to take care of.

Table: poll

Column Name	Data Type	Description
pollID	Integer	This will be our primary key for the table. We can use this to uniquely identify a given poll
question	String	This will be the question
posted	Integer	We'll use this column to hold the Unix timestamp for the date on which a given poll was posted
option1	String	The text for the first option
option2	String	The text for the second option
option3	String	The text for the third option
votes1	Integer	The number of votes for option 1
votes2	Integer	The number of votes for option 2
votes3	Integer	The number of votes for option 3

With all the specification and design preamble out of the way we can get down to the serious business of actually building the application.

Building our User Poll Application

As usual, before we go anywhere I'll give you a preview of exactly what our final poll will look like...

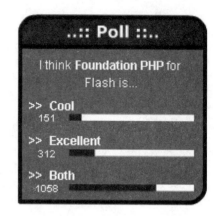

As you can see, we've taken the concept we sketched out earlier and fleshed (or *flashed*) it into a nice and clean user interface that fits in with the styling of everything we've met so far in the book.

We'll have our main display section where the user can see the question and choose from the three options listed for that poll. Once the vote has been cast we can display the current results for the poll. There are a couple of loading screens in there somewhere too, but we'll cross that particular bridge when we come to it.

Making Progress

Before we get stuck into the main Flash movie proper, we're going to spend a few minutes building our little percentage bars shown in the screenshot above.

Since we're going to be using this three times we'll create it as a separate movie clip that we can use in other movies too - should we want to!

So, first things first, we need to actually create the movie clip that we'll put everything in.

1. Select Insert > New Symbol from the main menu or press CTRL+F8 to create the movie clip. Call it Percent Bar and hit OK.

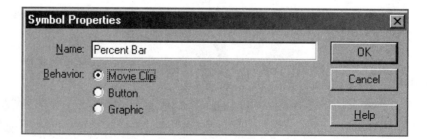

2. Now we need to create the layer and frame structure for the movie clip. This is going to be relatively simple since everything's going to be on the one frame.

Use the diagram below as a guide.

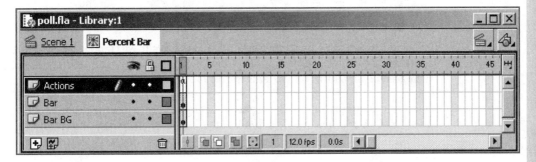

Don't worry about the ActionScript on the Actions layer for the moment, we'll come back to that soon enough.

3. We'll now turn our attention to the Bar BG layer. As the name may suggest, this'll be where we put the background for our percentage bar.

In our case this is a simple white rectangle.

Obviously you can style this as you see fit but you'll need to make sure that it's a shape that can be stretched in the horizontal without distortion – the reason for this shall become clear in the next step.

4. It's now time to create the actual bar that will indicate the percentage on the Bar layer.

Since when the bar is at 100% it should be exactly the same size and shape as the background above, your best bet is to copy that shape and use the Edit > Paste in Place option to paste the new copy on the Bar layer in exactly the same place.

Once it's pasted in place we'll want to change its color to something that contrasts with the Bar BG layer. I've chosen a funky dark blue to fit in with the design but if luminous pink takes your fancy then go for it!

5. If you're puzzling over how we're going to get the bar to change size according to what percentage we want it to represent, here's your answer.

   Each movie clip has an `_xscale` property and, fortunately for us, it is specified as a percentage. However, we can't scale the whole Percent Bar movie clip since we'd also scale the background we created in the Bar BG layer too.

   So what do we do about this little dilemma? Well, we simply convert the contents of the Bar layer into its own movie clip so that we can reference that separately from all the other items in this movie clip.

6. Select the contents of the Bar layer and select Insert > Convert to Symbol or press F8. Give the new movie clip a suitable name, such as Bar, and hit the OK button.

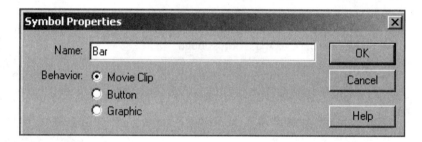

7. Once we've created our Bar movie clip we need to manipulate it a little so that it'll scale properly.

   What I mean by this is that when we modify the `_xscale` property of a movie clip, the scaling takes place relative to the center mark of the movie clip (the little cross).

   Now, at the moment the center mark for the Bar movie clip is ... well ... at the center of the rectangle shape. What we need to do is to align our movie clip so that the center mark is actually at the left hand edge of the rectangle.

8. Select our new Bar movie clip and choose Edit > Edit Symbols (or CTRL+E) from the main menu.

9. Ensure that the blue rectangle is selected and use the Align panel to align the left hand edge of the selection to the center mark for the movie clip.

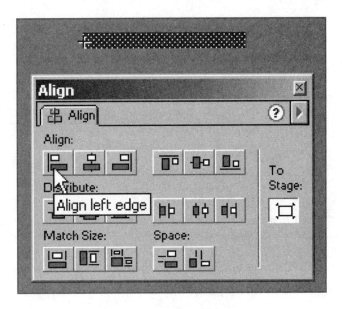

10. Having done all that, return to the Percent Bar movie clip and you'll notice that our nice blue bar has moved over a tad. This is as a result of the above step so we'll need to move it back over, in line with our background for the percent bar.

   To do this we'll use the Align panel again. Simple select our Bar movie clip and hit the center align button.

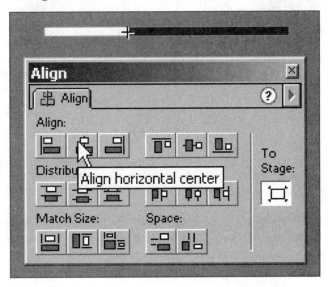

11. We now need to give our instance of the Bar movie clip a name so that we can reference it from ActionScript.

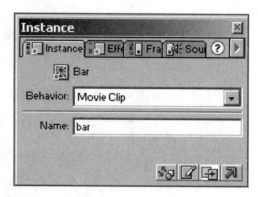

12. All that's left to do now is to create a function in our movie clip that'll enable us to set the percentage from outside.

This is where, as promised, we return to the ActionScript we noticed on the timeline screenshot way back at stage 2 of creating this movie clip.

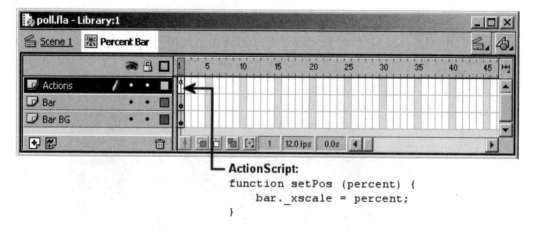

ActionScript:
```
function setPos (percent) {
    bar._xscale = percent;
}
```

The ActionScript simply defined a function named `setPos` that'll take a single argument of the percentage we need to set the bar for. Since the `_xscale` property of a movie clip is specified as a percentage, we can simply assign the value passed in to the `_xscale` property of the instance of our movie clip named `bar`.

13. That's it, our Percent Bar movie clip, and the other little clip inside it, are ready to be used. We'll drag and name instances of this movie clip as appropriate, but for now return to the main timeline by selecting Edit > Edit Movie or pressing the Scene 1 tab above the timeline.

Make Your Vote Count

Having got our Percent Bar movie clip sorted it's time to turn our attention to the main movie proper. We'll be building up the user interface over a number of stages, just as we have with previous projects.

1. Again, we're going to be using an `onClipEvent` handler to take the appropriate action once all the data has been loaded from a call to `loadVariables`. You know what that means by now so get creating that movie clip!

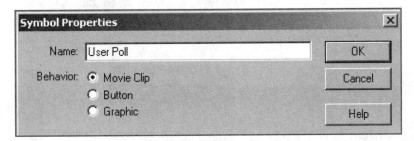

2. The next step, as always, is to rough out the layer and frame structure. Since we're going to be doing a fair amount in this movie it's a little more complicated than previous ones but it's not too bad – honest!

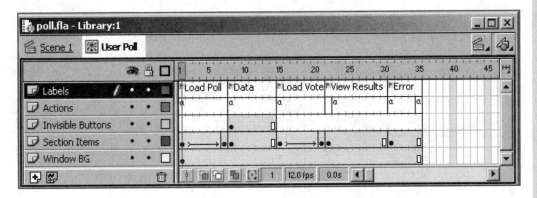

We'll worry about the details such as all the ActionScript a little later. For now let's just be content with mimicking the above structure.

3. Next up we need to create the styling for the Window BG layer. As mentioned earlier, I've used the same design as throughout this book but whatever takes your fancy will be fine!

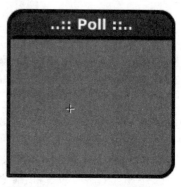

4. Once we've got that sorted we can move on to the Section Items layer of the Load Poll frame. Basically this is going to contain the same loading type screen with the animated clock face that I've been using since the very first application.

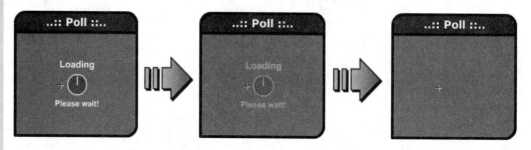

The motion tween between frames 1 and 7 simply fades the animation out.

5. Finally for this frame we need to add some ActionScript on the Actions layer.

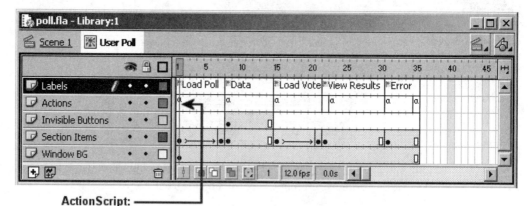

ActionScript:

```
randNum = int(Math.random() * 100000);
loadVariables("fetchpoll.php?" + randNum, this);
stop();
```

Here, on the first frame of the movie clip we've simply got some ActionScript to call the `fetchpoll.php` script we'll start playing with later on, loading all the resultant variables into the current timeline.

We're using our old trick of generating a random number to append to the URL in order to prevent the web browser delivering us a cached version of the script output.

Finally we're stopping the movie clip here so that the loading animation is shown until all data has been loaded, when we get the movie clip moving again with an `onClipEvent` handler.

6. Moving on to the Data frame things start to get a little more interesting. This is where the poll question will be displayed, along with the possible options to choose between. We'll also want to display the date that the poll was posted.

On the Section Elements layer we'll need to create the various text boxes to hold this information. Since we know that our poll can only have three options, we can design the form with this in mind.

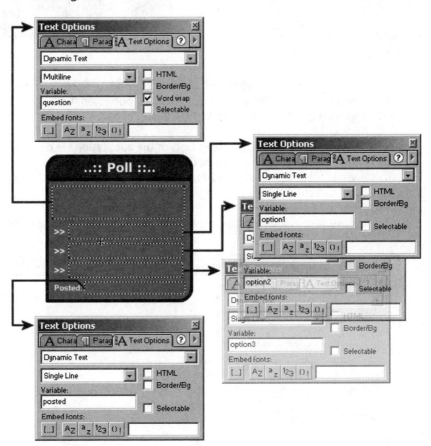

7. The one thing missing from the diagram on the previous page is the presence of buttons that the user can click to make their choice. If you've been particularly alert you may have seen an Invisible Buttons layer for this movie clip, and that may well give you a huge clue as to how we're going to implement this.

Let's take a look at what the stage will look like with the invisible buttons in place:

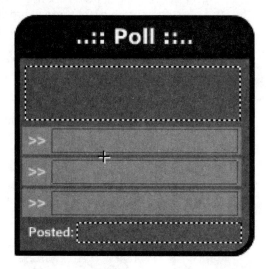

Hopefully you can see that the invisible buttons are represented as light colored rectangles. They're actually a light blue but given that the above shot is in grayscale you won't be able to see that!

8. If you look back to the screenshots of the application we discovered right at the start of this section, you'll notice that when the mouse moves over an option visual feedback is provided for the user via a semi-transparent bar highlighting the current option.

If we take a look at the timeline for our invisible button we can see how this works...

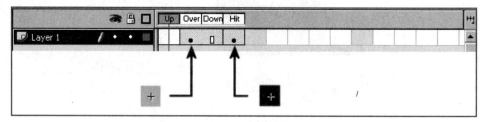

9. On the Hit frame for the button we create a simple black square to define the hit area. We then copy this square to the Over frame and change it to a cool navy blue color. Finally, we reduce the Alpha level of this blue square to 25%.

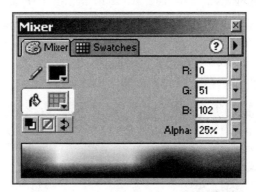

10. When you're done creating the invisible button above, drag three instances of it onto the Invisible Buttons layer of the Data frame. You'll need to position one over each of the options - stretching the size as necessary - as shown in the screenshot earlier.

11. For each button we then need to add the following ActionScript code:

```
on (release) {
    action = "vote";
    choice = 1;
    loadVariables ("vote.php", this, "POST");
    gotoAndStop ("Load Vote");
}
```

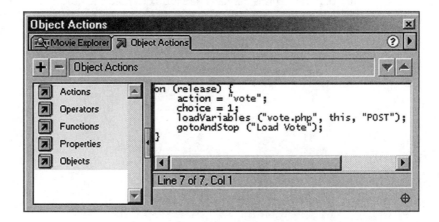

Obviously you'll want to change the **choice** line for each of the buttons to reflect the relevant option being chosen, but the basic idea is the same. We set a variable to indicate user choice and another to indicate the action we want the PHP script to take. We then call the PHP script and advance the movie to the Load Vote frame.

12. ...talking of which, the Load Vote frame is essentially the same as the Load Poll frame we developed earlier, with the exception that the ActionScript on the Actions layer has been changed to a simple stop action.

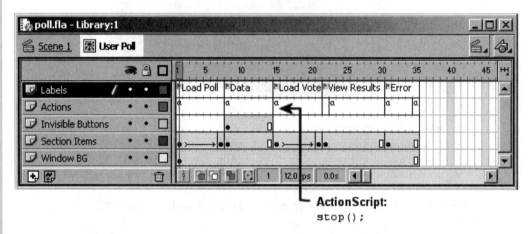

ActionScript:
`stop();`

13. Well, we're nearly there as far as the Flash movie is concerned. The penultimate frame we need to take care of is the View Results frame where we'll use some nice Percent Bar movie clips to display the results for the poll visually.

On the Section Items layer we need to create the various form elements that are required. This is basically a text box to hold the question, a text box for each of the options, and a further text box for each option to hold the vote count for that option.

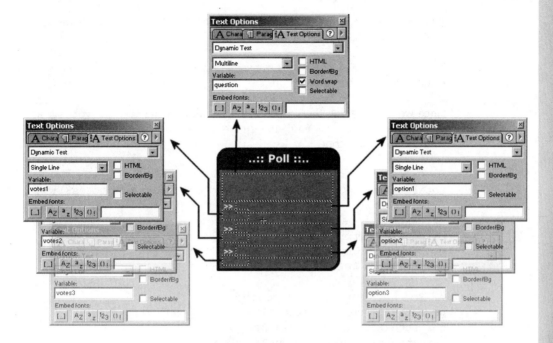

We can now add our three instances of the Percent Bar movie clip we developed earlier in the case study to the Section Items layer.

14. Drag three copies of the Percent Bar movie clip from the Library onto the Section Items layer and place as appropriate for each of the options.

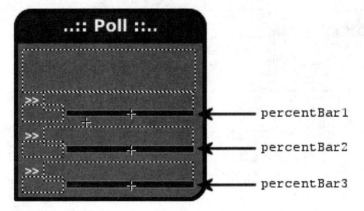

We'll also need to give each an appropriate instance name so that we can refer to it from ActionScript. The ones shown above should do just fine.

15. Now we need to address the ActionScript on the Actions layer of the frame *after* the View Results frame (frame 23).

This is where we're going to be calculating the percentage and passing the results on to the bars movie clip.

Since we'll be loading the votes for each option in the votes1, votes2, and votes3 variables we can easily determine the relative percentages for each bar with the following code.

```
// Calculate total votes cast
total = Number(votes1) + Number(votes2) + Number(votes3);

// Calculate percentages for each option
percent1 = (Number(votes1) / total) * 100;
percent2 = (Number(votes2) / total) * 100;
percent3 = (Number(votes3) / total) * 100;

// Set each option's percentage bar
percentBar1.setPos(percent1);
percentBar2.setPos(percent2);
percentBar3.setPos(percent3);

// Stop the movie from moving on
stop ();
```

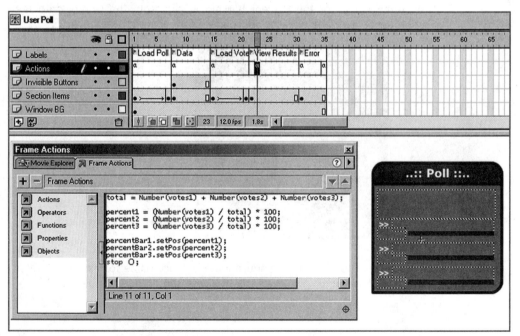

That should all look pretty straightforward to a Flash demon like you! Basically we're calculating the percentages for each bar, and then using the `setPos` function inside each instance to alter the percentage shown on the bar.

Why is it on the frame after the View Results frame? Well, I originally had it on the View Results frame but found that the percentage bars were not being set properly. It turns out that the function calls were failing for some reason so I had to move the ActionScript on one frame. It all comes down to trial and error at times like that!

16. Finally we create an Error frame to display any error message returned from the PHP scripts during the course of their operations.

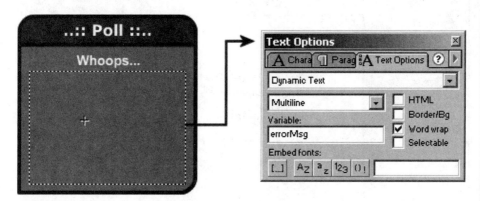

17. Just before we go, we need to drag a copy of our User Poll movie clip from the Library to the main stage, and attach the following ActionScript to handle incoming data.

```
onClipEvent (data) {
    // If operation successfull
    if (this.result == "Okay") {
        // Carry on with movie
        this.play();
    } else {
        // If user has already voted for the current poll
        if (this.result == "AlreadyVoted") {
            // Set action to a simple fetch
            this.action = "fetch";

            // Call vote.php to get results
            loadVariables("vote.php", this, "POST");
```

continues overleaf

```
                        // Go and wait at the loading screen
                            this.gotoAndStop("Load Vote");
                } else {
                    // Otherwise, something went wrong
                        this.gotoAndPlay("Error");
                }
            }
        }
```

Object Actions

Movie Explorer | Object Actions   ? ▶

+ − | Object Actions   ▼ ▲

Actions
Operators
Functions
Properties
Objects

```
onClipEvent (data) {
    // If operation successfull
    if (this.result == "Okay") {
        // Carry on with movie
        this.play();
    } else {
        // If user has already voted for the current poll
        if (this.result == "AlreadyVoted") {
            // Set action to a simple fetch
            this.action = "fetch";

            // Call vote.php to get results
            loadVariables("vote.php", this, "POST");

            // Go and wait at the loading screen
            this.gotoAndStop("Load Vote");
        } else {
            // Otherwise, something went wrong
            this.gotoAndPlay("Error");
        }
    }
}
```

Line 23 of 23, Col 1

> *This is a variant on our usual* onClipEvent *handler, designed to deal with the various kinds of incoming information. Follow the comments if you are unsure.*

That's it for the Flash movie. Save the hard work you've done so far and we can get motoring on to the PHP scripts that'll do all the hardest work for us!

Adding Some PHP Power

It's time to take a look at the PHP scripts that will be doing all the hard graft while the Flash front end just sits there looking sexy. We're actually going to be developing several scripts here, of which two will be for direct interaction with Flash, and two will be admin related, one setup script and a script that we'll use to hold some data that's common to all of the scripts.

The common.php Script

First up we've got the common.php script. This will contain the details that we'll need to access the database server, as well as a few common functions for performing various tasks. We can then use the include function we met in **Chapter 3** to add the PHP elements that are in this file to any other script that we desire, including scripts in the next chapter!

1. Let's get cracking with our common.php code. Firstly we set up some variables to hold our database access details. Obviously you'll need to change some of these details to suit your personal configuration, but you should get the basic idea!

```php
<?

// Database details
$dbHost = "localhost";
$dbUser = "user";
$dbPass = "pass";
$dbName = "phpforflash";
$table = "polls";
```

2. Next up we define a function called dbConnect. This function will perform the common "connect to database server and select our database" operation, outputting any necessary error messages as it goes.

You can see that we're registering a couple of global variables so that we can access them from our function.

```php
function dbConnect() {
   // Access global variables
   global $dbHost;
   global $dbUser;
   global $dbPass;
   global $dbName;
```

```
common.php                                                    _ □ ✕
 1  <?
 2
 3  // Database details
 4  $dbHost = "localhost";
 5  $dbUser = "user";
 6  $dbPass = "pass";
 7  $dbName = "phpforflash";
 8  $table = "polls";
 9
10  function dbConnect() {
11    // Access global variables
12    global $dbHost;
13    global $dbUser;
14    global $dbPass;
15    global $dbName;
```
Editor / HTML /

3. We then attempt to connect to the database server and check our link. If our link fails then we'll call the `fail` function – which we'll write in a moment – to output the error information back to Flash and exit the script.

    ```php
    // Attempt to connect to database server
    $link = @mysql_connect($dbHost, $dbUser, $dbPass);

    // If connection failed...
    if (!$link) {
        // Inform Flash of error and quit
        fail("Couldn't connect to database server");
    }
    ```

4. If all went well with the database server connection then we attempt to select our desired database. Again, if this fails we're using the `fail` function to output error information to Flash and exit the script.

    If we managed to select the database successfully then the link identifier for the database connection is returned.

    ```php
    // Attempt to select our database. If failed...
    if (!@mysql_select_db($dbName)) {
      // Inform Flash of error and quit
      fail("Couldn't find database $dbName");
    }

    return $link;
    }
    ```

5. Moving on to our now-infamous `fail` function, we can see that all this is doing is URL-encoding the error message and outputting that along with a fail message to the Flash movie. We then call `exit` to quit the script.

```php
function fail($errorMsg) {
    // URL-Encode error message
    $errorMsg = urlencode($errorMsg);

    // Output error information and exit
    print "&result=Fail&errormsg=$errorMsg";
    exit;
}

?>
```

```
common.php                                                    _ □ ✕
17    // Attempt to connect to database server
18    $link = @mysql_connect($dbHost, $dbUser, $dbPass);
19
20    // If connection failed...
21    if (!$link) {
22        // Inform Flash of error and quit
23        fail("Couldn't connect to database server");
24    }
25 // Attempt to select our database. If failed...
26    if (!@mysql_select_db($dbName)) {
27        // Inform Flash of error and quit
28        fail("Couldn't find database $dbName");
29    }
30
31    return $link;
32 }
33 function fail($errorMsg) {
34    // URL-Encode error message
35    $errorMsg = urlencode($errorMsg);
36
37    // Output error information and exit
38    print "&result=Fail&errormsg=$errorMsg";
39    exit;
40 }
41
42 ?>

 Editor ⟍HTML⟋
```

While that's it for our common.php *script, there's one important task you need to do before we can move on. Basically, you need to make sure that there are no whitespace characters either before the opening PHP tag or after the closing one. The reason for this will become clear soon enough but for now don't forget that a whitespace character can be a tab or a space, or even a newline. Happy hunting!*

The setup.php Script

This script is going to build the database and table structure for us so we don't have to mess about with the MySQL monitor!

We'll only need to run this script once so it'll be a simple case of uploading it or copying it to your web server and then opening it through your web browser.

1. The script kicks off by including the common.php file we've just created so that we can have access to the database connection variables.

    ```
    <?

    // Include config file
    include('common.php');
    ```

2. We then attempt to connect to the database server, displaying a nice error message if the connection fails.

    ```
    // Attempt to connect to database server
    $link = @mysql_connect($dbHost, $dbUser, $dbPass);

    // If connection failed...
    if (!$link) {
      // Inform user of error and quit
      print "Couldn't connect to database server";
      exit;
    }
    ```

    You may have noticed that we're not using the dbConnect function that we've just developed. The reason for this is that the database may not exist when the script is first run and if this is the case then we'd like to have a pop at creating it from PHP rather than halting the PHP script altogether.

We're also not using the `fail` function for our error message output since this was designed with Flash in mind. For us mere mortals a plain text based error message will suffice!

3. Next up, we have an attempt to create the database specified in $dbName using the `mysql_create_db` function. If this fails then we output an error message, but we DON'T exit since it could have failed if the database exists already. Of course, it may not have existed *and* there was a problem creating it meaning that it still doesn't exist - we'll weed this out in the next bit.

```
// Attempt to create database
print "Attempting to create database $dbName <br>\n";
if(!@mysql_create_db($dbName)) {
   // Inform user of error
   print "# Couldn't create database <br>\n";
} else {
   // Inform user of success
   print "# Database created successfully <br>\n";
}
```

If the database didn't exist, but was created successfully, then we'll get a nice message congratulating us on our success!

4. Once we've done our best to make sure that the database exists we can attempt to select it. Since we need to have a database selected to even have a stab at creating our desired table, we can safely exit the script if any problems were encountered when trying to select it.

```
// Attempt to select database
print "Attempting to select database $dbName <br>\n";
if(!@mysql_select_db($dbName)) {
   // Inform user of error and exit
   print "# Couldn't select database <br>\n";
   exit;
} else {
   // Inform user of success
   print "# Database selected successfully <br>\n";
}
```

Of course, if everything goes smoothly then we simply output a success message and cruise on our merry way though the rest of the script.

5. Talking of the rest of the script, we next formulate the query that we'll use to add the new table to our selected database. Note that we've used the table

mock-up we developed near the start of the case study as a guide for the various columns we need.

```
// Output message to tell user what stage in the setup
// process we're at.
print "Attempting to create table $table <br>\n";

$query = "CREATE TABLE polls (
            pollID INTEGER AUTO_INCREMENT PRIMARY KEY,
            question VARCHAR(255),
            option1 VARCHAR(255),
            option2 VARCHAR(255),
            option3 VARCHAR(255),
            votes1 INTEGER DEFAULT 0,
            votes2 INTEGER DEFAULT 0,
            votes3 INTEGER DEFAULT 0,
            posted INTEGER)";
```

6. We then execute the query, and output a message depending on its success or failure. We round the script off by outputting a message telling the user that we've reached the end of the setup script so it's safe to scarper off down the pub!

```
$result = @mysql_query($query);

if (!$result) {
  // Inform user of error
  print "# Error creating table <br>\n";
} else {
  // Inform user of euccess
  print "# Table created successfully <br>\n";
}

print "End of setup";

mysql_close($link);

?>
```

The fetchpoll.php Script

Finally, we get to the real meat of the PHP scripts. This script is particularly concerned with fetching the current poll and returning that information to the Flash movie. It'll also inform Flash of the presence of a cookie that we'll use to make sure that users can't vote more than once in a given poll.

1. The first thing we do here is to include our common.php file again so that we've got access to the database connection information.

```
<?

// Include config file
include('common.php');
```

2. We then call the dbConnect function we wrote a while back. will now be in action for the first time. We simply use this function call to take all of the hassle out of connecting to the database server and selecting the desired database. You'll come to appreciate the value of this when we meet the remaining scripts for the project.

```
// Connect to database
$link = dbConnect();
```

3. We then build our query to fetch the latest poll in the table. By using ORDER BY posted DESC we can be sure that we're returned the newest poll first, and the addition of the LIMIT clause ensures that we only get the single newest poll.

```
// Build query to fetch latest poll
$query = "SELECT pollID, question, option1,
          option2, option3, posted
          FROM polls ORDER BY posted DESC LIMIT 1";
```

Since we're not concerned with how many votes there are for each option at the moment, we're leaving them out of the list of columns for which we want information returned. This doesn't make a great deal of difference performance-wise with a database this simple but it's good to get into the habit of coding efficiently.

4. Having built the query, it's time to execute it. We check to see if the query has failed, and, if so, we call our fail function again to tell Flash that something's gone wrong and then exit the script.

```
// Execute query
$result = @mysql_query($query);

// If query failed...
if (!$result) {
    // Inform Flash of error and quit
    fail("Error executing query");
}
```

5. If we get this far then the query must have been a success, so we can extract our poll information from the result set as an array, using the `mysql_fetch_array` function.

```
// Fetch the returned poll at array
$poll = mysql_fetch_array($result);
```

6. We now add a `foreach` loop to remove any automatically escaped quotation characters from any of the elements in the `$poll` array.

```
// Remove any slashes from each element of $poll
foreach($poll as $key => $value) {
   $poll[$key] = stripslashes($value);
}
```

7. Following this, we use the `strftime` function to convert the UNIX timestamp that represents the date that the poll was posted into something a bit more manageable. We've met this function several times before so if you're unsure of its operation have a flick back to **Chapter 7**.

```
// Format posted date to something readable
$posted = strftime("%A %d/%m/%y", $poll['posted']);
```

8. We then output all of the poll information to Flash, URL-encoding the output where it may be necessary:

```
// Output poll information to Flash
print "&pollID=" . $poll['pollID'];
print "&posted=" . urlencode($posted);
print "&question=" . urlencode($poll['question']);
print "&option1=" . urlencode($poll['option1']);
print "&option2=" . urlencode($poll['option2']);
print "&option3=" . urlencode($poll['option3']);
```

9. Next up, we've got a clever piece of code to check if the user has already voted in the current poll. You can see from this code that we're checking for a cookie named `lastPollID` and, if its value is a match for the current `pollID`, Flash is informed via the `result` variable. If no cookie is present, or the ID does not match then we just return as normal.

```
// If cookie says user has voted before...
if($poll['pollID'] == $HTTP_COOKIE_VARS['lastPollID']) {
    // Tell Flash movie
    print "&result=AlreadyVoted";
} else {
    // Otherwise return okay
```

```
        print "&result=Okay";
    }
```

10. Finally, being the good little coders that we are, we round off the script by closing our connection to the MySQL server before we exit. Remember your manners!

```
    mysql_close($link);

    ?>
```

The vote.php Script

This script is concerned with registering the users vote in a poll and fetching the results thus far. It'll also be responsible for setting the cookie that'll tell `fetchpoll.php` whether or not the user has already voted in the current poll.

11. As with `fetchpoll.php`, we kick this script off by including our `common.php` script, and then using the `dbConnect` function within, to perform the database connection and selection routines:

```
    <?
    // Include config file
    require('common.php');

    // Connect to database
    $link = dbConnect();
```

12. We then decide whether we need to register the users vote for the given poll (if the user hasn't voted before). This will be indicated by a variable from our

Flash movie called `action`, so if it's set to "`vote`" then we know we want to capture the user's vote.

```
if ($action == "vote") {
  // Build name of column to update from choice variable
  $fieldName = "votes" . $choice;
```

If we're registering the vote then we build the name of the column that needs to be updating by adding the value of the `choice` variable – which will be 1, 2 or 3 depending on which option was chosen – onto the end of the string "`votes`".

13. Next up we build the query that'll increment the value in the appropriate column for the current poll as identified by `$pollID` which, having been passed to Flash when the `fetchpoll.php` script was called, will be sent to this script from Flash.

```
// Build query to update votes for this poll
$query = "UPDATE polls SET $fieldName=$fieldName+1
        WHERE pollID = $pollID";
```

14. We then execute our newly built query and check to make sure that nothing has gone wrong. If something has then we inform Flash of the error and quit the script.

```
// Execute query
$result = @mysql_query($query);

// If query failed...
if (!$result) {
  // Inform Flash of error and quit
  fail("Error executing query");
}
```

15. Our final action inside this `if` statement is to set the cookie that will indicate to `fetchpoll.php` that this poll has been voted in by the current user. Note that we're setting the cookie for 365 days – should be long enough.

```
// Set cookie so user can't vote again
setcookie("lastPollID", $pollID, time() + (365 * 86400));
}
```

16. It's now time to build up a query to select the current votes for the current poll and execute this query. If the query fails then an error message is sent to Flash and the script will exit.

```
// Return votes to this poll
$query = "SELECT votes1, votes2, votes3
          FROM polls WHERE pollID = $pollID";

// Execute query
$result = @mysql_query($query);

// If query failed...
if (!$result) {
  // Inform Flash of error and quit
  fail("Error executing query");
}
```

17. Next we simply fetch the votes from the result set and output that information back to Flash, rounding off the script by closing the link to the MySQL server.

```
// Fetch the returned poll at array
$votes = mysql_fetch_array($result);

// Output poll information to Flash
print "&votes1=" . $votes['votes1'];
print "&votes2=" . $votes['votes2'];
print "&votes3=" . $votes['votes3'];
print "&result=Okay";

mysql_close($link);

?>
```

The addpoll.php Script

Finally we need to develop a script that will allow us to add a new user poll to our database. This script will include an HTML form to allow us to enter the information, as well as some PHP code to take that information and insert in into our database.

Like our mailing list admin section from **Chapter 9** we're going to be using HTML and PHP on the same page. The main point to remember when doing this is that anything enclosed inside our PHP tags will be treated as PHP code, and anything outside will be treated as HTML.

1. The first thing we do is add some initial HTML to set the title of the page as it will appear in the browser window, and add a large text header so that the user is in no doubt as to the function of the form.

```
<html>
  <head>
    <title>Add User Poll</title>
  </head>
  <body>
<font size="+2"><b>Add User Poll</b></font><br><br>
```

2. Having got that sorted we can launch into the PHP code section of the page. Here we're checking to see if the $action variable has been set, and we'll use this to determine whether the form has been submitted and therefore whether we need to take any action script-wise. We can assume that if this variable is set accordingly then we have all of the information we need to insert into the table.

   If the $action variable is set to "add" then the next thing we need to do is to include our file that contains the database access details and common functions.

   ```
   <?
   // If the form has been submitted...
   if ($action == "add") {
       // Include config file
       include('common.php');
   ```

3. We then use the dbConnect function to perform the database connection and selection operations.

   ```
   // Connect to database
   $link = dbConnect();
   ```

4. Having done that we use the time function to get the current time as a UNIX timestamp. We'll use this value as the posted date of our new poll.

   ```
   // Get date for new poll
   $posted = time();
   ```

5. We then build the query to insert the new poll into the table. This should be pretty self-explanatory but you should note that, with the exception of $posted, the variables we're referencing here will all be created from HTML form input. We'll get to this a little later on.

   ```
   // Build query to insert new poll
   $query = "INSERT INTO polls (question, option1, option2,
   ➡option3, posted)
                   VALUES('$question', '$option1', '$option2',
   ➡'$option3', $posted)";
   ```

6. Finally for the script section we execute the query and output a success or failure message according to the success of the query. Note that we're using some HTML font tags to make errors appear in red and success messages appear in blue.

```
// Execute query
$result = @mysql_query($query);

// If query failed...
if (!$result) {
    // Display error
    print "<font color=\"#ff0000\">Could not insert
➥poll</font><br>\n";
} else {
    print "<font color=\"#0000ff\">Poll
➥added</font><br>\n";
}
```

7. We then close the link to the MySQL server and use the closing PHP tag to signify the end of the PHP code.

```
    mysql_close($link);
}
?>
```

8. Now we create a basic HTML form to input all our data:

```
<form action="addpoll.php" METHOD="post">
  <table border="1" cellspacing="2" cellpadding="3">
    <tr>
      <td>Question</td>
      <td><input type="text" name="question"
➥size="50"></td>
    </tr>
    <tr>
      <td>Option 1</td>
      <td><input type="text" name="option1"
➥size="50"></td>
    </tr>
    <tr>
      <td>Option 2</td>
      <td><input type="text" name="option2"
➥size="50"></td>
    </tr>
    <tr>
      <td>Option 3</td>
```

continues overleaf

```
                              <td><input type="text" name="option3"
            size="50"></td>
                  </tr>
                  <tr>
                    <td colspan="2">
                      <input type="hidden" name="action" value="add">
                      <input type="submit" value="Add Poll">
                    </td>
                  </tr>
                </table>
              </form>
            </body>
          </html>
```

9. The only particularly interesting point to note above is the following line:

```
<input type="hidden" name="action" value="add">
```

We use this hidden input field to set the $action variable so that when the form is submitted, the PHP code is invoked (as detailed earlier).

Also, note that the action attribute for the form points to the same script – addpoll.php.

```
<form action="addpoll.php" METHOD="post">
```

10. This will give all you an HTML form like the following, which you can use to add polls.

 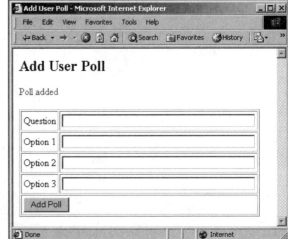

Summary

So, that's our first case study completed this fine evening – and we didn't even spill any of those strong PHP cocktails down our best clothes!

By now you should be gaining some kind of impression about how PHP provides a serious amount of backstage power, beefing up those oh-so-familiar web tools like HTML and Flash. Hopefully you will also be relaxing into the way of all things PHP, and not worrying when things appear to get complicated – I think you should know by now that it's all very easy, really!

Well, onward and upward. I've got to plan what I'm going to be doing after I finish this book, so a Flash and PHP **calendar** would go down a treat...

11

Case Study 2 – Event Planner

What we will build in this chapter

- An expandable **Flash interface** for our calendar application

- **Reusable** scripts to setup our database **connections** and define our **functions**

- A script to fetch the events from our **database** and pass them to our Flash movie

- An HTML-embedded **administration module** to add new events to the database

If you're anything like me then you'll subscribe to the theory that memory capacity (of the human variety) is inversely proportional to the amount of time you spend in front of your computer – leaving me with the memory capacity of a goldfish!

If this all sounds a little familiar to you then you're in need of the next application we're going to build – an online events calendar.

Although this project was born out of necessity, it's still worth looking around to see if you can pick up some ideas from other online calendars, if you can find them. My inspiration for this application was taken from an old personal organiser program I had on my Commodore Amiga.

Let's take a look at the basic steps our application will go through. Note that all this is presented without concern for implementation, meaning that we don't say where we load the data from, how we load it in or even what we load it into. This is generally a good idea when you're designing an application as it allows you to take the same general design and implement it using other technologies.

Anyway, enough waffle and on with those steps. In this calendar application, we'll want to...

- Set year to view as current year
- Load number of events for each month of the year
- Display calendar to user
- When user picks a given month, load the event details for that month
- Display that month's events to the user
- User hits a button to return to step 2

In addition to all this we'd like to give the user the ability to view events from previous years and events that are happening in future years – especially for all those forward planners out there.

Also, once the user gets to stage **5** above it might be nice to enable them to move on to view the events of adjacent months without having to return to the main calendar display. Without this functionality our calendar would be a little too rigid. We want it to be user friendly, and not merely usable!

Planning It All Out

It's time to get handy with the old pen and paper and start thinking about what our user interface will look like. We need to take into account all the steps the application should go through and make sure that there is adequate provision for them.

Looking at the list of steps we came up with in the previous section we can see that we're going to require two main sections for our user interface.

The first, known as the Year View, will basically show the number of events in each month of the currently selected year. We'll need to incorporate some method by which the user can select the year, and we also need to provide a way for the user to tell the Flash movie which month they would like to view event details for.

With all this in mind, we might come up with something like the following sketch...

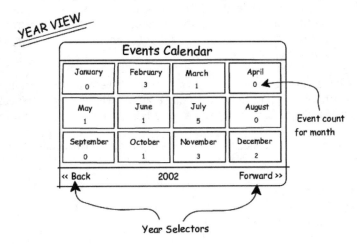

This includes all of the features we require from the Year View. Each of the twelve boxes displays the month name and the number of events for that month, and will have a button covering them so that the user can just click on the month they want to view. We can use that to load the details for the relevant month. We also have the Back and Forward buttons to enable the user to browse through the years.

Once the user has selected the month they want to view event details for, our movie will go off and fetch the events. When everything's loaded we need some mechanism for displaying the events to the user.

Enter the Month View...

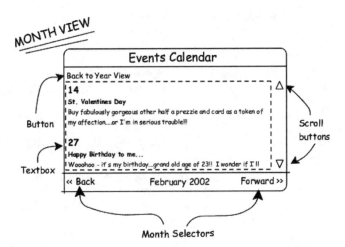

Here we've got a multiline text box to hold all of the events for the chosen month, and we've got some new Back and Forward buttons to allow the user to move through the months without going back to the Year View. We've also got a button to take the user back to the Year View if they want it and some nice scroll buttons linked to the main text box.

In addition to these two main sections we'll also have a loading screen or two and a section for displaying errors. Since these are fairly passive parts of the user interface it isn't essential that they be designed before we actually build them. However, this is as much a matter of personal taste as anything, so if you want to put in a design for these then go with your own personal flow!

Having designed the user interface we should have a pretty clear idea of the kind of information we're going to need to store and, having honed our database skills in the previous few chapters, we're going to use **MySQL** as our storage solution of choice.

So, what kind of information do we want to store? How about the following list for starters...

- Date of event
- Title for event
- Main event information

It would also be nice to have a mechanism for uniquely identifying a given event. You might think on first glance that the date will be just fine for this but we could well end up with multiple events on the same day. This makes the date unsuitable for uniquely identifying an event so we have to invent an extra item of information to do this for us.

With the above list in mind we should come up with a table that looks something like the following:

Table: events

Column Name	Data Type	Description
eventID	Integer	This will be our primary key for the table. We can use this to uniquely identify a given event.
year	Integer	The year the event is set for
month	Integer	The month the event is set for
day	String	The day the event is set for
title	String	The title text for the event
event	String	The main text that will describe the event

Storing the different components of the event date separately allows us to only select the items in the table that we're interested in, rather than having to select them all and then filter through which ones are relevant and which are not.

Having gone through our design process it's time to roll up our sleeves and start getting our hands dirty.

As usual we'll start off by building the foxy Flash front end, creating the scripts that'll act as the muscle behind the application once we've got an idea of what's required of them from Flash.

Charting the Days in Flash...

Since we've already sketched out the main sections for this Flash movie before getting to this stage it shouldn't take us too long to polish the whole user interface off. That said, we're going to have to use some ninja Flash moves to get everything to work as it should so we might stretch our knowledge of Flash a little in this chapter.

First things first, we're going to be using our friend the onClipEvent handler for this application so we'll have to enclose the entire user interface in a movie clip.

1. Select Insert > New Symbol from the main menu or press CTRL+F8 to create the movie clip. Call it Events Calendar and hit the OK button.

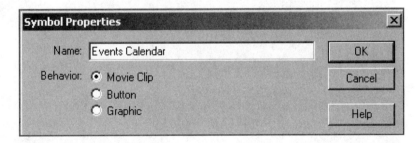

2. Having got that sorted, our next step, as always, is to create the layer and frame structure for the movie clip.

You should know the drill by now – use the screenshot below as a guide.

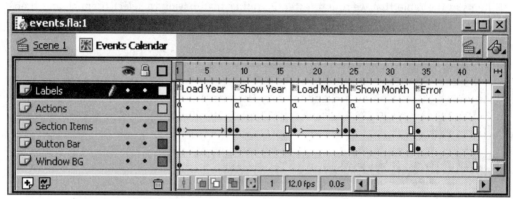

You'll probably recognize the motion tweens from previous applications but we'll get to these in a moment. We'll also come back and take a look at the ActionScript on the frames above in detail as we deal with each section of the movie clip.

As usual, the Window BG layer contains the background for the window. This has been carried over from the concept drawings we created earlier so there shouldn't be any surprises here.

As you can see I've left a fairly decent **client area** for the interface and I've accommodated the button bar at the bottom as per the designs we mocked up earlier.

3. Dealing with the Load Year frame first of all, the motion tween on the Section Items layer is ... yep, you guessed it ... the fading out of the clock face animation that I've been using since **Chapter 1**.

4. We've also got some ActionScript on frame 1 of the Actions layer. It is here that we'll need to invoke the PHP script to fetch the number of events for each month of the current year.

Let's take a look at the ActionScript and then we'll discuss exactly what it does.

```
// If no year selected
if (!year) {
   // Set year to current
   now = new Date();
   year = now.getFullYear();
}

// Setup action and call script...
action = "geteventcounts";
loadVariables("fetchevents.php", this, "POST");

// Halt movie clip
stop();
```

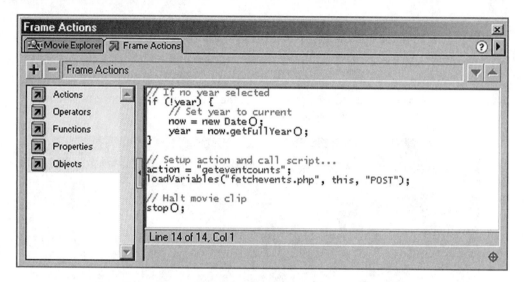

When the movie clip is first loaded there will be no currently selected year. If this is the case then we use the `new Date` object to fetch the current year according to the local time system.

Once that's done we set the action we want our script to perform and invoke the script using a call to `loadVariables`. Finally, we halt the movie clip until data has been received – although that functionality is provided by an `onClipEvent` handler we've yet to create.

5. Moving on to the Show Year frame we encounter our first items on the Button Bar layer.

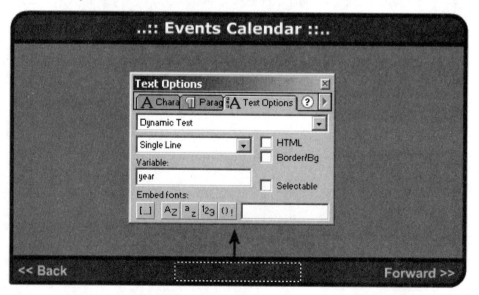

As you can see we've got a small text box in the middle of the button bar, and by giving it a variable name of `year` it will automatically tie in with the variable we first created in the previous step, displaying the currently selected year.

6.   We also have Back and Forward buttons here, so go ahead and add the following code:

```
//Back
on (release) {
    // Load previous year
    year—;
    gotoAndPlay ("Load Year");
}
```

and

```
//Forward
on (release) {
    // Load next year
    year++;
    gotoAndPlay ("Load Year");
}
```

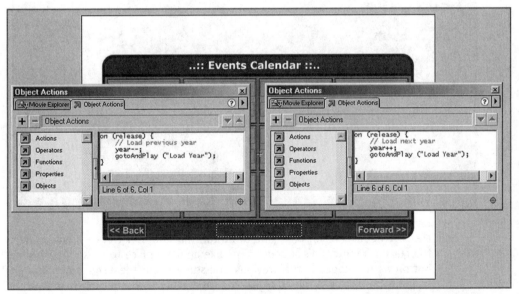

Because the job of loading the currently selected year is performed on the Load Year frame, all we have to do with these buttons is to appropriately alter the currently selected year and then play that frame.

7. Now we come to possibly the most complex aspect of the entire movie clip. Basically we now need to create the boxes that represent each of the months in the currently selected year, displaying how many events are in each.

   We could have done this in the same way as we built the User Poll interface in the first case study; creating 12 text boxes to hold the month names, 12 text boxes to hold the event count for that month and then 12 buttons which set the `month` variable appropriately and invoked `loadVariables`.

   However, given that we've done that kind of thing once, I thought it'd be good to push the boundaries of our Flash knowledge. Basically, we're going to use a generic movie clip for each of the month boxes, using ActionScript to assign the appropriate values. Now this is the stuff real Flash bloods use!

8. First up we draw a rectangle, mine being slightly darker than the window background so that it shows up better. We then need to add a couple of simple dynamic text boxes to display the relevant information for the month.

9. Next we need to have some kind of button that the user can click on to select the current month. This sounds to me like an ideal place to reuse the invisible button we developed in the previous case study. I've made a small modification to mine, namely that the color for the Over state is a semi-transparent white rather than semi-transparent blue.

10. The code we'll use for this button may not make too much sense at the moment but once we follow the next step it will, I promise! The code for the button is:

```
on (release) {
    // Set month to load to current
    _parent.month = this.month;

    // Load month details
    _parent.gotoAndPlay("Load Month");
}
```

11. Now we need to convert the whole of this month box into a suitable movie clip. Select the box, the text boxes and the new invisible button and select Insert > Convert to Symbol or hit the F8 key to convert the whole lot into a movie clip. Give it an appropriate name (such as Month Box) and hit the OK button.

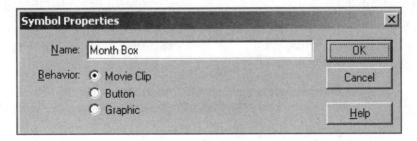

12. Finally we need to duplicate the instance of our Month Bar movie clip so that we have our rows of four to represent the twelve months of the year.

We also need to give each of these instances a meaningful instance name so that we can refer to them from our ActionScript.

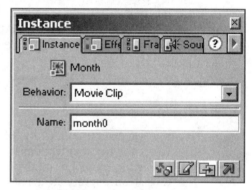

13. Starting with the top left corner and working your way left to right and top to bottom, name the instances as shown above so that you have instances ranging from month0 (top left) through month11 (bottom right). Names ranging from 0 to 11 may seem a little strange but there's a good reason for it, which we'll discover in a moment.

14. Now that these are all movie clip instances within our Events Calendar movie clip the ActionScript on the invisible button should make sense.

```
on (release) {
    // Set month to load to current
```

```
    _parent.month = this.month;

    // Load month details
    _parent.gotoAndPlay("Load Month");
}
```

Basically, _parent refers to the parent of the current movie clip instance, and in this case this is our Events Calendar movie clip. So you can see now that we're setting the month variable in the parent movie clip equal to the same variable in the current movie clip. Then we tell the parent movie clip to go and play the Load Month frame, which, cunningly, we'll use to load the currently selected month!

How does each of our Month Box instances know which month it represents? Follow me and all shall be revealed...

We need to define the ActionScript for the Show Year frame. We know that by the time we get here we have loaded all of the event counts for the currently selected year from the PHP script since we stopped the movie in the Load Year frame. This is because we're using an onClipEvent(data) handler to get it going again.

15. So it's time to set up the movie clips we've just created with meaningful data. Take a look at the following ActionScript code...

```
// Define month names
months = new Array("January", "February", "March", "April",
"May", "June", "July", "August", "September", "October",
"November", "December");

// For each month movie clip...
for (count = 0; count < 12; count++) {
    // Set month number
    this["month" add count].month = count;

    // Set month name
    this["month" add count].monthName = months[count];

    // Set number of events for month
    this["month" add count].eventCount = this["eventCount" add
count];
}

// Halt the movie clip
stop();
```

16. The first thing we do here is to create an array of month names called `months`. If you remember we named our Month Box instances starting from 0, and the reason for this is that the first element in an array is at index 0 – meaning that there's a direct correlation.

We then use a `for` loop to process each month in turn, setting the `month` and `monthName` variables within the relevant Month Box instance to their appropriate value.

Notice that we're using `this["month" add count]` to reference each instance of our Month Box movie clip in turn.

17. We also use a similar technique to get the event count for the current month, setting the `eventCount` variable of each Month Box instance accordingly. The variables that will be loaded in from the PHP script will be named thus:

```
eventCount0
eventCount1
    . . .
eventCount11
```

So we're using `this["eventCount" add count]` to fetch the correct value from the current timeline. Finally we round off by stopping the movie clip.

Back when we created the invisible button for the Month Box movie clip we referenced a frame called Load Month in the ActionScript. This frame will ask our PHP script to fetch the event details for the currently selected month, as determined by which button was pressed.

18. This frame is very similar to the Load Year frame, with the exception that the ActionScript on the Actions layer is a little different.

```
// Setup action and call script...
action = "geteventdetails";
loadVariables ("fetchevents.php", this, "POST");

// Halt the movie clip
stop ();
```

All that we've changed here is the value of the action variable, getting the PHP script to fetch the event details rather then event counts.

19. We now come to the business end of the application; the Show Month frame. The Button Bar layer contains a few features that we designed in right from the start.

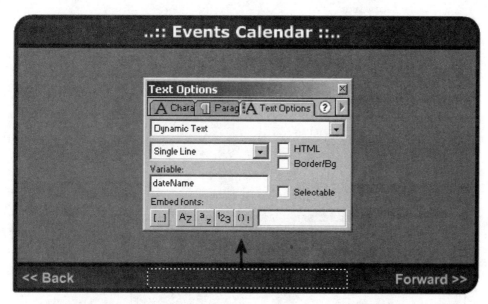

Here you can see we've got a simple dynamic text box for displaying the currently selected month and year. Unlike the similar text box on the Show Year frame we'll have to use some ActionScript to construct this text but we'll come to that in a moment.

Notice that we've also got on this layer some Back and Forward buttons as in the Show Year frame. However, the ActionScript on these has been edited to reflect that fact that we now want to load the adjacent months rather than previous and next years.

```
// Back
on (release) {
    // Load previous month
    month—;

    // If this was first month in year
    if (month<0) {
            // Load last month of previous year
            month = 11;
            year—;
    }
    gotoAndPlay ("Load Month");
}
```

and

```
//Forward
on (release) {
    // Load next month
    month++;

      // If this was last month of year
    if (month >= 12) {
            // Load first month of next year
            month = 0;
            year++;
    }
    gotoAndPlay ("Load Month");
}
```

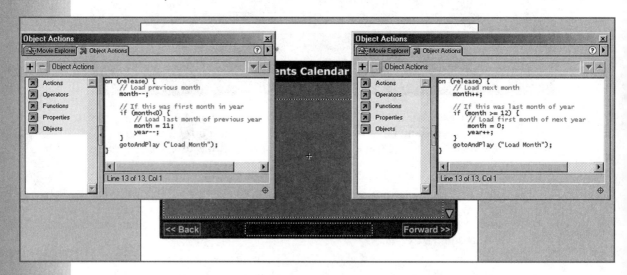

You can see that when the user clicks the relevant button on the first and last months of the year, they will actually be taken to the end/beginning of the previous/following year. This allows the user to browse through several years of event details without having to return to the Year View.

20. On the Section Items layer for this frame we have the various elements that go to make up the user interface for the Month View.

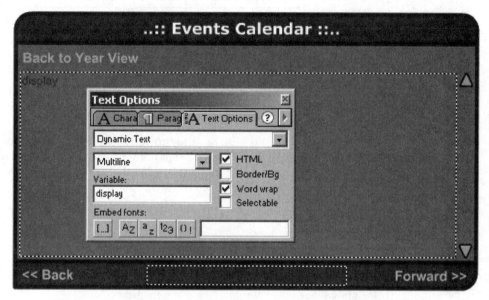

The most important factor to notice about the above screenshot is the fact that we've selected HTML for the text options of the display text box. We'll be using this feature to emphasize certain parts of the event text, namely the day on which events occur.

We've also got some scroll buttons linked to the display text box. These use the _scroll property of the text box to scroll the text.

21. Finally, we have our Back to Year View button, which, cunningly enough, takes us back to the year view.

```
on (release) {
    // Return to Year View for current year
    gotoAndPlay("Load Year");
}
```

22. Now we come to the real meat in the Flash sandwich – the ActionScript that takes the information returned from our PHP script and formats it nicely for

display in the `display` text box. We want to add this to the Show Month frame, on the Actions layer.

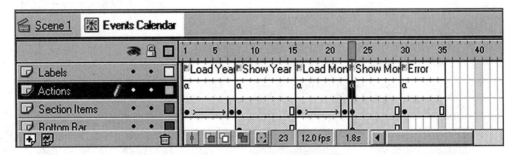

We'll go through this ActionScript bit by bit to make sure that we understand what's going on.

23. First of all, we use our old `months` array to fetch the month name for the currently selected month, and then we tack it onto the end of that the currently selected year. This all gets stored and displayed in the `dateName` text box.

```
// Construct datename
dateName = months[month] add " " add year;
```

24. We then check to make sure at least one event has been returned for the current month. If not, we set our display text box to inform the user of the fact.

```
// If there are no events for chosen month...
if (eventCount == 0) {
    // Inform the user
    display = "<b>No events for this month</b>";
```

25. If there was at least one event returned for the current month then the first thing we need to do is to clear the `display` text box. We then initialize a variable that we'll use to keep track of which day of the month the previous event was for. We'll use this to make sure that we only display one date if there is more than one event for a given day.

```
} else {
    // Otherwise clear display textbox
    display = "";

    // Init var to hold day of month for prev event
    prevDay = 0;
```

26. We then use a `for` loop to process all the events returned for the given month. We assign some generic variables the value of the event detail variables we'll

return from our PHP script, allowing us to use them throughout the remainder of the `for` loop.

```
// For each event returned...
for (count=0; count<eventCount; count++) {

    // Fetch event info into generic vars
    day = this["event" add count add "day"];
    title = this["event" add count add "title"];
    event = this["event" add count add "event"];
```

27. We then bring our `prevDay` variable into play, making sure that we only print out one day of the month for multiple events.

```
    // If this day is different to the prev...
    if (day != prevDay) {
        // Display day in large letters
        display = display add "<font color=\"#ffffff\"
size=\"16\"><b>" add day add "</b></font><br>";

        // Remember current day
        prevDay = day;
    }
```

28. Now add the standard event information to the display text box, making sure to emphasize the event title in bold.

```
    // Add event information to textbox
    display = display add "<b>" add title add
➡ "</b><br>";
    display = display add event add "<br><br>";
    }
}
```

29. Finally, we stop the movie where it is, allowing the user to control where they go from here.

```
// Halt the movie clip
stop ();
```

30. The final frame we need to look at is the Error frame. This is where we'll display any errors that occur during the course of the application.

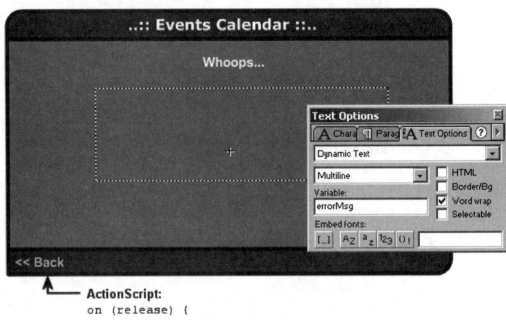

ActionScript:
```
on (release) {
    gotoAndPlay("Load Year");
```

31. Just before we go, we need to drag a copy of our Events Calendar movie clip from the Library to the main stage and attach the following ActionScript to handle incoming data:

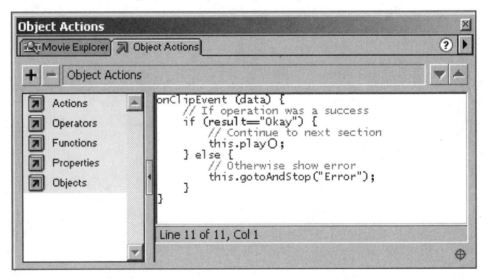

That's it for the Flash front end. Now it's time to flex our newly-grown code muscles!

Building the PHP Back End

Having constructed our nice swanky user interface we need to turn our attention to the PHP scripts that'll tie everything together.

We have four scripts in total to build, although the first two are pretty standard and we've covered them before. There should be nothing now you don't understand in these scripts, because all the component functions and statements have been covered earlier in the book. OK, let's get into these scripts...

The common.php Script

Since we're going to need more than one script for this application, we'll again use a separate script to hold any configuration information and common functions. The code presented here is exactly the same as in the previous case study, aside from the fact that we've changed the value of the $table variable to reflect the current application.

For this reason I'm just going to list the new script here with the usual comments. If you skipped the last case study then either go to the back of the class or flip back a few pages and read the explanation there!

```php
<?

// Database details
$dbHost = "localhost";
$dbUser = "user";
$dbPass = "pass";
$dbName = "phpforflash";
$table = "events";

// Common functions
function dbConnect() {
    // Access global variables
    global $dbHost;
    global $dbUser;
    global $dbPass;
    global $dbName;

    // Attempt to connect to database server
    $link = @mysql_connect($dbHost, $dbUser, $dbPass);

    // If connection failed...
```

continues overleaf

```
                if (!$link) {
                    // Inform Flash of error and quit
                    fail("Couldn't connect to database server");
                }

                // Attempt to select our database. If failed...
                if (!@mysql_select_db($dbName)) {
                    // Inform Flash of error and quit
                    fail("Couldn't find database $dbName");
                }

                return $link;
            }

            function fail($errorMsg) {
                // URL-Encode error message
                $errorMsg = urlencode($errorMsg);

                // Output error information and exit
                print "&result=Fail&errormsg=$errorMsg";
                exit;
            }

            ?>
```

The eventssetup.php Script

Next we need to build the setup script to create the database and table structure for our application. Again, the script here is very similar in structure to the one we built in the previous case study, with only the line where we define the table creation query actually being changed!

If the code needs any further explanation then take a look at the dissection of the setup script for **Chapter 10**.

```
            <?

            // Include config file
            include('common.php');

            // Attempt to connect to database server
            $link = @mysql_connect($dbHost, $dbUser, $dbPass);

            // If connection failed...
            if (!$link) {
```

```
        // Inform user of error and quit
        print "Couldn't connect to database server";
        exit;
}

// Attempt to create database
print "Attempting to create database $dbName <br>\n";
if(!@mysql_create_db($dbName)) {
        // Inform user of error
        print "# Couldn't create database <br>\n";
} else {
        // Inform user of success
        print "# Database created successfully <br>\n";
}

// Attempt to select database
print "Attempting to select database $dbName <br>\n";
if(!@mysql_select_db($dbName)) {
        // Inform user of error and exit
        print "# Couldn't select database <br>\n";
        exit;
} else {
        // Inform user of success
        print "# Database selected successfully <br>\n";
}


print "Attempting to create table $table <br>\n";

$query = "CREATE TABLE $table (
            eventID INTEGER AUTO_INCREMENT PRIMARY KEY,
            year INTEGER,
            month INTEGER,
            day INTEGER,
            title VARCHAR(255),
            event TEXT)";

$result = @mysql_query($query);

if (!$result) {
        // Inform user of error
        print "# Error creating table <br>\n";
        print mysql_error();
} else {
        // Inform user of euccess
        print "# Table created successfully <br>\n";
```

continues overleaf

```
}

print "End of setup";

?>
```

The fetchevents.php Script

1. Moving swiftly on we come to the real mover and groover of the operation. This script will handle all of the interaction between our Flash front end and the MySQL database server where our event information is stored.

   Although you've met all of the elements in this script before and could probably find your way around the code yourself, we'll go through this once together just to make sure that we understand what it's doing!

   If you feel like you're ready to take off those water wings, then feel free to have a stab at creating the script yourself using the design information we've already covered in this chapter, go for it! You can always come back if you get stuck!

2. As always, the first thing we need to do is connect to the database server. In order to do this, we first include our `common.php` file so that we have access to all the database connection details and common functions.

   ```
   <?
   // Include config file
   include("common.php");
   ```

3. We then use one of these functions, `dbConnect`, to connect to the database server and select our desired database.

   ```
   // Connect to database
   $link = dbConnect();
   ```

4. Next up, we need to determine which action the Flash movie has requested of the script. Depending on the value of the `$action` variable, which is passed from our Flash movie, we call the relevant function or return error information if the value is unknown.

   Note that the `$year` and `$month` variables will be passed in from our Flash movie.

   ```
   // Determine which action to take
   switch($action) {
        // Get event counts for year view
   ```

```
case "geteventcounts":
    getEventCounts($year);
    break;

// Get event details for month view
case "geteventdetails":
    getEventDetails($year, $month);
    break;

default:
    // Output error info to Flash and quit
    fail("Unknown action $action");
    break;
}
```

5. Finally, we do our good deed for the day and close the link to the database server.

```
// Close database connection
mysql_close($link);
```

```
fetchevents.php                                                    _ □ ×
 1  <?
 2  // fetchevents.php
 3  // Case Study 2 - Foundation PHP for Flash
 4
 5  // Include config file
 6  include("common.php");
 7
 8  // Connect to database
 9  $link = dbConnect();
10
11  // Decide which action to take
12  switch($action) {
13      // Get event counts for year view
14      case "geteventcounts":
15          getEventCounts($year);
16          break;
17
18      // Get event details for month view
19      case "geteventdetails":
20          getEventDetails($year, $month);
21          break;
22
23      default:
24          // Output error info to Flash and quit
25          fail("Unknown action $action");
26          break;
27  }
28
29  // Close database connection
30  mysql_close($link);
```
`Editor  HTML`

6. We now move on to the functions we've just mentioned. First up, we've got our getEventCounts function that will be used to fetch the number of events for each month of a given year. Here, we're just making sure that we've got access to the global variable that holds the table name for the application:

```
function getEventCounts($year) {
    // Register global variables
    global $table;
```

7. We then need to build our query to fetch all of the events for the given year.

```
// Build query to fetch all events for year.
$query = "SELECT month FROM $table WHERE year=$year";
```

> *Note here that we're only selecting the* month *column for each event. We've done this to make sure that the* SELECT *query is as efficient as possible, as we're only actually going to use the month information in this function.*

8. Once we've built the query we need to actually execute it and test to make sure that it was executed successfully. We've been using this piece of code for a while now so it should be familiar to you:

```
// Execute query
$result = @mysql_query($query);

// If the query failed...
if (!$result) {
    // Output error information to Flash and quit
    fail("Unable to fetch event information");
}
```

9. If everything went okay we need to set up some method of counting the number of events returned for each month. Here we're simply initializing a simple 12-element array, with each element representing the count for the relevant month:

```
// Setup array to hold event counts
$eventCounts = array(0, 0, 0, 0, 0, 0, 0, 0, 0, 0, 0, 0);
```

10. Next we go through each of the events returned by the query, subtracting the month information. We then use this value to increment the relevant element of our $eventCounts array.

```
// For each event returned...
while($event = mysql_fetch_array($result)) {
    // Extract the month for the event
    $month = $event['month'];

    // Increment the relevant element of our array
    $eventCounts[$month] ++;
}
```

11. We then loop through each of the elements in our $eventCounts array, outputting the information back to our Flash movie

The variables we return will be the eventCount1, eventCount2 (...and so on) that we discussed back when we were building the Flash front end.

```
// For each month of the year...
for ($count = 0; $count < 12; $count++) {
    // Output event count information to Flash
    print "&eventCount" . $count . "=" .
➡$eventCounts[$count];
    }
```

12. The final thing we need to do for the getEventCounts function is to report back to our Flash movie that the operation was a success.

```
// Output success
print "&result=Okay";
}
```

13. The getEventDetails function will be used to fetch the actual event details for a given month and year. As with the previous function, the first thing we need to do is to make sure that we've got access to the global variable that holds the name of the table for the application.

```
function getEventDetails($year, $month) {
    // Register global variables
    global $table;
```

14. We then build our query to select all of the events for the given month of the given year.

```
// Build query to fetch all events for month of year.
```

continues overleaf

```
$query = "SELECT * FROM $table WHERE year=$year
         AND month=$month ORDER BY day ASC";
```

The interesting thing to note about this query is that we're using an ORDER BY clause to make sure that the events are returned in chronological order. By specifying that earlier events should be returned first, we ensure that our calendar information displays properly in Flash, with events for the 11th day of the month being shown before events for the 17th!

15. The next step is to execute the query we've just built and handle any errors that crop up.

```
// Execute query
$result = @mysql_query($query);

// If the query failed...
if (!$result) {
    // Output error information to Flash and quit
    fail("Unable to fetch event information");
}
```

16. We then initialize a variable that, although slightly innocent looking at the moment, will play an important part in our script.

```
// Initialise count for output
$count = 0;
```

We'll use this variable to keep track of which event we're currently processing, and to output the event information into a unique variable when it's sent back to Flash. If this doesn't make absolute sense just now, then hopefully the next few snippets of code will make things a little clearer.

17. We set up a while loop to fetch each of the returned events. For each one, we then extract the event information into some variables, using stripslashes where appropriate to remove automatically added escape characters.

```
// For each event returned...
while($event = mysql_fetch_array($result)) {

    // Extract the event information
    $day = $event['day'];
    $title = stripslashes($event['title']);
    $event = stripslashes($event['event']);
```

> *Note here that we're not bothering to extract year or month information for the current event. The reason for that is the fact that the Flash movie must already know the year and month for these events since it passed that information to us in the first place.*

18. The next thing to do for each of the events returned is to output the information back to Flash. Notice how our mysterious $count variable is being used here to ensure that each event's information is output in sequentially named variables.

```
        // Output information to Flash
        print "&event" . $count . "day=" . $day;
        print "&event" . $count . "title=" .
➥urlencode($title);
        print "&event" . $count . "event=" .
➥urlencode($event);
```

19. The final stage of the while loop is incrementing our $count variable ready for the next go around the loop. The advantage of this method is that, once all of the events have been processed, $count will contain the total number of events processed.

```
        // Next event
        $count++;
    }
```

20. The very final act of this function is to use our $count variable to tell the Flash movie how many events we have returned to it, followed by a simple output to indicate the success of the operation … and that's the end of the script too!

```
        // Output number of events to Flash
        print "&eventCount=$count";

        // Output success
        print "&result=Okay";
    }
?>
```

The addevent.php Script

Lastly, we need some way of actually getting the event information into the database in the first place - otherwise our application is a perfect example of uselessness!

As with the previous case study, we're going to be building the user interface for this section using quick and easy HTML code since only the admin peeps will see it! This form could easily be replicated in Flash, so if you're feeling adventurous then feel free to give it a bash!

1. The code is pretty much self-explanatory, so I'll just list the script as is. That said, there are a couple of points in the script that'll need some closer discussion. These have been highlighted in **bold** and will be discussed at the end.

```
<html>
  <head>
    <title>Add Event</title>
  </head>
  <body>
  <font size="+2"><b>Add Event</b></font><br><br>

<?
// If the form has been submitted...
if ($action == "add") {
    // Include config file
    include("common.php");

    // Connect to database
    $link = dbConnect();

    // Correct 2 digit years
    if ($year < 60) {
        $year += 2000;
    } else if ($year < 100) {
        $year += 1900;
    }

    // Adjust month by 1
    $month--;

    // Convert newlines to <br> tags
    $event = nl2br($event);

    // Remove extra CR/LF characters
    $event = eregi_replace("[\n\r]+", "", $event);

    // Build query to insert new event
    $query = "INSERT INTO $table (year, month, day, title,
event)
                VALUES($year, $month, $day, '$title',
'$event')";
```

```php
    // Execute query
    $result = mysql_query($query);

    // If the query was successfull
    if ($result)
    {
        // Output success msg
        print "<font color=\"#0000ff\">Event
added</font><br>\n";
    }
    else
    {
        // Otherwise, inform user of failure
        print "<font color=\"#ff0000\">Couldn't add
event</font><br>\n";
    }

    mysql_close($link);
}
?>
```

```html
    <form action="addevent.php" METHOD="post">
      <table border="1" cellspacing="2" cellpadding="3">
        <tr>
          <td>Date</td>
          <td>
            Day <input type="text" name="day"
size="2">  
            Month <input type="text" name="month"
size="2">  
            Year <input type="text" name="year" size="4">
          </td>
        </tr>
        <tr>
          <td>Title</td>
          <td><input type="text" name="title"
size="50"></td>
        </tr>
        <tr>
          <td>Event</td>
          <td><textarea name="event" cols="50"
rows="5"></textarea></td>
        </tr>
        <tr>
```

continues overleaf

```
              <td colspan="2">
                <input type="hidden" name="action" value="add">
                <input type="submit" value="Add Event">
              </td>
            </tr>
          </table>
        </form>
      </body>
    </html>
```

2. The first section of the code that needs closer inspection is the following...

```
// Correct 2 digit years
if ($year < 60) {
    $year += 2000;
} else if ($year < 100) {
    $year += 1900;
}
```

Here we're simply making sure that years that have been entered into the form using just two digits actually get converted into four digit years.

To do this I've had to define some sensible cut-off points. Using the above code, if the user enters a 2 digit year between 0 and 59 we assume that they mean a date in the current century, adding 2000 to convert it to a full 4 digit year. In the same way, if a user enters a 2 digit year between 60 and 99 we assume that they're referring to the previous century, and add 1900.

Of course, if the year entered is 100 or greater then it will be taken literally as the full year and requires no manipulating.

3. Next up we need to look more closely at the following snippet of code...

```
// Adjust month by 1
$month—;
```

Here we're adjusting the month entered into the form, decrementing it. This may seem a little weird until you consider that in a lot of the code for this application we're using arrays, and that the first index of an array is 0, not 1. Indeed, if you remember when we were building the Flash movie we mentioned that we were numbering our months starting from zero to fit in with the arrays.

Now when a user goes to enter date information, it would be a little awkward to ask them to subtract one from the date they're entering - it would just look plain weird having my birthday being displayed as [27] [01] [1979] when I was born in February!

To resolve this situation we simply decrement the submitted month and store that value in our database!

4. The final section of code that may require closer examination is the following...

```
// Convert newlines to <br> tags
$event = nl2br($event);

// Remove extra CR/LF characters
$event = eregi_replace("[\n\r]+", "", $event);
```

What this code does is to insert an HTML linebreak (<br>) tag just after each newline character (\n) in the submitted $event variable using the nl2br function. Although we haven't met this function up until now, it's simple enough in its operation that we can accept it for what it is – or rather what it does.

The next step is to remove any extra characters that may be interpreted by Flash as an end of line character, including the newline characters themselves.

We need to do this because Flash will interpret both newline (\n) and carriage return (\r) characters as end of line markers, and if we don't whip them out we will end up with double spaced event text – not good!

That's it, your nice new addevent.php script should look something like the following when loaded through your web browser:

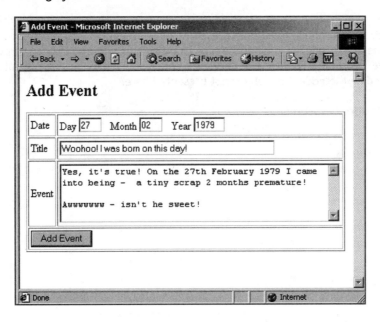

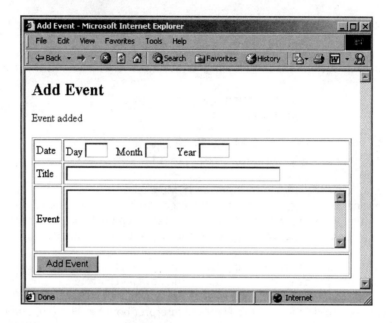

Summary

Well, that's all for this case study. We've taken another application from concept through to realization - and a useful application it is too!

Before you go take a well-deserved break you might want to consider some features that are missing from the application presented here. The only things I can think of are actually on the admin side, as it would be nice to be able to edit and delete the events should it prove necessary. This should be well within your capabilities and would only involve extending the addevent.php script presented here.

Don't worry! Experiment!

12 Case Study 3 – Forum

What we'll build in this chapter

- *A **masterplan** of how this complex project will take shape*

- *A full **Flash interface** for the forum, allowing users to **read** and **write posts**, **reply** to existing **threads** and even **register** their details*

- *Scripts to handle **posts**, **threads** and **registration** details, storing information in our **MySQL database** and retrieving it when needed*

You've probably been too busy building cool applications to notice, but our long journey through PHP is coming to an end. As a grand finale to the book we'll be building that most sought-after of applications – a message board system! Yes, it's time for the **Flash Forum** I've been promising you since ... well, since the back cover!

This will be a culmination of the techniques we've covered the whole way through the book. We'll also be using some intermediate to advanced ActionScript techniques on the Flash side of things, but when this crops up I'll explain exactly what we're doing and why we're doing it! Oh yes, we're mixing with the big boys now!

But before we can go anywhere we need to talk about a few concepts that we'll be using in this case study.

- **Post**
  A post is a single message on our message board.

- **Thread**
  A thread is a collection of posts on a single topic. For example, if I posted a question on the average lifespan of monkeys, that and all the replies to that message would make up a single thread.

  By using the concept of threads we can group related posts together, allowing us to present them to the user as complete discussions.

- **Forum**
  A forum is a collection of threads. Some message boards have many forums, each with a general topic under which threads can be grouped. The message board that we're going to build in this chapter only supports a single forum and so in this instance, our case study can be described as both. Two for the price of one – now I can't say fairer than that, can I?

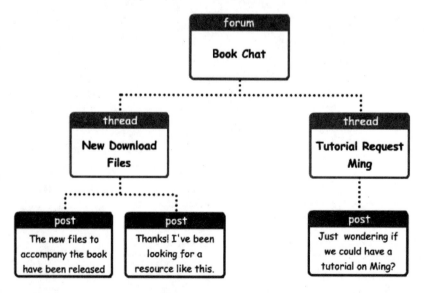

With this in mind, let's take a look at the basic steps our application will go through. Note that all this is presented without concern for implementation, meaning that we don't say where we load the data from, how we load it in or even what we load it into. This is generally a good idea when you're designing an application as it allows you to take the same general design and implement it using other technologies.

So, what we need to do is:

- Fetch list of threads for forum
- Display forum to user
- When user selects a thread, fetch list of posts for that thread
- Display thread to user
- Enable user to hit back button to return to forum view

In addition we need to handle the registration of new users, and we have to allow users to post new threads and reply to existing ones.

Drawing Up a Masterplan

It's time to get handy with the old pen and paper again and start thinking about what our user interface will look like. We need to take into account all the steps the application should go through (as we just outlined) and make sure that there is adequate provision for them.

Looking at the list of steps we came up with in the previous section we can see that we're going to require five main sections for our user interface:

- Forum View
- Thread View
- Post New
- Post Reply
- Register

We'll deal with each of these in turn.

Forum View

The Forum View will show a list of threads for the forum. In addition to displaying the threads, we need to allow the user to refresh the view to check for new threads in the forum. Also we need to have a think about the user's ability to post a new thread in the forum, and come up with some convenient way for the user to get to the registration section.

Of course it's obvious what we need, isn't it? We need a **button bar**! This will be a small section at the bottom of the interface that contains the buttons for controlling everything we could possibly want to do with this application.

Let's take a look at a rough sketch...

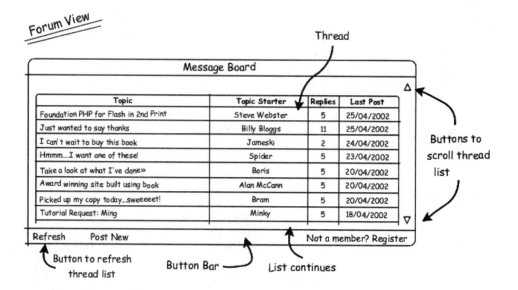

That's pretty much all we need, I'd say. What we've got here is exactly what we said we wanted.

The bulk of the area for the section is taken up with the list of threads in the forum. Now, we could be so popular that we have more threads than we can display on the screen at any one time, so we're going to have to add some kind of scrolling facility to enable the user to scroll down through the list of threads. That sounds to me like a practical Flash issue, so let's consign it to the Pending pile and worry about it later.

Of course it's totally up to us how we present our information, but I think it would be handy to adopt some conventional forum layouts, so we don't have to be concerned about inventing the wheel before we can get rolling. To this end I've used the sorts of columns you see in most forums: the topic under discussion, whoever started the thread, the number of replies, and the date of the last post.

Adopting this convention at least helps us figure out exactly what information we want to be storing in our database. You'll also note that I've taken on board another forum standard: the most recent posting goes first. That little feature is entirely down to how we play with the information in our database – we could arrange it how we want – but convention is our friend at this early stage. You gotta learn the rules to break 'em!

One last thing to note is our button bar at the bottom. I'm very proud of this. This bar will contain different buttons depending on the section of the application that the user is visiting. For example, a Post Reply button would not make any sense in the Forum View since the user needs to first select a thread to reply to. It's all very logical, but it's going to make all the difference to our final application.

Thread View

So that's the Forum View out of the way. Next we've got our Thread View. This will show all of the posts that belong to the thread that has been selected by the user. Again, we're going to want to display some appropriate buttons on the button bar to provide the necessary facilities for this section.

To my way of thinking, the Thread View is going to look pretty similar to the Forum View. There's no need to go overboard on our design variation, because that could make things look swampy. Here's my take on it:

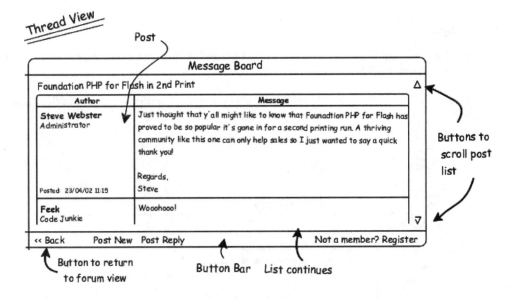

In a way I suppose we have zoomed in on the previous table, concentrating on the individual postings of the selected thread. The left hand side of each post gives information on the user who made that post as well as when it was posted. The right hand side consists entirely of the message posted.

> *Although not demonstrated here, it's extremely worthwhile pointing out that, while threads are shown with the newer ones towards the top, it is generally accepted that posts should be shown in true chronological order (the order in which they were posted). If you find that a little strange then try reading the next paragraph backwards and see how much sense it makes! By displaying the posts in order, the user can follow the conversation from start to finish.*

The Refresh button of the button bar has been swapped for a Back button, and this will take us back to the Forum View if the user clicks on it. We've also got an extra button – Post Reply. When the user hits this button they'll be able to post a reply to the current thread. Notice that we've still got our Post New button so the user doesn't have to return to the Forum View to post a new thread. Now that's what I call ergonomic satisfaction! Anyway, moving on...

Post New

Now that we know how our users are going to view the message board we need to design the user interface where they can post new threads.

This view will consist of a simple form built in Flash, and a handful of buttons in the button bar. There's nothing particularly special to worry about here so let's take a look...

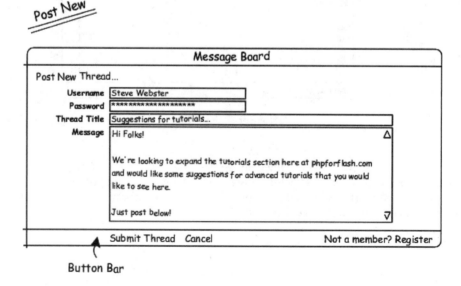

You can see here all of the form elements we'll need to provide for the user to post a new thread on our message board. This form pretty well represents an amalgamation of the main elements of each of the three tables for our message board.

First of all we have the **username** and **password** that will be used to make sure that the user is registered, and these details will be checked against those on file to ensure that the user has the permission to post on the boards.

Finally we have a spaces for the title of the thread and the main message. We need both of these details because not only are we creating a new thread but we'll also need to create a new post to go with that thread.

You can also see that we have the Submit Thread button on the button bar to invoke the posting process, a Cancel button just in case the user has a change of heart, and a Register button so the user can easily rectify the problem of having not yet registered.

Post Reply

The user interface for the Post Reply section is almost exactly the same as that for the Post New section. The reason behind this is that we need to provide the same basic information for each.

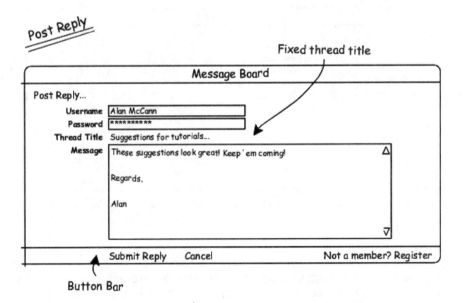

The only notable difference is that the thread title is no longer an editable text box. If the user has chosen to reply to a thread, they've got to stick to it! If they want to start their own thread, let them do it in the proper window! What we want to do is stamp the existing thread title up there for all to see so the more forgetful users remember what they're replying to!

Note that we've also switched the Submit Thread button for a Submit Reply button and we'll need to perform different actions on here to perform the desired operation.

Register

The Register section of the application will be where our users will come to sign up for the message board. The bare minimum of information we'll need to handle is:

- username
- password
- e-mail address

You can go to town and add as many things as you like to this but we'll stick with the basics for now. So, without further ado let's have a look at what kind of sketch that conjures:

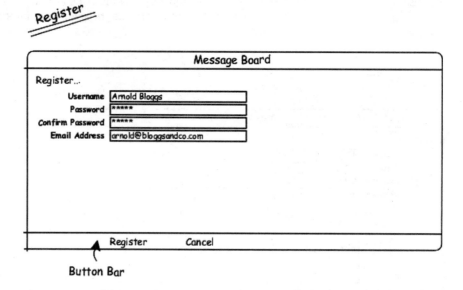

You can see that this section of our application is looking pretty threadbare by design. There are all sorts of extra things you might want to insert in here, and in particular some kind of Terms & Conditions that the user must agree to if they want access to the forums would be a good idea!

Arranging Our Tables

I'd say we've been pretty good to brainstorm the user interface so thoroughly before trying to do anything more advanced. Now we don't have to worry about whether it's going to work as a concept, and we can code with confidence. We should have a pretty clear idea of the kind of information we're going to need to store and, having practised our database manoeuvres in the previous case study, we're going to use MySQL as our storage solution of choice.

So, what kind of information do we want to store? How about the following list for starters:

Users
- Username
- Password
- Title
- E-mail Address

Posts
- User who creates post
- Message body
- The date the post was created

Threads
- Topic of thread
- User who created the thread
- The number of replies to the original post
- The date of the last post in thread

Since we need to keep information on so many different things I thought it wise to split the above into logical tables (Users, Posts, and Threads). With this in mind we should come up with tables that look something like the following:

Table: forumUsers

Column Name	Data Type	Description
userID	Integer	This will be our primary key for the table. We can use this to uniquely identify a given user.
username	String	The username for the user
password	String	The password for the user
email	String	The email address for the user
title	String	A title for the user, just as Administrator

Table: forumThreads

Column Name	Data Type	Description
threadID	Integer	This will be our primary key for the table. We use this to uniquely identify a given thread.
userID	Integer	This is the userID of the user who created the thread.
topic	String	The topic for the thread
replies	Integer	The number of replies to the original post in the thread
lastPost	Integer	The date of the last post made in this thread, stored as a Unix timestamp.

Table: forumPosts

Column Name	Data Type	Description
postID	Integer	This will be our primary key for the table. We can use this to uniquely identify a given post.
threadID	Integer	This is the threadID of the thread to which the post belongs.
userID	Integer	This is the userID of the user who created the post.
message	String	This is the main message body of the post.
posted	Integer	The date the post was made, stored as a Unix timestamp.

You may have noticed looking through these tables that they are all related in some way or another. For example, in the above forumPosts table, we're using the primary key of the forumThreads table (threadID) to identify to which thread a given post belongs. In the same table we use userID to identify the author of a given post.

We can visualize these relationships with the diagram below...

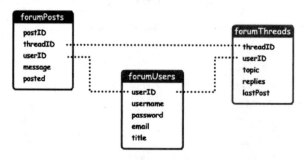

The Flash Movie: A Few Thoughts

Having done all the planning bits we need to do, it's time to go back to that Pending pile and start building the Flash movie that'll run the whole show!

The movie we'll develop for this Flash forum will be somewhat more complicated than the previous movies we've developed, due to the nature of what we're trying to do. That said, every step in this tutorial is explained with the "why" as well as the "how" so you should be okay!

Again, it's best not to get carried away with all this, so first off we need to exercise discipline by musing over exactly how we're going to visually represent the list of threads for the forum and the list of posts for a given thread. Although there are many ways in which this could be accomplished, by far the most polished is using the attachMovie method, which first surfaced in Flash 5.

We'll use attachMovie to create an instance of a given movie clip from the library for each thread or post that we need to be displayed.

The syntax for attachMovie is as follows:

```
someMovieClip.attachMovie(idName, newname, depth);
```

This function will attach an instance of the movie clip from the Library with an identifier of idName to the movie clip someMovieClip. The new instance of idName will be called newname, and we can use depth to control the depth of the movie clip.

> The depth property is very handy to be aware of in Flash. If you try to create more than one movie clip instance at a given depth then you'll overwrite the old one with each new one you add – instances cannot share a depth! Keeping this in mind is guaranteed to save headaches at a later date.

When I first met attachMovie I thought that in the idName slot I could enter my movie clip's name (the one I'd already defined in the Symbol Properties dialog). How wrong I was. The fact is you have to enter an exciting new district of Flash, known as **Symbol Linkage**. If you're at a loss as to what I'm going on about, let me explain.

Normally if a movie clip appears in the library but is not used anywhere in the Flash file then it is not included in the SWF file when you publish your Flash movie. However, in Flash 5 we can specify that certain movie clips should be exported *regardless* of whether they're used in the movie. This technique is known as Symbol Linkage.

What we have to do when we submit a movie for Linkage is specify an **Identifier** for that movie:

It is through this Identifier that we can reference it using attachMovie. So you see how it all comes together?

I'm not going to get into the mechanics of how we build the thread and post lists just now – I'll leave that to their proper section – but you should be aware that we'll be using this technique in our movie so you can get comfortable with it before we start chucking it about.

Interestingly, building the thread and post lists in this way brings up another point - if we've got more threads than can be displayed then won't they overlap our nicely crafted window?

The answer to this question is that they would...but only if we let them. What we're going to do is use a blank movie clip (we'll call this our canvas) onto which we can attach (using attachMovie) the thread, or post movie clips as appropriate for each view. All we need do after that is mask the canvas so that only the portion we desire is visible.

Take a look at the diagram below to see what I mean:

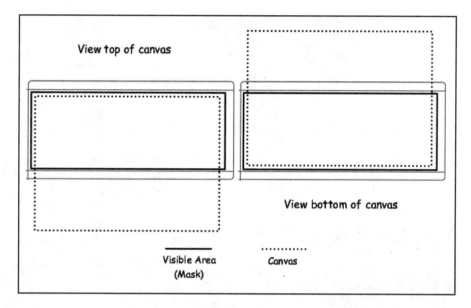

You can see that when the canvas is taller than the visible area (or mask), it's not all visible. If we want to scroll down to see whatever's at the bottom of the canvas then we need to decrease the _y property of the canvas movie clip until the very bottom of the canvas is within our viewable area.

This is a relatively straightforward process and won't take more than a line or two of ActionScript to accomplish.

Building The Forum in Flash

Having got the preliminary head scratching out of the way we can turn our attentions to getting our keyboards dirty. Yes, it's time to create the main Flash file. Of course there will be problems along the way – we're always going to have to keep on our coding toes – but at least we can now jab confidently at those keys, rather than hesitantly dabbling our way through weak ideas!

I think you've got the picture. So:

1. First things first, we're going to be using our old friend the onClipEvent handler for this application so we'll have to enclose the entire user interface in a movie clip.

Create the movie clip give it a suitable name and hit the OK button.

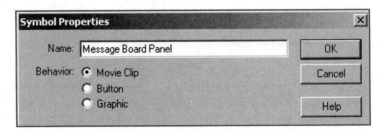

2. We now need to create the layer and frame structure for the movie clip. Although this one's a bit of a monster you should be able to identify with the frame labels for the different sections since we built mock-up shots of them earlier.

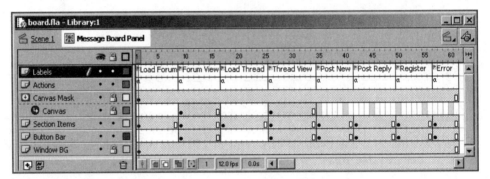

3. As usual, our Window BG layer contains the background for the application.

4. The Section Items layer of the Load Forum movie clip contains my favorite little clock face animation to give the user some feedback that the data is actually loading.

5. The final thing we need to take care of for the Load Forum section is the ActionScript on the Actions layer.

This is where we'll be calling the PHP script to fetch the list of threads for the forum. We're also going to define a function here that we'll be using throughout the movie.

```
// Create random number to append to URL
randNum = Math.random()*1000000000;

// Call PHP script to fetch forum information
loadVariables ("viewforum.php?" add randNum, this);

// Halt the movie clip until data loaded
stop ();
```

As far as the loading of the forum goes, that's all there is to it. Basically we're just setting up a random number to append to the URL of the PHP script so that the web browser doesn't serve us up a cached version of the file output. The reasons for this were of course outlined way back in **Chapter 1**.

What we do is add this random number onto the end of the url portion of the loadVariables call to viewforum.php (which we'll be looking at later on). Then we halt the movie clip so it doesn't go anywhere while the information is loading. We'll set up an `onClipEvent` handler to get it going again right at the end of this section.

6. Lastly for this frame we define a function that takes a single argument (`threadID`) and calls the `viewthread.php` script passing the desired thread ID along as it goes.

```
// ***********[ FUNCTION HEADER ]**************
// * viewThread()                                    *
// * Loads the thread with the specified threadID *
// *********************************************
function viewThread (threadID) {
    // Create random number to append to URL
    randNum = Math.random()*1000000000;

    // Load thread
    loadVariables ("viewthread.php?threadID=" add threadID add
"&" add randNum, this);

    // Wait for data to load
    gotoAndStop ("Load Thread");
}
```

Notice that we're using our random number trick again to prevent caching – just one of those things in life you wonder how you did without!

7. We now tell the movie clip to go to and wait on the Load Thread frame. This is so that once the movie clip is started again (when all of the data has been loaded) we move directly into the Thread View.

8. Okay, let's have a look at the Forum View frame. Here we encounter our first entry on the Button Bar layer.

Refresh   Post New   Not a member? Register..

The code for the above buttons is as follows:

```
Refresh
on (release) {
    gotoAndPlay("Load Forum");
}
```

Post New
```
on (release) {
    gotoAndPlay("Post New");
}
```

Register
```
on (release) {
    gotoAndPlay("Register");
}
```

These are all pretty straightforward – the bracketed definitions ensure we are taken to the relevant frame on the timeline.

9. We now need to add our "canvas" onto which we'll be attaching movie clips. As I said before a canvas is simply an empty movie clip so create one by pressing CTRL+F8. Give it the name of Canvas and hit the OK button.

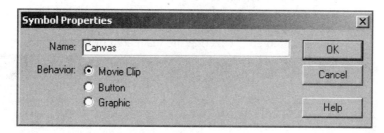

Once you've created the movie clip return to the timeline of our Message Board Panel movie clip.

10. Making sure that the Canvas layer is selected on the Forum View frame, drag a copy of our new Canvas movie clip from the Library onto the stage. Since the movie clip is empty it will appear as a small white circle. Select this circle and position it near the top left corner of the main section of our movie clip.

Ensuring that our instance of Canvas is still selected we need to give it an instance name so we can refer to it from ActionScript.

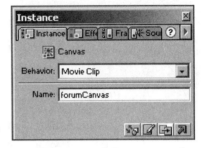

I've called it forumCanvas because we'll want two instances of Canvas, one for the Forum View frame and one for the Thread View frame.

11. Copy and paste this instance onto the Canvas layer of the Thread View frame and fix its instance name as threadCanvas.

12. Moving on, it's time to create the mask on the Canvas Mask layer. This, as we noted, will enable us to hide the bits of Canvas we don't want to see. Ensuring that the Canvas Mask layer is selected, pick a nice contrasting color (it doesn't really matter which) to that of the Window BG layer and draw a large rectangle almost completely covering the main area of our application.

13. Having done that make sure that the layer is selected as a mask by right clicking on the layer name (or CTRL+CLICK for Mac) and selecting Mask.

The mask and the canvas will disappear and their layers will become locked. Just use the layer icons to get at them again if you need to.

14. Before we go anywhere else we need to construct the movie clip that will be attached to the forumCanvas to form the thread list. To achieve this we need to create three movie clips, all of which will require exactly the same width, with the center point positioned at the top left corner.

Forum Header

15. The first of the three we are going to tackle is the Forum Header. Its only real function is to show the column names for the Forum View display but it also caps the thread list off nicely. Create a movie clip similar to the following and name it Forum Header

Note that the center point of the movie clip is in the top left corner. This is a necessity due to the method we'll be using to build the Forum View so make sure that this is the case.

Forum Footer

16. The purpose of this clip is to provide a nice bottom to the thread list rather than just cutting off at the end of the last thread. Create a movie clip like the following and name it Forum Footer.

Forum Thread

17. This is the main movie clip that will be attached to our canvas many times to show all of the threads in the forum. For this we'll need the invisible button we built in the previous case study, so go and pinch it from there if you don't fancy creating it from scratch again.

First of all we'll create the background and the lines representing the columns. This is best copied from the Forum Header movie clip as we'll want to be consistent with our column widths.

18. We then need to add some text boxes on top of it to hold the thread information:

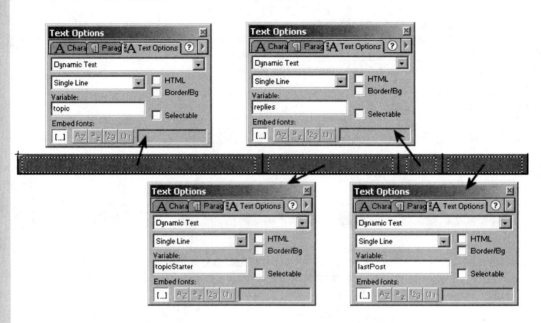

19. Finally we need to add an invisible button that covers the whole thread area. This will allow the user to click on the thread of their choice to view it.

20. ...and we need to add the code for the button too...

```
on (release) {
    _parent._parent.threadID = threadID;
    _parent._parent.topic = topic;
    _parent._parent.viewThread(threadID);
}
```

In this code the `_parent._parent` *section is necessary because this movie clip will be nested inside the* Canvas *movie clip, which in turn is nested inside the* Message Board Panel *movie clip – whose timeline we want to reference.*

So what we're doing here is setting two variables on the timeline of our Message Board Panel movie clip and then calling the `viewThread()` function we set up earlier - cool, huh?

Once all of these movie clips have been created we need to set their Symbol Linkage properties to make sure that they're exported with the movie clip when we publish it.

21. For each of the Forum Header, Forum Footer, and Forum Thread movie clips, right-click and select Linkage. Select the Export this symbol radio button and enter the following Identifiers respectively...

- Forum Header
- Forum Footer
- Forum Thread

22. We can now return to the Section Items layer for the Forum View movie clip and add some scroll buttons. Add the following code to the buttons:

Scroll Up
```
on (release) {
    if (forumCanvas._y < -140) {
        forumCanvas._y += 20;
    }
}
```

Scroll Down
```
on (release) {
    if (forumCanvas._y + forumCanvas._height > 110) {
        forumCanvas._y -= 20;
    }
}
```

This will allow us to scroll the canvas to view threads that are "off the page".

23. Now we come to a real meaty chunk of ActionScript on the Actions layer of the Forum View frame. This ActionScript actually builds the Forum View from the variables that will be passed in from our PHP script.

First we hide the canvas so the user doesn't see the thread list being built:

```
// Hide the forum canvas
forumCanvas._visible = false;
```

24. We then use `attachMovie` to attach an instance of our Forum Header movie clip to the forumCanvas movie clip.

```
// Attach a header MC to the canvas and set title
forumCanvas.attachMovie("Forum Header", "header", 255);
```

25. Since instances attached using `attachMovie` are always added with their center point at position (0,0) in the movie clip we need to keep track of the current height of the canvas and therefore what `_y` value we need to give our next movie clip. We're taking one away from the height of the forum header here to make sure there aren't any gaps when we attach the next movie clip instance.

```
// Set variable to keep track of where to put next
// MC on the canvas
nextY = forumCanvas.header._height - 1;
```

26. We then loop through each of the threads returned from the PHP script, attaching an instance of our Forum Thread movie clip and setting the (x,y) position accordingly.

```
// For each thread returned from PHP script...
for (count=0; count<threadCount; count++) {
    // Attach a thread MC to the canvas
    forumCanvas.attachMovie("Forum Thread", "thread" add
count, count);

    // Set X and Y positions for thread MC
    forumCanvas["thread" add count]._x = 0;
    forumCanvas["thread" add count]._y = nextY;
```

27. Now we take all of the items for this thread and copy them into the instance of Forum Thread we've just created. This will fill in the text boxes and set some variables that aren't visible such as the `threadID`

```
    // Set thread details
    forumCanvas["thread" add count].threadID = this["thread"
➥add count add "ID"];
    forumCanvas["thread" add count].topic = this["thread" add
➥count add "Topic"];
    forumCanvas["thread" add count].topicStarter =
➥this["thread" add count add "TopicStarter"];
    forumCanvas["thread" add count].replies = this["thread"
➥add count add "Replies"];
    forumCanvas["thread" add count].lastPost = this["thread"
➥add count add "LastPost"];
```

28. The final thing we do is to update our `nextY` variable, adding on the height of the newly attached movie clip instance so we know where to put the next instance.

```
// Set next MC to be put just below this on canvas
    nextY += forumCanvas["thread" add count]._height - 1;
}
```

29. Once all of the threads have been processed we add an instance of our Forum Footer movie clip on to the bottom of the thread list.

```
// Attach a footer to the canvas and it's position
forumCanvas.attachMovie("Forum Footer", "footer", count);
forumCanvas.footer._x = nextX;
forumCanvas.footer._y = nextY;
```

30. We can now show the canvas, and we halt the movie clip where it stands.

```
// Show thread canvas
forumCanvas._visible = true;

// Halt movie clip
stop ();
```

31. Moving on to the Load Thread frame, this is the same as the Load Forum frame in all but for the ActionScript on the Actions layer:

```
// Halt the movie clip
stop();
```

Since we've written the function earlier to load the thread for us all we have to do is to stop here.

32. The Thread View frame is very similar to the Forum View frame, and we've already got our threadCanvas movie clip on the Canvas layer.

Before we get to the ActionScript we need to add another button. If you look at the sketches we made earlier, you'll see that we want to add a Post Reply button for this frame with the following ActionScript:

```
on (release) {
    gotoAndPlay ("Post Reply");
}
```

This simply whisks us away to the appropriate section of our movie clip.

33. Before we go anywhere else we need to create the movie clips that will be attached to the threadCanvas to form the post list. Once again we've got three movie clips to create – all once more with the same width and top-left center point.

Thread Header

34. First on the list is the Thread Header movie clip. It's slightly different to the Forum Header because we've only got two columns and there's a text box at the top that will be used to show the thread topic. Again it also caps the post list off nicely. Create a movie clip similar to the following and name it Thread Header.

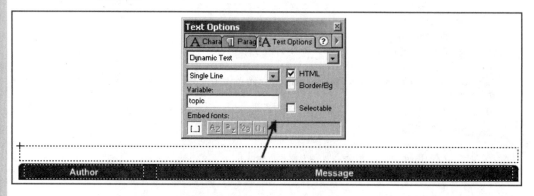

> *Again, note that the center point of the movie clip is in the top left corner. This is a necessity due to the method we'll be using to build the* Thread View *so make sure that this is the case.*

Thread Footer

35. Once again it's aesthetics I have on my mind. The only purpose of this clip is to provide a nice bottom to the post list rather than just cutting off at the end of the last post. Create a movie clip similar to the following and name it Thread Footer.

Forum Post

36. This is the movie clip that we'll be giving the `attachMovie` treatment to, smattering it all over our canvas, thereby showing all the posts in the chosen thread. First we'll create the background and the lines representing the columns. This is best copied from the Thread Header movie clip as we'll want to be consistent with our column widths.

37. We then need to add some text boxes to hold the post information:

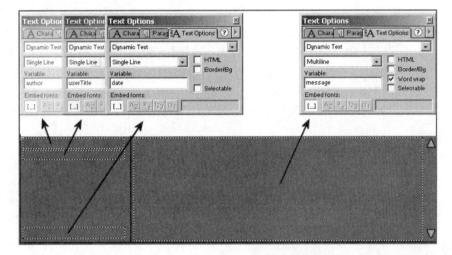

38. Finally we need to add the scroll buttons to allow us to scroll the message:

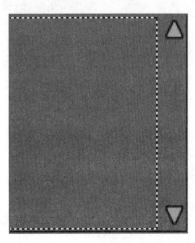

39. Add to that the ActionScript for the buttons:

Scroll Up
```
on (release) {
    message.scroll++;
}
```

Scroll Down
```
on (release) {
    message.scroll—;
}
```

Once all of these movie clips have been created we need to set their Symbol Linkage properties to make sure that they're exported with the movie clip.

For each of the Thread Header, Thread Footer, and Forum Post movie clips, right-click and select Linkage. Select the Export this symbol radio button and enter the following Identifiers...

- Thread Header
- Thread Footer
- Forum post

40. Now we add the ActionScript on the Actions layer. It's basically the same as the previous code and it's pretty well commented, but if you're unsure look back at the Forum View section.

```
// Hide the thread canvas
threadCanvas._visible = false;

// Attach a header MC to the canvas and set title
threadCanvas.attachMovie("Thread Header", "header", 255);
threadCanvas.header.topic = topic;

// Set variable to keep track of where to put next
// MC on the canvas.
nextY = threadCanvas.header._height - 1;

// For each post in thread...
for (count=0; count < postCount; count++) {
    // Attach post MC to canvas
    threadCanvas.attachMovie("Thread Post", "post" add count,
count);

    // Set X and Y positions for post MC
    threadCanvas["Post" add Count]._x = 0;
```

```
        threadCanvas ["Post" add Count]._y = nextY;

        // Set post details
        threadCanvas ["post" add Count].author = this ["post" add
    count add "Author"];
        threadCanvas ["post" add Count].userTitle = this ["post" add
    count add "UserTitle"];
        threadCanvas ["post" add Count].date = "Posted: " add
    this ["post" add count add "Date"];
        threadCanvas ["post" add Count].message = this ["post" add
    count add "Message"];

        // Set next MC to be put just below this one on canvas
        nextY += threadCanvas ["post" add count]._height - 1;
    }

    // Add footer to canvas and set position
    threadCanvas.attachMovie ("Thread Footer", "footer", count);
    threadCanvas.footer._x = 0;
    threadCanvas.footer._Y = nextY;

    // Show thread canvas
    threadCanvas._visible = true;

    // Halt movie clip
    stop ();
```

!! COFFEE BREAK !!

If you're looking for a convenient place to stop and have a rest then this is it. I'm having one anyway!

Finishing Off Our Forum in Flash

We now have just a handful of sections left to do! The first of those is the Post New section. This is where new threads will be created – or at least where we'll get PHP to create the thread. This section is little more than a simple Flash form with a button or two thrown in for good measure.

1. Create the text boxes on the Section Items layer as shown below:

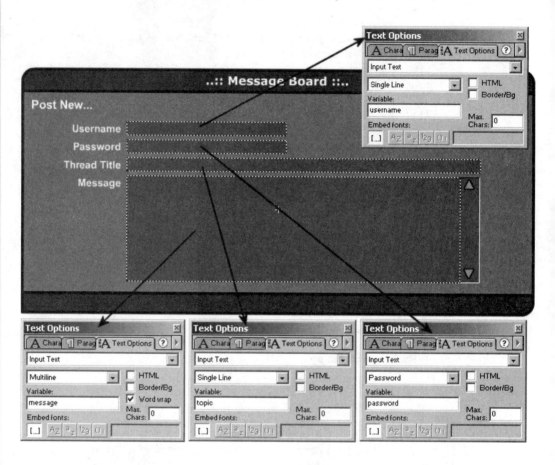

2. Now we need to add the scroll buttons for the message text box, including the obligatory ActionScript:

Scroll Up
```
on (release) {
    message.scroll++;
}
```

Scroll Down
```
on (release) {
    message.scroll—;
}
```

3. We also need to create the buttons on the Button Bar layer...

Submit Thread   Cancel   Not a member? Register...

4. ...and the code for them...

```
Submit Thread
on (release) {
    loadVariables("postnew.php", this, "POST");
    gotoAndPlay ("Load Forum");
}

Cancel
on (release) {
    gotoAndPlay ("Load Forum");
}
```

The script on the Actions layer for this frame is a simple `stop` action.

5. The Post Reply frame is very much the same as the previous one with the exception that the text field for the Thread Title is no longer editable and the button bar has a Submit Reply button instead of a Submit Thread button.

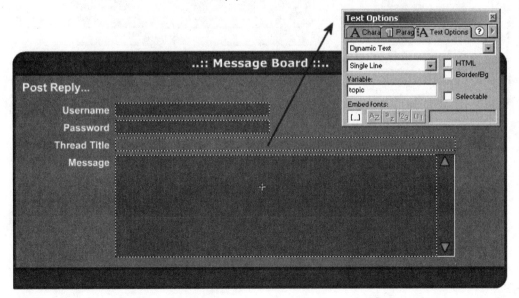

The ActionScript on the buttons is:

```
        Submit Reply
on (release) {
    loadVariables("postreply.php", this, "POST");
    gotoAndPlay ("Load Thread");
}


        Cancel
on (release) {
    gotoAndPlay ("Load Thread");
}
```

6. Moving on to the Register frame, we again have a very simple Flash form here as shown below:

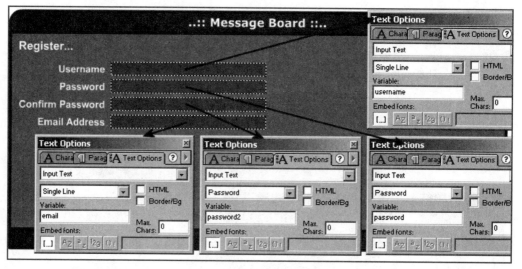

7. The buttons on the Button Bar layer have changed too, now reduced to Register and Cancel functions.

The code for the Register button is:

```
on (release) {
    if (username == "" || password == "" || password2 == ""
|| email == "") {
```

```
            errorMsg = "Passwords do not match";
            gotoAndPlay("Error");
    } else {

        if (password != password2) {
            errorMsg = "Passwords do not match";
            gotoAndPlay("Error");
        } else {
            loadVariables("register.php", this, "POST");
            gotoAndPlay("Load Forum");
        }
    }

}
```

What this code does is check that the required form elements have been filled out. If not then we set an error message and go to the Error frame.

If the required fields are filled out then we check to make sure that both passwords entered are the same. This is a security measure to make sure that users haven't typed in the wrong thing by mistake. Since they're unlikely to make the same mistake twice in a row this is a good way of trapping errors.

If everything is fine then we call the `register.php` script and then return to the Load Forum frame.

The Cancel button just takes you straight back to the Forum View

```
on (release) {
    gotoAndPlay("Load Forum");
}
```

8. The script on the Actions layer is, again, a simple `stop` action.

9. The last frame we need to deal with is the Error frame. This frame is an easy single text box, single button affair.

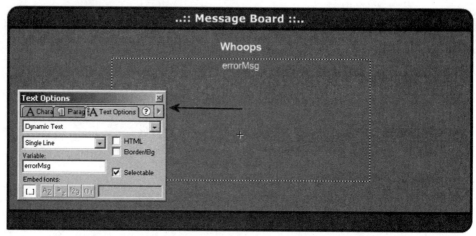

The only thing we really need worry about on this frame is the ActionScript on the Back button on the Button Bar layer. This takes us straight back to the main Forum View – which is a nice familiar place if we're having problems!

```
on (release) {
    gotoAndPlay ("Load Forum);
}
```

One final thing to note! The ActionScript on the Actions layer – another simple `stop` action!

Just before we go we need to drag a copy of our Message Board Panel movie clip from the Library to the main stage and attach the following ActionScript to handle incoming data:

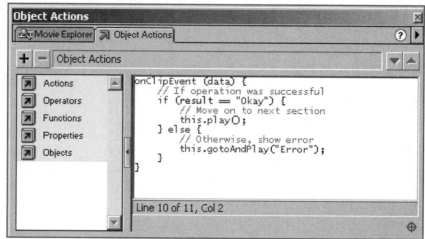

The PHP Scripts

In this section we're going to create the PHP scripts that run behind the fancy Flash front-end.

We've got a whole seven PHP scripts to develop in this section and before we get started we're just going to return to our good habits of taking a breather and spending a minute or two looking at what each one will do.

The scripts we'll be creating are:

`common.php`
> This script will contain configuration information and common functions to be used across the other scripts.

`setup.php`
> Before we can begin playing with our application we'll need to make sure that the database exists (and we are going to have to create it if necessary) and attempt to create all of the tables that our application requires.

`viewforum.php`
> We'll require a separate script to fetch the list of threads in the forum for display in our Flash movie. The sole focus of this script is to perform that operation.

`viewthread.php`
> Similar to `viewforum.php`, this script will fetch all of the posts for a given thread.

`postnew.php`
> When the time comes for the user to post a new thread in our message board we'll need some PHP code to process that data. This script will handle the posting of new threads.

`postreply.php`
> Similarly to the previous, this script will handle the posting of replies to existing threads.

`register.php`
> Last, but by no means least, we need to provide some way for our users to register for access to the message board. This script will take care of registering users.

You'll notice that these scripts are fairly specialized, and if you were thinking that we could have done it all in just two or three scripts then you'd be right. However, writing small, specialized scripts like these means that the script becomes far more legible and easy to understand, and it also means that we don't end up executing any unnecessary code.

On with the show...

The common.php Script

As with the previous multi-script applications, we're going to store all our database details and common functions in a single file and use the include function to add them in to each of the remaining scripts

1. The first part of the script is exactly the same as we've developed before so I'll leave you to your own devices to unpick it – there are comments in there and you can always skip back to the full explanation in **Case Study 1** if you're a bit stuck!

```php
<?
// Database details
$dbHost = "localhost";
$dbUser = "user";
$dbPass = "pass";
$dbName = "phpforflash";


// Common functions
function dbConnect() {
    // Access global variables
    global $dbHost;
    global $dbUser;
    global $dbPass;
    global $dbName;

    // Attempt to connect to database server
    $link = @mysql_connect($dbHost, $dbUser, $dbPass);

    // If connection failed...
    if (!$link) {
        // Inform Flash of error and quit
        fail("Couldn't connect to database server");
    }

    // Attempt to select our database. If failed...
    if (!@mysql_select_db($dbName)) {
        // Inform Flash of error and quit
        fail("Couldn't find database $dbName");
```

```
        }

        return $link;
    }


function fail($errorMsg) {
    // URL-Encode error message
    $errorMsg = urlencode($errorMsg);

    // Output error information and exit
    print "&result=Fail&errormsg=$errorMsg";
    exit;
}
```

2. For the purposes of our message board application we've also added another function to this file – a function to validate a user's username and password against the details in the database. Continue to add to the script you already have here.

```
function auth($username, $password) {
```

You can see from this line that our function is called auth and that we'll be passing the username and password details into it in order to have them validated.

3. Let's perform some simple encryption on the password that's been provided. The reason we need to do this is that we're going to be storing an encrypted version of the password that the user supplies when they sign up, and in order to compare the supplied password with the details in the database we need to encrypt it.

```
    // Encrypt the password
    $crypt = md5($password);
```

The md5 function uses an established algorithm to create what is known as an **md5 hash** and is applied to strings. You can think of this hash as a unique but one-way encrypted version of the original string

4. Once we've got our encrypted password we need to build the query to see if any of the entries in our forumUsers table match the supplied details.

```
    // Build query
    $query = "SELECT userID FROM forumUsers WHERE
        username = '$username' AND password = '$crypt'";
```

continues overleaf

5. We then execute the query and test the return value of the `mysql_query()` function to see if we found a match. If a match was found in the database then the `userID` of the matching row is extracted from the results. If no match was found then we set `$userID` to -1 so that we can detect that the user is not authorised.

```
// Execute the query
$result = mysql_query($query);

// If we found a match...
if (mysql_num_rows($result) == 1) {
    // Extract user ID from the results
    $user = mysql_fetch_array($result);
    $userID = $user['userID'];
} else {
    // Otherwise set username to -1
    $userID = -1;
}
```

6. Finally for the function we return the value of our `$userID` variable to the calling function.

```
// Return user ID
return $userID;
}

?>
```

7. We're also going to add one more function that we can use to check the validity of e-mail addresses. We're going to use a complex **regular expression** for this but fortunately it was the one we dissected in **Chapter 5**.

```
function checkEmail($email)
{
    // Define regular expression
    $regexp = "^[_a-z0-9-]+(\.[_a-z0-9-]+)*@[a-z0-9-]+(\.[a-
z0-9-]+)*(\.[a-z]{2,3})$";

    if (eregi($regexp, $email)) {
        return true;
    }
    else
    {
        return false;
    }
}
```

Basically this function will return `true` if the e-mail appears to be valid and `false` otherwise. We won't use this function until the very last script we develop but it's a worthwhile function having around if ever you need it!

The setup.php Script

Next up we need to build the setup script to create the database and table structure for our application. Again, the script here is very similar in structure to the one we built in the first case study, with the only exception being that we need to create *three* tables instead of just the one.

If the code needs any further explanation then take a look at the dissection of the setup script for **Case Study 1**.

```
<?
// setup.php
// Case Study 3 - Foundation PHP for Flash

// Include config file
include('common.php');

// Attempt to connect to database server
$link = @mysql_connect($dbHost, $dbUser, $dbPass);

// If connection failed...
if (!$link) {
    // Inform user of error and quit
    print "Couldn't connect to database server";
    exit;
}

// Attempt to create database
print "Attempting to create database $dbName <br>\n";
if(!@mysql_create_db($dbName)) {
    // Inform user of error
    print "# Couldn't create database <br>\n";
} else {
    // Inform user of success
    print "# Database created successfully <br>\n";
}

// Attempt to select database
print "Attempting to select database $dbName <br>\n";
if(!@mysql_select_db($dbName)) {
    // Inform user of error and exit
```

continues overleaf

```php
        print "# Couldn't select database <br>\n";
        exit;
    } else {
        // Inform user of success
        print "# Database selected successfully <br>\n";
    }


    print "Attempting to create tables<br>\n";

    // Attempt to create users table
    $query = "CREATE TABLE forumUsers (
            userID INTEGER AUTO_INCREMENT PRIMARY KEY,
            username VARCHAR(20),
            password VARCHAR(40),
            title VARCHAR(30),
            email VARCHAR(255))";

    $result = @mysql_query($query);

    if (!$result) {
        // Inform user of error
        print "# Error creating forumUsers table<br>\n";
        print mysql_error();
    } else {
        // Inform user of euccess
        print "# forumUsers table created<br>\n";
    }

    // Attempt to create threads table
    $query = "CREATE TABLE forumThreads (
            threadID INTEGER AUTO_INCREMENT PRIMARY KEY,
            userID INTEGER,
            topic VARCHAR(100),
            replies INTEGER DEFAULT 0,
            lastPost INTEGER)";

    $result = @mysql_query($query);

    if (!$result) {
        // Inform user of error
        print "# Error creating forumThreads table<br>\n";
        print mysql_error();
    } else {
        // Inform user of euccess
        print "# forumThreads table created<br>\n";
```

```
        }

        // Attempt to create users table
        $query = "CREATE TABLE forumPosts (
                postID INTEGER AUTO_INCREMENT PRIMARY KEY,
                threadID INTEGER,
                userID INTEGER,
                message MEDIUMTEXT,
                posted INTEGER)";

        $result = @mysql_query($query);

        if (!$result) {
            // Inform user of error
            print "# Error creating forumPosts table<br>\n";
            print mysql_error();
        } else {
            // Inform user of euccess
            print "# forumPosts table created<br>\n";
        }

        print "End of setup";

        ?>
```

The viewforum.php Script

Now we're beginning to move on to the more involved PHP scripts. The viewforum.php script will be solely concentrated on fetching all of the thread in the forum for display in Flash.

Now that you've become a regular PHP master you should be able to figure out the bits that we've already met before. To this end I won't go back over things that we've already encountered several times, and I'll provide a brief explanation of what that section of code it doing.

1. As usual we kick off the script by loading in our configuration file, connecting to our database server and selecting the desired database for our application.

    ```
    <?

    // Include config file
    include('common.php');
    ```

```
// Connect to database
$link = dbConnect();
```

2. We then build the query to fetch all of the threads in our forum. Notice that we're using an ORDER BY clause to make sure that newer threads are returned first.

```
// Build query to fetch forum
$query = "SELECT * FROM forumThreads ORDER BY lastPost
DESC";
```

3. We next attempt to execute our query, outputting an error message and quitting if anything goes wrong.

```
// Execute query
$result = mysql_query($query);

// If query failed...
if (!$result) {
    // Inform Flash of error and quit
    fail("Couldn't list threads from database");
}
```

If everything goes well then we fetch the number of threads in the forum using the mysql_num_rows function. If you remember from **Chapter 9** this function will return the number of results in a given resultset following the execution of a SELECT command.

```
// Find out how many threads in this forum
$threadCount = mysql_num_rows($result);
```

4. We then add the thread count as our first variable to be sent back to Flash. Notice that we're only adding this to a variable at the moment – we'll be adding yet more to it before we finally output it!

```
// Setup our variable to hold output
$output = "&threadCount=$threadCount";
```

5. We then start up a for loop to process each of the threads returned by the SELECT command.

```
// For each thread returned...
for ($count = 0; $count < $threadCount; $count++)
{
```

6. In this loop we fetch the next thread from the MySQL `resultset` into an array using the `mysql_fetch_array` function.

We the use this array to set some meaningfully named variables. This includes removing the slashes from any elements that may require it, and using the `strftime` function to convert the Unix timestamp that represents the time and date on which the thread was created.

```
// Extract post details from database
$thread = mysql_fetch_array($result);

$threadID = $thread['threadID'];
$userID = $thread['userID'];
$topic = stripslashes($thread['topic']);
$replies = $thread['replies'];
$lastPost = strftime("%d/%m/%y %H:%M",
➡$thread['lastPost']);
```

7. This next section may look a little strange but it's really just another query being executed, this time to fetch the username of the author of the current thread. We need a separate query to do this because we're only storing the `userID` of the user in the `forumThreads` table, and we use that value to `SELECT` the correct user in the `forumUsers` table.

```
// Build and execute query to fetch username of the
// user who created this thread
$query = "SELECT username FROM forumUsers WHERE userID =
$userID";
$result2 = @mysql_query($query);

// Extract user information from results...
$user = @mysql_fetch_array($result2);
$username = $user['username'];
```

8. The last thing we need to do for each thread is to add the details to our `$output` variable, ready to go back to our Flash movie. If you remember when we were creating the ActionScript for the Forum View frame of the Flash movie we discussed what format the output of our script would take so that we could handle the information effectively in Flash. You should be able to see that the code below matches that format!

```
// Add thread details to output
$output .= "&thread" . $count . "ID=" . $threadID;
$output .= "&thread" . $count . "Topic=" .
➡urlencode($topic);
$output .= "&thread" . $count . "TopicStarter=" .
```

continues overleaf

```
➥urlencode($username);
    $output .= "&thread" . $count . "Replies=" . $replies;
    $output .= "&thread" . $count . "LastPost=" . $lastPost;
}
```

9. Finally for this script we send the output we've been storing up back to Flash. In addition to this we add a variable to let Flash know that the operation was a success and then close the link to the MySQL server.

```
// Output all threads in one go
echo $output;

// Inform Flash of success
print "&result=Okay";

// Close link to database server
mysql_close($link);

?>
```

The viewthread.php Script

It's now time to build the script that will fetch all of the posts for a specified thread. This is the script that will be called when the user clicks on one of the threads in the Forum View.

Again we'll have met a lot of this code before so explanations may be a little thin on the ground in places. If you're unsure of anything then flip back to the relevant chapter in the book!

1. As usual we kick off the script by loading in our configuration file and then connecting to our database server and selecting the desired database for out application. This should be old hat to you by now and you'll be seeing this little snippet of code in your sleep!

```
<?

// Include config file
include('common.php');

// Connect to database
$link = dbConnect();
```

2. We then need to build the query to pull all of the posts for the chosen thread (as identified by the `$threadID` variable that is passed from our Flash movie) and return them to Flash.

```
// Build query to fetch thread
$query = "SELECT * FROM forumPosts WHERE threadID =
$threadID ORDER BY posted ASC";
```

3. We then attempt to execute our query as usual, outputting an error message and quitting if anything goes wrong.

```
// Execute query
$result = @mysql_query($query);

// If query failed...
if (!$result) {
    // Inform Flash of error and quit
    fail("Couldn't fetch posts from database");
}
```

4. If everything goes well then we fetch the number of posts in the thread using the `mysql_num_rows` function.

```
// Find out how many posts in this thread
$postCount = @mysql_num_rows($result);
```

5. We then add our post count as our first variable to be sent back to Flash.

```
// Setup our variable to hold output
$output = "&postCount=$postCount";
```

6. Next we start up a `for` loop to process each of the posts returned by the `SELECT` command.

```
// For each post returned...
for ($count = 0; $count < $postCount; $count++) {
```

7. The first thing we need to do in this loop is to fetch the next post from the MySQL `resultset` into an array using the `mysql_fetch_array` function.

```
// Extract post details from database
$post = mysql_fetch_array($result);

$userID = $post['userID'];
$message = stripslashes($post['message']);
$posted = strftime("%d/%m/%y %H:%M", $post['posted']);
```

Once more we set the relevant variables. This includes removing the slashes from any elements that may require it, and using the `strftime` function to convert the Unix timestamp.

8. **Y**ou should recognize this little piece of code from the previous script. This is fetching the details of the user who created the post, using the $userID stores in with the current post in the forumPosts forum.

```
// Build and execute query to fetch username and
// title  of the author of this post
$query = "SELECT username, title FROM forumUsers WHERE
➥userID = $userID";
$result2 = @mysql_query($query);

// Extract user information from results
$user = @mysql_fetch_array($result2);
$username = $user['username'];
$userTitle = $user['title'];
```

9. Rounding off each post we need to add the details to our $output variable, ready to go back to our Flash movie.

```
// Add post details to output
$output .= "&post" . $count . "Author=" .
➥urlencode($username);
$output .= "&post" . $count . "Date=" .
➥urlencode($posted);
$output .= "&post" . $count . "UserTitle=" .
➥urlencode($userTitle);
$output .= "&post" . $count . "Message=" .
➥urlencode($message);
}
```

10. Finally send the output we've been storing up back to Flash. In addition to this we add a variable to let Flash know that the operation was a success and then close the link to the MySQL server.

```
// Output all posts in one go
echo $output;

// Inform Flash of success
print "&result=Okay";

// Close link to database server
mysql_close($link);

?>
```

The postnew.php Script

Having sorted the scripts that'll handle the viewing aspects of the application it's time to turn our attention to those that'll be inserting and manipulating the table data.

The first of these to fall under the microscope is the `postnew.php` script. This script will work hand in hand with the Post New section of our Flash movie to facilitate the creation of new threads on the message board.

1. Hands up all those who recognise this next bit of code! That'll be everyone then! Let's move on shall we...

    ```php
    <?

    // Include config file
    include('common.php');

    // Connect to database
    $link = dbConnect();
    ```

    > *Just think if we hadn't created the* `common.php` *file how many times you'd have typed out all that database connectivity stuff!*

2. Once we've connected to the database we can use the `auth` function that we wrote way back when we were developing the `common.php` file to verify that the details provided from the Flash movie match those of a registered user.

    ```php
    // Attempt to authorize user with database
    $userID = auth($username, $password);
    ```

    > *Just to recap, if this function finds a match in the database for the supplied details then the* `userID` *of the matching user is returned. If no match is found then the function will return a value of -1...*

3. We can check for this value to determine whether or not user authentication was successful. If no match was found for the details supplied then we output our error message to Flash and quit.

```
// If authorisation failed...
if ($userID == -1) {
    // Inform Flash and quit
    fail("Invalid username and/or password");
}
```

4. Next we fetch the current time as a Unix timestamp, as used in our queries to provide the date and time at which the new thread and post were created.

```
// Fetch the current time
$posted = time();
```

5. We then set about building the first of two queries necessary in this script. This particular query will perform the task of creating a new thread.

```
// Build query to insert new thread
$query = "INSERT INTO forumThreads (userID, topic, lastPost)
VALUES ($userID, '$topic', $posted)";
```

We then attempt to execute this query. If this operation fails then the thread could not be inserted. We inform Flash of this error and quit.

```
// Attempt to execute query
if(!mysql_query($query)) {
    fail("Error inserting thread");
}
```

6. We now come to a MySQL related function we haven't met before (mainly because it didn't really fit in anywhere else). The mysql_insert_id function is a clever little bean indeed. It'll return the last integer generated for a column specified as AUTO_INCREMENT using the current database connection.

```
// Fetch the threadID of the new thread
$threadID = mysql_insert_id();
```

In our case the threadID column of the forumThreads table is designated as AUTO_INCREMENT, and we use mysql_insert_id after successfully inserting the new thread (as just described) so that we can use the $threadID when adding the new post to go with the new thread (which we'll sort out next).

7. It's now time to build our query to insert the new post into the forumPosts table. We use the $threadID that we captured using mysql_insert_id in the previous section to associate this new post with the newly created thread.

```
// Build query to insert new post
$query = "INSERT INTO forumPosts (threadID, userID, message,
```

```
posted) VALUES ($threadID, $userID, '$message', $posted)";
```

8. We then attempt to execute this query. If this operation fails then the post could not be inserted, and we inform Flash of this error and quit.

```
// Attempt to execute query
if(!mysql_query($query)) {
    fail("Error inserting post");
}
```

9. To round off the script we inform Flash of our success and close the link to the MySQL database.

```
// Inform Flash of success
print "&result=Okay";

// Close link to database server
mysql_close($link);

?>
```

> *Well, it's five down and two to go. Some scripts are probably becoming old hat to you already, but doesn't that show just how much you've picked up in a relatively short space of time!*

The postreply.php Script

This script will handle all of the requests to add a reply to an existing thread. It is very similar in operation to the postnew.php function because of the nature of what they both do – add posts to the forum! The main difference is that this script updates a row in the forumThreads table rather than creating a new one since, if we're replying to a thread, it must already exist!

1. We start with our old friends.

```
<?

// Include config file
include('common.php');

// Connect to database
$link = dbConnect();
```

continues overleaf

```
// Attempt to authorise user with database
$userID = auth($username, $password);

// If authorisation failed...
if ($userID == -1) {
    // Inform Flash and quit
    fail("Invalid username and/or password");
}
```

Once we've connected to the database we again use the auth function to verify that the details provided from the Flash movie match those of a registered user. If not we inform Flash of the error and quit!

2. Next we fetch the current time as a Unix timestamp.

```
// Fetch the current time
$posted = time();
```

3. We then build and execute the query to insert the new post into the forumPosts table, outputting error information if necessary. This is exactly the same as the code from the previous script, only this time the $threadID variable is provided by the Flash movie.

```
// Build and execute query to insert new post
$query = "INSERT INTO forumPosts (threadID, userID, message,
posted) VALUES($threadID, $userID, '$message', $posted)";

if(!mysql_query($query)) {
    fail("Error inserting thread");
}
```

4. Then we build and execute the query to update the details of the thread in forumThreads specified by $threadID. Basically we're adding one to the number of replies for the thread and updating the lastPost timestamp.

```
// Build and execute query to update reply count for thread
$query = "UPDATE forumThreads SET replies = replies + 1,
lastPost = $posted WHERE threadID = $threadID";

if(!mysql_query($query)) {
    fail("Error inserting thread");
}
```

5. To round off the script we inform Flash of our success and close the link to the MySQL database.

```
// Inform Flash of success
print "&result=Okay";

// Close link to database server
mysql_close($link);

?>
```

Just the one left to go...!

The register.php Script

```
<?

// Include config file
include('common.php');

// Connect to database
$link = dbConnect();
```

1. Our aim with this next piece of script is to set up a title that will be given to new users who sign up. A user's title appears under their name in the Thread View and is generally used as an indication of their status on the board. For our purposes we're just going to use a single title for all users aside from the administrator account we created earlier, so you can change this to whatever takes your fancy!

```
// Set up title for new users
$title = "Code Junkie";
```

Back when we were developing the auth function in the common.php script we said that we would be storing the password in the database in encrypted form. We chose (well, okay, I chose) to go with the md5 hash function as it's simple to use and provides good one-way encryption.

Thus, before we can go any further we'll need to encrypt the password supplied to the script form the Flash movie.

```
// Encrypt password
$crypt = md5($password);
```

Next we check to make sure that the e-mail address supplied is a valid one using our `checkEmail` function from `common.php`.

```
// If email is invalid...
if (!checkEmail($email)) {
    // Output error to Flash and quit
    fail("Invalid email address");
}
```

2. We then need to make sure that the specified username doesn't already exist in the `forumUsers` table. If it does then we report the error back to the Flash end and quit!

```
// Build query to search for duplicate usernames
$query = "SELECT * FROM forumUsers WHERE
username='$username'";

if(!mysql_query($query)) {
    fail("Couldn't search database for duplicates");
}

// If a match was found...
if (mysql_num_rows($query) != 0) {
    // Inform Flash of error and quit!
    fail("Username $username already registered");
}
```

3. It is then time to build the query to insert the new user into the `forumUsers` table. Notice that we're using `$crypt` instead of `$password` so that we store the encrypted version of the original password and that, because it's still a string, we need the single quotes around it!

```
// Build query to add user
$query = "INSERT INTO forumUsers (username, password, title,
email) VALUES ('$username', '$crypt', '$title', '$email')";

if(!mysql_query($query)) {
    fail("Username $username already exists");
}
```

4. Finally we report our success to Flash and close the connection to the database server.

```
// Inform Flash of success
print "&result=Okay";
```

```
// Close link to database server
mysql_close($link);

?>
```

That's it – all of the scripts are finished, and you should now be able to upload and run them.

So, that's about everything we should be able to muster from the previous chapters. How does it feel to be nifty at PHP? Actually, I've got to tell ya, I know exactly how it feels: pretty darned good! So let's have a quick resume of what we did in that final case study:

- We were very sensible and planned exactly what we were going to do before filthying up the keyboard

- We considered exactly which technologies would help us out – namely MySQL and Flash – and which parts of those technologies would be the most appropriate

- We constructed all of the interface elements in Flash, paying particular attention to making the whole thing user friendly

- We rattled through the seven PHP scripts that provide the functionality to the whole thing

What we have developed there (and throughout this book) is the classic pattern for developing a PHP-powered Flash application; it's planning, followed by framework, and finally the electricity behind the whole thing.

I hope that this crescendo is going to inspire you to go off and make waves in the PHP world!

A Installing PHP and MySQL

Installation: It's Easy PHPeasy!

This is a guide to installing the software you will need to tackle the tutorials in this book. Obviously there can be teething problems when it comes to installing any type of software and the chances of anticipating every one of them are pretty slim. However, this installation section will mop up the vast majority of installation spills. For further information, check out the online documentation that comes with your software, and browse the various web sites and forums (listed in the resources section at the back of this book). Check also for installation updates and troubleshooters on our site www.phpforflash.com.

Yes, I know you're just going to dive in anyway and hope for the best – and let's face it, that's usually the fruitful option – but it's handy to be aware in case things go pear-shaped.

*There are also some set-up tools listed in **Appendix C**, and these tools can even install PHP, MySQL and Apache for you!*

Installing Apache & PHP for Windows

To some, the thought of installing PHP may seem a daunting task. Now, add to that the perceived complexities of an Apache web server and you can almost smell the fear.

And do you know what I'm going to say now? Exactly what you want me to. It's not so hard. Think of it. If you're the sort of person that can sift through a bunch of computer titles and opt for a classy book on PHP, then the task of installing this stuff is just peanuts. To really nail it down, we'll cover the entire process of installing both Apache and PHP on Windows step by step.

Users of the Windows platform may be surprised to discover that both Apache and PHP are free for both commercial and non-commercial use. This fact alone has contributed to the success of both Apache and PHP – not to mention the functionality offered by both products. It's a winning combination!

Before you can begin the installation you need to make sure you have the latest versions of the software. You can download these directly from the developer's web sites, shown below:

Downloading Apache

http://httpd.apache.org/dist/httpd/binaries/win32/

The current version at the time of writing is 1.3.20. Version 2.0.16 is due to be released shortly.

We'll be using 1.3.20 as it's been around for some time now and has proven stability. Download the Win32 binary version of the software; this is a windows specific version, providing amongst other things a nice friendly installation wizard.

Downloading PHP

http://www.php.net/downloads.php

The current version at the time of writing is 4.0.6, and with each new release comes improvements and of course the inevitable bug fixes. For this reason it's important to keep your PHP installations up to date where possible. Plus it's free so there's no reason not to get the latest one!

There are two types of installation files available from the PHP web site:

PHP 4.0.6 zip package [4,859Kb] 23 June 2001
(CGI binary plus server API versions for Apache, AOLserver, ISAPI and NSAPI. MySQL support built-in, many extensions included, packaged as zip)

PHP 4.0.6 installer [755Kb] - 23 June 2001
(CGI only, MySQL support built-in, packaged as Windows installer to install and configure PHP, and automatically configure IIS, PWS and Xitami, with manual configuration for other servers. N.B. no external extensions included)

For the purposes of this chapter we'll be getting our hands a little bit dirty and using the zip package and installing PHP manually. This isn't nearly as scary as it sounds and it means we become more familiar with how PHP is organised than we would with a point-and-click installer - which can only be a good thing!

Assuming that you downloaded both Apache and PHP installation files from their respective sites successfully we're ready to begin our installation.

Installing Apache Web Server for Windows

1. To begin, double click the installation file to start the Installation wizard.

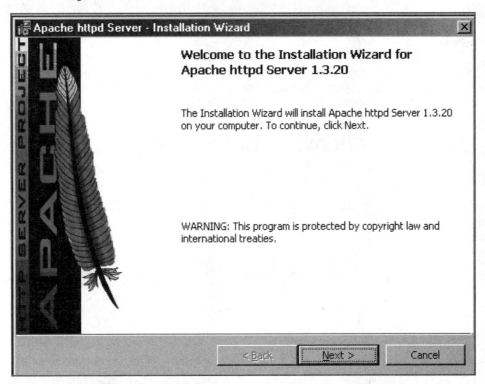

The image above shows the Apache Installation wizard, displaying the version of Apache we're about to get friendly with. Click Next to continue with the installation.

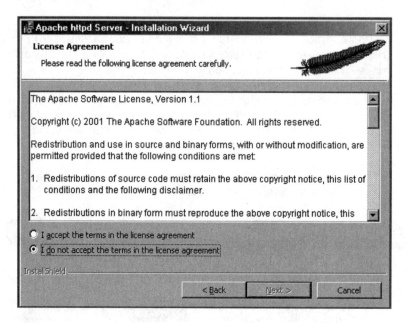

2. Next you'll see the Apache License Agreement screen. Read through the agreement before you accept. Because Apache is freely available the restrictions of the agreement apply mainly to those wanting to re-distribute the Apache software but as with all software it's important to read the terms and conditions of use.

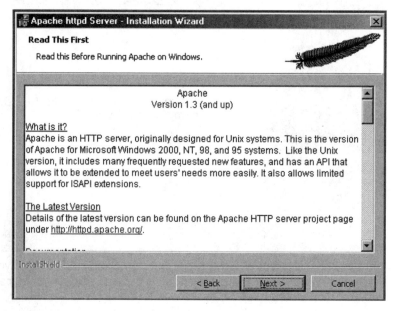

3.   You should pay close attention to this screen especially if you intend to use your Apache server as a production web server.

The Windows version of Apache is not considered by its developers to be a production-ready product. Firstly, the code has not been optimized for performance, and secondly there are a few remaining security issues, however for development purposes it's fine.

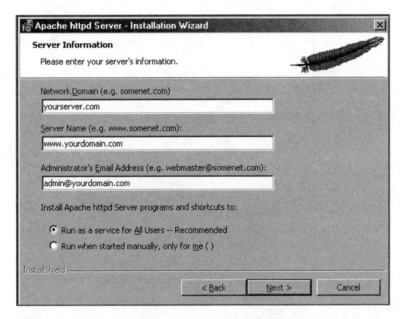

4.   OK, that's the initial froth out of the way – here's the interesting bit of the installation. The image above shows the Server Information screen. This is where you'll configure your web server.

Replace the contents of the text boxes with your settings, your server name, your domain and so on.

> We use the `mail` function in PHP in **Chapter 3**, so be sure to enter your proper mail address.

5.   The final part of the Server Information screen allows you to install the server icons and start-up options for all users, either on a shared system or simply for the current user. If you select the Run as a service for All Users on an NT or Windows 2000 system the Apache server runs as a service in the background and you don't need to worry about starting the server before you can use it.

If you are using Windows 95/98/ME you can select either of the options – however Apache will not run as a service and will need to be started manually. You can replicate the functionality offered by running the web server as a service by adding the `apache.exe` to your start-up menu, that way it will start every time you start your computer.

6. Click Next and you'll be presented with the screen below:

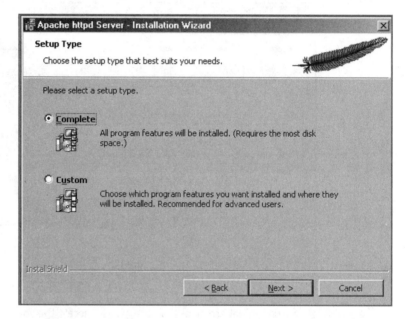

On the previous screen you provided all the information the Apache installer requires to complete a successful installation. The above screen displays the Setup Type options, and unless you want remove the Apache documentation I recommend you select the Complete option.

7. Click Next to select where your web server will be installed. Note that by default it will be installed to `C:\Program Files\Apache Group\`. It's as good a place as any and I recommend you use the default path where possible as it will make troubleshooting easier if something does go wrong at a later date.

8. Click Install and the installer will go off and do its worryingly will-it-won't-it thing for a moment. When it's stopped all its toil, click Finished. Well done! Your first Apache Web Server install is complete. That's all there is to it, contrary to popular belief I'm sure you'll agree that it was easy.

9. Now for the acid test: Does our web server actually work?

Open a browser window and type `http://localhost` into the address field. `localhost` is a way of referring to the local machine – in this case our Apache web server.

If all went well you'll see the Apache test page in your browser:

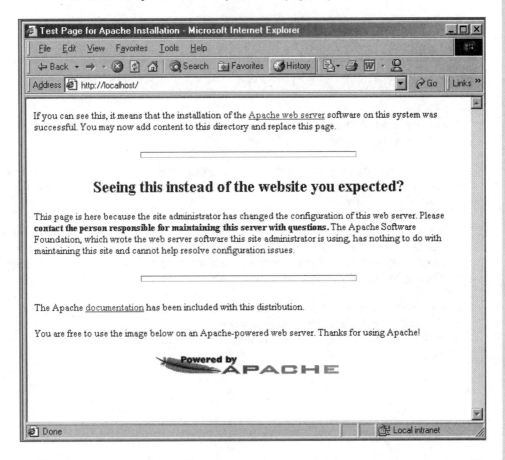

10. If your browser looks like the one above, perform one final, crucial step: Sit back, put your hands behind your head and smile smugly. Your Apache install was completely successful.

Troubleshooting Tips

If you don't see the Apache test page then you need to check that your web server is running. When running Apache **not as a service** you'll see it running on your Windows task bar (see image below).

It's important to remember that all modifications to the conf file require a restart of the web server.

If you don't see Apache running in your task bar, you can start it from the Start >> Programs Menu >> Apache httpd Server.

It's worth noting that if you start the server manually the DOS command line window will remain on screen while the web server is running, please don't sit waiting for the DOS window to vanish: it won't.

If you installed Apache on WindowsNT\2000 as a **service** then check that the Apache service is running in Control Panel > Services (NT) Control Panel > Administration > Services(Windows2000). If the service is not running start the service and then try connecting to localhost in your browser again.

If you're still having problems with your web server you'll find lots of support information on the Apache website at http://www.apache.org. And if you were wondering, yes we all think that's going to be us, sulkily traipsing off to the support site when it hasn't worked. Don't worry! You'll be fine...

Installing PHP on Apache for Windows

As we've already successfully completed the Apache web server installation your confidence levels should be sky high right now, so while we're on a roll let's dive straight into installing PHP.

1. Double click the PHP4 installation file we downloaded earlier; you'll need Winzip or something similar to extract the files. For ease of use we'll extract them to `c:\php`.

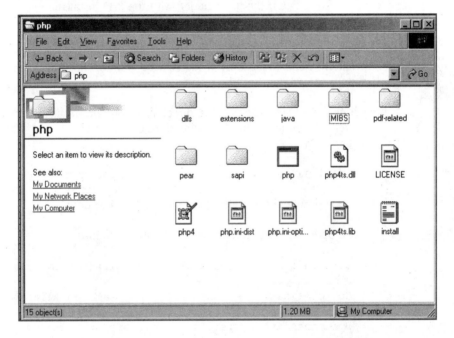

2. If all went well the contents of c:\php should look something like the image above.

3. Now, I don't know about you, but I feel that when you start messing about with the files themselves, you're crossing a definite boundary. After all, one can get very used to double-clicking stuff and having it all unpack before our very eyes. Wouldn't it be nice if suitcases had that facility?

   Anyway, I digress. We are going to have to sort our own underwear and put them in the right drawers when it comes to PHP. But that's no need to get jumpy. It's really no big deal.

4. First up we need to rename the file `php.ini.dist` to `php.ini` and drag it over to our main windows directory (it'll be called C:\WINDOWS or C:\WINNT for NT based systems.).

5. Now, copy the files `mscvrt.dll` and `php4ts.dll` to your Windows system directory – for example C:\WINDOWS\SYSTEM or C:\WINNT\SYSTEM32 for NT based systems.

The file `mscvrt.dll` is used by many Windows applications and therefore may already exist in your system directory, if this is the case only copy the file over the existing one if the file included with the PHP installation is newer than the existing one. If in doubt, always leave the existing one.

6. OK, we're almost there, so far we've installed the Apache web server and PHP4. What we need to do now is tell Apache that we have installed PHP on our system and where it can be found.

For this we need to go to the directory where we installed the Apache web server C:\Program Files\Apache Group\apache\conf and open the file `httpd.conf`.

We need to modify this file. I know, I know, it's another threshold we're passing, but it's only one *little* change, and it is *absolutely necessary*. Moreover, you can use any simple old text editor such as **Notepad** to do it.

Once open we need to find the section shown below:

```
# ScriptAlias: This controls which directories contain
server scripts.
# ScriptAliases are essentially the same as Aliases, except
that
# documents in the realname directory are treated as
applications and
# run by the server when requested rather than as documents
sent to the client.
# The same rules about trailing "/" apply to ScriptAlias
directives as to
# Alias.
```

7. At the end of the section shown above we need to add the following lines:

```
ScriptAlias /cgi-bin/ "C:/Program Files/Apache
Group/apache/cgi-bin/"
ScriptAlias /php/ "C:/php/"
```

The paths in quotes should represent the paths where you installed Apache and PHP. This may be different to that shown above depending on where you installed the applications.

> Note the use of forward slashes "/" where normally in windows you would use back slashes "\" – this stems back to Apaches UNIX roots.

8. Now find the section shown below:

```
# AddType allows you to tweak mime.types without actually
editing it, or to
# make certain files to be certain types.
#
# For example, the PHP 3.x module (not part of the Apache
distribution - see
# http://www.php.net) will typically use:
#
#AddType application/x-httpd-php3 .php3
#AddType application/x-httpd-php3-source .phps
```

At the end of the section shown above we need to add the following lines:

```
AddType application/x-httpd-php .php
AddType application/x-httpd-php .php4
```

This tells apache what file extensions to treat as PHP files in this case anything that ends in .php or .php4.

9. Now find the section shown below:

```
# Action lets you define media types that will execute a
script whenever
# a matching file is called. This eliminates the need for
repeated URL
# pathnames for oft-used CGI file processors.
# Format: Action media/type /cgi-script/location
# Format: Action handler-name /cgi-script/location
```

At the end of this lot we need to add the following line:

```
Action application/x-httpd-php /php/php.exe
```

10. OK, let's recap on what we've achieved so far. By modifying the `httpd.conf` file we've told Apache about our PHP installation, we've also now told Apache what file extensions to treat as PHP files.

11. It's now time to test our installation. If Apache is already running manually or as a service you need to stop it and then restart it for the modifications we've just made to take effect.

    We need a simple PHP script to test our installation. Feel those nerves jangling! Below is a sample script, this is about as simple as PHP scripts get.

12. Create a new file in your text editor and type the following into the file.

    ```
    <? phpinfo(); ?>
    ```

13. Save this file as `phpinfo.php` into the root directory of our web server. If you followed the installation instructions to the letter this will be C:\Program Files\Apache Group\apache\htdocs.

14. Open a web browser window and type the following into the address field.

    ```
    http://localhost/phpinfo.php
    ```

    The image below shows the results of running our `phpinfo.php` script.

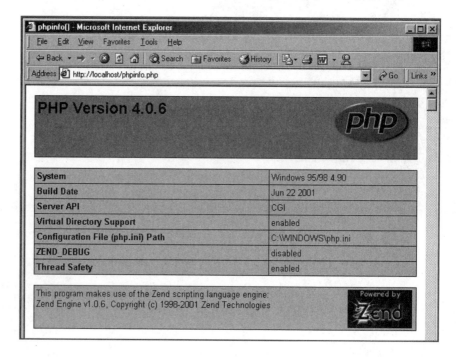

15. If your browser window looks like the one shown then you're onto a winner. Assume the position of self-satisfaction.

> Note how the `localhost` in the address just replaces the long file path to your web root.

Troubleshooting

If your installation failed, here's couple of things to try:

Check that all modifications made to the `httpd.conf` file use the forward slash syntax instead of the normal backslash:

```
ScriptAlias /cgi-bin/ " C:/Program Files/Apache/Apache
Group/Apache/cgi-bin "
```

Ensure that you restarted the web server after making changes to the configuration file. Changes to the configuration only take effect when you restart the web server.

If you're still having problems you can get support from the developer's web sites:

- Apache – www.apache.org

- PHP – www.php.net

And also don't underestimate the usefulness of the supplied documentation and installation READMEs, or of our own support forums.

Installing Apache & PHP for UNIX

In this section we'll cover installing the Apache web server and PHP on a UNIX operating system.

I'll be using LINUX for the installation, but for most flavors of UNIX the installation process is identical. Only the installation file is operating system specific so Solaris, HPUX and IRIX users should feel equally at home.

We'll start by installing Apache, as a UNIX user you should be familiar with the Apache web server. In the UNIX world it has legendary status, beating off many of its commercial rivals to sit at the top of the web server tree of popularity.

Before we can begin the installation we need to make sure we have the latest versions of the software. The best way to do this is to visit the developer's site and start downloading.

Downloading Apache

http://httpd.apache.org/dist/httpd/binaries/
The current version at the time of writing is 1.3.20. Version 2.0.16 is currently in beta testing and will be released shortly.

We'll be using 1.3.20 as it's been around for some time now and has proven stability.

If you visit the URL shown above you'll be presented with a list of folders containing Apache Web Server installation files for almost every operating system known to man. Select the relevant one for your OS.

The Installation

1. Once we've downloaded the file we need to copy it into the directory where we want to install the software. We do this using the command below.

   ```
   cp apache_1.3.20.tar.gz /usr/local
   ```

2. Now we need to change directory to where we copied our installation file.

   ```
   cd /usr/local/
   ```

   You'll notice that the file we downloaded has the .gz extension this means that the file has been zipped up (compressed). Before we can use this file we need to uncompress the file using the command below.

   ```
   gunzip apache_1.3.20.tar.gz
   ```

3. Now we have the unzipped file `apache_1.3.20.tar` (an archive file) we need to untar it, expanding it to its original structure:

```
tar -xvf apache_1.3.20.tar
```

Your screen will be filled with the contents of the archive file as it's unarchived, and it should only take a moment to complete.

4. We now have the Apache web server directory structure we need for the rest of the installation. We first need to change directory to the parent directory that the archive created.

```
cd apache_1.3.20
```

5. From here we can begin to build our installation using the command below.

```
./configure --prefix=/usr/local/apache_1.3.20 --enable-
module=so
```

> Note: If your apache_1.3.20 directory resides elsewhere then this should be reflected in the command above.

6. Your system will then start the configure script, checking the configuration and creating the **make** files needed for the installation. During this process your screen will fill with output from the configure script. After a tense moment or two you'll be returned to the prompt. Hey, trust me!

7. We now need to run the make files created by the configure script.

```
make
```

This process also creates a substantial amount of output to the screen but a moment or two later when the process is complete you'll be returned to the prompt.

8. To complete the installation process we need to type `make install` at the prompt.

```
make install
```

This does pretty much what it says – it actually installs the Apache web server from the files we have created with the commands used earlier.

As with the previous commands, it takes a few moments to complete the installation, you will see the install progressing via the screen output and on completion you'll be returned once again to the prompt.

9. Before we can use our web server we need to make a few changes to the configuration. For this we need to edit the `httpd.conf` file, which is located in the `conf` directory. If you followed the install to the letter, your path to the `httpd.conf` is shown below.

   `/usr/local/apache_1.3.20/conf/`

   Open the `httpd.conf` file in your text editor of choice.

   We need to find the `ServerAdmin` setting in the file and change the e-mail address to your e-mail address.

   `# ServerAdmin you@youraddress.address`

10. Next we need to find the `ServerName` line of the file

    `# ServerName new.host.name`

    We'll change the value of the server name to `localhost`. Once you've made these changes, save the file and it's time to test our installation!

11. Fortunately our Apache install comes complete with a couple of utilities for starting and stopping our web server. To start the web server ensure you're in the Apache installation directory

    `/usr/local/apache_1.3.20`

12. At the command prompt type the following:

    `./bin/apachectl start`

    If all is well you'll see a message in the output to screen that reads

    `httpd started`

13. To stop the web server simply type:

    `./bin/apachectl stop`

14. To test our installation, we must firstly make sure the web server has been started. We then need to open a web browser to connect to our web server.

In the address field of the web browser we need to type the following:

`httpd://localhost`

...where `localhost` refers to the `ServerName` we set in the `httpd.conf` file earlier.

If all is well then you'll be presented with the Apache test page, an example of which is shown below. And that, my dear friends, is your lot.

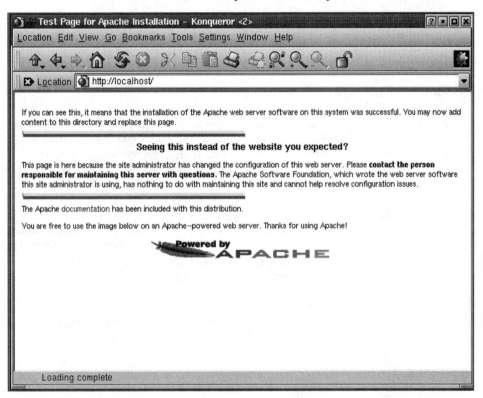

Installing PHP on UNIX

Installing PHP4 on UNIX contrary to popular belief isn't difficult at all. I mean to say, we've just installed the Apache web server without any problems so installing PHP should be a walk in the park!

There are three ways of installing PHP4 on Apache for UNIX. Details of each method – along with the pros and cons – are listed below.

CGI-Binary

This option is not advised for UNIX users, although one of the most popular methods for Windows users, running PHP in this way is a drain on server memory and CPU resources. The CGI-binary method brings with it poor server performance, hence the reason we will not be covering this installation method here.

Static Module

Installing PHP in this manner keeps resource usage to a minimum; PHP appears as just another Apache module keeping performance to a maximum. The downside of installing PHP as a static module is that if you wish to add additional PHP functionality such as MySQL support you will have to recompile both PHP and the Apache web server. It's not the end of the world but it's not something you'd want to do everyday, a little forward planning will eliminate the need to do this very often.

Dynamic Module

This is the best method of installing PHP and it's the method we'll be using in this chapter. The dynamic method has all the pluses of the static module with one additional feature. Because the module is dynamic, when you change the configuration of PHP you need only recompile PHP, you no longer need to recompile Apache, a restart of the web server is all that's required.

The latest version of PHP for your operating system can be downloaded from the developers web site.

Downloading PHP

PHP is available from – http://www.php.net/downloads.php

The current version at the time of writing is 4.0.6, with each new release comes improved stability and of course the inevitable bug fixes, for this reason it's important to keep your PHP installations up to date where possible.

You need to download the full source version of PHP – the largest of the available downloads – which include the entire source code plus extensions.

Starting Installation

Assuming you have downloaded the appropriate installation file we'll begin the installation.

1. We'll start by copying the installation file to the directory we want to install the software, to keep things simple we'll use /usr/local

   ```
   cp php-4.0.6.tar.gz /usr/local/
   ```

2. As with the Apache file, our PHP installation file is in compressed format (.gz). Before we can uncompress the file we first of all move to the directory where we copied the file.

   ```
   cd /usr/local
   ```

3. Then we use the gunzip command to uncompress the file.

   ```
   gunzip php-4.0.6.tar.gz
   ```

4. We now have an archive file (.tar), we'll use the command below to unarchive the file.

   ```
   tar -xvf php-4.0.6.tar
   ```

   Following the above command, the contents of the archive will be extracted; this process will create the directory structure and files we need for the rest of the installation.

5. Change directories to the newly created PHP directory:

   ```
   cd php-4.0.6
   ```

   Once inside the PHP directory we can start the build process, which is almost identical to the Apache process.

   > NOTE: Users wishing to add MySQL support to the PHP installation may do so using the configure command below where mySQLpath is the path to your MySQL installation for example /usr/local/mysql/.
   >
   > ```
   > ./configure --with-
   > apxs/usr/local/apache/apache_1.3.20/bin/apxs
   > ```

6. Once the `configure` process is complete you'll be returned to the prompt. Type:

```
make
```

After a short while and lots of screen output you'll be returned to the prompt.

7. Here we type:

```
make install
```

A few moments later and again lots of output to the screen you'll be returned to the prompt.

8. Next, you... Oh, wait. That's it! We have completed our PHP installation, which really could not be a whole lot simpler.

9. However, before we can test our installation we need to tell Apache that we have installed PHP. It's really not too much to ask, is it? We do this by modifying the `httpd.conf` file which can be found in the `conf` directory of your Apache installation – for example /usr/local/ apache_1.3.20/conf.

10. Once open, locate the lines below:

```
# AddType application/x-httpd-php  .php
# AddType application/x-httpd-php  .phps
```

We need to uncomment the lines by removing the "#" symbol from both lines. These lines define the file extensions apache needs to recognise as PHP files so that they can be passed to the PHP parser for processing.

Remember that when you make any changes to the web server's configuration it needs to be restarted before the changes take effect so let's restart the web server using the commands we learned earlier.

11. Ensure you're in the Apache parent directory /usr/local/apache_1.3.20 and type the following commands to stop and then restart the web server.

```
./bin/apachectl stop
```

```
./bin/apachectl start
```

12. Now let's just test the PHP installation. In order to do this we'll create a very simple PHP file. In your chosen text editor (trusty old **Wordpad** or some such applicationette) type the following:

```
<? phpinfo() ?>
```

13. Save the file as phpinfo.php and move it into the web server's root directory.

/usr/local/apache_1.3.20/htdocs/

14. If we now open a web browser and in the address field type...

http://localhost/phpinfo.php

...we'll see the PHP information page which includes all the information about our PHP installation (shown below).

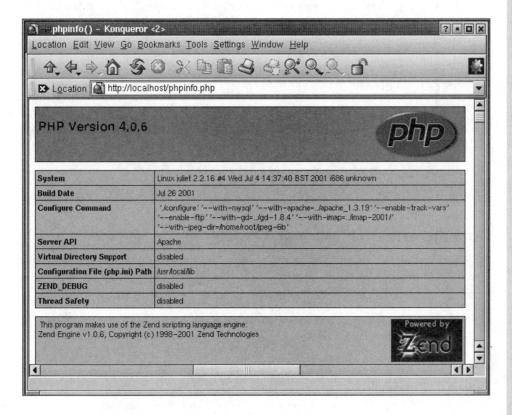

Troubleshooting

In the unlikely event that you don't see the above screen when you test the PHP installation, below are a couple of trouble shooting tips that may cure your problem.

Check the file permissions on your phpinfo.php file. Users of your web site must have the permission to execute the file. For development purposes you can change the permissions using the following command.

chmod 755 phpinfo.php

> Note: A full explanation of the chmod function is beyond the scope of this book, for more information chmod consult your manual pages using the command **man chmod**.

Also check that you have carried out all the changes to the httpd.conf file as discussed earlier, ensure that ALL the lines discussed have been uncommented.

Ensure that you restart the web server *every* time you make changes to the configuration file. Changes made to the configuration do not take effect until the web server is restarted.

Check, recheck and then check again the paths entered into the configuration file. This is one of the most popular causes of failure.

If you've checked all of the above and you're still experiencing problems installing either Apache Web Server or PHP then you can get support from the developer's web sites and the online documentation.

Apache – www.apache.org
PHP – www.php.net

Apache and PHP for Mac OS X

Users fortunate enough to have the all-singing, all-dancing Mac OS X installed on their machine may or may not be aware that you already have both the Apache web server and PHP 4 installed on your machine.

You can start and stop your Apache web server using the Sharing option in System Preferences (see image below).

Web Sharing Off

 Click Start to turn on Web Sharing and allow other users to access Web pages in Sites folders.

Max OS X users wishing to take advantage of PHP can do so by making some very simple modifications to the httpd.conf file usually found in /etc/httpd/.

1. Open the file in a terminal window using "vi" or similar if you prefer to use something else. We need to find the following line in our file.

```
# LoadModule php4_module
```

Note: You need to be "root" to make the changes to the file.

The line is currently commented out and is therefore ignored by Apache, to activate it we need to remove the '#' symbol from the beginning of the line.

2. Next, find the following lines and again remove the '#' symbol from the beginning of each line.

```
# AddModule mod_php4.c
# AddType application/x-httpd-php .php
# AddType application/x-httpd-php .phps
```

3. When all the lines have been modified, save the file and restart the web server so that the changes can take effect.

4. To test our PHP installation we need to create a simple PHP file. Create a new file in your chosen text editor and enter the following line of PHP code into it.

```
<? phpinfo() ?>
```

5. Save the file as phpinfo.php to your own web site directory, for example if your user name is mickeym your directory will be /users/mickeym/sites.

6. Once saved, we can test the file in a web browser by entering the following text into the address field replacing of course mickeym with your user name.

```
http://127.0.0.1/~mickeym/phpinfo.php
```

PHP Version 4.0.4pl1

System	Darwin smallsoldiers 1.0 Darwin Kernel Version 1.3: Thu Mar 1 06:56:40 PST 2001; root:xnu/xnu-123.5.obj~1/RELEASE_PPC Power Macintosh powerpc
Build Date	Jun 27 2001
Configure Command	'/SourceCache/apache_mod_php/apache_mod_php-5/php/configure' '--prefix= /usr' '--mandir=/usr/share/man' '--infodir=/usr/share/info' '--with-apxs'
Server API	Apache
Virtual Directory Support	disabled
Configuration File (php.ini) Path	/usr/local/lib
ZEND_DEBUG	disabled
Thread Safety	disabled

Troubleshooting

There's not much to go wrong here, all the hard work was done by the OS X install, all you have to worry about is the modifications to the configuration file so make sure that you have made changes correctly.

Always ensure that you restart the web server following modifications to the web server, changes to the configuration will only take effect when you restart.

If you're still experiencing problems, take a look at the developer's web sites for support and online help.

Apache – www.apache.org
PHP – www.php.net

Installing, Configuring and Running MySQL on Win32

Before we can start using MySQL we first need to install and configure it on our system. The instructions given here assume that you're using the pre-compiled Win32 binary version of MySQL. The latest version at the time of writing is 3.23, and you can download all the necessary files direct from the MySQL website at http://www.mysql.com/downloads/index.html.

Installation

The installation files for MySQL come packaged in a ZIP file so the first thing we'll need to do is unzip them to a temporary directory. For this you can use a tool like **WinZip**, (a trial version of which is available from www.winzip.com).

Once the files have been unzipped you'll need to locate and run the setup.exe file. This will start an install wizard that will guide you through the rest of the installation procedure.

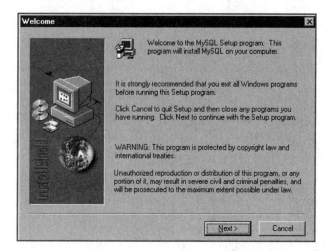

During the install process you will be asked where on your system you would like MySQL installed. It's a good idea to install it to the default c:\mysql\ directory suggested for the sake of compatibility with other software and ease of configuration for MySQL itself!

> Installation instructions for other operating systems and platforms can be found in the online MySQL documentation at http://www.mysql.com.

Once the wizard has completed its task and MySQL has been installed, it's time to find out how to control the MySQL daemon from within Windows.

The MySQL Daemon

The MySQL daemon – perhaps we should call it mysqld from here – can be thought of as a listening device. It is a program whose job is to sit around and listen for client requests for our MySQL server. When such a request is received, mysqld will fetch the required information and return a response to the calling client.

So, the first thing we need to do is to start mysqld. Firstly, you will need to navigate to your chosen installation directory for MySQL. That's the one we just suggested as being c:\mysql\. You should see a directory structure along the lines of the one shown below:

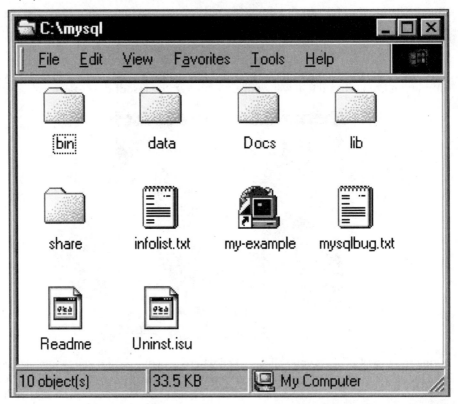

Open the bin directory and locate and double-click on the mysqld.exe file to unleash the MySQL beast. Note that mysqld runs as a background process and there will be no outwardly visible sign that it's running. The easiest way to ensure that it *is* doing what it's told is to check the Windows Task Manager by pressing CTRL-ALT-DEL on your keyboard – you should see an entry labelled mysqld. Alternatively, you can use the **MySQL monitor** program, which will be covered in the next section.

To stop mysqld gracefully you will need to open up an **MS-DOS Command Prompt** and navigate to your MySQL directory (so, type "cd \mysql" if you've been following these instructions to the letter). Next, type the below, followed by the ENTER key.

```
bin\mysqladmin shutdown
```

Use the **Windows Task Manager** again to confirm that mysqld has indeed been shut down.

Note that you could have used the Windows Task Manager to kill the process but this can have some unpredictable results. At best, mysqld will be shut down and you will keep all of your data intact – at worst, you could scramble your databases and your data would be toast!

On Windows NT and 2000 machines you should install mysqld as a service as follows:

```
mysqld -nt —install
```

You can now start and stop mysqld as below:

```
NET START mysql
NET STOP mysql
```

Note that in this case you can't use any other options for mysqld! You can remove the service as follows:

```
mysqld -nt —remove
```

MySQL Monitor

Although it has a fairly grand name, the MySQL monitor is little more than a console interface to MySQL. It does, however, allow you to perform almost all MySQL related tasks, including the creation and manipulation of databases, tables and data.

To start the MySQL monitor you will again need to open an MS-DOS Command Prompt and navigate to the MySQL directory (again, "cd \mysql"). Then, type the below code, followed by the ENTER key.

```
bin\mysql
```

If the MySQL monitor can connect to the MySQL daemon then you will see something like the following output:

```
MS MYSQL                                                          _ □ ×
C:\WINDOWS>cd \mysql

C:\mysql>bin\mysql
Welcome to the MySQL monitor.  Commands end with ; or \g.
Your MySQL connection id is 2 to server version: 3.23.41-max-debug

Type 'help;' or '\h' for help. Type '\c' to clear the buffer.

mysql>
```

If the mysqld program isn't running when you attempt to start the MySQL monitor then you will see something like the following output.

```
C:\mysql>bin\mysql
ERROR 2003: Can't connect to MySQL server on 'localhost' (10061)
```

If you get this output then mysqld is not running on the local machine. Please return to the previous section on starting the MySQL daemon and try again.

To escape from the MySQL Monitor simply type exit followed by the ENTER key. You will be returned to the command prompt.

None Shall Pass: MySQL Security

MySQL has a strict set of security features. You can restrict who can access your databases, where they can access from, which databases they can access, what they can do with the databases and much more. This is an extremely important feature to get to grips with if you're going to be letting the general public loose on your servers.

However, such configuration has been known to fill whole books even bigger than this one. For this reason we will not be discussing the security features of MySQL in this section. However, if you're interested in the security aspects of MySQL then check www.phpforflash.com, for more information.

Well folks, that should see you right. Remember that the installation process for the simplest of applications can seem a little daunting. But if you got PHP on your machine, then you really should know no fear! Don't forget that as with the other technologies we've installed, there is a comprehensive set of documentation supplied and online.

B PHP and Object-Oriented Programming

In this appendix, I will introduce you to some more advanced programming techniques that have not been covered so far in this book. The main area that I'm going to cover is **Object-Oriented Programming**, although I'm going to cover some other interesting functions and techniques along the way.

Hopefully, this appendix should trigger some ideas of your own, and rather than going into too much depth it should encourage you to find out more about object orientation in PHP.

At the end of this appendix, I'll be taking you through a very simple object oriented shopping basket system.

OOPs!

Just to give you a bit of background, Object-Oriented Programming (OOP) is a style of programming first introduced in the Sixties with the Simula language. Since then, more and more object-oriented languages have appeared on the scene and nowadays most commercial languages are based around OOP principles, such as Java, C++ and Visual Basic.

But what exactly is Object-Oriented Programming?

Well, in any program there are variables that hold data, and functions that perform some kind of operation using those variables. In traditional programming these variables and functions are thought of as separate entities. In OOP however, variables and functions can be grouped together in distinct modules, called **classes**.

A class is made up of any number of **properties** (data) and **methods** (functions). Once you have defined a class, you can make any number of **objects** that belong to that class, much as you can create any number of variables of the integer data type.

PHP itself is not a true Object-Oriented language, but, as it allows programming in an object-oriented style, we'll assume that it is one.

OOP by Example

In OOP, we can look at programming in a similar way to the way in which we view the world around us. We are surrounded by self-contained objects, with which we interact on a day-to-day basis.

Your computer is an object, your car, your television, even your friends down the pub are objects. All of these objects have a number of properties and functions that they can perform, sometimes at your request and sometimes just on their own accord. Your car starts when you turn the ignition, your computer loads a program, and your friends fall over when you've bought them enough drinks.

What's important is that you don't need to know about the complex internal workings of all of these things. You don't need to be a mechanic to start your car, you don't need to be a programmer to work a computer, and you certainly don't need to be a genius at biology to calculate how many beers it would take to make your friends fall over.

This concept underlies OOP, and to help you get to grips with it, we're going to look at the theoretical example of a television set.

Properties

If we look at a television set, apart from catching a few interesting shows occasionally, we can see that all televisions share some common properties. Let's just list a few of them:

- **Make** – The manufacturer of our television
- **Channel** – What station the television is currently tuned in to.
- **Volume** – How loud the sound is.
- **State (On / Off)** – Whether the set is turned on or off at the moment.

In OOP we would call these **properties** of the **class** Television. The syntax for declaring this in PHP would be:

```
<?
   class Television {
           var $make;
           var $channel;
           var $volume;
   }
?>
```

> *In order to use classes in a PHP script, you must first define them, and list all of their properties and methods.*

So, we've defined the properties of our Television class, but how do we actually use it? Well, the answer is that we can't until we've defined its methods.

Methods

Let's look at the kinds of actions we could perform on our Television:

- Change the channel
- Turn the volume up
- Turn the volume down
- Turn the set on or off

On any television set, these options are generally easy to find on the remote control, and we can change the channel just by pressing a button.

But, if you look at the code above, one of the properties of Television is **make**, and there definitely isn't a button on any television that I know of to change its make! Only some of an object's properties can be changed, whilst others remain constant.

If we add these methods to our Television definition, we get:

```
<?
class Television {
        // Class properties
        var $volume;
        var $channel;
        var $make;

        // Class methods
        function increaseVolume() {
                //Add one to the current volume

                $this->volume++;
                }

        function decreaseVolume() {
                //Subtract one from the current volume

                $this->volume—;
                }

        function setChannel($newChannel) {
                //Set channel to newChannel
                $this->channel = $newChannel;
                }

        function getChannel() {
                //Just return the current channel

                return $channel;
                }
        }
?>
```

As you can see, defining the methods for a particular class is the same as defining any other function in PHP. We use the function keyword and declare the function within curly braces.

You've probably also noticed that the function declarations appear within the class definition – inside its curly braces. This is very important, because if you declare them outside of the class, they just won't work!

In our first method, **increaseVolume**, we are attempting to increment the current volume value by one. You'll recall the ++ operator we've used in previous chapters, but you may not be familiar with the term $this.

`$this` is a special variable that refers to the current instance of a class. Each copy of the `Television` object has its own set of variables that are not shared with other `Television` objects. We use the `$this` keyword to state that we are interested in only the current object.

The other piece of notation that might be unfamiliar is the "`->`" operator. In PHP, we use this to access properties and methods of objects. So, in our example, `$this->channel` refers to the channel variable of the current `Television` object.

The remaining functions are very similar, and change the value of their respective variables as you might anticipate – `decreaseVolume` subtracts one from the current volume, `setChannel` sets the value of the `$channel` property, while `getChannel` simply returns the value of the current channel.

This is quite a difficult concept to get your head around at first, so let's just have a look at an example of our `Television` in action.

Instantiation

```
$myTV = new Television;
    $myTV->setChannel(2);

    $anotherTV = new Television;
    $anotherTV->setChannel(4);

    print "My TV : " . $myTV->getChannel()."<br>\n";
    print "The other TV : " . $anotherTV->getChannel();
```

If we take it from the top, we've got a `Television` object called `$myTV`. Whenever we want to make an object in PHP, we use the `new` operator. This is a little bit different from how we would normally create a variable, and is called **instantiation** – we are creating an **instance** of the class `Television`, just like in Flash!

OK, then we call the `setChannel` method of `$myTV`. If you have a look at the code for our `Television` class, all this method does to set the value of `$channel` to the argument of `setChannel`. We could achieve exactly the same thing by forgetting about the `setChannel` method, and doing this:

```
<?
    //This is really bad practise!!
    $myTV->channel = 2;
?>
```

This would work, but it is very bad practise. Working in this kind of way is like rooting around inside your real-world television, finding the bit of electronics that changes the channel, and crossing the wires!

Generally in OOP, you should always use **access functions** like `setChannel` and `getChannel` instead – the equivalent of having some nice buttons and knobs on the front of your television. We do this so that we can ensure that, no matter who uses our code, they will use it in the way that it has been designed. This improves the general reusability and robustness of our code, and makes us happy designers!

Right, if we rewind to the example, you'll see that we create another `Television`, call it `$anotherTV`, and set its channel to 4.

What this means is that we've now set two `Televisions` to two different channels, which may seem simple. However, this is one of the most powerful features of OOP. If you wanted to do the same thing in a traditional way, the script would be very complicated. We would probably have to set up some kind of array, and loop through each to get a similar result.

Constructors

Usually when we instantiate a class, it is important to set some of the new object's properties to an initial value, or to run certain functions.

In the case of our `Television` class, we have so far omitted to mention the `$make` property. As we said previously, the make of a TV should be constant once it has been manufactured, and we shouldn't be able to change it.

To make sure our `Television` class behaves in a similar way, we define a **constructor**. We add the following function to our class definition:

```
function Television ($theMake) {
        $this->make = $theMake;
}
```

A constructor is a function that is always run when an instance of a class is first created. It must have exactly the same name as the class, and you can define whatever parameters you like for it.

If we were using the above constructor, we would have to adapt our code for making a new `Television` object to the following:

```
$myTV = new Television("A well-known brand");
        $myTV->setChannel(2);
```

```
$anotherTV = new Television("A competitor brand");
$anotherTV->setChannel(4);
```

All this does is set the value of $make in $myThirdTV to A well-known brand, and $anotherTV to A competitor brand.

Inheritance

Well, that's the basics of OOP over and done with. Don't worry if you haven't quite understood all of it – we're working towards a real-world example at the end of this appendix.

There are a few other points to note about OOP, and they are somewhat more advanced, and the first is called **inheritance**. We won't be using this in our example, but it's a very important part of OOP, and is something that you might find very useful in your future PHP projects.

If you imagine a family tree of televisions, right at the top we have the humble Television class we've been working on, and underneath that are a number of different types of television – the Black & White Television, the Widescreen Television, Color Televisions, Color Widescreen Televisions, and so on.

To state the obvious all of these types of televisions are based around the simple Television, but with specific peculiarities. For instance, Black & White Televisions only show pictures in black & white, Widescreen Televisions can switch between widescreen and 16x9 modes.

Let's assume that we wanted to make a new class for Widescreen Televisions. Most of the functionality is exactly the same as a normal Television, with just a few additions.

We could simply copy and paste the code from the Television class, and add the extra functionality that we need. This would work fine, but what happens if we discover that we've made a mistake in some of our original Television code? We would have to amend it in two different places, because we have copied and pasted from it. And if in the future we wanted more and more different types of television, this method would replicate any errors over and over.

A much better approach would be to re-use the bits of the Television class that we need, and just add on the extra functionality. And guess what? OOP is perfect for this.

```
<?
class WideScreenTelevision extends Television {
    var mode;

    function WideScreenTelevision($theMake) {
```

continues overleaf

```
                            $this->make = $theMake;
                            $this->mode = true;
                    }

            function toggleWideScreenMode() {
                    $this->mode = !$this->mode;
            }
        }
    ?>
```

In this example, I have defined a new class `WideScreenTelevision` which **extends** the `Television` class. The word **extends** is a special keyword, and means that the new class being defined has access to all of the methods and properties of the parent class, in this case the `Television` class.

So, the new class can use all of `Television`'s methods and functions as well as all of any new ones it declares.

In my example, I've implemented a simple switch that flips the television between Widescreen mode and Normal mode.

It might interest you to note that you can't extend a class in PHP and remove any of its methods or properties. This is something that is possible in other object oriented programming languages, but not PHP.

Let's Go Shopping!

So, by now you should have at least a passing understanding of what objects do, what they are for, and how they are implemented. I'm now going to take you through an example of how to use objects in practice, with an example of a simple shopping basket.

Most online shops in the world are based around a surprisingly similar system for buying goods. I'm sure you're familiar with buying online but, if not, the process is as follows:

- The user visits the site, and is presented with a virtual shopping basket which will hold their purchases.

- The user moves around the web site until the product they are interested in is found.

- Usually, there is an Add to basket button next to the product, and the user clicks this.

- The user's choice is recorded in the shopping basket.

- The user then carries on looking around the store, perhaps adding more and more objects to the basket.

- Once the user is happy with the products in their basket, they hit the Checkout button, enter a few credit card details and, hey presto, their purchases land up on their doorstep within a few days.

> *Maybe you bought this book by doing just that!*

This process seems quite simple, but there are a number of complex issues lurking in the shadows.

The whole process relies on the fact that the web site can *remember* the user, and distinguish between one user and another. So far we have come across one simple way of recording a user's information with the use of cookies in **Chapter 6**. In the following example, we will extend this concept and show you a useful implementation.

When implementing a shopping basket in Flash, some developers record a user's purchases in Flash variables. This is all well and good, but Flash variables have a life span limited to one viewing of a particular web site. In some instances, should you press the Refresh button mid-purchase, you would lose all of these purchases because Flash would reset all of its variables.

So it's a good idea to store any variables that need to last an entire 'session' (one visit to a site) on the server.

We could do this by setting a cookie on the user's computer with a unique user ID, and then storing all of the purchases in a MySQL database. This is a good solution, but it can be too complicated for some uses.

A simpler approach is to use something called a **session variable**, which is a variable that we can access consistently from one script to another. We will be using that once we have designed the structure of our application, which we'll start now...

> *It's worth mentioning at this point that at the time of going to press, there are bugs in the Macintosh Internet Explorer implementation of the Flash plug-in which will cause this example to fail. I would recommend using Netscape for this example if you are developing on a Macintosh.*

Creating a Shopping Basket

We'll start with the Flash, and the screenshot below shows what we are aiming for. The section on the left is a list of products that we'd have on our web site, and the section on the right will hold our selections.

By clicking on one of the items in the left-hand window, it will be added to our basket, and the contents of the basket will be displayed in the window on the right.

There is also an Empty Basket button, which allows our users to realize they don't have the bucks to spend. Finally, there's a box to display the total cost of the items in the basket.

The Flash Bit

1. As with the other applications we've built, we're going to put everything in a movie clip, so let's make one. Call it Shopping Basket, and press OK.

2. The timeline for this movie is going to be very simple, and as we have done in previous examples, we'll separate the form and the background graphics onto two separate layers.

   Recreate the layer structure below:

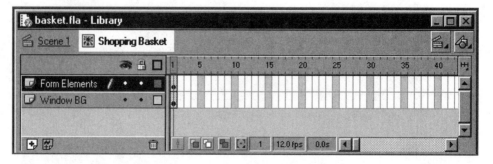

3. The next step is to create the background graphics for our shopping basket. I've used the same style as I have been using throughout the book, but you can use any style you like. Either way, here's what mine looks like:

4. Now we need to add the form elements onto the Form Elements layer. Use this diagram as an outline:

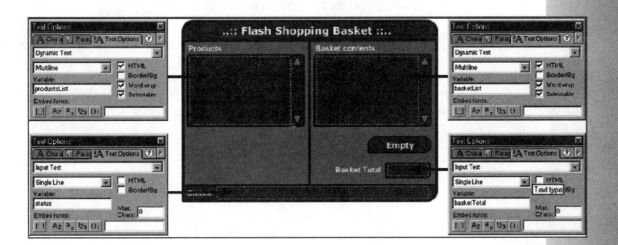

5. Now we need to add the ActionScript for our buttons. Start with the scroll bars for both text areas – you can probably copy and paste these from the Cookie Cutter example in **Chapter 6**.

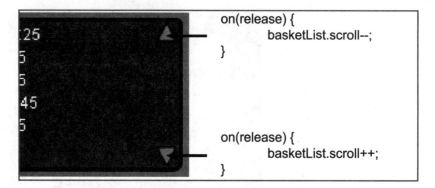

```
on(release) {
        basketList.scroll--;
}
```

```
on(release) {
        basketList.scroll++;
}
```

6. Now we need to create the Empty button. Create a new button symbol, or even better, copy and paste a button from a previous example.

The ActionScript for this button is very simple, because we are going to declare the removeAll function later on in our code:

```
on (release) {
        removeAll();
}
```

7. Now drag an instance of our Shopping Basket on to the main timeline. We're going to define the functions that our Shopping Basket is to perform by attaching some actions to it:

```
onClipEvent (load) {
    status = "Loading products...";
    LoadVariables("products.php", this, "POST");

    action = "";
    LoadVariables("basket.php", this, "POST");
```

This first part of the onClipEvent(load) function displays the message Loading products... in the status bar, and then loads products.php, which will install a list of products into the left hand area of our Flash movie. We then set the variable action to a blank string and load basket.php to retrieve the contents of the basket, should we be coming back to our movie having added items to the basket on a previous visit.

8. Now have a look at this chunk of code:

```
function addItem(parameters)        {
        action = "addItem";
        status = "Adding product to basket...";

        properties = parameters.split("|");
        description = properties[0];
        price = properties[1];

        LoadVariables("basket.php", this, "POST");
}
```

The function addItem is called when the user clicks on one of the products in the left hand window. This is done by using a very useful trick. Assuming that you have some knowledge of basic HTML, you will be familiar with what a hyperlink looks like:

```
<a href="http://www.somewhere.com">Click here</a>
```

When you click on this link in a web browser, you will be taken to the URL (web address) www.somewhere.com. It is also possible to do other more interesting things with the URL area of a link, and in Flash we can have special links that can call ActionScript functions. The format for a hyperlink which can call an ActionScript function is:

```
<a href="asfunction:myFunction,myParameter">Click here</a>
```

When the user clicks on this link, it will invoke a function called myFunction, with myParameter as an argument: the equivalent of a button with the following ActionScript:

```
on(release) {
        myFunction(myParameter);
}
```

You might be wondering why this is useful. Well, it means that we can have links inside HTML text boxes in our Flash applications. All will become clear when you see it in action.

An extension of this is to send multiple parameters to your function. You can do this by using an arbitrary separator, such as the "|" character, and split up the parameter afterwards in Flash. So, if we have a look at our function again, we can use the split function to achieve this:

```
properties = parameters.split("|");
```

```
            description = properties[0];
            price = properties[1];
```

9. Anyway, that's enough beating around the bush. The next function, `removeItem` is also called in this way, but only requires one parameter – we will look at this in the PHP.

```
function removeItem(theItem) {
        action = "removeItem";
        status = "Removing product from basket...";
        itemNumber = theItem;
        LoadVariables("basket.php", this, "GET");
}
```

10. The last function is `removeAll`, which as its name suggests, will empty the shopping basket.

```
function removeAll() {
        action = "removeAll";
        status = "Removing all items...";
        LoadVariables("basket.php", this, "GET");
}
```

The PHP Bit

Phew! That's the Flash side of things over and done with, so it's time we had a look at the PHP script. In its simplest form, a shopping basket class needs only one property – an array of purchases. In terms of methods, we will need the following:

- A constructor (to **make** a new basket)

- A function to **add** an item to the basket

- A function to **remove** an item from the basket

- A function to **empty** the entire basket

- A function to **print** out the contents of the basket

- And finally a function to get the **total** price for the items in the basket

We're also going to create a new class called Item, which will hold all the necessary information for an item in our shop.

An item can be as simple or as complicated as necessary for your site, but in this case we're just going to store a textual description of the item and a price. These two variables will be the properties of this class.

The methods for our Item class are very few indeed:

- A constructor, with which we will set price and description

- A function to get the price of an item

- A function to get the description

So, let's have a look at this in PHP. You'll need to make a text file in the same directory as your Flash movie, and it needs to contain the following PHP script:

```php
<?
  // Basket and Item classes

  // The item class
class Item {
    var $description;   // A textual description
// of the item
    var $price;                // The numeric price
// of the item
```

continues overleaf

```php
   // Class constructor
   function Item($description, $price) {
     $this->price = $price;
     $this->description = $description;
   }

   // Get the price of the item
   function getPrice() {
     return $this->price;
   }

   // Get the description of the item
   function getDescription() {
     return $this->description;
   }
 }

 // Basket class
 class Basket {
   // Class properties

         var $items;   // This property will hold all of
// the contents of the basket.
// Each item in this array will
// be an instance of Item.

   // Class Methods

   // Constructor Function
   function Basket() {
     // Set up $items as an array
     $this->items = array();
   }

   // Add an item to the basket
   // $description: A description of the
   // $price: The price of the item to add
   function addItem($description, $price) {
       // Create a new instance of the Item object
       $newItem = new Item($description, $price);

       // Add the object to the $items array
       $this->items[] = $newItem;
   }

   // Remove a specific item from the basket
```

```php
    //   $itemNumber: The array number of the item
       function removeItem($itemNumber) {
         // Remove this item from the $items array
         unset($this->items[$itemNumber]);
       }

       // Remove all items from the basket
       function removeAll() {
         // To do this, we reset the $items array
         $this->items = array();
       }

       // Print out the contents of the basket for Flash
       function getContents() {
         // Print out the total cost of the items
print "&basketTotal=".$this->getTotalPrice();

    // Rewind the $items array back to the beginning
    reset($this->items);

    // Check if there are any items in the basket,
    if (count($this->items) > 0) {
      print '&basketList=';

      // Loop through the items in the basket
      while(list($itemNumber, $currentItem)=each($this->items)) {
// Print out the item's price and description
        print '<p>'.$currentItem->price.'
    <b>'.$currentItem->description.'</b></p>';
      }
    }

else {
        // If there are no items in the basket,
// print a message saying so

        print '&basketList=<p>Your basket is empty.</p>';
            }
        }

  // Get the total price of the objects in the basket
  function getTotalPrice() {
      $total = 0;

      // Rewind the $items array back to the beginning
```

continues overleaf

```
                reset($this->items);

                // Loop through the items in the basket
                while(list($null, $currentItem) = each($this->items)) {
                    // Get the price of the current item and add it to
        the total
                    $total += $currentItem->price;
                }

                // Return the total price of the items
                    return $total;
                }
            }
    ?>
```

Okay, go get a pair of scissors – we're going to cut this into pieces, and I'll explain each piece as we go.

1. I've started off by declaring our Item class, which is quite simple – it consists of two properties: $description and $price; two methods: getDescription and getPrice; and finally the constructor: the function Item.

2. We can create a new Item with a simple constructor, for example:

```
<?
            $anExampleItem = new Item("A pair of shoes",
➥15.99);
?>
```

This piece of code creates a new instance of the Item class with the description set to "A pair of shoes" and a price of 15.99. OK, so let's all stop laughing about the average cost of my shoes.

The Item class is quite simple, and is more or less just a method of holding data in an efficient way. It would be relatively straightforward to adapt our Item class to include more information for each product – product IDs, sizes, colors, etc. And because we're using OOP, we can do this without affecting our Basket class!

3. So, on to the Basket class. At first glance this can look quite complicated, but don't let that deter you. By breaking it down into its constituent parts it becomes very intuitive.

    The first thing is to have a look at the class properties, and in this case, there is just the one – $items, which is an array of instances of the Item class. This stores all of the Item objects that are added to the basket.

The constructor is also quite simple, and does not accept any parameters:

```
function Basket() {
        // Set up $items as an array
        $this->items = array();
}
```

The only thing to note is that when you have an array in a class you must always create it in your constructor function. The same thing also applies to any other types of variables that you want to set – always do this in the constructor.

4. Let's have a look at the addItem function. It takes two parameters – $description and $price. Using these two variables, it first creates a new Item object and then adds it to the items array.

```
function addItem($description, $price) {
        // Create a new instance of the Item object
        $newItem = new Item($description, $price);

        // Add the object to the $items array
        $this->items[] = $newItem;
    }
```

5. The next logical method to look at is how to remove items once they have been added:

```
function removeItem($itemNumber) {
        // Remove this item from the $items array
        unset($this->items[$itemNumber]);
    }
```

This is a little bit more complex than addItem, and uses a function we haven't come across before: unset.

What unset does is remove an item from an array based on its position in the array. So unset($this->items[3]) would remove the fourth item in the items array, because array items are always numbered from zero.

6. Let's look now at the removeAll method:

```
function removeAll() {
        // To do this, we reset the $items array
        $this->items = array();
    }
```

This method resets the items array, effectively emptying it of its contents.

7. Now, let's have a look at what happens when our user has finished shopping:

```php
function getContents() {
        // Print out the total cost of the items
print "&basketTotal=".$this->getTotalPrice();

            // Rewind the $items array back to the beginning
            reset($this->items);

            // Check if there are any items in the basket,
            if (count($this->items) > 0) {
                print '&basketList=';

                    // Loop through the items in the basket
                    while(list($itemNumber,
$currentItem)=each($this->items)) {
// Print out the item's price and description
                            print '<p>'.$currentItem->price.'
      <b>'.$currentItem->description.'</b></p>';
                    }
            }

else {
    // If there are no items in the basket,
// print a message saying so

    print '&basketList=<p>Your basket is empty.</p>';
            }
    }
```

In our Flash movie, we've defined the basket area as HTML, so that we can control formatting and layout. This function first prints out the total value of the basket and then returns it as the variable `basketTotal`. It then loops through each item in the items array, printing out each one as a line of text with the description in bold.

If the basket is empty, it sets `basketList` to `<p>Your basket is empty.</p>`

8. The last method in our `Basket` class is `getTotalPrice`, which unsurprisingly returns the total of all of the items that are currently in the basket.

```php
function getTotalPrice() {
        $total = 0;

            // Rewind the $items array back to the beginning
```

```
        reset($this->items);

        // Loop through the items in the basket
        while(list($null, $currentItem) = each($this-
➥>items)) {
                // Get the price of the current item and add
➥it to the total
                $total += $currentItem->price;
        }

        // Return the total price of the items
        return $total;
    }
```

I've implemented this by looping through each item in the `items` array, and adding its price to the `$total` variable, then returning it.

9. Now that we've defined our classes, we need to finish off with the code that will actually interact with our Flash movie. This involves those **session variables** we were talking about. Copy the following code into `basket.php`:

```
// Start session variables and register the variable
// $myBasket as a session variable
   session_start();
   session_register(myBasket);

   // If this is the first time running this script,
// make $myBasket into an instance of the class "Basket"
   if (!isset($myBasket)) {
          $myBasket = new Basket;
   }
```

Earlier in this appendix I said that we would introduce another system for remembering the contents of the user's basket. The piece of code above uses a session variable to create that memory. A session variable, as we established, is a variable that can be used from one script to another and over a period of time, without having to declare it every time we wish to use it.

The first line sets up PHP so it is able to use session variables. It is necessary to do this before any other output has been initiated – before you send any variables back to Flash, and also before any white space occurs in your script. It is a common mistake to accidentally print out an occasional line break or space before using session variables, which will cause your script to fail in the same way as this occurs when using cookies.

It's not really important to understand fully how session variables work, but you can think of them in the same way as cookies. A small piece of information is recorded, which is then matched up to data stored on the server. You can store any variable as a session variable, including an object such as our basket.

Once sessions are enabled, we use the session_register function to state that we want to declare the variable $myBasket as a session variable. Note that we don't use the dollar ($) symbol when registering a session variable.

10. It may seem a little bit counter-intuitive, but after we set up our session variable, we have to make sure that it is an instance of our Basket class. We first check to see if the variable is set using the isset function, and if it is not set we create a new instance of the class. The reason we do this after all of the session stuff is that we will only need to do this once, so we need to check for an existing session variable before we set up a new one, which would actually over-write the existing variable should it already exist.

11. The final part of the script is a switch statement that controls what to do in certain situations. Rather than having separate files for adding to, removing from and displaying the basket, we use the same file, but set the variable $action to choose between them.

```php
// Now for the actions
switch($action) {
        case "addItem":
                $myBasket->addItem($description, $price);
                break;
        case "removeAll":
                $myBasket->removeAll();
                break;
        case "removeItem":
                $myBasket->removeItem($itemNumber);
                break;
}

$myBasket->getContents();

?>
```

As you'd expect, we call the appropriate function depending on the value of $action, and afterwards call getContents so that the contents of the basket are always kept up to date.

12. OK, that's the hard bit finished with. Now all we need to do is set up some example products to use with our applications. You need to copy the following code into a file called products.php.

```
<?
    // Set up the products in two arrays

    $productName[]="Shoes";
    $productPrice[] = 45;

    $productName[]="Shirt";
    $productPrice[] = 15;

    $productName[]="Socks";
    $productPrice[] = 5;

    $productName[]="Shorts";
    $productPrice[] = 25;

    $productName[]="Skirt";
    $productPrice[] = 35;

    // Now output these variables for Flash

    print "&productsList=";

    for ($counter=0; $counter < count($productName);
➥$counter++) {
        print '<p><a href="asfunction:
➥addItem,'.$productName[$counter].'|'.$productPrice[$counter
➥].'">
<b>'.$productName[$counter].'</b> —
➥£'.$productPrice[$counter].'</a></p>';
    }

?>
```

This code is a very simplified way of doing things. Strictly speaking, in the real world you would probably want to store the product information in a MySQL database, but we're not really dealing with MySQL in this chapter, we're concentrating on OOP instead, so I'm just using two arrays – one to hold the names of the products, and the other to hold their prices.

The for loop at the end of the script simply loops through the arrays and prints them out to Flash in the productsList variable, corresponding to the text area on the left in our movie. Again, it's an HTML text area, so we have to make sure we format the output with <p> and <b> tags.

Here is where we use the `asfunction` URL that I discussed earlier, and this is the part of the script that allows the user to click on an item and add it to the basket. For example, a line that is output from this script is:

```
<p><a href="asfunction:addItem,Shirt|45"><b>Shirt</b> —
£45</a></p>
```

Once you've finished coding up the two scripts, run the SWF file from a web server, and admire the results. Also, try reloading the Flash movie, or visiting another web site and going back to it to see the shopping basket stay constant over a number of visits.

Summary

We've covered some pretty advanced PHP subjects in this appendix, and hopefully it will have triggered a few ideas and shown you that a lot can be achieved with the language.

You've taken your first steps into Object-Oriented Programming, but there is plenty more to learn on the subject. You can read more on the many Flash and PHP resource web sites, a few of which are listed in our **Resources** section.

You'll notice that I left one major area of functionality out of our shopping basket application – the `remove` function. I've written the ActionScript function and the PHP function, but I've deliberately left the rest to you as a challenge. Another area you might want to look into is storing quantities of products, rather than just having a list.

My advice to you is to look through a few more tutorials and read as much as possible on the subject – object orientation can really help you make robust, reusable and timesaving code.

C Resources

I thought this would be a pretty good place to spread the word about some helpful resources on the web. I'd like to think that by the time you get to the end of this book, your mind is buzzing with ideas and you're on the hunt for fresh inspirations.

If so, take yourself to some of the following places and look for web pages with the file extension .php.

Foundation PHP for Flash links

www.phpforflash.com

www.friendsofed.com

Author's homepage

www.codejunkie.co.uk

Sotware homepages

www.php.net

www.mysql.com

www.apache.org

www.macromedia.com

www.zend.com

Setup Tools

www.phpgeek.com/phptriad.php

www.firepages.com.au/dev4.htm

These sites offer special installation and setup packages, installing PHP, MySQL and Apache on your system with a minimum of fuss.

Also try http://mysql.com/doc/I/n/Installing.html for installation instructions for MySQL on Unix.

PHP Editors

http://soysal.free.fr/PHPEd

www.phpide.de

Easy to use (and free) PHP code editors.

PHP Street Corners and Forums

Know that you are not alone in your newfound PHP patronage. If you want to check out the development patterns of like-minded souls, and perhaps take on a few hints and tips about where to go from here, check out some of the following links:

www.phpbuilder.com

http://phphead.com

www.phpstarter.com

http://thephploft.com

PHP Web Resources

www.phpworld.com
  Newsy, comprehensive PHP site, offering articles, information and feedback.

http://back-end.org
  This site offers a separate application aimed at intermediate PHPers (that's you!)

http://php.resourceindex.com

Bringing attention to everything that's new in the PHP world, with plenty of complete scripts and useful tips.

http://screaming-penguin.com

Ah, the Temple of the Screaming Penguin – a valuable site dedicated to open content, open information and open source, which is exactly where we have pitched ourselves by getting involved with PHP and MySQL!

http://sourceforge.net

More commitment to open source development, claiming the largest repository of open source code and applications.

www.scriptsearch.com

A great resource for all code-loving designers, offering scripts on every language in the coding rainbow, with an extensive section on PHP.

www.webmonkey.com/programming/php

Resources on everything web-related, including a great PHP section, with tutorials and tips.

Hosting Companies Supporting PHP

To publicly display your new piece of dynamic art, you'll need a web host that supports PHP and MySQL (support for these usually comes as a pair). They can also supply you with the user information you'll need to insert into your scripts to access the database. There are any number of companies out there that offer PHP-inclusive web space.

The PHP for Flash web site at www.phpforflash.com is hosted by *Xcalibre Communications*, who have built up many of their back-end systems using PHP. They also fully support MySQL and can be found at www.xcalibre.co.uk or www.webhoster.co.uk.

You could also try the following:

www.successfulhosting.net
www.phpwebsites.com
www.1stcom.com
www.phphost.com

For a comprehensive list, plus some reviews of the services, check out:

http://hosts.php.net/msgboard/

Index

The index is arranged hierarchically, in alphabetical order, with symbols preceding the letter A. Many second-level entries also occur as first-level entries. This is to ensure that users will find the information they require however they choose to search for it.

▶

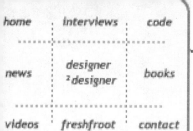

home · interviews · code

news | designer ²designer | books

videos · freshfroot · contact

friendsof

DESIGNER TO DESIGNER™

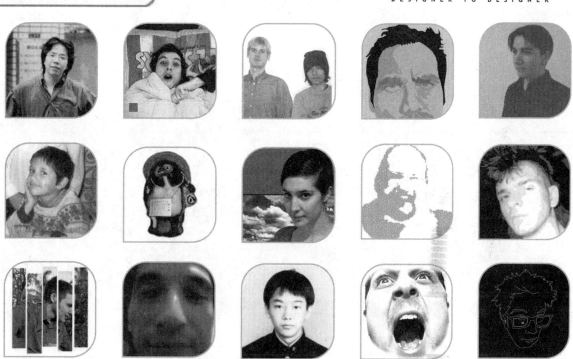

You've read the book, now enter the community.

friendsofed.com is the online heart of the designer to designer neighbourhood.

As you'd expect the site offers the latest news and support for all our current and forthcoming titles – but it doesn't stop there.

For fresh exclusive interviews and videos every month with our authors – the new and future masters like Josh Davis, Yugo Nakamura, James Paterson and many other friends of ED – enter the world of D2D.

Stuck with a design problem? Need technical assistance? Our support doesn't end on the last page of the book. Just post your query on our message board and one of our moderators or authors will make sure you get the answers you need – fast.

Welcome to friendsofed.com. This place is the place of friends of ED – designer to designer. Practical deep fast content delivered by working web designers.

Straight to your head.

www.friendsofed.com

FreshFroot
www.freshfroot.com

get it o

freshfroot #2 advertisement created by mike cina
esigner, typographer, master of scrapbook mayhem
ike, you shine brighter than most.

mikecina.com
trueistrue.com
weworkforther

DESIGNER TO DESIGNER™

friends of ED writes books for you. Any suggestions, or ideas about how you want information given in your ideal book will be studied by our team.

Your comments are valued by friends of ED.

For technical support please contact support@friendsofed.com.

Freephone in USA	800.873.9769
Fax	312.893.8001
UK contact: Tel:	0121.258.8858
Fax:	0121.258.8868

Registration Code : | 01608TT2C8716001 |

Foundation PHP for Flash - Registration Card

Name ....

Address ....

....

....

....

City .... State/Region ....

Country .... Postcode/Zip ....

E-mail ....

Occupation ....

How did you hear about this book? ....

☐ Book review (name)..

☐ Advertisement (name) ....

☐ Recommendation ....

☐ Catalog ....

☐ Other ....

Where did you buy this book? ....

☐ Bookstore (name) .... City...........

☐ Computer Store (name)..................................

☐ Mail Order...

☐ Other..

What influenced you in the purchase of this book?

☐ Cover Design

☐ Content

☐ Other (please specify)....................................

How did you rate the overall content of this book?

☐ Excellent ☐ Good

☐ Average ☐ Poor

What did you find most useful about this book? ....

....

What did you find the least useful about this book? ....

....

Please add any additional comments ....

....

What other subjects will you buy a computer book on soon?

....

What is the best computer book you have used this year?

....

Note: This information will only be used to keep you
updated about new friends of ED titles and will not be used for
any other purpose or passed to any other third party.

friendsof

D E S I G N E R   T O   D E S I G N E R ™

NB. If you post the bounce back card below in the UK, please send it to:

friends of ED Ltd.,
30 Lincoln Road,
Olton,
Birmingham.
B27 6PA